THE UNIVERSAL STRUCTURE OF CATEGORIES

Using data from a variety of languages such as Blackfoot, Halkomelem, and Upper Austrian German, this book explores a range of grammatical categories and constructions, including tense, aspect, subjunctive, case, and demonstratives.

It presents a new theory of grammatical categories – the Universal Spine Hypothesis – and reinforces generative notions of Universal Grammar while accommodating insights from linguistic typology. In essence, this new theory shows that language-specific categories are built from a small set of universal categories and language-specific units of language.

Throughout the book the Universal Spine Hypothesis is compared to two alternative theories – the Universal Base Hypothesis and the No Base Hypothesis. This valuable addition to the field will be welcomed by graduate students and researchers in linguistics.

MARTINA WILTSCHKO is a Professor in the Department of Linguistics at the University of British Columbia.

T0371449

In this series

Earlier issues not listed are also available

CAMBRIDGE STUDIES IN LINGUISTICS

The Universal Structure of Categories

THE UNIVERSAL STRUCTURE OF CATEGORIES

TOWARDS A FORMAL TYPOLOGY

MARTINA WILTSCHKO

University of British Columbia, Vancouver

CAMBRIDGE
UNIVERSITY PRESS

Shaftesbury Road, Cambridge CB2 8EA, United Kingdom

One Liberty Plaza, 20th Floor, New York, NY 10006, USA

477 Williamstown Road, Port Melbourne, VIC 3207, Australia

314–321, 3rd Floor, Plot 3, Splendor Forum, Jasola District Centre, New Delhi – 110025, India

103 Penang Road, #05–06/07, Visioncrest Commercial, Singapore 238467

Cambridge University Press is part of Cambridge University Press & Assessment,
a department of the University of Cambridge.

We share the University's mission to contribute to society through the pursuit of
education, learning and research at the highest international levels of excellence.

www.cambridge.org
Information on this title: www.cambridge.org/9781009342452

First published 2014
First paperback edition 2022

A catalogue record for this publication is available from the British Library

Library of Congress Cataloging-in-Publication data
Wiltschko, Martina.
The universal structure of categories : towards a formal typology / Martina Wiltschko.
    pages   cm – (Cambridge studies in linguistics ; 142)
ISBN 978-1-107-03851-6 (Hardback)
1. Categorial grammar.   2. Structural linguistics.   3. Language, Universal.   I. Title.
P161.W58 2014
415–dc23   2014011843

ISBN   978-1-107-03851-6   Hardback
ISBN   978-1-009-34245-2   Paperback

Dedicated to my elders
Gertrude, Thea
Yámelot, Th'áth'elexwot
and Tootsinaam

Contents

Figures

Tables

Acknowledgements

First and foremost I wish to thank the speakers of the main languages that I discuss here. They provided the data as well as their expertise, their comments, and insight into their fascinating languages. For Upriver Halkomelem, this was the late Rosaleen George (*Yámelot*) and the late Dr. Elizabeth Herrling (*Th'áth'elexwot*). I wish I could tell them how much they taught me. For Blackfoot, this is Beatrice Bullshields (*Tootsinaam*). She opened up yet another world for me, the prairie world of Blackfoot. One day we will have a conversation in Blackfoot. I do hope that the way I have come to analyse the data is true to these speakers' insights.

The theoretical ideas that I develop here did not emerge in isolation. Many people have shaped my thinking: my mentors, my collaborators, and my students.

My mentors from the days when I was only working on German (Martin Prinzhorn, Edwin Williams, and Wolfgang U. Dressler) have shaped the ways I identify and approach problems. And the mentors I have found at the University of Bitish Columbia have helped me to find my way into the Salishanist and the Algonquianist world (the late M. D. Kinkade, Henry Davis, Lisa Matthewson, and Rose-Marie Déchaine).

I feel very fortunate to have ongoing collaborative relations with two linguists I admire immensly: Rose-Marie Déchaine and Betsy Ritter. Their ways of thinking about language have shifted mine many times in important ways. This book would look much different if I hadn't had the opportunity to work with them so closely. I am grateful for their intellectual generosity as well as their friendship.

I also have benefitted greatly from the annual meetings with some of my friends and colleagues across Canada: Jila Ghomeshi, Diane Massam, Éric Mathieu, and Ileana Paul.

My students were essential in the way my thinking about categories has evolved: Solveiga Armoskaite, Heather Bliss, Christiana Christodoulou, Atsushi Fujimori, Peter Jacobs, Olga Steriopolo, Sonja Thoma, and James

Thompson. While I hope I have taught them a thing or two, I know that they have taught me much more than they would ever imagine. Much of their work is reported here.

Special thanks are due to Heather Bliss, Erin Guntley, and the brave first-year undergraduate student Eric Laylock for taking the time to proofread the manuscript, catching typos, errors, inconsistencies, and lots of superfluous hyphens.

I also wish to thank the anonymous reviewer for constructive feedback.

Finally, I am most grateful to my family. Konrad who thought it was cool that I worked on my book manuscript during our vacation in Guatemala. I do hope he will find his passion. And Strang-Dr.-Dexterous-Burton, linguist, thinker, radical skeptic, inventor of the "kobe-beef-approach to writing," and strict enforcer of the "you-have-to-write-every-day-at-least-for-15-minutes-rule." I would not think the way I do, let alone have written a book without him. *Thank you, eh!*

A note on the core languages of investigation

There are four main languages I investigate here: Blackfoot, Halkomelem, Squamish, and Upper Austrian German. If not otherwise indicated, the data from these languages come from my own fieldwork. All data are presented in the practical orthography of each language. The key to the Blackfoot orthography can be found in Frantz (1991); the key to the Halkomelem orthography can be found in Galloway (1993).

The particular choice of these languages is based on my expertise: Blackfoot and Halkomelem are the two languages I have conducted extensive fieldwork on. Blackfoot is a Plains Algonquian language, consisting of four mutually intelligible dialects, spoken on three reserves in southern Alberta and one reservation in northwestern Montana. In Alberta, the three dialects are Siksiká (aka Blackfoot), Kaináá (aka Blood), and Piikani (aka Peigan), and in Montana, the dialect is Blackfeet. Data from my own fieldwork stems from the Kaináá dialect. I wish to thank Heather Bliss for help with fieldwork, data glossing, formatting, and proofreading the data.

Halkomelem is a Central Coast Salish language, consisting of three mutually intelligible dialects: Halq'eméylem (aka Upriver Halkomelem), Hən̓q̓əmin̓əm (aka Downriver Halkomelem), and Hulq'umín'um' (aka Island Halkomelem). It is spoken in the lower mainland of British Columbia and on Vancouver Island. Data from my own fieldwork stem from the Upriver dialect. I wish to thank Strang Burton for proofreading the data.

As for Squamish (Skwx̱wu7mesh), another Central Coast Salish language, I was fortunate enough to supervise Peter Jacobs' (2011) UBC dissertation on control in Squamish. Most data on Squamish come from his fieldwork.

And finally Upper Austrian German is my native language. It is spoken in the province of Upper Austria (Oberösterreich). The judgments reported here are my own; they have been confirmed with four other speakers of the same dialect.

Abbreviations

1	1st person
2	2nd person
3	3rd person
4	4th (obviative) person
acc	accusative
accom	accompany
adhort	adhortative
agr	agreement
ai	animate intransitive
Asp	Aspect
AspP	AspectPhrase
assert	assertion
aux	auxiliary
caus	causative
cl	clitic
clas	classifier
cnj	conjunction
cn	common noun connective
coin	coincidence
comp	complementizer
conj	conjunct
D	determiner
dat	dative
deic	deictic
dem	demonstrative
deon	deontic
dep	dependent tense
det	determiner
dir	direct
dist	distal
DP	determiner phrase

ds	different subject
ECM	Exceptional Case Marking
emph	emphatic
EPP	Extended Projection Principle
erg	ergative
Ev	event
Eval	evaluation world
evid	evidential
excl	exclusive
exis	assertion of existence
fe	final event
fem	feminine
FOC	focus
fut	future
gen	genitive
hab	habitual
horiz	horizontal
ic	initial change
Ident	identity
ie	initial event
ii	inanimate intransitive
imp	imperative
impf	imperfective
imprs	impersonal
inan	inanimate
inch	inchoative
incl	inclusive
ind	indicative
inf	infinitive
int	intensifier
inv	inverse
irr	irrealis
lc	limited control
LCA	Linear Correspondence Axiom
LF	logical form
link	linker
loc	local person
locv	locative
masc	masculine

mid	middle
NBH	No Base Hypothesis
neg	negative
neut	neuter
nmlz	nominalizer
nm.term	nominal terminative
nom	nominative
nonaff	non-affirmative
nonfact	non-factive
nonloc	non-local person
NP	noun phrase
nv	non-visible
obj	object
obl	oblique
obv	obviative
om	object marker
part	participle
pass	passive
perc	perceived
perf	perfective
PF	phonological form
pl	plural
pnp	perfective non past
poss	possessive
PoV	point of view
prep	preposition
pres	present
prn	pronoun
prosp	prospective aspect
prox	proximate
prt	particle
prtv	partitive
pst	past
q	question
redup	reduplicant
refl	reflexive
rep	reportative
rl	realis
s	subject

sg	singular
SpecDP	specifier of Determiner phrase
SpecIP	specifier of IP
SpecKP	specifier of Kase phrase
ss	same subject
subj	subjunctive
ta	transitive animate
TAM	tense aspect mood
ti	transitive inanimate
top	topic
TP	tense phrase
tr	transitive
UBH	Universal Base Hypothesis
UG	Universal Grammar
unr	unreal
UoL	Unit of Language
USH	Universal Spine Hypothesis
Utt	utterance
VP	verb phrase
WALS	*World Atlas of Language Structures*

1 *The universal structure of categories*

No amount of experimentation can ever prove me right;
a single experiment can prove me wrong.   Albert Einstein

Those who make many species are the 'splitters',
and those who make few are the 'lumpers'.   Charles Darwin

1.1   What is a category and how do we find one?

Linguistic descriptions of natural languages typically make reference to grammatical categories (*c*). This monograph addresses three questions: What are grammatical categories? How do we identify them? And are they universal?

What is labeled a grammatical category in individual grammars is not a homogeneous class. Specifically, it includes (but is not limited to) words, morphemes (meaningful units that may be smaller than words), features (that may or may not be associated with an overt expression), as well as certain construction types. These are exemplified below on the basis of categories that are attested in English.[1] To refer to this heterogeneous set of categorizable entities, I use the term *Unit of Language* (UoL).

(1)   Categorizable Units of Language
          a. Words: DETERMINERS, COMPLEMENTIZERS, AUXILIARIES, ...
          b. Morphemes: POSSESSIVE, PROGRESSIVE, ...
          c. Features: TENSE, NUMBER, CASE, ...
          d. Clause-types: IMPERATIVE, SUBJUNCTIVE, ...

We talk about a *category* when we can make generalizations over the distribution of a whole set of UoLs. For example, if we know that a word belongs to a certain category *c*, then we automatically know the distribution of this word. Crucially, this distribution cannot be determined based on either the meaning

---

[1] The classification in terms of words, morphemes, features, and clause-types is meant for illustrative purpose only. These notions, as we shall see, have no theoretical status.

or the sound of the word. But where does this categorial identity come from? Is it part of a universal repository of categories that is part of our genetic endowment, i.e., part of a universal grammar? Or does it emerge as a matter of language use?

To explore this question it is essential to know whether all languages make use of the same categories, and if not, what the range of variation is. But how can we tell whether categories are universal and if they are universal, how do we identify them? Answering these questions is not a trivial task.

To appreciate its complexity, consider first a more modest question: how do we identify the categories of individual languages? Since its categorial identity determines the morphological and syntactic distribution of a given UoL, we can use distributional criteria to identify categories. For example, we identify a word as an auxiliary if it precedes a main verb (2), if it inflects for tense (3) and subject agreement (4), and if it participates in subject–auxiliary inversion (5).

(2)   a. *Edward **has** blown the whistle.*
      b. *Edward **is** blowing the whistle.*

(3)   a. *Edward **had** blown the whistle.*
      b. *Edward **was** blowing the whistle.*

(4)   a. *They **have** blown the whistle.*
      b. *They **were** blowing the whistle.*

(5)   a. ***Has** Edward blown the whistle?*
      b. ***Is** Edward blowing the whistle?*

Based on these diagnostics, we can identify *have* and *be* as belonging to the category auxiliary, as in (6), where π stands for the representation of its phonetic form.

(6)   a. c:AUXILIARY $= \pi$:*have*
      b. c:AUXILIARY $= \pi$:*be*

The diagnostic tests for individual categories are always language-specific. For example, not all languages make use of an inflectional category tense. Similarly, subject–auxiliary inversion is not universally attested. Hence neither tense inflection nor subject–auxiliary inversion can function as universal diagnostics for a category auxiliary.

But if criterial diagnostics for categories are language-specific, how do we discover universal categories? In order to identify universal categories, we need universal diagnostics.

And in fact, as I will now show, there are certain formal characteristics of grammatical categories that cut across language-specific patterns in that they go beyond individual sound–meaning associations. These characteristics concern the way UoLs relate to their interpretation. What we observe is that the categorial identity c of a given UoL (i.e., its distribution) plays a critical role in the way this UoL relates to its interpretation. That is, the relation between a UoL and its interpretation is mediated by its categorial identity c. This suggests that the existence of c is a linguistic reality.

1.1.1 Patterns of multifunctionality

To see how c mediates the relation between a UoL and its interpretation, consider again the UoLs *have* and *be*. Based on language-specific criteria, they are classified as auxiliaries, as we have seen above. However, there are also occurrences of these particular forms (*have* and *be*) that do not satisfy the criterial diagnostics for auxiliaries. For example, in (7), they do not precede a main verb: in fact they behave themselves like main verbs. And in (8), we observe that only *be* but not *have* undergoes subject–auxiliary inversion.

(7)   a. *Edward **has** courage.*
        b. *Edward **is** the whistle-blower we have been waiting for.*

(8)   a. *Does Edward **have** courage?*
        b. ***Is** Edward the whistle-blower we have been waiting for?*

What we observe here is that, both *have* and *be* can be used in two different ways: as main verbs and as auxiliaries. In their use as main verbs, their meaning can roughly be characterized as indicating possession and identity, respectively. This is illustrated in (9), where Σ represents their substantive content[2] and the curly brackets around π and Σ reflect the fact that they create a unit in the form of an unordered set.

(9)   a. c:VERB $= \{\pi$: *have*, Σ:possession$\}$
        b. c:VERB $= \{\pi$: *be*, Σ:identity$\}$

In their use as auxiliaries, their meaning is hard to pin down. They are not associated with any kind of substantive content, at least not in any obvious way, as indicated by ? in (10). Instead they serve a grammatical function: to form complex tenses.

---

[2] I use the term *substantive content* to refer to the type of conceptual content whose interpretation is independent of the linguistic context.

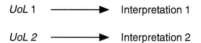

Figure 1.1 *Multifunctionality as homophony*

(10)   a. *c*:AUXILIARY = {π:*have*, Σ:?}
        b. *c*:AUXILIARY = {π:*be*, Σ:?}

A commonly held view in light of this multifunctionality is to treat it as an instance of accidental homophony (at least synchronically), such that there are two distinct UoLs each associated with a different interpretation, as in Figure 1.1.

But this type of multifunctionality is pervasive across unrelated languages. For example in Halkomelem (Salish) the UoLs π: *i* and π: *li* can be used as lexical verbs (*be here* and *be there*) and as auxiliaries. Consequently they can co-occur within the same sentence, as illustrated in (11)–(12).

(11)   a. *lí = chap ole   í?*
           AUX-2PL PRT be.here
           'You folks are here, eh?'

                                                                        Galloway 2009: 100

        b. *li   í   the-l   tàl?*
           AUX be.here DET.FEM-1SG.POSS mother
           'Is my mother in?'

                                                                        Galloway 2009: 100

(12)   a. *í:-lh = tsel   lí.*
           AUX-PST-1SG.S   be.there
           'I was there.'

                                                                        Galloway 2009: 103

        b. *lí-lh = a = chxw   lí.*
           AUX-PST-Q-2SG.S   be.there
           'Were you there?'

                                                                        Galloway 2009: 217

Thus, the Halkomelem auxiliaries show the same pattern of multifunctionality as those of English, as illustrated in (13)–(14).

(13)   a. *c*: VERB = {π: *í*, Σ:be.here}
        b. *c*: VERB = {π: *lí*, Σ:be.there}

(14)   a. *c*: AUXILIARY = {π: *í*, Σ:?}
        b. *c*: AUXILIARY = {π: *lí*, Σ:?}

The verb–auxiliary multifunctionality is a case where a lexical category does double duty as a grammatical category. But patterns of multifunctionality are not restricted to this type. We also find cases where a single form may instantiate two different types of grammatical categories. It is, for example, a common pattern across unrelated languages that demonstratives serve double duty as complementizers. This is illustrated on the basis of English in (15); representations of the two instances of this UoL are given in (16).[3]

(15)   a. *I know **that** guy.*
        b. *I know **that** this guy is courageous.*

(16)   a. *c*:DEMONSTRATIVE $= \{\pi$:*that*, Σ:?$\}$
        b. *c*:COMPLEMENTIZER $= \{\pi$:*that*, Σ:?$\}$

The patterns of multifunctionality illustrated here are often viewed as a result of a grammaticalization path (Heine 1994; Heine and Kuteva 2002; Hopper and Traugott 2003; see Roberts and Roussou [2003] and van Gelderen [2004] for a generative approach towards grammaticalization). But the grammaticalization approach is not itself an explanation for the affinity between certain categories or why certain UoLs are more prone to a recategorization than others. Moreover, the fact that similar grammaticalization paths are attested across unrelated languages suggests that there is something universal about these *recategorization* processes. And consequently, we may conclude that there is something universal about *categorization* processes.

The postulation of a categorial label that mediates between a UoL and its interpretation serves as a necessary step towards an explanation for the pervasive patterns of multifunctionality. The pervasiveness goes beyond these patterns of polysemy we have just observed. Other patterns of multifunctionality that are determined by the syntactic context include *expletives* (loss of interpretation), *syncretism* (one UoL occupying multiple cells within a paradigmatic organization), and *fake forms* (partial loss of interpretation). We shall see instances of these patterns of multifunctionality throughout this monograph. What they share in common is that the same UoL is interpreted one way in one syntactic context but another way in a different syntactic context. Since the syntactic distribution of a particular UoL is an indication

---

[3] From a descriptive point of view, the demonstrative version of *that* seems to have more semantic content than the complementizer *that:* the former includes a notion of displacement (*there* rather than *here*) which is absent in the latter. Leu (2008) argues that this displacement feature in demonstratives is supplied by a silent *there* which is overtly realized in many languages (see Section 6.4.3.2. for discussion).

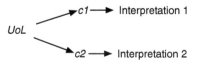

Figure 1.2 *Categorial identity mediates the relation between a UoL and its interpretation*

of its categorial identity we may conclude that c affects the interpretation of a given UoL, as illustrated in Figure 1.2.

If this is on the right track, we have in turn evidence for the linguistic reality of c.[4] In the course of exploring what this reality looks like we will address the question as to how exactly it influences the interpretation of a given UoL and in so doing we will be able to shed some light on the nature of grammatical meaning.

Crucially, patterns of multifunctionality of this sort can be used as universal diagnostics for categorical patterns.

1.1.2   Patterns of contrast

A second diagnostic for the presence of a category that can be universally applied has to do with the classic structuralist notion of *contrast* (Trubetzkoy 1939). As Saussure famously argued, language is defined by contrast: *'Dans la langue il n'y a que des différences ... sans termes positifs'* ['In a language there are only differences, and no positive terms'] (Saussure 1967 [1916]: 166).

To see contrast at work, consider English plural marking in (17). While the plural is marked with the suffix -*s*, the singular is morphologically unmarked. And crucially, this unmarked form is not compatible with a plural interpretation as evidenced by its incompatibility with a numeral of cardinality greater than 1, as shown in (18).[5]

(17)   a. *They planted the bug.*
        b. *They planted the bug-s.*

(18)   a. **They planted three bug.*
        b. *They planted three bug-s.*

---

[4] Whether this linguistic reality corresponds to a psychological reality as well is a different question that I will set aside here. See Cohen and Lefebvre (2005) for relevant discussion on this issue.

[5] Though as we shall see immediately below, the unmarked form is not universally associated with a singular interpretation. Rather unmarked forms are often interpreted as an instance of *general number*.

Table 1.1 *A paradigmatic contrast*

Base	Marked by ...	Interpreted as ...
N	{π:Ø, Σ:singular}	singular
N	{π:-s, Σ:plural}	plural

Table 1.2 *An interpretive contrast*

Base	Marked by ...	Interpreted as ...
N	–	singular
N	{π:-s, Σ:plural}	plural

So how does the unmarked noun trigger a singular interpretation? A number of answers have been proposed. They can be classified into two types. On one view, the singular interpretation arises in the presence of a dedicated UoL, which enters into a *paradigmatic contrast* with the overt plural marker but happens to be zero. This is illustrated in Table 1.1.

On the other view, the singular interpretation arises solely due to the absence of plural marking. This is illustrated in Table 1.2.

There are several ways to derive the presence of what appears to be a dedicated interpretation in the absence of a dedicated UoL. The singular interpretation can be considered a *default* that need not be directly encoded (Harley and Ritter 2002). Or else it may come about as an instance of Gricean-style reasoning (Sauerland 2008). This is grounded in the assumption that speakers are always as specific as possible. Thus, in light of the absence of plural marking, an addressee may conclude that the speaker must intend a non-plural interpretation, and non-plural equals singular. Essentially the same idea can also be modeled as a morphological principle instead of a pragmatic one, namely in terms of *the blocking principle*.[6] Only the most specified form compatible with a particular interpretation can be used. So even though the unmarked form may in principle be compatible with a plural interpretation, the existence of a more specified form (the plural marked form) blocks its use.

---

[6] This is also known as the elsewhere principle, Panini's principle, or the subset principle (Kiparsky 1973; DiSciullo and Williams 1987; Noyer 1992; Williams 1994, 1997; Halle 1997; Wiese 1999; Stump 2001).

Table 1.3 *Two ways of being unmarked*

Base	Marked by ...	Interpreted as ...	Markedness status
N	–	general number	truly unmarked
N	{π:Ø, Σ:singular}	singular	zero marked
N	{π:-s, Σ:plural}	plural	overtly marked

No matter how the interpretive contrast in Table 1.2 is implemented, it faces a fundamental problem. Not all morphologically unmarked forms are interpreted as singular. For example, in the context of a compound (19), the unmarked noun (*bug*) is not associated with a dedicated singular interpretation. Instead it is compatible with a plural interpretation. A bug spray is not a spray against a single bug as is obvious from the continuing sentence in (19).

(19)   **Bug spray** *won't help. There are bugs everywhere.*

This suggests that not all unmarked nouns trigger a singular interpretation. The compatibility of the unmarked form with both a singular and a plural interpretation is sometimes referred to as *general number* (Corbett 2000; Rullmann and You 2006). The accounts based on interpretive contrasts may still be rescued, however. Since plural marking is not allowed within compounds, the unmarked form is not blocked in this context. However, unmarked nouns in Halkomelem Salish are compatible with a plural interpretation (20a), even outside of compounds where plural marking can otherwise occur (Wiltschko 2008).

(20)   a. *te   lhíxw   swíweles*
            DET   three   boy
            'the three boys'

        b. *te   lhíxw   swóweles*
            DET   three   boy.PL
            'the three boys'

Wiltschko 2008: 642 (3)

This indicates that nouns not marked as plural are not all treated equally: some unambiguously trigger a singular interpretation, while others are compatible with both a singular and a plural interpretation. We thus have to recognize two ways of being unmarked (Table 1.3). In Wiltschko (2008), I argue that unmarked nouns in Halkomelem (and inside English compounds) are truly unmarked (i.e., they are not marked as singular) while singular nouns in English are marked as singular, albeit not by an overt UoL, but instead by a zero marker (Ø).

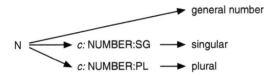

Figure 1.3 *Categorial identity mediates between form and interpretation*

But how do we distinguish between a zero-marked noun and a truly unmarked noun? We are facing yet another problem of multifunctionality: at least on the surface, the UoL used for the singular interpretation is identical to the UoL used for the general number interpretation. And again, this difference is syntactically conditioned. In the context of a compound an unmarked noun is truly unmarked while in the context of a nominal phrase (introduced by a determiner) an unmarked noun is in fact marked as singular. As with other cases of syntactically conditioned multifunctionality, we can model this difference by postulating the presence of a category. In particular, the singular interpretation in the absence of overt marking is indicative of the presence of a category, while the absence of a dedicated interpretation (general number) is indicative of the absence of such a category. Furthermore, associating the singular interpretation with a categorial identity predicts that there are other instances of the same category. And this is indeed the case: plural marking is another instance of the same category, which is typically identified as *c:*NUMBER. This is schematized in Figure 1.3.

The presence of a categorial identity not only mediates between form and interpretation and licenses zero marking; it also is syntactically active in that it participates in syntactic relations (such as agreement).

This contrasts with the Halkomelem pattern where unmarked forms are always truly unmarked and therefore are never associated with categorial identity. This is consistent with the fact that the plural marker does not form a class with other UoLs, zero marking is not available, and it does not participate in syntactic relations (Wiltschko 2008). Instead the plural marker, a simple sound–meaning correspondence (marked as {π,Σ}) in Figure 1.4 combines with a noun to trigger the plural interpretation.

We have now seen two types of patterns where the presence of a categorial identity mediates the relation between UoLs and their interpretation:

(i) multifunctionality
(ii) zero marking licensed by a categorial contrast.

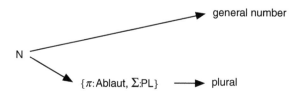

Figure 1.4 *Direct mapping between a UoL and interpretation*

In both cases, the UoL acquires a distinct interpretation by being associated with a particular categorial identity (*c*). These patterns are attested across categories and across languages, as we shall see. This suggests that UoLs are categorizable as a matter of the universal language faculty, i.e., *Universal Grammar* (UG). But at the same time, *c* does not seem to be an intrinsic property of UoLs in that they can exist without a categorial identity. This lies at the heart of both categorical patterns. Multifunctional UoLs are intrinsically without *c* but may be classified by two (or more) different categorial identities. And truly unmarked UoLs instantiated by general number nouns may or may not be classified as *c*:NUMBER. The question is how does *c* come about?

In what follows I discuss two opposing answers. On the one hand, we have the *Universal Base Hypothesis* according to which *c* comes about as a matter of UG. Accordingly, UG makes available a set of universal categories. This hypothesis, however, faces problems in light of much variation in the categorial inventories of the languages of the world. This is the starting point for the opposing view, which I dub the *No Base Hypothesis*, according to which there is no set of universal categories. I discuss each of these hypotheses in turn.

1.2   The Universal Base Hypothesis

In this section I introduce the Universal Base Hypothesis and the problems it presents.

1.2.1   The universal base as a repository of categories

The Universal Base Hypothesis (henceforth UBH) goes back to the early days of generative grammar (Chomsky 1965; Bach 1968; Lakoff 1970; Ross 1970 [1968]), but has been revived and updated over the years. In its early days, the *base* comprised both lexical rules and phrase structure rules. The former set of rules was responsible for the *categorization* of words (e.g., N → *dog*) whereas the latter was responsible for *word order* (e.g., NP → Det A N). According to early instantiations of the UBH the base is identical across all languages, with differences reducing to surface phenomena. The particular formulation in (21) is due to Ross (1970[1968]: 260).

(21)   The Universal Base Hypothesis
        The deep structures of all languages are identical, up to the ordering of constituents immediately dominated by the same node.

While more recent instantiations of the UBH no longer assume a base in this early sense, they nevertheless assume a universal structure for all languages.[7] For example, Kayne (1994) dispenses with variation in the way structure is built. Instead, according to this proposal, all phrases must be head-initial and adjunction is always to the left, though in Kayne's version of the UBH categorial identity plays no role. Universality of linearization **and** categorization is explicitly reintroduced in Cinque (1999), a framework that has come to be known as *cartography* and which has become a prolific research agenda. Its main thesis is that all languages have the same functional structure and that every projection in this structure is associated with a precise semantic interpretation, as in (22).

(22)   [[Mood$_{speech-act}$ [Mood$_{evaluative}$ [Mood$_{evidential}$ [Mod$_{epistemic}$ [T$_{past}$
        [T$_{future}$ [Mod$_{irrealis}$ [Mod$_{necessity}$ [Mod$_{possibility}$ [Asp$_{habitual}$ [Asp$_{repetitive}$
        [Asp$_{frequentative(I)}$ [Mod$_{volitional}$ [Asp$_{celerative(I)}$ [T$_{anterior}$ [Asp$_{terminative}$
        [Asp$_{continuative}$ [Asp$_{perfect(?)}$ [Asp$_{retrospective}$ [Asp$_{proximative}$ [Asp$_{durative}$
        [Asp$_{generic/progressive}$ [Asp$_{prospective}$ [Asp$_{sg.completive(I)}$ [Asp$_{pl.completive}$
        [Voice [Asp$_{celerative(II)}$ [Asp$_{repetitive(II)}$ [Asp$_{frequentative(II)}$
        [Asp$_{sg.completive(II)}$]]]]]]]]]]]]]]]]]]]]]]]]]]]]]]
                                                            Cinque 1999: 106

In this particular version of UBH, the answer to the question how *c* comes about is simple: via UG. In particular, UG is conceived of as a repository of categories available to individual languages, as in (23).

(23)   a. $C_{UG} = \{c_1, c_2, c_3, \ldots c_{n+1}\}$

        b. $C_{Lg1} = \{c_1, c_2, c_3, \ldots c_{n+1}\}$
            $C_{Lg2} = \{c_1, c_4, c_5, \ldots c_{n+1}\}$
            . . .

Though scholars differ in how many of these categories they postulate and what their precise content is, a survey of the labels used by generativist linguists reveals that content comes in (at least) four flavors: (i) substantive content (e.g., *tense* or *number*); (ii) word class (e.g., *determiner* or *complementizer*); (iii) morphological type (e.g., *inflection* or *clitic*); and

---

[7] See Section 2.4 for a brief overview of what happened to the base.

traditional grammatical category (*mood* or *aspect*). In what follows, I evaluate the UBH. I discuss three unexpected patterns of variation in categorial inventories.

1.2.2   Problem #1: Hypothesized universal categories are not universally attested

Our assumptions about universal categories are shaped by the categories we encounter in the languages most often studied. For example, tense and number are among the categories often assumed to be universal. This is because they are among the pervasive categories in the Indo-European languages. But not all languages use morpho-syntactic categories associated with this content (temporality or plurality). In other words, the languages of the world differ in the content of the features that are systematically expressed. They differ in the formal organization of meaning (Sapir 1921).

To see this consider first an Indo-European language like English. In matrix indicative clauses, the verb must be inflected for tense (present or past) as shown in (24); in noun phrases introduced by a determiner or a quantifier, a count noun must be inflected for number (singular or plural), as shown in (25).

(24)   Tense marking on verbs
      a. *Yoshi play-**ed** with his ball yesterday.*
      b. **Yoshi play-s* with his ball yesterday.*
      c. **Yoshi play with his ball.*
      d. **Yoshi playing with his ball.*

(25)   Number marking on nouns
      a. *He has five ball-**s**.*
      b. **He has five ball.*

The categories tense and number are among the functional categories commonly assumed to be universal. However, in many North American languages, tense and number are not among the pervasive morpho-syntactic categories. For example, in Blackfoot (Algonquian), tense is not part of the inventory of morpho-syntactic categories.[8] To see this, consider the sentences in (26). The same form can be used independently of whether the event holds in the present or in the past.[9]

---

[8] See Chapters 4 and 5 for more detailed discussion.

[9] This holds for states and imperfective marked eventives, but not for unmarked eventive predicates (Reis Silva and Matthewson 2007; Louie, forthcoming).

(26) a. *Anna*   *Mai'stoo*   *isttso'kiniwa.*
          ann-wa   Mai'stoo-wa   isttso'kini-wa
          DEM-PROX   Raven-PROX   hungry.AI-PROX
          'Mai'stoo is hungry.' OR 'Mai'stoo was hungry.'

      b. *Anna*   *Mai'stoo*   *áíhpiyiwa.*
          ann-wa   Mai'stoo-wa   á-ihpiyi-wa
          DEM-PROX   Raven-PROX   IMPF-dance.AI-PROX
          'Mai'stoo is dancing.' OR 'Mai'stoo was dancing.'

                                                  adapted from Louie 2008

Number marking, too, is not a language universal. For example in Mandarin, a classifier language, nouns are not inflected for number as shown in (26), where the numbers indicate tone.

(27) a. *yi4*   *zhi1*   *mao1*
          one   CLASS   cat
          'one cat'

      b. *san1*   *zhi1*   *mao1*
          three   CLASS   cat
          'three cats'

                                                  Chenhao Chiu p. c.

Similarly, not all languages have categories identified based on word class or function such as *complementizer* and *determiner*, typically labeled C and D, respectively. For example, Blackfoot has no UoLs dedicated for introducing complement clauses. A few illustrative examples are provided in (28).

(28) a. *Nitsikannistsikssimmstaawa*   *nitssisstsiikoohsi.*
          nit-iik-annist-ikssimmstaa-wa   nit-sistsikoo-hsi
          1-INT-MANNER-think.AI-PROX   1-tired.AI-CONJ
          'I think I am tired.'

      b. *Aniiwa*   *otaissistsikoohsi.*
          wanii-wa   ot-a-sistsikoo-hsi
          say.AI-PROX   3-IMPF-tired.AI-CONJ
          'He said he was tired now.'

      c. *Nitsíksstaa*   *nááhksoy'ssi.*
          nit-iik-sst-aa   n-ááhk-ooyi-hsi
          1-INT-want-AI   1-NONFACT-eat.AI-CONJ
          'I want to eat.'

      d. *Nitaanistaa*   *oomaahkootooyakstsissi.*
          nit-waanist-a-wa   ot-m-ááhk-go-yáakihtsiiyi-hsi
          1-say.TA-DIR-PROX   3–3-NONFACT-go-go.to.bed.AI-CONJ
          'I told him to go to bed.'

e. **Nitsítssáyoyihtopi**   *nitáaksoyi*   *ánnohka.*
   nit-it-say-Ioyi-htopi   nit-yáak-Ioyi   annohka
   1-then-NEG-eat-UNREAL   1-FUT-eat.AI   now
   'If I hadn't eaten then, I'd eat now.'

adapted from Frantz 1991: 115, ex. x

Similarly, not all languages have dedicated UoLs to introduce nominal phrases (e.g., determiners). This is illustrated in (29) for Polish where word order determines definiteness.

(29)   a. *Student lubi Marie.*
        student likes Mary
        'The student likes Mary.'

        b. *Marie lubi student.*
        Mary likes student
        'A student likes Mary.'

Zlatic forthcoming: (2)

And finally, not all languages have categories defined based on morphological type such as *inflection* or *clitic*. That is, among the hypothesized categories of UG we often find a category labeled INFL (for *inflection*, see Section 2.2). Not all languages have inflectional morphology however. For example isolating languages such as Mandarin are languages with no inflectional categories. It follows that morphological type such as inflection cannot identify universal categories.

This presents us with the first problem for this version of the UBH: not all languages use the same morpho-syntactic categories. This is of course not a new discovery as can be gleaned from the following quote from Tomasello (2003: 5):

> *Typological research has also established beyond reasonable doubt that not only are specific grammatical constructions not universal, but basically none of the so-called minor word classes of English that help to constitute particular constructions (e.g.. prepositions, auxiliary verbs, conjunctions, articles, adverbs, complementizers, and the like) are universal across languages either.*

What do we do in light of this variation in categorial inventories? If we want to maintain the strict version of the UBH introduced in (23) we have to assume that all categories are present in all languages. Categories that appear to be missing could be instantiated by silent UoLs or by a silent instantiation of the missing *c*, or else we may identify *c* as a syntactic pattern or construction. On this view then, language variation in categorical inventories reduces to a superficial difference: c may or may not be associated with an overt UoL $\{\pi,\Sigma\}$.

(30)   a. $C_{UG} = \{c_1, c_2, c_3, \ldots c_{n+1}\}$

   b. $C_{Lg1} = \{c_1\ c_2, c_3, \ldots c_{n+1}\}$
   $UoL_{Lg1} = \{\{\Sigma_1\ \pi\}, \{\Sigma_3\ \pi\}\ldots\}$
   $C_{Lg2} = \{c_1, c_2, c_3, \ldots c_{n+1}\}$
   $UoL_{Lg2} = \{\{\Sigma_2\ \pi\}, \{\Sigma_3\ \pi\}\ldots\}$

Alternatively, we may view variation in the inventory of morpho-syntactic categories across languages as indicating a parametric choice. While we may maintain a universal base, i.e., a universal set of categories (C_{UG}), we may hypothesize that individual languages can chose among them. If so, the set of language-specific categories (C_{Lg}) must be a subset of C_{UG}.

(31) $C_{UG} \supseteq C_{Lg}$

Note that both ways of dealing with variation in morpho-syntactic categories are still versions of the UBH. This is because UG is still conceptualized as including a repository of universal categories. And there are problems for the UBH that affect both of these versions. In particular, while the UBH may not predict that all languages have the same categories, it does make two other predictions: (i) categories of the same type will behave in a universal fashion; and (ii) any language-specific category must also be part of the universal repository. I now show that neither of these predictions is borne out.

1.2.3   Problem #2: Hypothesized universal categories are not formally identical

There is a second – more subtle – problem with the UBH. UoLs associated with the same content (e.g., temporality or plurality) do not behave in a formally identical manner. We have seen an example of this type of variation in Section 1.1.2. While both English and Halkomelem have UoLs that express plurality, they differ in their formal properties. In English plural morphology is an obligatory inflectional category, while in Halkomelem it is optional. It serves as a modifier.

A similar difference can be observed with the morpho-syntactic marking of past. While both English and Halkomelem have UoLs that express past time, they too differ in their formal properties. In English past morphology is an obligatory inflectional category, while in Halkomelem it patterns as an optional modifier. That is, unlike in English where all indicative matrix clauses must contain a tense-inflected verb, Halkomelem verbs need not be so marked. Past tense may be overtly marked (32a) but at the same time, the unmarked form is compatible with a present and past interpretation (32b).

(32)   a. *í-lh*   *qw'eyílex*   *tú-tl'ò.*
       AUX-PAST   dance   DET-PRN
       'He was dancing.'

       b. *í*   *qw'eyílex*   *tú-tl'ò.*
       AUX   dance   DET-PRN
       'He is/was dancing.'

Ritter and Wiltschko forthcoming: (2)

While both English and Halkomelem have UoLs that express the same substantive content (Σ: past), only the English UoL displays a categorical pattern. But if they do not have the same distributional properties across the two languages, we have to conclude that they do not instantiate the same category. **Distributional properties are the hallmark of categorial identity** and if their distribution differs, then presumably their categorial identity differs as well.

We reach the same conclusion when it comes to categories defined by word class or morphological type. Take for example *pronouns*. Across and within languages, pronouns show different distributional and morpho-syntactic properties. For example, English pronouns can function as bound variables, as shown in (33). Their reference is dependent on the quantified expression (*every man*). In contrast, pronouns in Halkomelem cannot be so dependent. As shown in (34a), the pronoun *tútl'ò* can only refer to a contextually salient individual and is not dependent on the interpretation of the quantified expression. The bound variable interpretation is only available in the absence of the pronoun (34b).

(33)   *Every man$_i$ is happy when he$_i$ sings.*

(34)   a. *mékw'*   *ye*   *sí:wí:qe$_i$*   *xwoyí:wel*   *lhi-s*   *t'í:t'elém **tú-tl'ò$_i$**.*
       every   DET.PL   men.PL   happy   when-3S   singing   DET-3PRN
       'Every man$_i$ is happy when he$_{*i/j}$ sings.'

       b. *mékw'*   *ye*   *sí:wí:qe*   *xwoyí:wel*   *lhi-s*   *t'í:t'elém.*
       every   DET.PL   men.PL   happy   when-3S   singing
       'Every man$_i$ is happy when he$_i$ sings.'

Wiltschko 1998: 17 (49)

This shows that even though the word class pronoun is available both in English and in Halkomelem, it differs in distribution (Déchaine and Wiltschko 2002; Wiltschko 2002b). And, again, if distributional differences are indicative of categorical differences, we have to conclude that we are not dealing with a universal category.

1.2.4   Problem #3: Unexpected categories

The last problem for the UBH I discuss here has to do with categories that are not part of the hypothesized set of universal categories. Consider for example the system of *direct/inverse* marking in Blackfoot as in (35).

(35)   a. *Nitsinóáwa.*
             nit-ino-**aa**-wa
             1-see.TA-**DIR**-PROX
             'I see him/her.'

         b. *Nitsinóóka.*
             nit-ino-**ok**-wa
             1-see. TA-**INV**-prox
             'S/he sees me.'

Bliss et al. 2011: (2)

From an Indo-European perspective, what is unusual about (35) is the fact that the same 1st person marker (*nit-*) is used independently of whether the 1st person participates in the event as the agent or the patient.[10] The parallel sentences in English differ in their agreement pattern as is obvious from the translations in (35). If the first person serves as the agent (*I see him*) no overt agreement marker is found on the verb; in contrast if a 3rd person serves as the agent, the verb is suffixed with the 3rd person singular agreement marker -*s* (*He see-s me*). Despite the fact that the agreement system does not co-vary with the switch in participants, the sentences are nevertheless unambiguous in Blackfoot. Direct/inverse marking on the verb serves to disambiguate the two sentences: if the 1st person functions as the agent, the verb is suffixed by -*aa* (the direct marker); in contrast, if the 3rd person functions as the agent, the verb is suffixed by -*ok* (the inverse marker).[11] So how do we analyze the direct/inverse system within a universalist approach? Given the logic of the UBH it must be part of the universal base. But if so, the cartographic structure in (22) will have to be modified to include the universal category instantiated by Blackfoot direct/inverse marking.

---

[10] In Blackfoot, there is no straightforward evidence for the grammatical relations subject and object that is independent of their thematic role (see Bliss, forthcoming for detailed discussion).

[11] See Chapter 7 for a detailed discussion of the direct/inverse system.

Crucially, the list of such examples is too extensive to be ignored. I here add two examples from Squamish, another Salish language. Salish languages – like Algonquian languages – present us with many categories unfamiliar from Indo-European languages. For example, in Squamish, the verb is overtly marked by a suffix which not only marks transitivity but which also appears to encode whether or not the agent is in control of the event (Jacobs 2011).[12]

(36) a. *chen*   *kw'lh-**at***   *ta*   *tiy.*
         1SG.S   pour-TR   DET   tea
         'I poured the tea.' (on purpose)

      b. *chen*   *kw'élh-**nexw***   *ta*   *tiy.*
         1S.SU   spill-LC.TR   DET   tea
         'I spilt the tea.' (accidentally)

                                                    Jacobs 2011: 1 (1)

Similarly, in the nominal domain, Squamish requires that a determiner be marked according to the location of the referent. For example, the neutral determiner *ta* can be used when the referent is close to the speaker, close to the addressee, or far away from both. In contrast, the proximate determiner *ti* can only be used when the referent is close to the speaker, but not otherwise (see Gillon 2006, 2009).

(37) a. *Chen*   *tákw-an*   ***ta***   *stákw.*
         1SG.S   drink-TR   DET   water
         'I drank the water.'

            ✓water near speaker
            ✓water near addressee
            ✓water far away from speaker and addressee

      b. *Chen*   *tákw-an*   ***ti***   *stákw.*
         1SG.S   drink-TR   DET   water
         'I drank the water.'

            ✓water near speaker
            ✗ water near addressee
            ✗ water far away from speaker and addressee

                                            Gillon 2009: 9f. (12–14)

None of these categories must be expressed in Indo-European languages. While deictic contrasts are quite frequent – but not always obligatory – among

---

[12] See Chapter 7 for a more detailed discussion of the system of control marking.

the world's languages,[13] control marking is considerably rare. It is these rare categories, which posit a particular challenge to UBH.

In sum, the UBH faces at least three problems:

(i) Some categories are missing in language L
(ii) Some categories have different distributional properties in different languages
(iii) Some categories of L have no correlate in C_{UG}.

1.3 The No Base Hypothesis and its problems

Similar arguments against the UBH are made by linguists who deny the existence of a universal base: there are no universal categories or word-order effects. I will refer to this as the No Base Hypothesis (henceforth NBH). In the absence of a universal base, we expect languages to differ unsystematically. This is in fact the position of Joos (1957: 96): *"languages could differ from each other without limit and in unpredictable ways."* More recently, Haspelmath (2007: 119) argues that the existence of typologically rare categories is detrimental to a universalist approach towards categories because *"almost every newly described language presents us with some 'crazy' new category that hardly fits existing taxonomies."*

The argument is simple. If Joos and Haspelmath have a point, then the number of categories (c) is potentially infinite. But if C_{UG} is a non-finite set, then the postulation of a UG will no longer be explanatory in our understanding of how children categorize.[14]

Above we have seen that morpho-syntactic categories – if defined based on content – are not universal. Since most categories that have been argued to be universal are defined in these terms, it is not surprising that researchers have concluded that there are no universal categories. That is, as illustrated in (38), a universal repository of categories is not attested (38a). And consequently, languages use different categories (38b).

(38)   a. $*C_{UG} = \{c_1, c_2, c_3, \ldots c_{n+1}\}$

b. $Lg_1 = \{c_1, c_2, c_3, \ldots c_{n+1}\}$
$Lg_2 = \{c_4, c_5, c_6, \ldots c_{n+1}\}$

---

[13] See Chapter 6.

[14] A similar argument is found in Sampson (1974) with regard to the question whether phonetic inventories are universal. I am grateful to an anonymous reviewer for pointing me to Sampson's paper.

There are two different versions of the NBH. And they both face problems. The NBH is probably most forcefully held by many contemporary typologists. For example, Croft (2001: 34) concludes that *"Universal Grammar does not consist of an inventory of universal categories and relations available to all speakers."* Similarly, Dryer (1997: 117) argues that grammatical relations and word classes in a cross-linguistic sense are *"at most a convenient fiction."* And he concludes that there are no cross-linguistic grammatical categories of any type.

However, the NBH is not restricted to typologists. It has also become a prominent position among generativists to deny the existence of universal categories while still maintaining the existence of UG (or even a universal linearization device). What is often denied is the existence of prefabricated labels for categories (see Chomsky 1995; Collins 2002)

The denial of universal categories automatically takes care of the three empirical problems that characterize the UBH. Since there is no expectation that categories are universal, the absence of categories with certain content is not surprising, and neither is the fact that categories of the same content have different formal properties or that there are certain typologically rare categories. But the NBH comes with its own problems (see Newmeyer 2007).

The first thing the NBH misses is the fact that there are categories in all languages and that children appear to assume so very early on in the acquisition process (Labelle 2005). That is, there are certain distributional properties associated with sound–meaning correspondences. This is the essence of categories: they are associated with distributional patterns which are neither defined by sound nor by meaning. The presence of categories is reflected in the patterns of multifunctionality, contrast, and complementarity, as we have seen in Section 1.1. If the universality of categories is denied, then the universality of categorical patterns is somewhat surprising. It appears that categorization is a universally available operation and given the universality of categorical patterns it also appears to be constrained by some universal principles.

Not only is it the case that there are categories, which manifest themselves via contrast, it is also the case that these categories are organized into certain domains. And these domains are ordered relative to each other. This defines the second problem for the NBH. If there are no universal categories, then these domain effects require further explanation.

Models in generative grammar have always assumed the existence of certain syntactic areas or domains. These are typically identified with particular categories. For example the verbal phrase is identified with the area where event roles (also known as *thematic roles*) such as agent or patient are defined. The area where aspectual marking and tense marking are introduced is typically identified with the area where grammatical roles such as subject and object are defined.[15] And finally, the area where clauses are typed is often identified as the area where discourse roles such as topic and focus are defined.[16] Crucially, linear and hierarchical ordering relations (scope) are restricted by these universally ordered domains: UoLs that interact with the event domain appear closer to the verbal root than UoLs that interact with tense and the domain of grammatical roles. And UoLs which interact with clause-typing and the domain of discourse roles are typically marked farthest away from the verbal root.

This is exemplified below for English and Blackfoot – though the ordering restriction manifests itself in different ways. In English (39), wh-words (*who*), which mark a special kind of focus (Rochemont 1986), occur at the left periphery followed by an auxiliary verb which is marked for tense followed by the subject and the verb.

(39)   a. *Who did you see?*
        b. focus > tense > subject > verb

In Blackfoot, these relations are all marked on the verb itself via suffixation rather than by means of independent words. While the linear order differs, the ordering relative to the main verb remains the same. The so-called TA (transitive animate) marker is part of a system of markers (so-called *finals:* Frantz 1991) which classifies predicates as transitive or intransitive and it simultaneously indicates the animacy of one of the arguments. It thus has the characteristic properties of a marker that interacts with the event domain and indeed it is in the position closest to the verb. Next comes the *direct* marker, which we have already seen in Section 1.2.4 above. It interacts with the system of grammatical relations in ways that I describe later.[17] And finally, the rightmost UoL *wa* is classified as a *proximate* marker. It can roughly be characterized as a marker of *discourse roles* (see Bliss 2005, 2013 for detailed discussion and analysis).

---

[15] This is just a rough approximation. As we shall see in Chapter 4, tense is not universally associated with this area.

[16] A more appropriate term may be *information structural roles*. Though for convenience I continue using the term discourse role. See Section 2.3 for a more detailed overview of these areas.

[17] See Section 7.2.4.1.

(40)   a. *Nitsóóhtowawa.*
        nit-yooht-o-a-wa
        1-hear-TA-DIR-PROX
        'I heard him/her.'   Bliss 2013: 33 (8)

        b. ... verb < transitivity < direct < proximate

While the particular content of these categories differs from those found in English, they show a similar ordering effect: event-related categories are introduced before categories related to grammatical relations which in turn are introduced before categories related to discourse relations as illustrated in (41).[18]

(41)   Universal ordering effects of categories
        c:DISCOURSE > *c*:GRAMMATICAL > *c*:EVENT > *c*:VERB

The existence of these universal ordering effects suggests that there is something to be ordered. This in turn suggests that the UBH, while facing some of its own problems, may be on the right track after all. At least the basis for these ordering effects must be universal. But under the NBH these ordering effects are coincidental and thus their robustness requires further explanation.

In addition, it has long been observed that there is a parallel behavior of nominal and verbal categories (Chomksy 1970; Abney 1987).[19] This parallelism suggests the existence of a category-neutral spine, which defines the core functions associated with each domain. If there are no universal categories, then the universal nominal/verbal parallelism requires further explanation. Thus, under the NBH this parallelism would be missed.

While the NBH does not face any of the problems we have identified for the UBH, we have now seen that it faces problems of its own. In particular, if there were no universal categories, then we would not expect any of the universal characteristics summarized in (42).

(42)   a. There are universal *categorical patterns*

                Patterns of multifunctionality
                Patterns of contrast

        b. Categories show systematic universal *ordering effects*
        c. Nominal and verbal categories *parallel* each other in function and
           hierarchical organization

---

[18] Note that in terms of absolute linear ordering Blackfoot is the mirror image of English in that the TA marker precedes the direct marker which in turn precedes the proximate marker. This effect is known as the Mirror Principle (Baker 1985); see Section 2.1.2.2.

[19] For a detailed discussion of these parallels see Section 2.3.4.

These universal characteristics suggest that there are universal restrictions on categorization.

In what follows I introduce an alternative to the UBH and the NBH in the form of the *Universal Spine Hypothesis*.

1.4   The Universal Spine Hypothesis

In this section I introduce the Universal Spine Hypothesis (henceforth USH) and I show how it allows us to come to terms with the tension between the observed universality of categorical properties on the one hand and their variability on the other.

1.4.1   *A problem: universals and variation*
We have thus far arrived at two seemingly contradictory propositions:

(43)   Universals and variation
    i. There is evidence for the universality of categories
    ii. Languages vary in their categorial inventories

Unsurprisingly, the tension between these two propositions is reflected in lively debates about the universality of categories. Evans and Levinson (2009: 429) argue that in light of the observed variation the claim for universality has to be abandoned.

> *The true picture is very different: languages differ so fundamentally from one another at every level of description (sound, grammar, lexicon, meaning) that it is very hard to find any single structural property they share. The claims of Universal Grammar, we argue here, are either empirically false, unfalsifiable, or misleading in that they refer to tendencies rather than strict universals. Structural differences should instead be accepted for what they are, and integrated into a new approach to language and cognition that places diversity at centre [sic] stage.*

And relative to categories, they argue that: *"no two languages have any word classes that are exactly alike in morphosyntactic properties or range of meanings"* (Evans and Levinson 2009: 435).

The question of how to come to terms with the observation that there are universals and that there is variation has been at the heart of the generative enterprise for several decades. However, focus has been mostly on linear ordering, displacement, dependency relations, and grammatical constructions. Variation in the categorial inventories of individual languages has hardly been addressed from this perspective. The USH fills this gap.

The key problem, which leads to the tension between the two propositions in (42), lies in the assumption that the set of universal categories (C_{UG}) is to be defined as a repository of grammatical categories. Rather, we have to recognize that the set of categories in C_{UG} is fundamentally different from the set of language-specific categories (C_{Lg}). The proposal I develop here, based on generative theorizing, consists of two claims:

(i)   Language-specific categories (c) are constructed from a small set of universal categories κ and language-specific UoLs

(ii) The set of universal categories κ is hierarchically organized where each layer of κ is defined by a unique function.[20]

I discuss each of these claims in turn.

1.4.2   The universal categorizer

The central thesis behind the USH is that language-specific categories (c) are constructed out of language-specific Units of Language (UoL) and a limited set of universal categories (κ) as in (44).

(44) $c = \kappa + \text{UoL}$

Thus, the set of categories in C_{UG} (45a) is fundamentally different from the set of categories in C_{Lg} (45b). The former are primitives; the latter are derived (Déchaine and Wiltschko 2010).

(45)   a. $C_{UG} = \{\kappa_1, \kappa_2, \kappa_3, \kappa_4\}$
          b. $C_{Lg} = \{c_1: <\kappa,\text{UoL}>_1, c_2:<\kappa,\text{UoL}>, c_3<\kappa,\text{UoL}>...c_{n+1}:<\kappa,\text{UoL}>\}$

Accordingly, C_{UG} does not serve as a repository for language-specific categories. Since language-specific categories are constructed, we predict that they can be constructed in different ways, and hence categories vary. Nevertheless, κ constrains the derivation of language-specific categories, and hence categorial patterns are universal. Thus, the USH differs from the UBH in the assumption that the spine does not serve as a repository for language-specific categories. Instead it serves as the basis for the construction of categories, as a universal *categorizer*.

1.4.2.1   Making sense of variation in categorical patterns

Consider the patterns of variation we have observed in Sections 1.2.2 to 1.2.4.

(i)   Some categories are missing in language L

---

[20] Whether these functions are part of the language faculty in the narrow sense, or whether they are based on more general cognitive functions is an empirical question, which I do not address here.

(ii)   Some categories have different distributional properties in different languages

(iii)   Some categories of L have no correlate in current versions of C_{UG}

Each of these patterns of variation is expected under the USH. First, why do categories such as tense appear to be missing in some languages? According to the USH, tense is constructed based on an abstract κ and a language-specific UoL. The specific temporal content of this category can thus be analyzed as being supplied by UoL, as in (46a). USH further predicts that languages without c:TENSE have another category c constructed from the same abstract universal category, as in (46b) (Chomsky 1973). In Chapter 4, I show that this allows for a fruitful exploration of tenseless languages.

(46)   Missing categories
   a. $C_{Lg1} = \{c_1$:TENSE $<\kappa_1,\{\pi,\Sigma$:past$\}>...\}$
   b. $C_{Lg2} = \{c_1$:? $<\kappa_1,\{\pi,\Sigma$:?$\}>...\}$

Second, why do apparently identical categories such as plural or past marking have different distributional properties across different languages? As we have seen, in Halkomelem neither plural marking nor past marking is contrastive (see Sections 1.1.2 and 1.2.3, respectively). The key to understanding this pattern of variation lies again in the assumption that the conceptual content (Σ:plural and Σ:past, respectively) is associated with universal categories on a language-specific basis. Thus, just as the same universal category κ may be associated with different substantive content Σ, so too may a particular substantive content Σ associate with different universal categories κ. For example, while Σ:plural may associate with κ to construct c:NUMBER it may also serve as a modifier of other categories, in which case it is analyzed as a simple sound–meaning bundle (47b). Such a plural marker is not predicted to display categorical properties and we expect its distributional properties to differ from a plural marker that associates with κ, as in (47a).[21] Alternatively, Σ:plural may associate with κ, but in a different domain (47c). This yields another kind of number-based category, with yet another set of distributional properties.[22]

(47)   Categories with different distributional properties.
   a. $C_{Lg1} = \{c_1$:NUMBER $<\kappa_1,\{\pi,\Sigma$:plural$\}>...\}$
   b. $C_{Lg2} = \{\pi,\Sigma$:plural$\}$
   c. $C_{Lg3} = \{c_2$:NUMBER $<\kappa_2,\{\pi,\Sigma$:plural$\}>...\}$

---

[21] See Wiltschko (2008) and Chapter 3 for a formalization of this claim.
[22] See Butler (2012) for a typology of plural marking along these lines.

Now let us turn to the third question: how should we analyze categories that have no correlate in C_{UG}? As we have seen in Section 1.2.4, languages may have categories that are not among the set of hypothesized universal categories. In particular, we have seen Blackfoot direct/inverse marking and Squamish control marking. Given the USH, we expect that these language-specific categories are constructed based on κ and language-specific UoLs. But the question still remains **how** such categories are constructed. What is the universal category κ that serves as the basis for constructing these categories?

(48)   Unexpected categories
        a. $C_{Lg1} = \{c_1:\text{DIRECT} = \kappa_1 + \text{UoL}\}$
        b. $C_{Lg2} = \{c_2:\text{CONTROL} = \kappa_2 + \text{UoL}\}$

I will develop an answer to these questions in Chapter 7, where I argue that both of the categories in (48) are based on the same universal category as viewpoint aspect is in English.

In sum, the assumption that language-specific categories are constructed allows us to understand the patterns of variation we observe in the categorial inventories of the languages of the world. The core of this monograph is dedicated to exploring precisely how such language-specific categories are constructed.

1.4.2.2   Making sense of the universality of categorical patterns

We now turn to the universality of categorical patterns introduced in Section 1.1. These patterns include multifunctionality and contrast. According to the USH, these patterns are due to the presence of κ in the construction of language-specific categories. To see this, consider first the patterns of multifunctionality. The essence of multifunctionality, whereby a given UoL receives a different interpretation depending on the syntactic context, lies in the recognition that categorial identity mediates between a UoL and its interpretation. According to the USH, the categorial identity of a language-specific category is not just a matter of the UoL. Instead, the UoL is viewed as an ingredient in the construction of the category along with the universal categorizer κ. Consequently, the interpretive effect that correlates with a switch in categorial identity of a given UoL must be due to κ. This is consistent with the observation that in such patterns of multifunctionality, there is no dedicated UoL that serves to supply a meaning. We may therefore conclude that this meaning is supplied by the language faculty itself, more specifically by κ, as in Figure 1.5. In particular, as we shall see, each κ is associated with a unique function. Thus, κ not only regularizes the distribution of UoLs as well as

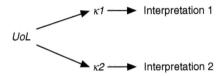

Figure 1.5 *κ mediates the relation between a UoL and its interpretation*

determining hierarchical structure, it also conveys meaning. In the core chapters of this monograph we will explore how.

The second universal categorical pattern we have discussed is contrast. In English nominal phrases, for example, the contrast between singular and plural nouns is exhaustive. Generally, if a count noun is not marked for plural, it must be interpreted as singular. For this reason, it is possible to infer the singular interpretation from the absence of plural marking, despite the absence of an overt UoL that would serve to mark singular. This pattern of contrast is mediated by the presence of categorial identity. And given the USH, this means that contrast reflects the workings of κ. I will assume that this is the result of an unvalued feature, which, in line with current minimalist assumptions, must be valued (either positively or negatively). It is this unvalued feature, which facilitates the construction of language-specific categories. In particular, it makes available the necessary interface for the interaction between a universal κ and a language-specific UoL. Again, exactly how this interaction comes about will be explored in the course of this monograph.

In sum, according to the USH, the fact that some UoLs have a categorial identity is a matter of UG. In this way, the USH sides with the Universal Base Hypothesis. However, it departs from the latter in that it does not postulate a universal repository of categories that languages make use of or choose from. Instead, language-specific categories are always constructed from universal categories and language-specific UoLs. So just as categories are not universally associated with sounds (π), they are also not universally associated with substantive content (Σ) (Ritter and Wiltschko forthcoming). Both sound and meaning, and their combinations $\{\pi,\Sigma\}$ are language-specific UoLs. Categorial identities κ come with particular functions, which reflect their position in the hierarchical organization of the set of κ, the universal spine, to which I turn next.

1.4.3   A syntactic spine with core functions
The UoLs of any language may combine with each other to form complex expressions and they do so in a hierarchically ordered fashion. As discussed in Section 1.3, the hierarchical organization of categories follows a universal

blueprint both in the nominal and verbal domain. These observations lead to the postulation of a universal syntactic spine. That is, the set of universal categories is hierarchically organized. This universal hierarchical organization is detectable based on the function associated with each of these universal categories (Déchaine and Wiltschko 2010). I shall refer to this as the *spinal function*. In particular, in line with current research (reviewed in Chapter 2), I assume four layers, as in (49). Furthermore, consistent with the observation that verbal and nominal projections parallel each other, I assume that the spine is inherently category-neutral. Its verbal or nominal character is derived. The lowest layer (*κ:classification*) is responsible for the classification of events or individuals; the second layer (*κ:point-of-view*) is responsible for introducing a viewpoint relative to which the event or individual is presented. The next layer (*κ:anchoring*) is responsible for anchoring the event or individual to the utterance; this may result in either deictic or anaphoric anchoring. And finally the spinal function of the outermost layer (*κ:discourse linking*)[23] is to establish a relation between the proposition or referent and the ongoing discourse.

(49) C_{UG} = *κ:discourse linking* > *κ:anchoring* > *κ:point-of-view* > *κ:classification*

On this view, the hierarchical organization of UoLs is mediated by the syntactic spine. That is, by virtue of associating with the spine, the arrangement of UoLs must be hierarchically organized, forming tree structures of the familiar kind.

The spinal function associated with κ is always relational. For example, the anchoring category (*κ:anchoring*) relates the event to the utterance. We can model this by assuming that κ is intrinsically transitive, relating two arguments, as in (50). The characteristics of these arguments are partly universal, though the particular flavor of a given argument can be affected by the content of the UoL that associates with κ, as we shall see.

(50)   The structure of κ

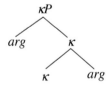

---

[23] Déchaine and Wiltschko (2010) take the outermost layer to be associated with the function of *clause*-typing. The relation between *typing* and *linking* has yet to be established.

As summarized in Figure 1.6, there are three ways in which categories are universally structured. The USH is meant to address all three aspects of the universal structure of categories. In the course of this monograph we explore each aspect relative to several case studies of categories that have proven difficult to analyze under current assumptions.

1.5 Methodological implications

This monograph is concerned with the universal structure of categories. There are a number of compelling reasons to explore the universality of categorial properties.

Linguistic universals may tell us something about the way the human mind works. At least that is the generative perspective. But there is something more basic we can glean from this exercise, something that is of interest even to a linguist that works on a single language, without the intention to compare or extract abstract universals. The question about the universal structure of categories has a *practical dimension*.

Assumptions about the general structure of categories are essential for the discovery of categories as well as for their analysis and presentation. To give but one example, consider the problem of glossing. Linguists need to be able to present the data they collect to other linguists. This is standardly done by means of presenting the data in various forms: (i) the string of sounds as they present themselves in the language; (ii) the morpheme breakdown of this string; (iii) the morpheme-by-morpheme glosses; and (iv) the translation. This is illustrated in (51), an example from Halkomelem.

(51) (i) *lílhachexw lí?*
      (ii) lí-lh = a = chexw   lí
      (iii) AUX-PAST = Q = 2SG.S   be.there
      (iv) 'Were you there?'

adapted from Galloway 2009: 217

The glossing problem presents itself as follows. According to the Leipzig glossing rules, "*Interlinear morpheme-by-morpheme glosses give information about the meanings and grammatical properties of individual words and parts of words.*"[24]

A problem arises with multifunctional words such as *lí* in (51): in sentence-initial position it functions as an auxiliary but in sentence-final position it functions as a main predicate. The way *lí* is glossed in (51) misses this generalization.

---

[24] See www.eva.mpg.de/lingua/resources/glossing-rules.php (preamble).

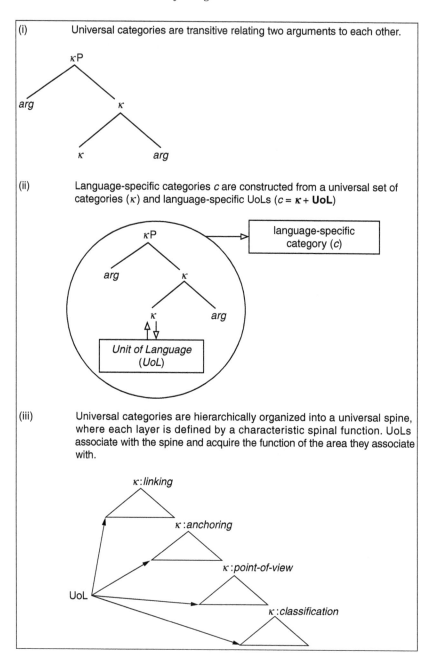

Figure 1.6 *The universal structure of categories*

The second problem has to do with patterns of contrast. Halkomelem past marking is not contrastive in the sense defined in Section 1.1.2.[25] Thus, its categorical properties are different from those of past marking in English. This is not reflected in the gloss. The Leipzig glossing rules acknowledge this indeterminacy of glossing:

> *It should also be noted that there are often multiple ways of analyzing the morphological patterns of a language. The glossing conventions do not help linguists in deciding between them, but merely provide standard ways of abbreviating possible descriptions. Moreover, glossing is rarely a complete morphological description, and it should be kept in mind that <u>its purpose is not to state an analysis</u>, but to give some further possibly relevant information on the structure of a text or an example, beyond the idiomatic translation.*[26]

While it is stated here that glossing is not to state an analysis, the decision to gloss a given morpheme as an auxiliary, for example, does involve an analysis. And indeed, the next paragraph states exactly that:

> *Glosses are part of the analysis, not part of the data. When citing an example from a published source, the gloss may be changed by the author if they prefer different terminology, a different style or a different analysis.*

What is this analysis that is involved? Recall that the diagnostic tests for individual categories are always language-specific. Thus, to decide whether a given UoL is an auxiliary we must apply language-specific diagnostics. But then, what is the basis for classifying and thus glossing it as an auxiliary? There seems to be an implicit assumption that language-specific categories can all be classified as instantiating some kind of *meta-category* (such as auxiliary). But if such meta-categories can indeed be postulated, independently of their language-specific instantiations, then this is no longer different from postulating universal categories.

This problem is exacerbated in the context of typological and generative research. Both seek to understand the range of variation languages display and they are thus intrinsically comparative endeavors. How do we compare languages without postulating such meta-categories? How do we know what to compare if we do not have conceptions of categories in mind that have somewhat universal scope?

---

[25] See Chapter 4 for explicit discussion.
[26] See www.eva.mpg.de/lingua/resources/glossing-rules.php (preamble) (emphasis MW).

Most typological approaches are characterized by the assumption that comparison must be based on the content of a given category. For example, according to Haspelmath (2007: 119), *"comparison cannot be category-based, but must be substance-based, because substance (unlike categories) is universal."* The fact that most glosses listed in the Leipzig glossing rules are indeed defined by their substantive content (e.g., DURATIVE, FUTURE, IMPERATIVE, LOCATIVE, PLURAL, ...) reflects this belief. Those categories that are not so defined are alternatively based on word class (AUXILIARY, COMPLEMENTIZER, DETERMINER, ...) or based on grammatical function (ABSOLUTIVE, OBJECT, INFINITIVE, ...). If indeed, as Haspelmath suggests, categories are not universal, then the question of glossing becomes acute for these categories that are not definable based on substance. How do we decide whether a given UoL instantiates an auxiliary, a complementizer, or a determiner and can thus be compared to instantiations of the same meta-category in other languages if there are no universally valid diagnostics?

The same conundrum arises in the context of generative research, which seeks to identify universals and variation mostly for the sake of exploring the cognitive underpinnings of the language faculty. It is clearly communicated in the following quote from Matthewson (2010), who deals with the problem of classifying a category as subjunctive.

> *This raises a terminological issue which arises in many areas of grammar. Should we apply terms which were invented for European languages to similar—but not identical—categories in other languages? For example, should we say 'The perfect/definite determiner/subjunctive in language X differs semantically from its English counterpart', or should we say 'Language X lacks a perfect/definite determiner/subjunctive', because it lacks an element with the exact semantics of the English categories? I adopt the former approach here, as I think it leads to productive cross-linguistic comparison, and because it suggests that the traditional terms do not represent primitive sets of properties, but rather potentially decomposable ones.* Matthewson 2010. 9:14, fn.10

And the problem is most acute when we encounter these rare categories that cannot in any straightforward way be classified in terms of any of the existing notions. This problem is highlighted by the following quote from Nordlinger and Sadler (2008), who deal with the question as to when a given temporal marker should be classified as tense. But, as they point out, this problem is not restricted to tense.

> *To put it in a broader perspective, when confronted with unfamiliar or previously undescribed linguistic phenomena, how do we know when to*

establish a new category to account for it, and when to redefine an existing one? To what extent is a category to be defined in terms of the internal oppositions of the language itself (that is, in terms of its positioning within the systems of the language under description), and to what extent should we impose preconceived notions of categories and their boundaries? These seem to us to be fundamental and difficult methodological points that we constantly face in linguistic research, most especially on underdescribed languages, and ones that warrant further discussion and reflection by the field as a whole.   Nordlinger and Sadler (2008: 329)

Thus, what is required is a set of assumptions and procedures that allow us to describe and compare language-specific categories. This is not a new argument. It goes back to Humboldt (1829), who recognized the necessity for a *tertium comparationis*, a third element in the comparison of two languages (see also Raible 2001).[27]

Die lichtvolle Erkennung der Verschiedenheit erfordert etwas Drittes, nämlich ungeschwächt gleichzeitiges Bewusstseyn der eigenen und fremden Sprachform. Dies aber setzt in seiner Klarheit voraus, dass man zu dem höheren Standpunkt, dem beide untergeordnet sind, gelangt sey, und erwacht auch dunkel erst recht da, wo scheinbar gänzliche Verschiedenheit es auf den ersten Anblick gleich unmöglich macht, das Fremde sich, und sich dem Fremden zu assimilieren.   Humboldt (1963[1829]: 156)

This third element may be called a *philosophical (universal) grammar*. The postulation of such a universal theoretical, rather than descriptive, grammar goes back to the *Grammaire générale et raisonnée de Port-Royal* by Claude Lancelot and Antoine Arnaud (Paris 1660). The latter is "general" in the sense that it seeks to capture all languages.

It is one of the goals of this monograph to start developing such a philosophical universal grammar based on insights rooted in the generative tradition. The USH is meant to provide a foundation for this endeavor. On the assumption that language-specific categories c are constructed ($c = \kappa + \text{UoL}$) the comparison among such categories brings about a new analytical challenge. We need to identify the ingredients of each category (UoL and κ) as well as the way these ingredients relate to each other: this comprises the structure of

---

[27] The enlightening recognition of differences requires a third element, namely unweakened simultaneous consciousness of one's own form of language as well as those of unfamiliar ones. But this presupposes in its clarity that one has reached the higher point of view, to which both are subordinated; and it awakens darkness where apparent complete divergence makes it impossible – at first sight – to assimilate the unfamiliar to oneself and oneself to the unfamiliar. (Translation MW.)

categories and provides the foundation for a formal typology. It is formal because it is based on the structure of categories, rather than their meaning.

In contrast, neither the UBH nor the NBH provides a third element for comparison. On the one hand the NBH denies the existence of a universal base altogether. The UBH, on the other hand, postulates the existence of a universal base, but crucially, the set of universal categories is conceived of as either identical to or a superset of the categorial inventory of a given language. In the absence of an independent third element for comparison, it comes as no surprise that the basis for comparison in both approaches is substance. But as we have seen, substance-based comparison leads to the identification of categories with very different formal properties. And this is precisely one of the reasons that proponents of the NBH deny the existence of categorical universals: categories do not seem to be universally defined. Instead, according to Comrie (1989), linguistic universals must always be viewed as prototypes with non-categorical, fuzzy boundaries. A prototype is defined by a set of features, but peripheral members of a particular category are not always associated with all of the features of the prototypical one (Croft 2003). This is illustrated in Figure 1.7.

It is my contention that the observed fuzziness is a direct consequence of the lack of a third element of comparison. Instead, the element of comparison is substance, as in Figure 1.8. Under the NBH this is all there is (as in the left-hand model), whereas under the UBH there is a universal repository of categories, which are defined by substance but which are also hierarchically organized (as in the right-hand model). Crucially, within both however, the methods of comparison are implicitly or explicitly substance-based.

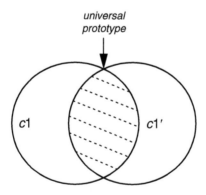

Figure 1.7: *Universal categories as prototypes*

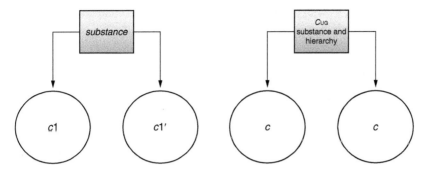

Figure 1.8 *Substance-based comparisons*

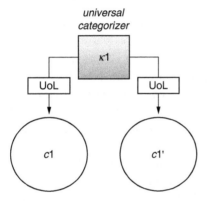

Figure 1.9 *Comparison based on κ*

It follows from the USH that substance-based comparisons will not yield a unified set of categories. Thus, when analyzing a given language, we cannot determine categorial identity on the basis of meaning (see also Newmeyer 2007). This should come as no surprise. We have long assumed this for the lexical categories (*nouns* and *verbs*). But when it comes to grammatical categories, substance-based comparisons are common.

According to the USH, substantive content is supplied by UoLs and thus necessarily language-specific. Consequently, the USH makes available a comparison set based on κ, as in Figure 1.9.

The set of κ is detectable on the basis of universal categorical patterns as well as the spinal functions.

In sum, the USH has theoretical consequences in that it allows us to draw conclusions about the universal structure of categories. At the same time the

USH provides us with a tool for discovery, analysis, and comparison. It makes for a novel way of approaching universality and diversity.

1.6   Overview

The goal of this monograph is to explore in more detail the idea that categories are constructed. The particular version of this idea I explore and test here is the Universal Spine Hypothesis (USH). The universal spine is characterized by a set of core categories κ that are defined by formal and functional properties. In Chapter 2 I introduce the history of ideas behind the main ingredients of the universal spine: structure, the labels of categories within the structure (functional categories), and the different areas in the spine, which are defined by their core function. I also review evidence that the spine dominating verbal categories (deriving clauses) is fully parallel to the spine dominating nominal categories (deriving nominal constituents). Once we recognize a universal spine that exists independently of words and morphemes (the units of language, UoLs) it becomes necessary to establish how the language-specific UoLs associate with the spine. At the end of Chapter 2, I introduce some of the existing ideas on how to model this relation. Thus, the purpose of Chapter 2 is to familiarize the reader with some of the core ideas that lead to the particular version of the universal spine I assume here. For readers that are already familiar with these ideas, this chapter may be skipped without affecting the readability of the remainder of this monograph.

Having identified the essential properties of the spine, I then move on in Chapter 3 to make explicit how the assumption of a universal spine can be exploited for the discovery, comparison, and analysis of language-specific categories. In particular, I introduce the logical possibilities for associating UoLs with the spine and the empirical effects they bring about. I also spell out more explicitly my assumptions regarding the structure of κ, which I assume in the remainder of the monograph.

The core Chapters (4–7) comprise a series of case studies of language-specific categories. In particular, I focus on categories that are difficult to define in terms of their substantive content and which therefore give rise to non-trivial problems for substance-based comparisons both within the UBH and within the NBH. In each chapter, I start by pointing out problems with both models (UBH and NBH) and then move on to detailed case studies adopting the USH. I show how USH can successfully derive the empirical properties of these categories. This includes categories that are not attested cross-linguistically, categories which are defined by different formal properties across languages, as well as the rare categories introduced above (direct/inverse and control).

In Chapter 4, I start by exploring tense and tenselessness.[28] If we ask whether all languages make use of a morpho-syntactic category tense, the answer is *"No!"* Some languages lack UoLs marking present and past; and in some languages past marking does not display categorical properties. Under the USH the absence of a particular language-specific category such as tense leads to a novel question: what else is there instead of tense? That is, the assumption that *c:*TENSE is constructed based on *κ:anchoring* prompts us to look for another *c* constructed from *κ:anchoring*. And what we find, based on the diagnostics developed in Chapter 3, is that other manifestations of *κ:anchoring* involve *c:*PERSON in Blackfoot, *c:*LOCATION in Halkomelem, and *c:*REALIS in Upper Austrian German.

Since the construction of the anchoring category differs in dependent and independent clauses, I explore independent clauses separately in Chapter 5. There are simply more factors at play in the construction of dependent language-specific categories. The category I explore in this chapter is the subjunctive, a category that is notoriously difficult to define based on its substance. It is shown that the categories labeled subjunctive across different languages (Blackfoot, Cypriot Greek, Halkomelem, and Upper Austrian German) are all constructed in different ways with predictably different empirical consequences.

In Chapter 6, I explore nominal categories that are based on *κ:anchoring*. These include certain pronouns, demonstratives, and case. The discussion of pronouns revolves around German personal pronouns. While this paradigm is familiar, the USH sheds new light on a peculiar pattern of multifunctionality that has largely been ignored. Thus, the USH is not only useful as a heuristic in the analysis of unfamiliar languages; it also invites us to reconsider familiar data. As for demonstratives, I explore the paradigm of so-called deictic determiners in Squamish (Salish). Here the USH sheds new light on the paradigmatic organization of this system, building on a pattern of multifunctionality which has to date been neglected. Pronouns and demonstratives manifest the nominal equivalent of the clausal anchoring categories found in independent clauses. I then move on to develop a theory of case, which is another category notoriously difficult to come to terms with in substance-based approaches towards categories. In particular, I argue that case instantiates a

---

[28] The core insight of this chapter draws from joint work with Elizabeth Ritter (Ritter and Wiltschko 2005, 2009, forthcoming).

form of dependent anchoring, similar to the subjunctives explored in Chapter 5. This novel way of approaching case allows for a new way to understand caselessness in some polysynthetic languages without recourse to a macro-parameter.

Finally, in Chapter 7, I investigate the construction of aspect. While the coding of aspectual information is widespread it is nevertheless not universally attested, nor are the formal properties of aspectual markers uniform. In line with the USH, I develop an analysis of aspect, which does not identify it with its substantive content (a form of temporal marking). Instead, the core function of aspect is to introduce a point of view from which the reported event is presented. However, this point of view need not be temporal. In particular, I show that the rare categories introduced in Section 1.2.4 (Blackfoot direct/inverse marking and Squamish control marking) can be analyzed as manifesting κ:*point-of-view*. The proposed analysis has implications for temporal aspect as well, which I briefly address.

Based on the case studies in Chapters 4–7, I draw conclusions about the universal structure of categories in Chapter 8. What are the universal aspects of κ and what is the range of variation we observe in the construction of language-specific categories? Note that the case studies are based on a few languages only: Blackfoot, Halkomelem, and Squamish (both Central Coast Salish), as well as German and one of its dialects (Upper Austrian German). Compared to other typological studies, this is a small sample, most likely too small to draw firm conclusions about universals. However, in contrast to substance-based analyses, comparison and analysis within the USH require in-depth exploration of the formal properties of categories and the UoLs that are used in their construction. In order to achieve the required depth, I cannot cover the entire range of categories found across the languages of the world. It is my hope that the ideas I explore in this monograph will inspire others to look at language-specific categories in this new way.

2 A history of ideas behind the spine

Recognition of function always precedes recognition of being.

Rita Mae Brown

2.1 Structure

What do generative findings tell us about what we may expect about individual language-specific grammars? One of the core findings of generative investigations is structure-dependence (Chomsky 1980). The units of language (UoLs) that make up a sentence, a phrase, or even a word are not simply assembled like beads on a string. Instead, evidence from many genetically and geographically unrelated languages points to the conclusion that these UoLs are hierarchically organized. But when confronted with a string of UoLs such as *Edward has blown the whistle,* how do we determine where and how each UoL is integrated into the syntactic hierarchy? Pre-generative linguistics recognized the existence of constituents and thus developed constituent tests. But the generative enterprise found hierarchical organization beyond constituent structure. There is a widely held assumption that language is fundamentally organized around a universal structure. This is often referred to as the *Universal Base Hypothesis.*

> *to say that the formal properties of the base will provide the framework for the characterization of universal categories is to assume that much of the structure of the base is common to all languages. This is a way of stating a traditional view, whose origins can ... be traced back at least to the [Port-Royal] Grammaire générale et raisonée.* Chomsky (1965 [1964]: 117)

In what follows, I explain how ideas about universal categories have changed throughout the history of generative grammar.

2.1.1 Structure dependence

That a string of morphemes and words is organized in ways that go beyond '*X precedes Y*' is virtually uncontroversial across all ways of approaching grammar. Thus, the existence of a relative hierarchy is an established fact within linguistic theory. Some morphemes and words are more tightly connected to each other than others – we call those tight connections of UoLs *constituents* or *phrases*. This had been established long before generative grammar emerged – and there are well-established discovery procedures for such phrases, namely tests for constituency.

Generative grammar, however, introduced the idea that there are rules deriving one sentence from another and – crucially for our purposes – that these rules are *structure dependent*. One of the early pieces of evidence for structure dependence came from *auxiliary inversion*. To derive a well-formed *yes/no*-question in English, the auxiliary must invert with the subject, as in (1).

(1)   a. *Edward has blown the whistle.*
        b. *Has Edward blown the whistle?*

On the basis of these examples only, we could formulate the hypothesis that *yes/no*-questions in English are formed by means of moving the first auxiliary to sentence-initial position. Such a rule is purely based on linear ordering. This rule, however, will fail to generate the right question when the corresponding declarative clause is more complex, as, for example, in (2a). If we move the first auxiliary to sentence-initial position, as in (2b), the result is not a well-formed *yes/no*-question. Rather, we need to recognize that the subject is complex, containing a relative clause. It is the auxiliary following the complex subject, which must be inverted to derive a well-formed *yes/no*-question, as in (2c).

(2)   a. *The guy that has blown the whistle has left the country.*
        b. **Has the guy that blown the whistle has left the country?*
        c. *Has the guy that has blown the whistle left the country?*

This type of evidence establishes that rules are structure-dependent; and if rules are structure-dependent, it follows that there must be some structure that they depend on. But ideas of how structure is composed or generated vary considerably. The kind of structure we minimally need to account for phenomena such as subject-auxiliary inversion requires us to recognize constituents: some words in a sentence form a unit to the exclusion of others. For example, subjects (S) and objects (O) form constituents in English as indicated by the brackets in (3).

(3)   [*The guy that has blown the whistle*]$_S$ *has left* [*the country*]$_O$.

This amount of structure is taken by many to be a language universal. Consequently, languages are often classified based on the order of such constituents (e.g., SVO, OVS, VSO, etc.). As we shall see in Section 2.3.1, however, in the generative tradition it is recognized that we also need to distinguish between various types of subjects and objects (e.g., thematic subjects versus grammatical subjects). Thus a formal typology of sentence structure must go beyond the traditional labels S, V, and O. Moreover, sentences do not consist only of subjects, verbs, and objects. What about the remaining UoLs in (3), namely the auxiliary and the complementizer? How are they integrated into the structure?

2.1.2   *Diagnosing structure*

It was one of the crucial findings of generative grammar that the object forms a constituent with the verb to the exclusion of the subject (and the auxiliary) as in (4).

(4)   The VP hypothesis

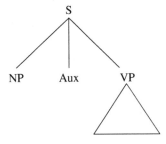

From our present perspective the postulation of the VP seems obvious at best and too simplified at worst.[1]

2.1.2.1 C-command

The postulation of the VP opened up a whole research agenda, which was to demonstrate that there are asymmetries in the distribution of subjects and objects. Subjects are structurally higher than objects in a way that makes it possible for objects to be dependent on subjects. Thus, for dependency relations such as, for example, reflexive binding (5), polarity licensing (6), or quantifier-variable binding (7), objects are generally found to be dependent on subjects and not vice versa.

---

[1] Not everyone agrees with the claim that a VP is universally available. For example on some accounts in the 1980s, non-configurational languages were characterized by lacking a VP (Chomsky 1981; Haider 1982; Hale 1982, 1983; É. Kiss 1987; see also Carnie [2005] for a more recent instantiation of this claim for Modern Irish, a VSO language).

(5)   a. *Edward$_i$ saw **himself$_i$** in the news.*
       b. ****Himself$_i$** saw Edward$_i$ in the news.*

(6)   a. *I don't know **anyone**.*
       b. ****Anyone** doesn't know me.*

(7)   a. *Everyone$_i$ loves **his$_i$** mother.*
       b. ****His$_i$** mother loves everyone$_i$.*

These kinds of dependencies have served as a generative discovery procedure ever since.

They are constrained by the structural relation of c(onstituent)-command (Reinhart 1976) defined as in (8).

(8)   Node A c(onstituent)-commands node B if neither A nor B dominates the other and the first branching node which dominates A dominates B.

                                                         Reinhart 1976: 32 (36)

Based on syntactic dependency relations, we are able to determine which constituent is generated higher in a given syntactic tree. We observe such asymmetries not only between subjects and objects but also between direct and indirect objects (Barss and Lasnik 1986).

(9)   a. *I showed John$_i$ himself$_i$ in the mirror.*
       b. **I showed himself$_i$ John$_i$ in the mirror.*

                                               Barss and Lasnik 1986: 347 (2), (3)

(10)   a. *I gave noone anything.*
       b. **I gave anyone nothing.*

                                              Barss and Lasnik 1986: 350 (18), (19)

(11)   a. *I denied each$_i$ worker his$_i$ paycheck.*
       b. **I denied its$_i$ owner each$_i$ paycheck.*

                                               Barss and Lasnik 1986: 348 (6), (7)

Facts like these have lead generative grammarians to develop a more articulated structured VP, one in which the direct object is generated in a position structurally higher than indirect objects. Specifically, Larson (1988) proposes an analysis of double-object constructions that implements an insight (dating back to Chomsky 1975[1955]) according to which the verb and the indirect object form a constituent to the exclusion of the direct object. According to Larson, a sentence like (12a) is associated with the underlying representation in (12b). To derive the observed linear order he further argues that the verb moves above the VP to the verbal head of another VP, as illustrated in (12c), where *t* represents the trace of movement.

(12)   a. *John sent a letter to Mary.*
        b. *John* [$_{VP}$ *a letter* [$_V'$ *send to Mary*]]
        c. *John* [$_{VP}$ *send$_i$* [$_{VP}$ *a letter* [$_V'$ *t$_i$ to Mary*]]]

Larson's (1988) analysis has come to be known as the *VP-shell analysis* and has played an important role ever since. What is crucial for our purpose is that c-command effects have long served as a useful discovery procedure for hierarchical structure.

2.1.2.2 Linear precedence

Another discovery procedure for hierarchical structure is the linear order of words and morphemes – at least under some assumptions. For example, according to the Linear Correspondence Axiom (henceforth LCA) (Kayne 1994) linear precedence derives from asymmetric c-command as in (13).

(13)   X precedes Y iff X c-commands Y and Y does not c-command X.

Assuming the LCA, the further left a given word is in the linear string, the higher it must be associated with the syntactic tree. In example (14), *John* linearly precedes *love*, which in turn linearly precedes *Mary*.[2] The linear order can (in part) be read off the hierarchical structure. The NP *John* associates with the highest position in the tree asymmetrically c-commanding and therefore preceding all other UoLs in the sentence. Next, the verb *love* asymmetrically c-commands Mary and thus linearly precedes it.

(14)   C-command maps onto linear precedence

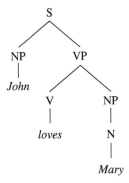

---

[2] For the purpose of this discussion, I abstract away from the labels associated with the projections and continue to use the labels S and VP. The label of the projection does not affect the logic of the LCA. We return to the issue of category labels in the next subsection.

In sum, according to the LCA, asymmetric c-command maps onto linear order and, as a consequence, the linear order of words can give us a clue about the hierarchical organization of the sentence.[3]

Similar considerations apply to word-internal syntax, i.e., morphology. In particular, according to some assumptions, the linear ordering of morphemes can give us a clue about the relative position in a given hierarchy. For example, according to Baker's (1985) *Mirror Principle*, the ordering of morphemes tells us something about the relative height of the morpheme. The closer a given morpheme appears to the root (i.e., the lexical core) in terms of its linear order, the lower this morpheme will be in the structural hierarchy.

(15)   The Mirror Principle
        Morphological derivations must directly reflect syntactic derivations
        (and vice versa).

                                                        Baker 1985: 375 (4)

To see this, consider the examples in (16) from Chamorro as discussed in Baker (1985) (data are originally from Gibson 1980). The plural marker *man/ fan* is restricted to intransitive predicates, as in (16a). In passive constructions such as (16b), the distribution of *fan* suggests that it is sensitive to the surface subject since the passive derives an intransitive predicate. In contrast, in causative constructions such as (16c), the distribution of *fan* suggests that it is sensitive to the underlying subject, since after causativization the predicate is no longer intransitive.

(16)   a. ***Man**-dikiki'*.
            PL-small
            'They are small.'

        b. *Para-u-**fan**-s-in-aolak*   *i*   *famagu'un*   *gi as*   *tata-n-niha.*
            IRR-3PL.S-PL-PASS-spank   the   children   OBL   father-their
            'The children are going to be spanked by their father.'

        c. *Hu-na'-**fan**-otchu*   *siha.*
            1SG.S-CAUS-PL-eat   them
            'I made them eat.'

                                                adapted from Baker 1985: 374 (2)

Thus, the interaction between plural marking and argument-changing processes suggests that plural marking happens after passivization but before causativization. Crucially, this correlates with the linear ordering of the

---

[3] Unlike Kayne (1994) I do not assume that asymmetric c-command always maps onto linear precedence. In particular, I assume that right-adjunction is an option; see Section 2.1.2.3.

plural marker relative to the passive and causative morphemes, respectively. In particular, the passive marker appears closer to the verb root than the plural marker, whereas the causative marker appears further away from the verb root. This is the essence of the mirror principle. The order of morphemes reflects the order of syntactic rules which in turn may be reinterpreted to indicate that the closer a morpheme appears to the verb root, the lower it will appear in the syntactic tree. Thus, the linear order of morphemes gives us a clue about syntactic structure.

Linear order is, however, not always a good predictor for structure. For example, the ordering of clitics has been argued to be governed by post-syntactic templatic information (Perlmutter 1971; Bonet 1991, 1995). As a result, there is massive cross-linguistic, as well as dialectal, variation to be observed. Thus, clitic ordering (at least in some languages) will not necessarily provide us with a clue about hierarchical structure.

Moreover, linear order tells us nothing about constituency. While in some cases, intonational phrasing coincides with syntactic constituency this is not always the case. Consider the examples in (17).

(17)   a. *He never completed% the list of references%*
        b. **He never completed the% list of references%*
                                            Taglicht 1998: 183 (2a/c)

The string of words (*the list of references*) functions as a constituent. Syntactic constituency here is matched by intonational phrasing. This can be seen on the basis of the fact that an intonational break (indicated by%) is well formed preceding the constituent *the list of references*. However, if the break occurs between the determiner *the* and the head noun *list*, the result is an ill-formed utterance. In this case the break would indicate hesitation, which in turn is not regulated by grammar (see Taglicht 1998: 183 for discussion).

Now consider the examples in (18) from Halkomelem and in (19) from Gitxsan (Tsimshianic).

(18)   *Osu   thíy-t-es=te   sil-áwtxw   s=kwtáxw=te   lálem*
        and.then   build-TR-3S=DET   cloth-house NMLZ-let.inside=DET house
        'So he built the tent inside the house.'
                                            Brown and Thompson 2006 (1)

(19)   *Hadixs=hl   gat=gi.*
        swim-CN   man=DIST
        'The man swam.'
                                            Rigsby 1986: 277

While the determiner-noun string forms a syntactic constituent in both languages, phonologically this is not so: the determiner encliticizes onto the preceding word in both languages – optionally in Halkomelem but obligatorily in Gitxsan. The result of this encliticization is a syntax–phonology mismatch. The existence of such mismatches is pervasive across many languages and ranges over a number of phonological processes, including stress assignment, tone assignment, sandhi rules, etc. (see Selkirk [2011] for an overview). For the purpose of our discussion it is important because it shows that constituency, and thus hierarchical structure, cannot be (always) read directly off of the phonological structure.

In sum, properties that are detectable purely on the basis of the *sound* of the string of UoLs (e.g., linear ordering, intonational patterns, etc.) can give us a clue about hierarchical structure but they are not sufficient. Instead, to determine the hierarchical organization of complex UoLs, we need to take *meaning* into consideration as well.

2.1.2.3   Scope

An important aspect of meaning relevant in this context is *scope*. Scope has figured prominently as a discovery procedure in the generative enterprise. This is because scope appears to be sensitive to the syntactic hierarchy, in the form of a c-command requirement, as summarized in (20).[4]

(20)   X has scope over Y only if X c-commands Y.

In the relevant literature, the term *scope* is used in two ways (Rice 2000): one is a general term and refers to the scope a given UoL has relative to the structure it combines with; the other one refers to *quantifier scope*, which is restricted to cases where the UoL entering into a scope relation is quantificational. Here I am concerned with the more general notion, which concerns semantic compositionality. That is, assuming strict binary branching (Kayne 1984), given three UoLs (X, Y, and Z) two of these UoLs must be combined with each other before the third one is added. The third UoL is then added to the constituent formed by X and Y, as shown in (21). In this configuration, Z has scope over X and Y.

(21)   [Z [X Y]]

---

[4] But see Barker (2012) as well as Bruening (forthcoming), who both argue against the relevance of c-command.

Crucially, scope cannot be reduced to linear order.[5] To see this, consider the scope of the adverb *quickly* in (22). *Quickly* is ambiguous between a manner reading (the act of talking was fast) and a temporal aspectual reading. The sentence is in the future because it is easier to distinguish the temporal aspectual reading from the manner reading. In particular, in the future, the event time of telling the story concerns the time it will take between the utterance time and the start time of the event (i.e., it won't be long before Peter tells the story) (see Travis [1988], Pustejovsky [1995], and Tenny [2000] for discussion).

(22)   *Peter will [quickly]*$_{\text{Adv}}$ *tell her the story.*
       ✓ manner reading
       ✓ temporal reading

Now consider the German examples in (23), discussed in Wiltschko (1995). The adverbial phrase *so schnell er kann* ('as fast as he can') can occur in two different positions. The temporal reading is available only if the adverb precedes the VP as in the (23a) example. This contrasts with the (23b) example, where the adverb precedes the verb only, and the only reading available is the manner reading.

(23)   a. *Peter wird [so schnell er kann]*$_{\text{Adv}}$ *Maria die   Geschichte erzählen.*
          Peter will   so fast   he can   Mary DET story   tell
          'Peter will tell Mary the story as quickly as he can.'

          * manner reading
          ✓ temporal reading

---

[5] The scope of quantifiers also cannot be reduced to linear order, at least not in all languages. Take for example the English sentence in (i):

   (i)   *Every man loves a woman.*

There are two readings associated with this sentence. First, for every man there may be a (different woman) who he loves (e.g., his mother). This is the reading where the universal quantifier *every* has scope over the existential quantifier *a*. This scope relation matches the linear ordering since *every* linearly precedes *a*. However there is also a second reading: there may be a certain woman (e.g., Marilyn Monroe) whom every man loves. This is the reading where the existential quantifier has scope over the universal quantifier despite the fact that the former linearly follows the latter. When the linear order does not correspond to the scope relation, we talk about *inverse scope*. Such inverse scope effects have been used to argue for an abstract level of representation (Logical Form) where quantifiers may occupy positions higher than their surface position (May 1985).

b.   *Peter wird Maria die Geschichte [so schnell er kann]*$_{Adv}$ *erzählen.*
     Peter will Mary DET story   so fast   he can   tell
     'Peter will tell Mary the story as quickly as he can.'
     ✓ manner reading
     * temporal reading

Wiltschko 1995: 175 (61)

The temporal reading arises when the adverb combines higher in the structure (namely with the functional category AspP); in contrast the manner reading arises when it combines lower (namely with the VP) (see Thompson 2006). Thus, one might expect that the temporal reading will correlate with a position of the adverb which is further left than its position in the manner reading. This is indeed the case. In English, *quickly* precedes the VP on the temporal reading but it follows the VP on the manner reading. In German, the adverbial phrase *so schnell er kann* precedes the VP on the temporal reading but it precedes the verb alone under the manner reading. If this was all there is to the mapping of linear ordering to syntactic structure we could simply say that linear precedence maps onto structural c-command (Kayne 1994). And thus scope can be read off of linear order. This is, however, not always the case. In particular, the situation is reversed in the context of right-adjunction, which is a structural configuration where a particular UoL (simplex or complex) is adjoined to the target in such a way that it is linearly realized to the right of the target. Adjunction is a structural configuration which is characterized by the fact that it does not alter the categorial identity of the target phrase.

To see the effects of right-adjunction on scope, consider the German example in (24). Here, the adverbial phrase occupies a position to the right of the verb. Assuming that in German the VP is head-final (Haider 1993), it follows that the adverbial must be right-adjoined. For right-adjoined structures, linear order tells us nothing about relative scope, and indeed in this case, both the manner and the temporal readings are available.

(24)   *Peter wird Maria   die Geschichte erzählen [so schnell er kann]*$_{Adv}$.
       Peter will Mary   DET story   tell   so fast   he can
       'Peter will tell Mary the story as quickly as he can.'
       ✓ manner reading
       ✓ temporal reading

Wiltschko 1995: 176 (63)

More importantly, if there are two right-adjoined phrases (a complement clause and the adverbial phrase) then the rightmost position corresponds to the higher scope position. That is, if the adverb follows the complement clause, we obtain the temporal reading as in (25a). If the adverb precedes the complement clause we obtain the manner reading, as in (25b).

(25)   a. *Peter wird Maria erzählen* ...
        Peter will Mary tell
        ... [*dass Hans ein Spion ist*][Adv *so schnell er kann*].
             that Hans a   spy   is   so fast   he can
        'Peter will tell Mary that Hans is a spy as fast as he can.'
                * manner reading
                ✓ temporal reading

        b. *Peter wird Maria erzählen* ...
        Peter will Mary tell
        ... [Adv *so schnell er kann*][*dass Hans ein Spion ist*].
                so fast   he can   that Hans a   spy   is
        'Peter will tell Mary as fast as he can that Hans is a spy.'
                ✓ manner reading
                * temporal reading

                                            Wiltschko 1995: 176 (64)

In sum, the pattern of adverb interpretation tells us that adverbial scope is determined by hierarchical structure, rather than by linear ordering. That is, in terms of hierarchical structure, both left- and right-adjoined adverbials follow the same pattern: the higher adverb receives the temporal reading, whereas the lower adverb receives the manner reading. This mirror image effect – schematized in (26) – is precisely what we expect from a hierarchical organization of sentence structure.

(26)   The symmetry of adverbial scope

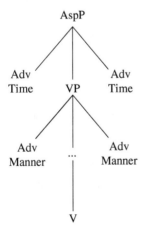

In contrast, this mirror-image effect of scope would be hard to capture in terms of linear order alone. Here leftness translates into higher scope if the adverb precedes the verb, but it translates into lower scope if the adverb follows the verb, as schematized in (27).

(27) $Adv_{manner} > Adv_{temporal} > V < Adv_{temporal} < Adv_{manner}$

In sum, we can get a clue from linear order about the relative height of a given UoL, but at the same time it is not sufficient to establish it definitively. To do so, we need to take scope into consideration, as well. This holds for both words and morphemes (Rice 2000).

2.1.2.4   Relative vs. absolute height

While linear ordering and c-command can give us a clue about the relative height of UoLs, this is not enough to provide us with the full picture. Consider the examples in (28). Both *they* and *what* are found in sentence-initial position and are thus both expected to be in the highest position within the clause; but the leftmost position in each of the two sentences turns out not to correlate with the same hierarchical position. Under most current analyses, *they* in (28a) occupies a position lower than *what* in (28b).

(28)   a. *They have seen the movie.*
        b. *What have they seen?*

The sentence-initial position in (28a) is classified as an A-position (SpecIP) whereas the sentence-initial position in (28b) is classified as an A′-position. The two types of positions impose different distributional properties onto the constituents that occupy them. To see this, consider verb agreement. In both sentences in (28), the verb agrees with the subject *they*. This can be seen on the basis of the fact that the agreement differs in both sentences if we replace the plural pronoun with a singular pronoun as in (29).

(29)   a. *He has seen the movie.*
        b *What has he seen?*

Since agreement is syntactically conditioned, it is generally assumed that it is regulated by syntactic positions. In particular, subject–verb agreement is often considered to be associated with the syntactic head that is associated with the grammatical subject role (see Section 2.3.1). In (28) and (29) the subject pronouns (*they* and *he*) occupy the syntactic position for grammatical subjects, no matter whether they appear in sentence-initial position (as in the [a] examples) or in a position following the auxiliary (as in the [b] examples).

This further suggests that despite the fact that the pronoun in the (a) examples and the wh-word in the (b) examples both occupy the highest position in relative terms, as shown in (30), they do not occupy the same syntactic position in absolute terms, as shown in (31).

(30)   Same relative position

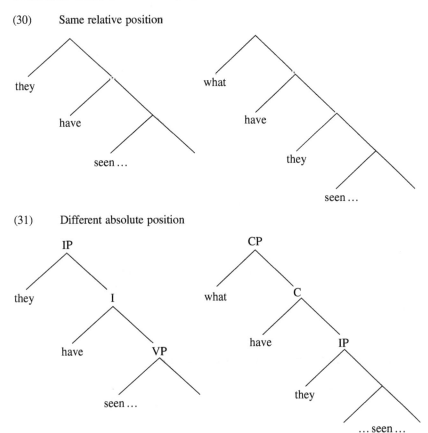

(31)   Different absolute position

We conclude that relative height alone is not sufficient to determine the absolute position a given UoL. Consequently, while linear ordering (and other purely sound-based criteria), as well as scope, may give us clues about the relative hierarchical organization of UoLs, these diagnostics cannot tell us much about the absolute position within the syntactic hierarchy. To determine the absolute position within the hierarchical organization of a sentence we need a labeling function. That is, we need to know the categorial identity of the position that a given UoL associates with. Much research has been devoted to explore in more detail the layers of structure that constitute a sentence as well as nominal argument expressions. I turn to an overview of this research in the next section.

2.2   Labels in the structure: functional categories

While it is relatively uncontroversial that phrases and sentences are hierarchically organized, i.e., structured, the precise form of this structure and how it is derived is a matter of debate. I here adopt the view that there is a universally determined structure, namely the *universal spine*. A key ingredient of the Universal Spine Hypothesis is the assumption that lexical categories are dominated by several layers of functional categories. In this section, I introduce some of the core characteristics of functional categories, which constitute the essence of the universal spine. We start by introducing some core assumptions regarding the content of functional categories as conceived of within the generative tradition (Section 2.2.1). We then proceed to discuss assumptions about the way functional categories are structured (Section 2.2.2).

2.2.1   What are functional categories?

Functional categories have been a central object of investigation within the generative tradition for several decades now. And they also constitute the core of our investigation into the universality of categories. That is, we are here concerned with grammatical categories rather than lexical categories such as noun and verb. But what exactly do we mean by *functional category*? In this subsection I briefly discuss some of the basic assumptions that have led to current conceptualizations of functional categories.

Many of the widely assumed functional categories were first introduced on the basis of word classes. For English, which constituted the main language of investigation within the generative tradition, three functional categories were originally recognized: AUX, COMP, and DET. I briefly discuss each of these categories in turn.

Sentences such as (32) appear to be made up of lexical categories only: a proper noun which simultaneously functions as a noun phrase and combines with a verb phrase, which in turn may or may not combine with another noun phrase. And in fact the sentence structure of such examples did not used to include functional categories, as shown in (33): S consists of NP and VP.

(32)   a. *Yoshi runs.*
        b. *Yoshi likes food.*

(33)   [NP VP]$_s$

However, to form complex tenses (34), to introduce negation (35), and to form a question (36), function words need to be introduced, namely in the form of *auxiliaries*. If no auxiliary is present in the positive declarative then *do* is inserted to form questions and negative statements, as in (35) and (36), respectively.

(34)   a. *Yoshi is running.*
        b. **Yoshi running*

(35)   a. *Is Yoshi running?*
        b. **Runs Yoshi*
        c. *Does Yoshi run?*

(36)   a. *Yoshi is not running.*
        b. **Yoshi runs not*
        c. *Yoshi does not run.*

The way auxiliaries were initially integrated into the clausal architecture is simply with another node (AUX) as sister to both NP and VP (Chomsky 1957). The result is a ternary branching structure as in (37).

(37)   Integrating AUX into S

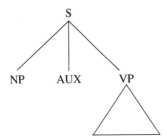

However, AUX appears to be more than a node that can host a single function word. Auxiliaries may be inflected for tense (38a). A single clause may contain more than one auxiliary (38b). And modal verbs may occur in the same position (38c).

(38)   a. *Yoshi **had** taken the ball.*
        b. *Yoshi **has been** taking the ball.*
        c. *Yoshi **will** take the ball.*

To account for this distribution, Chomsky (1957) suggests that AUX may host several categories including *tense* (T), and *modals* (M), as well as *perfective* (perf) and *progressive* (prog) aspect. This is illustrated in (39).

(39)   The structure of AUX

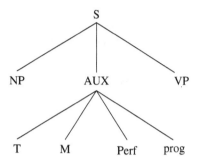

Note that the categories hosted by AUX are a heterogeneous word class. While all belong to the system of tense, aspect, and mood (often abbreviated as TAM), they have different distributional properties within and across languages. But if the UoLs hosted by AUX do not constitute a unique category, in what sense is AUX a category? The answer has to do with its *function*, hence the label *functional category*. Thus, while the label AUX suggests a category based on a word class, its actual function is in fact more complex. It encompasses all of the functions auxiliaries may be associated with, and these functions (such as tense) may be realized independently of the presence of the actual word class. And it turns out that the functions associated with AUX are hierarchically organized in a way that is not reflected by the flat structure in (39) (Cinque 1999).

The crucial problem with the structure in (39), which has led the field to abandon the category AUX, is the fact that all other phrases were endocentric. That is, phrases based on lexical categories (N, V, A, and P) are all headed by a category-determining UoL. A VP contains a V head (40a), an NP contains an N head (40b), an AP contains an A head (40c), and a PP contains a P head (40d).

(40)   Phrases are endocentric
    a. [*walk*~V~ *the dog in the rain*]~VP~
    b. [*a very cute* **dog**~N~]~NP~
    c. [*extremely* **proficient**~A~]~AP~
    d. [**with**~P~ *a leash*]~PP~

This observation led to the formulation of X′-theory according to which the projection of all lexical categories is restricted by the same blueprint (Jackendoff 1977) (see Section 2.2.2 below for discussion). A head combines with a phrase known as the *complement*. And the newly formed syntactic object, labeled X′ in (41), combines with another phrase known as the *specifier*.

(41)   X′-theory

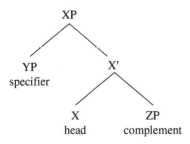

Turning now to constituents that are not based on lexical categories, such as the clause S in (39), there is a problem. Here, S does not appear to be endocentric: there is no head that determines the categorical identity of S. Conversely, there is no phrase which AUX projects. This situation was rectified in Chomsky (1986) where X′-theory was generalized to functional categories. At the core of generalized X′-theory is the observation that, in English, all matrix declarative clauses require one and only one inflected verb. This is the hallmark of a head: obligatoriness and uniqueness. And thus, INFL was introduced as the head of the clause (Travis 1984).

(42)   Introducing I(NFL)

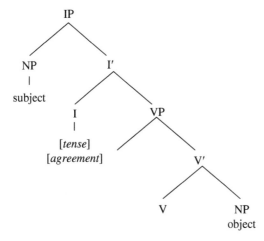

As indicated in (42), INFL was assumed to bear two features: *tense* and *agreement*. This reflects the fact that in English (and many other Indo-European languages), the verb in a matrix indicative clause is inflected for tense and agreement.

(43)   a. *Yoshi play-s.* → present 3rd person singular
        b. *Yoshi play-ed.* → past

In his seminal paper, Pollock 1989 introduced the idea that the functional head INFL should be split into two distinct functional categories, each corresponding to one of the features associated with the INFL head: TENSE and AGR, as illustrated in (44)

(44)   The split INFL hypothesis (Pollock 1989)

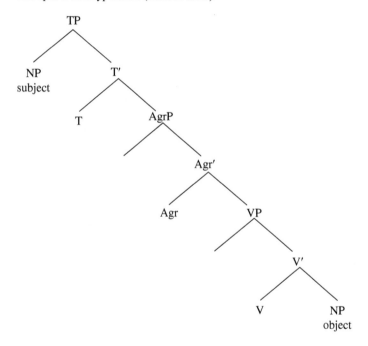

The split INFL hypothesis paved the way for two common assumptions about the essence of functional categories:

(i)   there is a single feature associated with a particular functional category; and
(ii)   functional categories may be identified with the substantive content of the feature they host (e.g., *tense*).

These assumptions have spawned much research over the past few decades (see van Gelderen [1993] for an overview) peaking in the cartographic approach towards functional structure developed by Guglielmo Cinque and his colleagues (Cinque 1999 and subsequent work). The essence of this approach is the elaborate structure of hierarchically organized functional categories in (45). This structure has a dual function: it hosts heads and hosts phrases in their specifiers. In the clausal architecture, the heads are occupied by inflection, (inflected) auxiliary verbs, or simply verbs that have moved into the head position. The phrases are considered to be adverbials. The function of each adverb is constrained by the content in the head it combines with.

(45)   Functional categories in cartography
        [[Mood$_{\text{speech-act}}$ [Mood$_{\text{evaluative}}$ [Mood$_{\text{evidential}}$ [Mod$_{\text{epistemic}}$ [T$_{\text{past}}$ [T$_{\text{future}}$
        [Mod$_{\text{irrealis}}$ [Mod$_{\text{necessity}}$ [Mod$_{\text{possibility}}$ [Asp$_{\text{habitual}}$ [Asp$_{\text{repetetive}}$ [Asp$_{\text{frequentative(I)}}$
        [Mod$_{\text{volitional}}$ [Asp$_{\text{celerative(I)}}$ [T$_{\text{anterior}}$ [Asp$_{\text{terminative}}$ [Asp$_{\text{continuative}}$ [Asp$_{\text{perfect(?)}}$
        [Asp$_{\text{retrospective}}$ [Asp$_{\text{proximative}}$ [Asp$_{\text{durative}}$ [Asp$_{\text{generic/progressive}}$ [Asp$_{\text{prospective}}$
        [Asp$_{\text{sg.completive(I)}}$ [Asp$_{\text{pl.completive}}$ [Voice [Asp$_{\text{celerative(II)}}$ [Asp$_{\text{repetitive(II)}}$
        [Asp$_{\text{frequentative(II)}}$ [Asp$_{\text{sg.completive(II)}}$]]]]]]]]]]]]]]]]]]]]]]]]]]]]]]]]]]
                                                                        Cinque 1999: 106

To sum up, the very concept of a functional category is rooted in the classic division between (closed class) function words (such as auxiliaries) and (open class) content words (such as nouns and verbs) (Fries 1952). The way functional categories have been conceived of has changed substantially over the decades, as witnessed by the fact that we started with a single (non-projecting) node AUX with some now assuming a substantial series of functional projections (see also the *nano-syntactic* approach developed by Michal Starke and his colleagues in Tromsø: Starke 2009).

The other major functional category (COMP) had a similar fate. Its origins trace back to Rosenbaum (1967), who introduces the label COMP (short for *complementizer*) for the function words that serve to introduce a complement clause as for example *that* in (46).

(46)   *They think [**that** Edward is a spy]*.

Before the introduction of generalized X'-theory in Chomsky (1986), the label of the complement clause introduced by COMP was S' as in (47) where COMP combines with S forming S'.

(47)   S'→ COMP S

This phrase structure rule, however, also violates the endocentricity requirement for phrases. There is no head that corresponds to the phrase S'. Just as

INFL replaced S, the situation was rectified in Chomsky (1986) by assuming that COMP (now reduced to C) serves as the head of the clause determining its label (CP), as in (48).

(48)   CP → ... C ...

While C may host individual words that are often classified as complementizers (e.g., *that, if, for*), it is not restricted to such words. In particular, in the context of inversion triggered by question formation, auxiliaries are usually assumed to move to C, as shown in (49a). In German this type of inversion has been generalized, resulting in the obligatory verb second configuration: in matrix clauses the finite verb has to move to C (den Besten 1977), as illustrated in (49b).

(49)   a. [*What*   [*did*]$_C$ [$_{IP}$ *you eat last night*]]]?

    b. [*Den*   *Ball*   [*hat*]$_C$ [$_{IP}$ *der*   *Yoshi*   *verloren*]].
       DET.ACC   ball   has   DET.NOM Yoshi   lost
       'Yoshi lost the ball.'

This suggests that word-class membership is not a necessary condition to associate with C. Instead, it can be occupied by other word classes via movement.

   That word-class membership is also not a sufficient condition to associate with C can be gleaned from the fact that there are languages that allow for, or even require, a clause to be introduced by more than one complementizer. For example, some dialects of Italian allow for multiple occurrences of complementizers (Poletto 2000). The following example is from Turin Piedmontese.

(50)   *A venta che*   *gnun*   *ch'a*   *fasa*   *bordel.*
        It needs COMP t   nobody   COMP=CL   do.SUBJ   noise
        'It is necessary that nobody makes noise.'
                                                Cocchi and Poletto 2000: 66 (20)

Since there are two complementizers, it follows that they cannot both occupy the same head position, since heads are always unique. Facts like this have been used to develop a more articulated analysis of the C-domain. Instead of a single functional projection, several are postulated, including ForceP, FocusP, TopicP, Fin(iteness)P (Rizzi 1997).

(51)   An articulated structure for COMP

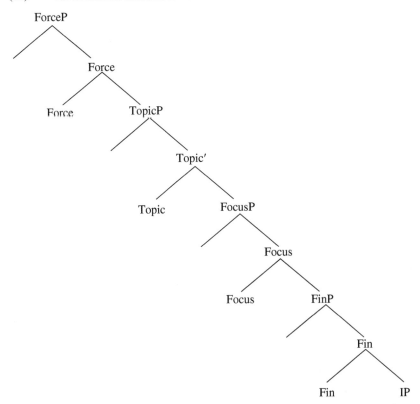

In sum, while the very concept of a functional category is rooted in the distinction between content words and function words as well as inflectional morphology, it cannot be identified with either function words or inflectional morphology. That is, neither function words nor inflectional morphology of a particular category map onto functional categories in a one-to-one fashion. On the one hand, UoLs that do not belong to the corresponding word class or inflectional category may occupy functional heads. On the other hand, the functional categories that were based on the word classes *auxiliary* and *complementizer* have all been shown to be associated with a more articulated structure. The essential ingredients of this structure are the topic of the next subsection.

2.2.2   *The structure of functional categories*
In Section 2.1, we saw evidence that UoLs are hierarchically organized: some constituents are higher than others. They stand in a relation of dominance to

each other. The question I address in this subsection concerns the essence of hierarchical organization. How are these constituents hierarchically organized?

According to the Universal Spine Hypothesis, the functional categories provide the scaffolding for the hierarchical organization of constituents. The relation among constituents is mediated by functional heads, as in (52).

(52)   The structure of a functional category

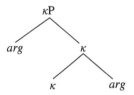

It is in this sense that functional categories are themselves structured. The theoretical assumptions about the nature and the sources of hierarchical organization differ, but some assumptions are common across many theories of phrase structure, at least those that recognize the notion of a functional category. These assumptions, which I shall adopt here, are summarized in (53).

(53)   a. endocentricity
        κ and its complement construct a complex κ, which bears the same label as κ
        b. extendability
        A complex κ may be extended to include another UoL without changing the label of the newly formed expression

Endocentricity and extendability have been important components of phrase structure rules for several decades. As mentioned above, the endocentricity property of lexical categories served as one of the key impulses for the generalization of X′-theory to functional categories (Chomsky 1986). Extendability is another property well grounded within X′-theory.[6] On the assumption that flat structures are excluded on principled grounds and that syntactic structure adheres to binary branching (as in [52]: Kayne 1984) any additional UoLs that associate with κ must do so by associating with the topmost node (structure building). Under the generalized X′-theory, which essentially serves as a blueprint for the construction of phrases, this position is known as the *specifier* position. Since Stowell's (1981) seminal work on the origins of phrase structure, specifiers are explicitly assumed to host *subjects* across different

---

[6] See for example Chomsky's extension condition according to which the operation Merge always extends its target (Chomsky 1993: 22–23).

lexical categories as well as functional categories (Williams 2003) – though with a generalized notion of *subject* in place. On this view, then, functional categories may be viewed as relating specifiers to their complements.

In addition to specifiers, heads, and complements, standard X'-theory optionally made available another position, namely one for modifiers. The question as to *where* such additional UoLs (i.e., *adjuncts*) can be added to a head-complement structure and *how many* has received different answers over the years. As for the locus of adjunction, they might be added to intermediate projections of κ (known as the X'-levels since Jackendoff [1977]) or else they might be added to the topmost phrasal layer (κP, known as Chomsky-adjunction). As for the number of possible adjuncts, scholars differ as to how many they allow. For example, Jackendoff (1977) proposes three layers both in the clausal and in the nominal domain which are identifiable by semantic characteristics of the modifiers that are associated with each layer.

Thus, one of the original motivations for the postulation of X'-theory was the layering effects associated with modifiers: roughly, adverbials in the projection of the clause and adjectival modifiers in nominal projections. These layering effects have received different treatments over the years, just like the layering effects associated with the auxiliary complex discussed in the last subsection. Specifically, with the introduction of functional categories, different layers with different functions are made available. In other words, functional categories mediate the relation between phrases and their modifiers.

In an attempt to constrain the relation between dominance and linear ordering, Kayne (1994) argues that the latter may be derived from the former. In so doing, he was able to derive the essence of X'-theory, though in ways that place several constraints on the number of phrases that a head may relate to. Specifically, Kayne does not distinguish between specifiers and adjuncts, and furthermore, the number of phrases that may be associated with a head-complement structure is restricted to two. This assumption also lies at the heart of cartography: according to Cinque (1999), adverbs are best analyzed as occupying specifier positions of functional categories. Though – as we have seen in (45) – the cartographic structure dominating the lexical core is much more articulated than the standard CP–IP–VP structure.

To sum up, while details differ, there emerge some core assumptions about the structure made available by functional categories. In addition to making available a head position, κ also serves to relate phrases (subjects, complements, and adjuncts) to each other. Thus the hierarchical organization of functional categories serves as the backbone for the hierarchical organization of constituents. This is what I refer to as the universal spine.

2.3   The areas of the spine and their functions

Thus far, we have introduced and reviewed some of the core ideas of generative grammar about the underpinnings of the hierarchical organization of UoLs. Constituents are hierarchically organized internally and relative to each other. Moreover, the relation among constituents is mediated by functional categories – the main object of our investigation. In this section, I turn to another assumption about the essence of structure. In fact, one of the principal arguments for the existence of a universal spine is the fact that the functional structure dominating lexical categories introduces a series of fixed areas, sometimes referred to as domains. Within each domain, arguments, modifiers, as well as the functional heads that relate them are affected in specific ways. These areas have been most clearly established in the verbal extended projection, i.e., the clause. In particular, generative analyses since Government and Binding Theory (Chomsky 1981) recognize at least three areas, which can roughly be described as follows.

(i)   the **thematic domain**,[7] where lexical[8] categories introduce thematic arguments, such as *agent* and *theme*

(ii)   the **A**(rgument)-domain where functional categories such as INFL and ASPECT license the thematic arguments via **grammatical relations**, such as subject and object, which are typically marked by case and/or agreement.

(iii)   the **A′**-domain where functional categories such as C license **discourse relations**, such as topic or focus.

I here review some of the most prevailing properties of these domains. As one may expect, the different domains affect the construal of the arguments and modifiers, as well as the heads that are associated with them, respectively. I discuss properties of the arguments associated with each domain in Section 2.3.1. In Section 2.3.2, I discuss the characteristics of the UoLs instantiating the functional heads in each domain. In Section 2.3.3, I isolate the functions that lie at the core of each of the domains identified on the basis of the heads and phrases that comprise them. And finally, in Section 2.3.4, I discuss the

---

[7] The *thematic domain* is more recently referred to as the *event domain* because it is where the roles of event participants are determined (van Hout 1996, 2000).

[8] The notion 'lexical category' here includes those that are labeled with small letters such as *v*. These categories are currently assumed to introduce arguments and are sometimes referred to as *semi-lexical categories* because they have characteristics of both lexical and functional categories (see Corver and van Riemsdijk [2001] for a recent overview).

parallels between the domains in both the verbal and nominal extended projections. It goes without saying that in this brief overview I cannot do justice to the work that has been done in each of these areas. Instead, I will focus on some of the milestones – relevant to the Universal Spine Hypothesis – abstracting away from important details.

2.3.1 The roles of arguments

The development of an articulated series of functional projections, i.e., the spine, made it possible to understand a striking and pervasive property that unrelated languages have in common: the existence of several distinct roles that the nominal dependents bear relative to the predicates that introduce them.

To appreciate this property, let us consider the examples in (54).

(54)   a. *Yoshi buried the bone.*   ACTIVE
         b. *The bone was buried (by Yoshi).* PASSIVE

According to traditional typological descriptions, this English sentence instantiates an SVO order: the subject (S) precedes the verb (V), which in turn precedes the object (O). One of the key insights of generative grammar is the recognition of several distinct levels of subjecthood and objecthood. For example, in (54a), *Yoshi* is the agent of the event of *bone-burying*, and it has the grammatical properties of a subject. The key insight here is that the grammatical role *subject* cannot be equated with the semantic role *agent*.[9] This can be gleaned from the passive sentence in (54b) where the grammatical subject is not the agent but instead the theme. The agent is only optionally realized as a prepositional phrase. The same is true for the relation between themes and objects. To see this, consider the sentences in (55) and (56).

(55)   a. *Yoshi wants **him** to play.*
         b. ***He** plays.*

(56)   a. *I gave the ball to **him**.*
         b. *I gave **him** a ball.*

In (55), the pronoun *him* is simultaneously the agent of *play* and the grammatical object of *want* as evidenced by the fact that it is realized as accusative case. This means that objects cannot be equated with themes. Similarly, in (56) we observe that the benefactive argument (*him*) may be realized either as a

---

[9] Semantic roles are also known as *logical* roles, *thematic* roles, *theta* roles, *underlying* roles, or *event* roles.

prepositional phrase (i.e., an indirect object) (56a) or as a direct object in a position immediately adjacent to the verb (56b). Again, this suggests that semantic roles are not mapped onto grammatical roles in a one-to-one fashion.

This indicates that we have to identify two separate roles: the grammatical subject and object role on the one hand, and the semantic agent and theme role on the other hand. In some cases the two roles are simultaneously instantiated by the same nominal phrase. But it is the mismatches between form and interpretation that tell us that we need to keep them apart. It is these mismatches that serve as common diagnostics for grammatical relations. The most common ones are listed below.

> (i)   *Expletive subjects.* In the absence of a thematic role that could map onto the grammatical subject relation, an expletive subject (i.e., the neuter pronoun *it*) must be inserted.

(57)   a. ***It** is raining.*
        b. ***It** seems that he is really sick.*

> (ii) *Mismatches between thematic and grammatical relations.* As we have seen above, in passives, the thematic object (patient) is realized as the grammatical subject. In exceptional case marking (ECM) constructions,[10] the thematic subject (agent) is realized as the grammatical object of the embedding predicate (58). This suggests that there is a grammatical relation that is not definable by means of thematic relations.

(58)   a. ***He** played.*
        b. *She wanted **him** to play.*

> (iii) *Agreement is conditioned by grammatical relations.* Subject–verb agreement is triggered by the grammatical rather than the thematic subject relation, as evidenced by the passive sentence in (59).

(59)   a. ***He** was chased.*
        b. *They **were** chased.*

At least on the basis of English, we can conclude that we must recognize grammatical relations that are partially independent of thematic relations.

The dissociation between thematic and grammatical roles can be implemented in different ways. In the early days of generative grammar, it was

---

[10] In classical grammars based on Latin, these are known as *accusative cum infinitive* constructions.

achieved by the assumption that there are (at least) two levels of representation. Specifically, it was assumed that thematic roles are assigned at D-structure while grammatical roles are assigned at S-structure, as illustrated in (60).

(60) a. D-structure   b. S-structure

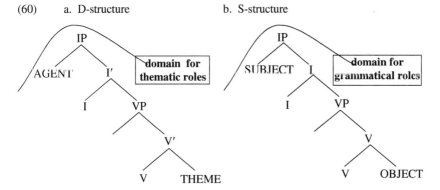

Mismatches between thematic and grammatical roles can be understood by means of a transformation that maps the underlying theme argument to the surface subject position.

On this approach, the two roles (agent and subject) are assigned to the same structural position, but at different times in the derivation. With the introduction of several layers of functional structure it has become possible to associate the different roles with different areas in a single syntactic structure.[11] On the one hand, semantic roles are typically assumed to be assigned within the VP (or an articulated version thereof). On the other hand grammatical roles are assumed to be assigned in the functional structure dominating the VP. For concreteness, I present in (61) a particular version of this idea, which reflects a certain consensus in the field, though there are of course variations. In particular, for the assumption that agents are introduced VP-internally see Koopman and Sportiche (1991); for the assumption that the VP is more articulated, introducing arguments in different layers, see Larson (1988), Chomsky (1995), Kratzer (1996), and Ramchand (2010); for the assumption that accusative case is assigned in SpecAspP see Borer (1994, 2005) and Megerdoomian (2000); and for the assumption that nominative case is assigned by INFL see Chomksy (1980). Assuming that the assignment of structural case correlates

---

[11] See van Riemsdijk and Williams (1981) for the assumption that there are three levels of representation: deep structure, NP-structure, and wh-structure. On this view, each layer of the structure in (64) would be associated with a separate level of representation. See also Williams (2003) for a recent reincarnation of the multilevel representation approach.

with the realization of grammatical roles, we may conclude that thematic roles are assigned in an articulated VP (also known as the thematic domain) and grammatical roles are assigned in the structure dominating it (also known as the A-domain), as illustrated in (61).

(61)   The structural dissociation of semantic and grammatical roles

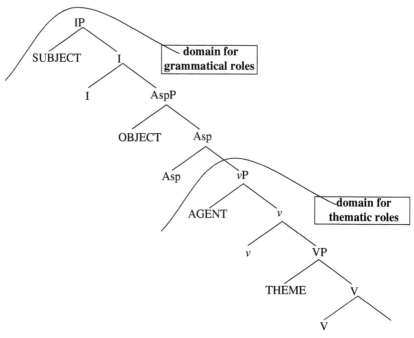

The assumption that different roles are associated with different areas in the syntactic spine makes superfluous the assumption that different roles are assigned at different levels of representation. This is consistent with current minimalist assumptions according to which there are indeed no levels of representations beyond those that are independently required as interfaces to the interpretive components (PF and LF, respectively: Chomsky 1995).

There are several advantages of the articulated structure in (61), over the simpler one that relies on the postulation of more than one level of representation as in (60). First, it is now possible to uniquely identify particular roles with particular structural positions. This is a welcome result, because such roles are not always encoded on the nominal constituents that instantiate them. In fact, the pervasive absence of such marking provides us with an argument for the existence of a universal spine: the syntactic properties and the semantic interpretation of nominal dependents is influenced by their position in the spine without being overtly coded as such. This suggests that at the initial state of language acquisition, we come equipped with some expectations about the interpretive correlates of structural positions. This provides us with exactly the kind of architecture we need to account for the puzzle we ended up with in Section 2.1.2.4. There we concluded that determining the relative position of a given constituent is not sufficient to uniquely identify its syntactic properties. Consider the contrast in (62) and (63).

(62)   a. **Your dog** buried the bone, *(didn't **he**?)*
       b. *Your dog buried **the bone**, (*didn't **it**?)*

(63)   a. **The bone**, *your dog buried, (*didn't **it**?)*
       b. *The bone, **your dog** buried, (didn't **he**?)*

In (62), the sentence-initial phrase *your dog* is the grammatical subject and is thus the constituent that the pronoun in a tag-question relates to. The object *the bone* cannot be the antecedent for this pronoun. In contrast, in (63), the object is topicalized to sentence-initial position. However, the pronoun in the tag-question must still be co-referent with the subject, even though it is no longer in initial position. Its relative height is different but its absolute height is the same. The importance of absolute hierarchical positions (in addition to relative ones) highlights the need for a spine.

The other lesson we learn from these sentences is that the structure in (61) is not sufficient to account for all of the data. We need to recognize yet another area in the spine. This area is generally known as the A′-domain and is associated with the functional category C. Given what we have seen about the properties of the two domains already discussed, we expect that the A′-domain as well may be associated with a particular set of well-defined roles. This is indeed the case. In particular, the phrases that appear in the A′-domain are often characterized by functions such as *topic* and *focus* (Rizzi 1997), which may broadly be characterized as *discourse* roles, that is, roles that are defined in terms of the ongoing discourse. That is, they serve to structure the information flow in the ongoing conversation. Again, the postulation of discourse roles distinct from grammatical or event roles is justified by the fact that the former cannot be defined based on the latter two. While subjects often bear the topic role, this is not necessarily so, as evidenced by the data in (63), where the grammatical object serves this function.

Abstracting away from the details of the structure, this leaves us with three commonly assumed areas in the clausal architecture, as schematized in (64).

(64)   The areas in the spine

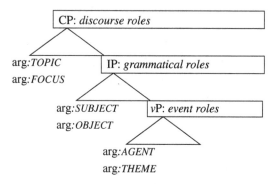

Like the structures associated with event roles and grammatical roles, the structure associated with discourse roles has developed from an area with a single position (C) to an articulated structure with several layers. For example, Rizzi (1997) proposes to recognize at least Force, Topic, Focus, and Finiteness (see [51] above). From the present perspective, the important aspect of this proposal is that there are again roles, which are not directly encoded on the DPs that bear them, but which are instead uniquely identifiable by the structural position they occupy. The possibility for a structural definition of the different roles a nominal dependent may bear is made possible by the postulation of a functional structure dominating the lexical core. This predicts that we should find evidence for head positions which introduce these roles. I now turn to a brief discussion of such evidence.

2.3.2   The heads

If there are indeed distinct heads associated with each of these domains it is predicted that they may be associated with distinct UoLs. This is indeed the case. Consider first the lexical domain where thematic roles are introduced. While in English there is no direct morphological evidence for the existence of a separate head that introduces the agent role, there is in other languages (Hung 1988; Kratzer 1996). Halkomelem is such a language, wearing its argument structure on its morphological sleeve. Verbs that come with a theme argument only (i.e., *unaccusative* verbs) are realized as bare roots, (65) and (66). Any predicate that comes with an agent role is morphologically complex. One set of suffixes is used to derive agent-oriented intransitive predicates, i.e., *unergatives* (65) while another set of suffixes is used to derive transitive predicates (66) (Gerdts 1988; Galloway 1993; Wiltschko 2003).

(65)   a. Unaccusative predicates

lhíkw'	'hooked, gaffed'
yéqw	'burn'
líw	'be inside sthg'
qw'él	'cooked; ripe'

Galloway 1993: 251f.

   b. Unergative predicates.

*lhekw'-**áls***	'to hook (e.g., fish)'
*yeqw-**áls***	'perform burning'
*lewíl-**ém***	'go into an opening'
*qw'él-**em***	'barbecue, roast'

Galloway 1993: 251f.

(66)   a. Unaccusative predicates

q'óy	'die'
íkw'	'lost'
tós	'get hit, mashed'
qw'és	'fall into water'
tl'éx̱w	'covered'
x̱élh	'hurt'

Galloway 1993: 245–247

   b. Transitive predicates

*q'óy-**t***	'kill sthg/so'
*íkw'-**et***	'throw sthg away, discard sthg'
*tás-**et***	'mash sthg (berries)'
*qw's-**et***	'push sthg/so into water'
*tl'x̱w-**et***	'cover so/sthg'
*x̱lh-**et***	'hurt so'

Galloway 1993: 245–247

As illustrated in (67), an articulated VP structure where each role is introduced by a separate verbal head provides us with the required head positions that may host the argument-introducing morphology.[12]

---

[12] We must assume however that the agent-oriented intransitives are concealed transitives (Hale and Keyser 2003). And indeed there is language-internal evidence for this assumption: agent-oriented intransitives may optionally co-occur with a theme argument. Though this theme argument may not be associated with the grammatical object role (see Chapter 4 for discussion).

(67)   Morphological evidence for a layered VP structure

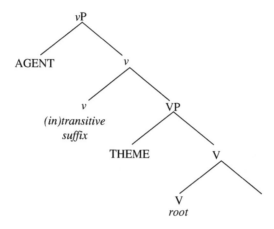

Next we turn to the functional layers within the area of the spine where grammatical roles are introduced. According to the structure introduced above, these layers include INFL (or tense) and (viewpoint) aspect.

That viewpoint aspect instantiates a syntactic head (Asp) immediately above the verb phrase (i.e., *v*P) and immediately below INFL is now commonly assumed (Demirdache and Uribe-Etxebarria 1997; Travis 2010). In addition to its contrastive nature (which we shall discuss in Chapter 7), there are several other criteria that support the view that aspect functions as a syntactic head, at least in English. For example, aspect interacts with case in a way that is indicative of a syntactically active head that supports a phrasal position (i.e., its specifier). In Finnish, different aspectual properties of a predicate correlate with different case-assigning properties (Kiparsky 1998; Svenonius 2002). In particular, predicates in the perfective aspect assign accusative case to the internal argument, whereas predicates in the imperfective aspect assign dative case.

(68)   a. *hän*   *luki*   *kirjan.*
             he   read   book-ACC
             'He read the book.'

         b. *hän*   *luki*   *kirjaa.*
             he   read   book-DAT
             'He was reading the book.'

Comrie 1976: 8

Another case-related correlate of aspect is found in Hindi. Here we find a split between a nominative/accusative case system and an absolutive/ergative case system, which is driven by viewpoint aspect (Dixon 1994). In particular, in the imperfective we find a nominative/accusative alignment, as in (69a). In this case, the verb agrees in gender with the nominative argument (i.e., the external argument). In contrast, in the perfective aspect we find an ergative/absolutive alignment, as in (69b). In this case, the verb agrees in gender with the absolutive argument (i.e., the internal argument).

(69)   a. *Raam*   *roTii*   *khaataa*   *thaa.*
             Ram.MASC   bread.FEM   eat.IMPF.MASC   be.PST.MASC
             'Ram (habitually) ate bread.'

        b. *Raam-ne*   *roTii*   *khaayii*   *thii.*
             Ram.MASC-ERG   bread.FEM   eat.PERF.FEM   be.PST.FEM
             'Ram had eaten bread.'

Mahajan 1990: 76, 78

This supports the view that the grammatical object role (marked as accusative case) is introduced by a functional head, which we may identify as (viewpoint) Aspect.

A similar point can be made for grammatical subjects. In English, for example, the presence of a nominative subject depends on the presence of tense inflection on the verb. To see this, consider the examples in (70). If the embedded clause is finite with a verb inflected for tense, then a nominative subject is required (70a); if the embedded clause is non-finite and the verb is not inflected for tense, then the agent role may not be realized as a grammatical subject (70b). Instead, it may optionally be realized as the grammatical object of the higher predicate (70c). (Note that this is another instance where thematic roles and grammatical roles do not coincide, supporting the view that they need to be distinguished.)

(70)   a. *Yoshi said that *(he) played.*
        b. *Yoshi wanted [(*he) to play].*
        c. *Yoshi wanted (him) to play.*

The pattern in (70) (among others) suggests that it is tense which serves to license the realization of the grammatical subject role. Consequently, it is assumed that tense features are associated with the functional head that introduces subjects. This assumption is sometimes taken to be a linguistic universal. We will discuss it in detail in Chapter 4.

Finally let us turn to the domain of discourse roles. According to Rizzi (1997), there are two types of heads that may be found in this area of the spine: a head that introduces the illocutionary force of the sentence, and another one that is sensitive to finiteness distinctions in the IP domain. Both head positions may be occupied by complementizers. And indeed there are languages where two complementizers are simultaneously realized in a single clause, as we have already seen in Section 2.2.1 (ex. [50] repeated below as [71]).

(71)   *A venta **che***   *gnun*   ***ch'a***   *fasa*   *bordel.*
        it needs COMP   nobody   COMP=CL   do.s   noise
        'It is necessary that nobody makes noise.'

                                                           Cocchi and Poletto 2000: 66 (20)

2.3.3   *The core functions associated with the areas in the spine*

The purpose of this subsection is to review evidence for the assumption that the functional structure above the VP can be divided into several distinct areas. In particular, we have seen evidence that each area is associated with a particular set of roles that the nominal arguments introduced in the VP may bear. In addition to the thematic roles defined by the predicates that introduce them, arguments may bear grammatical roles (subject and object) as well as discourse roles (topic and focus).

(72)   The areas in the spine

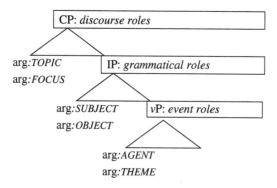

The three areas correspond to the classic division into theta-positions, A-positions, and A′-positions, which each of these roles occupy. The roles themselves are tightly connected to the head positions available in each area: *v*, INFL (or T) and C.

Additional evidence for the areas defined by the heads and the roles they introduce comes from the syntax and semantics of adverbial modifiers. Some adverbs modify aspects of the VP, some modify aspects of the area where grammatical roles are introduced, and a third class modifies aspects of the area where discourse roles are introduced (Jackendoff 1977). Below is a sample of some of these adverbs; the classification is in fact much more fine-grained (Cinque 1999; Ernst 2002).

(73)   a. Event-oriented adverbs
        *The door **quietly** closed.*

        b. Subject oriented adverbs
        *The guard arranged the surveillance cameras **cleverly**.*

        c. Speaker-oriented adverbs
        ***Frankly**, he should quit his job.*

In fact, adverbs are treated as an important window into the universal functional architecture. Their semantic properties, along with their linear ordering effects, have led to the development of the articulated structure known as cartography (Cinque 1999 and subsequent work). In particular, cartographic diagnostics for relative height involve the linear ordering of adverbs relative to each other but also relative to verbs, auxiliaries, and modals. The labeling convention for the categories that host the adverbs crucially derive from the semantic content that the adverbs and the heads they relate to share. However, crucially, the cartographic approach does not recognize the three areas of the spine that we defined on the basis of the roles the nominal arguments bear. That is, by introducing a fine-grained distinction based on the semantic content of adverbs, the cartographic approach misses a broader distinction based on argument roles. Accordingly, we would have to introduce a mechanism to recognize such domains, even in an articulated cartographic structure (see Grohmann's [2003] notion of *prolific domains*).

The assumption that the roles arguments bear are characteristic of several domains (however articulated they may be) is further supported by the fact that we can identify a core function with each of these domains. To see this, consider the difference between thematic roles on the one hand, and grammatical and discourse roles on the other hand. When arguments are first introduced in the *v*P-projection, they are immediately associated with an interpretation (the semantic role), which specifies the way the argument relates to the event. In fact, argument structure in the traditional sense may be reduced to event-structure (van Hout 1996, 2000; Borer 2005; Ramchand 2008). Crucially, the roles that are introduced in the functional superstructure do not introduce new event participants. Instead, the nominal arguments already introduced in the VP are now associated with additional roles that are independent of the event or participant roles associated with the *v*P-domain. In other words, the subject, for example, is not an argument of INFL (or T) and the object is not an argument of Aspect. It is, however, sometimes assumed that tense and aspect are themselves argument-introducing predicates (Zagona 1990, 1995, 2003; Stowell 1995; Demirdache and Uribe-Etxebarria 1997). However, the arguments introduced by tense and aspect are not participant arguments, but instead temporal arguments (i.e., times) In particular, Demirdache and Uribe-Etxebarria (1997) argue that aspect relates the event time to some reference time, while tense relates the reference time to the utterance time. They further propose that these abstract temporal arguments are represented in the syntactic configuration – though they are not overtly manifested. This is illustrated in (74).

(74)   Tense and aspect order times

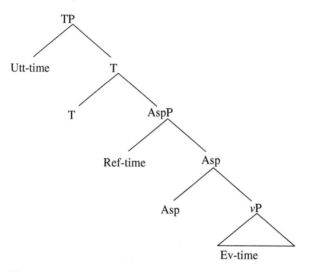

As we will see through the remainder of this monograph, abstract arguments such as the temporal arguments in (74) may be construed as the essential characteristic of universal functional categories (Speas 2010). What these abstract arguments are, and how they are introduced into the spine, will be discussed in detail in the chapters to come. For now, let me emphasize two points. First, we may identify a core function with each of the areas in the spine (Travis 2006: 327; attributed to Ken Hale MIT classes in the 1980s). I refer to these functions as the spinal functions. And second, the spinal functions are tightly connected to the abstract arguments. In particular, within the (articulated) projection of the VP, the event is introduced and classified – hence I refer to this as the domain of *classification*. The next domain serves to locate the event in time. In terms of its function, this domain may be split into two sub-domains. Aspect introduces a reference time, which serves as the point of view from which the event is characterized. Hence I refer to this domain as the *point-of-view* domain. Tense introduces the utterance time, which serves to anchor the event to the utterance. I refer to this domain as the *anchoring* domain. And finally, the domain for discourse roles is a domain where the existing structure is linked to the larger structure. Hence I shall refer to this domain as the *linking* domain. The spine with the functional domains it defines is schematized in (75).

(75)   The areas in the spine

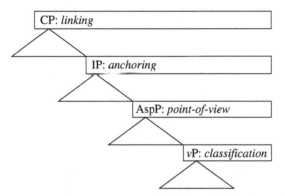

The fact that the spine may be divided into the areas in (75) provides us with key evidence for the existence of such a spine. Thus, (75) is a good candidate for a linguistic universal, though it may only be observed if we abstract away from the particular substantive content that the categories in each domain are associated with. That is, I will show that anchoring, for example, is not universally mani-fested in the form of tense. Instead, languages may choose different types of substantive content to fulfill the anchoring function. If indeed the spinal functions are universal, then we may conclude that the spine itself is an integral part of UG. Further support for this conclusion stems from the fact that there is a striking parallel between the functional structure that dominates verbs and the functional structure that dominates nouns. This is the subject of the next subsection.

2.3.4   Nominal and verbal instantiations of the spine
The parallel between nominal and verbal projections has been well docu-mented in the generative tradition. This parallelism has informed linguistic theorizing at least since Chomsky's (1970) *Remarks on Nominalization* where it was established based on data such as in (76)–(78).

(76)   a. *John is eager to please.*
        b. *John has refused the offer.*
        c. *John criticized the book.*

(77)   a. *John's being eager to please*
        b. *John's refusing the offer*
        c. *John's criticizing the book*

(78)   a. *John's eagerness to please*
       b. *John's refusal of the offer*
       c. *John's criticism of the book*

Chomsky 1970: 187 (ex.s 2–4)

The relevance of these data lies in the fact that the same types of arguments are possible both for the verbal (76) and for the nominal version (77) and (78) of the same root. Nominalizations differ in how these arguments may be realized; and this difference sheds light on the locus of nominalization. In Chomsky's (1970) analysis, the gerundive nominalization (77) is derived syntactically while nominalization via derivational morphology (by *-ness, -al,* and *-ism* (78)) is derived in the lexicon. In current terms, these differences may be understood in terms of the domains where nominalization applies (Abney 1987; Kratzer 1996).

Both types of nominalization differ from their verbal counterparts in the way the subject is realized. While subjects of verbs are realized with nominative case (*John*$_{\text{NOM}}$ *has refused the offer*) the subject of a nominalization is realized with genitive (possessive) case (*John's*$_{\text{GEN}}$ *refusing the offer, John's*$_{\text{GEN}}$ *refusal of the offer*). This suggests that the domain where subjects are licensed is not part of the nominal projection. That is, nominalization has to occur *before* the IP is projected.

As for objects, here is where the two types of nominalizations differ. In gerund nominalizations, the complement is realized in the same way as in their verbal counterparts (*John has refused the offer, John's refusing the offer*), suggesting that the domain where objects are licensed (i.e., Aspect) is present. In nominalizations via derivations, the complements must be introduced by the dummy preposition *of* (*John's refusal of the offer*) suggesting that nominalization occurs before Aspect is introduced as illustrated in (79): Gerund nominalization applies at AspP where accusative is available but nominalization via derivation applies at *v*P (or below) where accusative is not yet available. But both types of nominalization apply lower than IP and therefore nominative case is not available in either.

(79)   Domains for nominalization

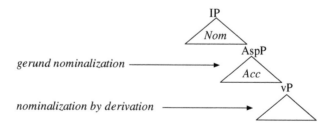

Table 2.1 *Patterns of nominalization*

	Verbal clause	Gerund nominalization	Nominalization via derivation
THEME	✓	✓	✓
AGENT	✓	✓	✓
OBJECT	✓	✓	✗
SUBJECT	✓	✗	✗

The empirical differences between verbal clauses and the two types of nominalizations are summarized in Table 2.1.

The fact the thematic subjects may be realized as either nominative subjects (in the clausal projections) or as genitive possessors suggests that there is an affinity between the two roles such that possessors may be construed as the nominal equivalent of clausal subjects (Szabolcsi 1983). Since the grammatical subject role is assumed to be introduced by a functional head, we can conclude that this is also the case for the nominal equivalent. This (among other facts) led Abney (1987) to assume a similar functional architecture dominating both verbs and nouns. In particular, he argues that the functional position occupied by the possessive morphology may be viewed as the nominal equivalent of INFL. And since (in English) possessive morphology is in complementary distribution with determiners, this position has been identified as D (see Leu [2008] for a recent discussion). Interestingly, D does indeed serve some of the same functions as INFL, in that it serves to relate the individual to the utterance. For example, in languages that encode definiteness, it relates the referent to the discourse by marking whether it serves as a novel or a familiar discourse referent (Heim 1988). In this way, D functions as the nominal anchoring category.

Similar parallels have been established for the other categories of the spine (Alexiadou and Stavrou 1998; Cardinaletti and Starke 1999; Bernstein 2001, 2008; Grimshaw 2005; Koopman 2005; Rijkhoff 2008, *inter alii*). In particular, verbal Aspect is parallel to nominal number (Travis 1992; Megerdoomian 2008 and references therein); the verbal classification system known as *Aktionsart* finds its nominal equivalent in classifications based on *mass/count* and are labeled *Seinsart* in Rijkhoff (1991); finally the verbal system of complementizers is replicated by some case-assigning elements such as the dummy preposition *of*, which we may analyze as occupying K (Lamontagne and Travis 1987; Bittner and Hale 1996).

(80)   The parallelism between the nominal and verbal spine

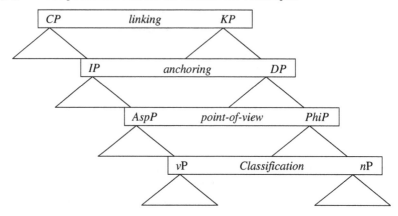

The parallel between the nominal and the verbal domains illustrated in (80) supports the Universal Spine Hypothesis. Since both verbal and nominal projections are dominated by functional structure with identical spinal functions, it follows that the spine is intrinsically category-neutral. It may be instantiated by nominal or verbal categories. This predicts that we should find some patterns of category-neutrality in the domain of functional categories. It has often been claimed that lexical roots are intrinsically category-neutral in that they are not lexically specified as either nouns or verbs (Marantz 1997; Borer 2005). Consequently they can be equally realized as nouns or verbs, as in (81). Their categorial identity is determined by the syntactic context.

(81)   a. *I like to **dance**.*
        b. *I like that **dance**.*

It is in this sense that roots are category-neutral. But a similar pattern is also observed with function words, suggesting that category-neutrality is not restricted to lexical roots. For example, there is a common pattern in the lexicalization of complementizers such that a nominal functor (i.e., a demonstrative) does double duty as a complementizer, as in (82).

(82)   a. *I've heard **that** story.*
        b. *I've heard **that** Edward wants to stay in Russia.*

A similar pattern of category-neutrality with functional morphemes is found in Yupik agreement morphology. Here, the same form (*-t*) can be used in the nominal and verbal domain: it is used for subject agreement, ergative marking, a and possessive agreement.

(83)   a. *Angute-t*   *kiputa-a-t.*
           man-ERG.PL   buy-OBJ-S
           'The man bought it.'

        b. *angute-t*   *kuiga-t.*
           the man-ERG.PL.   river-s
           'the men's river'

                                                Abney 1987: 28 (24)

Similarly, in Hebrew pronouns may do double duty as copula verbs (Ritter 1995).

(84)   a. *Dani*   ***hu***   *ha-more.*
           Dani   he   DET-teacher
           'Dani is the teacher.'

        b. *Hu malax*   *'al*   *jisra'el.*
           he reigned.3MASC.SG.   over   Israel
           'He reigned over Israel.'

                                                adapted from Katz 1996: 86 (1)

Note that the pronoun–copula connection is not an isolated case unique to Hebrew. Many languages display this type of multifunctionality. It is also found in Russian (Pereltsvaig (2001)), Haitian Creole (Deprez 2003), and Pulaar (Cover 2006), among others.

This establishes that category-neutrality is not restricted to lexical roots but is also found with functional words and morphemes, supporting the claim that the spine is intrinsically category-neutral (Bliss 2013; Wiltschko 2014).

2.4   When do the units of language associate with the spine

Thus far we have introduced some of the empirical findings and generalizations that support the assumption of a universal spine. One of the main points I wish to establish in this monograph is that the categories based on word classes, inflectional type, and substantive content are not part of the spine, and are thus not expected to be universal. Instead the categories of the spine are defined in terms of their core function (*classification, point-of-view, anchoring,* and *linking*). The spine constrains the language-specific categorization patterns but does not uniquely determine them. This means that language-specific categories are not expected to be universal. The question remains, however, how the language-specific units of language (UoLs) (words, morphemes, features, etc.) associate with the universal spine. In this section I briefly review some previous assumptions about the relation between language-specific UoLs and syntactic representations. Since these questions are fundamentally about the relation between different modules, they have implications for the architecture of grammar.

In the early days of generative grammar the relation between language-specific UoLs (conceived of as words) and syntactic representations was regulated by lexical rules (85). Alongside phrase structure rules, such as those in (86), the lexical rules constituted the *base*, which in turn constituted the input for transformational rules as shown in Figure 2.1.

(85)   V → *buried*
        N → *dog*
        N → *bone*
        Det → *the*

(86)   S → NP VP
        VP → V NP
        NP → Det N
        NP → N

The shift from a rule-based to a principle-based grammar that defined the shift between the Standard Theory and the Principles and Parameters framework led to the rejection of lexical rules. Instead, a separate module – the lexicon – was postulated (Figure 2.2).

The conceptualization of the lexicon has changed over the years, and is still a matter of much debate. There are two principal questions that arise if we separate the lexicon from the syntax:

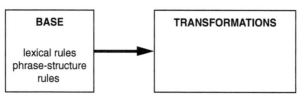

Figure 2.1 *The base and the transformational component*

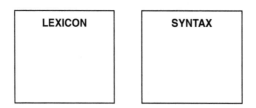

Figure 2.2 *Separating the lexicon from the syntactic component*

(i) What is in the lexicon?

(ii) How do lexical entries relate to the syntax?

I briefly discuss how these two questions have been answered within the generative tradition (see Harley [forthcoming] for a recent overview of these issues).

Once we postulate a lexicon, which functions as a repository of building blocks for a given language, we need to ask what counts as a building block. Several answers have been proposed.

One possible answer can roughly be characterized as 'The-lexicon-contains-all-words-hypothesis'. It includes simplex as well as complex words. Given that word formation is productive, it follows that the lexicon itself will also contain rules for forming complex words. What characterizes this view – known as *lexicalism* – is that whatever was created in the lexicon is treated as an unanalyzable unit in the syntax. This is sometimes referred to as the *Lexical Integrity Hypothesis* (Lapointe 1980) or *lexical atomicity* (Williams 1981). To ensure that these lexical units match syntactic requirements, certain correspondence rules must be postulated (to regulate, for example, the distribution of inflected words, which must match the syntactic derivation). Thus, the model of grammar that emerges looks something like in Figure 2.3.

A second possible answer can roughly be characterized as 'The-lexicon-contains-some-words-hypothesis'. This is a weaker version of lexicalism. It is associated with Aronoff (1976, 1994) and Anderson (1992). The reason underlying the split in the repository of words has to do with the fact that words formed by derivational morphology are formed independent of their syntactic context, whereas inflectional morphology is sensitive to the syntactic context. This leads to the postulation that the lexicon contains simplex words as well as derivational word-formation rules. The output of the lexicon so

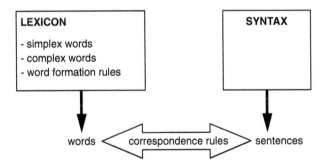

Figure 2.3 *Lexicalism*

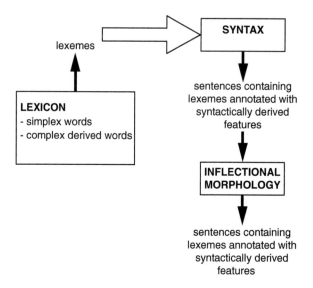

Figure 2.4 *Weak lexicalism (split morphology)*

conceived is so-called *lexemes*. These enter into the syntactic computation where they may be annotated with inflectional features. In a second post-syntactic repository these annotated lexemes become fully inflected words. Thus on this view the morphological component is split, as illustrated in Figure 2.4.

On this view, the correspondence rules of strict lexicalist theories are replaced by the assumption that there are two split morphologies: one feeds syntax (it is *pre-syntactic* or *projectional*), and the other one is fed by syntax (it is *post-syntactic* or *realizational*). On the classical approach these two types of morphologies define derivation and compounding on the one hand vs. inflection on the other. But not all theories divide up the lexicon in this particular way.

For example, the framework of Distributed Morphology (Halle and Marantz 1993) may be characterized as a 'The-lexicon-contains-only-simplex-units-hypothesis'. The core assumption that sets this framework apart from the previous two is that all word-formation rules are restricted to the syntactic component. Consequently, the initial repository of building blocks contains simplex units only. These units consist of morpho-syntactic features, which are, however, not yet associated with phonological information. On some versions of Distributed Morphology, simplex sound meaning bundles (known as √roots) are also part of this pre-syntactic lexicon. This repository is known as the *list*. It feeds syntax, which in turn computes the morpho-syntactic

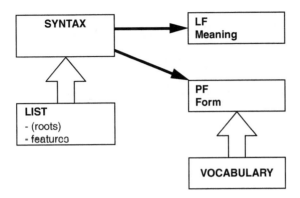

Figure 2.5 *Distributed morphology*

features. Another repository is found after syntactic derivation. The fully inflected forms here are known as the *vocabulary*. The Distributed Morphology model may be roughly represented as in Figure 2.5.

The separation of the module that derives morpho-syntactically complex forms from the module which produces the phonological form that realizes these morpho-syntactic expressions is not unique to Distributed Morphology. It is also found in Sproat (1985), Beard (1995), and Jackendoff (1997), among others.

Such models contrast with purely projectional ones (such as Lieber [1992, 2004]), according to which all UoLs are intrinsically associated with sound and meaning and are inserted early.

We have seen that our view of how words are assembled to form sentences has changed over the last few decades. This has to be reflected in a formal typology, which seeks to provide a framework for how sound, meaning, and category are associated with each other. What is important from our point of view is that there are two logical possibilities for the association between sound–meaning correspondences and the syntactic spine. The association may be early or late. In developing the formal typology based on the universal spine, I will assume that UoLs may be both pre- and post-syntactic.

3   The universal spine as a heuristic for the identification of grammatical categories

Under heaven all can see beauty as beauty only because there is ugliness.
All can know good as good only because there is evil.
Therefore having and not having arise together.
Difficult and easy complement each other.
Long and short contrast each other.
High and low rest upon each other.
Voice and sound harmonize each other.
Front and back follow one another.   Lao Zi, fourth century BC

3.1   Units of language associate with the spine

We started in Chapter 1 with three questions: (i) What are grammatical categories? (ii) How do we identify them? (iii) And are they universal? In response to question (i), the central thesis of this monograph is that the grammatical categories found in the languages of the world are constructed. In particular, they are constructed from a universal categorizer κ and a language-specific UoL, as in (1). I refer to the elementary operation that combines κ with UoL as *Associate*.

(1) $c = \kappa + \text{UoL}$

Since categories are constructed, it follows that they can be constructed in different ways and therefore will have different formal properties. Hence Universal Grammar cannot be viewed as a repository of categories. This yields an answer to the third question. Language-specific categories are not universal, but the foundational ingredient for categorization (κ) is.

The goal of this chapter is to address the second question: how do we identify grammatical categories? The task is to make explicit the consequences of (1) for the discovery of language-specific categories. What sets this approach towards categorization apart from most existing approaches is the assumption that categories are not associated with substantive content as a

84

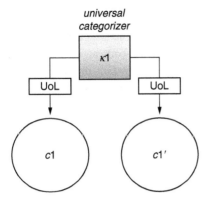

Figure 3.1 *Comparison based on κ*

matter of UG. Just like sound (π) is part of a UoL, so too is substantive content (Σ). In other words, there is no universal relation between κ and UoL or any of its ingredients (Σ or π). For this reason, substance-based comparisons do not work (see Section 1.5).[1] Instead, I propose that it is the universal spine, which serves as the comparison set, as illustrated in Figure 3.1 (repeat of Figure 1.9 above). In particular, rather than comparing language-specific categories (c1 and c1′) directly with each other, they are decomposed into the UoL and the universal core (κ) that serve to construct them.

If this is on the right track, then the identification of any grammatical category *c* requires not only identifying the relevant UoLs but we must also know **how** these UoLs associate with κ.

This chapter is organized as follows. In Section 3.2, we explore the logic of the association relation between UoL and κ. The association relation is defined along three parameters. UoLs differ in *how, where,* and *when* they associate with κ. Differences in actual association relations have predictable consequences for the distribution and interpretation of a given UoL. It is these differences that we can use as heuristics to discern the nature of the association relation from a particular UoL. In Section 3.3, these criteria are introduced. In section 3.4, I conclude by making explicit the implications for the identification of *c*, which will guide the case studies in the chapters to come.

---

[1] For the same reason, sound-based comparisons will not work either, though to the best of my knowledge, unlike meaning-based heuristics, sound-based heuristics have not been employed.

3.2   The logic of Associate

In Chapter 1 (Section 1.1.2), we saw that grammatical categories have different formal properties even if their substantive content appears identical. For example, plural and past marking in Halkomelem differ significantly from their English counterparts in their distributional properties. The hypothesis I put forward here is that these differences result from differences in the way UoLs associate with the spine. There are three parameters that define the association relation. That is, for any given UoL we can ask the following questions:

(i)   ***How*** does the UoL associate with the spine?
(ii) ***Where*** does the UoL associate with the spine?
(iii) ***When*** does the UoL associate with the spine?

Here I briefly introduce the logic behind each of these questions. The first parameter of variation has to do with *how* a given UoL associates with κ, its *manner of association*. There are two logical possibilities, as illustrated in (2).[2] One possibility is for a UoL to associate with κ in a way that can be characterized as an "*is-a*" relation (2a): the UoL is a κ. In this case we have the impression that κ is intrinsically associated with the substantive content supplied by the UoL. I adopt Ritter and Wiltschko's (2009) terminology and refer to this as *substantiation*.

Alternatively, a UoL may associate with κ in a way that can be characterized as a relation of *modification* (2b): the UoL modifies κ.

(2)   Manner of association

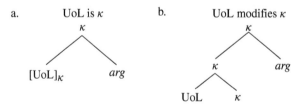

---

[2] I will abstract away from the possibility that a UoL could associate with a complex κ. This may be either phrasal (κP) or a *span* of several distinct κs (in the sense of Williams [2003]). I have no reason to believe that these logical possibilities are ruled out on principled grounds. However, the data I have investigated thus far did not require me to explore this type of association relation in more detail.

In more traditional terms the difference between these two options is referred to as a difference between *substitution* (2a) and *adjunction* (2b). In the former, the UoL becomes a syntactic head (the UoL *is-a* κ). Thus, the UoL itself becomes categorized. I represent this by means of the familiar labeled bracket convention, which expresses the "*is-a*" relation (3a). In the alternative strategy (adjunction) the UoL merely modifies κ. When no tree structures are given, I represent this type of association as an unordered set (3b).

(3)   Representing two different manners of association
         a. [UoL]κ
         b. {κ, UoL}

The second parameter of variation has to do with **where** along the spine a given UoL associates with κ, its *place* of association. As introduced in Chapter 1 (Section 1.4.3), the universal spine is a set of recursive κs, each associated with a distinct abstract function. A UoL may associate with the spine across all four domains as illustrated in (4).

(4)   Place of association

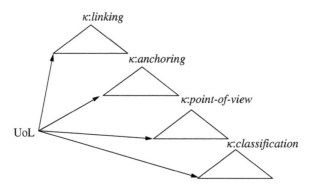

In this respect, the USH does not differ from previous approaches in any substantial way (apart from the assumptions regarding the nature of the spine).

When no tree structures are given, I represent the place of association as an ordered pair where the first member is the UoL and the second member is κ, annotated with its function (e.g., κ:*f*).[3]

---

[3] In fact, either UoL or κ can serve as the first member in this ordered pair corresponding to a difference in the timing of association. I discuss this immediately below.

(5)   Representing the place of association
    a. <UoL, *κ:linking*>
    b. <UoL, *κ:anchoring*>
    c. <UoL, *κ:point-of-view*>
    d. <UoL, *κ:classification* >

The third parameter of variation concerns the *timing of association*. A UoL may associate with the spine either *before* or *after* the syntactic computation, as schematized in (6). The arrow from UoL towards *κ* indicates an early association relation, while the arrow from *κ* towards UoL indicates a late association relation.

(6)   Timing of association

    a. UoL associates early   b. UoL associates late

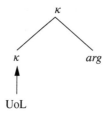 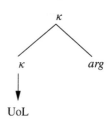

In traditional terms, the difference between early and late association corresponds to *projectional* morphology or *early insertion* versus *realizational* morphology or *late insertion* (see Chapter 2, Section 2.4). Many current frameworks consider these two alternatives to be exclusive in the sense that UoLs are either all projectional or all realizational.[4] Here I assume that there is no intrinsic reason for this to be so. Instead I assume that UoLs may associate either early or late with predictable consequences for their distribution. When no tree structures are given, I represent the timing of association as an ordered pair: if the UoL associates early, it constitutes the first member (7a); if the UoL associates late it constitutes the second member (7b).

(7)   Representing the timing of association
    a. Early association: <UoL, *κ*>
    b. Late association: <*κ*,UoL>

In sum, to identify the grammatical categories of a given language, we must not only identify the UoLs but also the ways they associate with *κ*. We have here introduced the logical possibilities for the association relations. The question we

---

[4] See de Belder (2011) for recent discussion within the framework of Distributed Morphology.

Table 3.1 *Two ways of being unmarked*

Base	marked by ...	Interpreted as ...	Markedness status
N	–	general number	truly unmarked
N	{π:Ø, Σ:singular}	singular	zero marked
N	{π.-s, Σ:plural}	plural	overtly marked

have to address now is how we can diagnose the association relations that define a particular grammatical category. I turn to this question in the next section.

3.3   Categorizing the Units of Language

When faced with a particular UoL, how can we tell how, where, and when it associates with κ? In what follows, I introduce some of the diagnostics that are used in the case studies to follow. In particular, the association relations involved can be gleaned from the way in which κ contributes to the interpretation of the UoL.

As we have seen in Chapter 1 (Section 1.1) the contribution of κ to a given UoL manifests itself most clearly in patterns of contrast and patterns of multifunctionality. In both cases, there is a mismatch between the form of the UoL and its interpretation. This mismatch can be understood on the assumption that a UoL exists independently of κ and that κ contributes to the interpretation of the UoL. But it does so in different ways depending on the manner, place, and timing of association.

3.3.1   *Diagnosing the manner of association*

The two patterns of contrast introduced in Section 1.1.2 serve to diagnose the manner of association (Wiltschko 2008). Recall that the difference between these two patterns manifests itself most clearly in the way the absence of marking is interpreted. Specifically, sometimes the absence of a particular UoL is associated with a dedicated interpretation. As summarized in Table 1.3, repeated from Chapter 1 as Table 3.1, in some contexts, in English, the absence of plural marking receives a dedicated interpretation (singular). In other contexts, the absence of plural marking is characterized by the absence of a dedicated interpretation (general number). Consequently the latter is compatible with both a singular and a plural interpretation.

Table 3.2 *Surface effects of κ-contrast*

Surface effects	Manner of association	
	κ-categories	κ-modifiers
Obligatory (relative to κ)	✓	✗
Syntactic head effects (c-selection, agreement, ...)	✓	✗
Allows for zero marking	✓	✗
Allows for expletive interpretation	✓	✗

The difference between being zero marked and being truly unmarked is indicative of different association relations. In particular, zero marking is only licensed (i.e., recoverable) if the marked UoL associates with κ by means of the "*is-a*" relation. That is, if κ is involved, it allows for the triangulation of meaning even in the absence of a corresponding overt form. I refer to this type of contrast as *κ-contrast*.

If the UoL that marks a particular meaning modifies κ, but does not itself substantiate κ, then its absence does not substantiate κ either. Hence, in this case the absence of marking cannot be associated with a dedicated interpretation – it is simply not recoverable as a form of zero marking. Thus, it is the interpretation of the unmarked form, which reveals the pattern of contrast most clearly, as summarized in (8).

(8)   The contrast diagnostic
       a. UoL associates with κ via the "*is-a*" relation if...
          ... the distribution and interpretation of the unmarked form *complement* the distribution and interpretation of the marked form

       b. UoL associates with κ via the *modification* relation if...
          ... the distribution and interpretation of the unmarked form *include* the distribution and interpretation of the marked form

These two patterns of contrast yield a number of surface effects, which in turn can be used to diagnose the association relation, and thus grammatical categories (Wiltschko 2008).[5] These include *obligatoriness*, syntactic head effects, possible licensing of *zero marking*, and possible licensing of an *expletive* interpretation. This is summarized in Table 3.2.

---

[5] See Steriopolo (2006) for an application of these diagnostics to diminutives in Russian.

A few words about the status of these diagnostics are in order. First consider *obligatoriness*, which is commonly used to identify grammatical categories. For example, in a recent dissertation on person, de Schepper (2012: 9) defines a *"grammatical category as a semantic concept that is obligatorily encoded on a subset of linguistic items in one or more of the world's languages."* However, obligatoriness itself is not as straightforward to identify as it may sound. In particular, the obligatoriness of a given grammatical category is dependent on the syntactic context. Take for example tense marking. While it is obligatory in English in matrix indicative clauses, it is not in certain embedded clauses (e.g., in infinitives), and in some clauses its form is present, but its interpretation differs (e.g., in counterfactuals). The former clause-type is sometimes analyzed as tenseless and the latter is sometimes analyzed as involving *fake* past marking (see Chapter 4). Similarly, number marking in English is only obligatory for count nouns in nominal phrases. In contrast, mass nouns are not marked for number and inside of compounds number marking is typically not available. Thus, obligatoriness may not be absolute but must instead be relativized to particular syntactic contexts.

Next we turn to syntactic head effects. Associating UoL with κ via the *"is-a"* relation causes the UoL to display the distribution of a syntactic head. And as a consequence, it may interact with other heads within the syntactic spine. In particular, we may observe c-selectional restrictions and head movement effects, and the UoL may trigger agreement.

Finally we turn to the licensing of zero marking and expletive interpretations. It is one of the crucial effects of associating UoL to κ via the *"is-a"* relation that in this case the UoL is characterized by three ingredients: π, Σ, and κ. As a consequence of the obligatory presence of κ, in certain syntactic contexts either π or Σ may remain uninterpreted. If π remains uninterpreted, the result is zero marking and thus a complementary interpretation; if Σ remains uninterpreted, the result is zero interpretation (i.e., expletiveness).[6] Note that expletiveness is a special form of multifunctionality. In particular, the same UoL may or may not be interpreted, depending on the linguistic context. This captures the phenomenon that UoLs that may be used as expletives are never dedicated as such.

---

[6] This derives what is sometimes referred to as a generalized EPP feature (Chomsky 2000), occurrence feature (Chomsky 2001), or edge feature (Chomsky 2008). The purpose of these features is to ensure the obligatory occurrence of a UoL in a particular syntactic position. It is here generalized to derive the possibility for zero marking and expletive interpretations.

In conclusion, the difference in the manner of association has different distributional and interpretive effects supporting the claim that κ mediates the relation between form and meaning. The manner of association derives two types of categories. Under some definitions of grammatical categories only those defined by the "*is-a*" relation are recognized as categories (since those are the ones that display obligatoriness; see the quote from de Schepper [2012] above). Here the term category covers both types. If it is necessary to distinguish the two types of categories, I will use the term *κ-category* for those that are characterized by the "*is-a*" and the term *(κ-)modifier* for those that are characterized by the modification relation.

3.3.2   *Diagnosing the place of association*

In addition to establishing *how* a given UoL associates with the spine, we must also establish *where* it associates with the spine. In particular, there are (at least) four distinct areas in the spine, which are defined in terms of a core function: *κ:linking, κ:anchoring, κ:point-of-view*, and *κ:classification*. Thus, in addition to the classic diagnostics for structural position (c-command, linear order, and scope; see Chapter 2, Section 2.1.2) we may also use the spinal function of a particular UoL to diagnose its structural position. Recall that the classic tests diagnose relative structural position only, but they are not always sufficient to diagnose absolute position. Instead, to determine the absolute position of a given UoL, we need to establish which of the spinal functions it realizes. Thus, in addition to formal diagnostics, the USH requires and enables us to use some functional criteria as well.

In this way the USH differs from the other two approaches that we compare it to. On the one hand, in many instantiations the Universal Base Hypothesis (UBH) identifies categories by their content, which in turn derives their function. For example, the widely assumed functional category tense is defined by its temporal content. But at the same time it is defined as a deictic category, thus instantiating the anchoring function (see Enç 1987). The USH differs in that it dissociates content from function: while function is intrinsically associated with particular instantiations of κ, substantive content is not. Consequently, while the UBH has to use content to determine the absolute position of a given UoL, the USH can use function (without content) to do so.

Within the other alternative, the No Base Hypothesis (NBH), there is no absolute position that one would have to identify. Under the minimalist version of the NBH (i.e., label-free syntax) (Uriagereka 1999; Chomsky 2000, 2001; Collins 2002; Seeley 2006), prefabricated positions do not exist. Rather, UoLs are merged with each other to build structure without a mediating spine.

On this view then, identifying structural relations reduces to determining relative positions only.

Using the function of UoLs as a way to diagnose categorial identity is thus unique to the USH, at least within the generative tradition. Function as a crucial identifier for categories is of course commonly used in functional approaches, with an important difference, however. As discussed in Section 1.5, functionalism denies the existence of universally valid categorical distinctions in favor of a prototype approach. In addition, in the USH, formal criteria such as c-command are not replaced by functional ones, but instead they are supplemented in this way. In sum, the USH makes available the function as a heuristic to identify the absolute position of a particular UoL.

(9)   The function diagnostic
        The absolute position of a given UoL can be diagnosed by identifying its
        function, which is independent of its content.

The dissociation of function from content also predicts a certain pattern of multifunctionality. Specifically, if a given UoL appears to be associated with a given function, such as for example deictic anchoring, the USH predicts that this function is contributed by the spine (i.e., κ). This pattern of multifunctionality is similar to expletiveness, in that it is characterized by an apparent loss of meaning; however, in this case, it is only a particular aspect of meaning that appears to be lost, namely its function. Such patterns of multifunctionality are sometimes described as *fake* marking. For example, counterfactual conditionals in English are formally marked with past tense morphology, but this marking is not interpreted as past tense (see Chapter 5 for discussion). Similarly, 1st and 2nd person pronouns are typically interpreted as indexicals, referring to the speaker and addressee, respectively. However, in some contexts, this indexical interpretation is lost (Partee 1989), resulting in so-called *fake indexicals* (Kratzer 2009). Under the USH, fake indexicality is indicative of the contribution of κ (Déchaine and Wiltschko forthcoming). Accordingly, it is not the UoL itself that is indexical, but instead it acquires an indexical interpretation by virtue of its position in the spine, namely κ: *anchoring*.

Thus, the apparent loss of meaning of a given UoL (i.e., fake patterns) is among the effects derived from the place of association of a given UoL. This is because its particular position in the syntactic spine may add a particular meaning component, namely the function associated with κ, to UoL. So if a given UoL is associated with a different position it will appear as if its meaning is lost. This is however only possible if the UoL is associated with κ early.

Patterns of multifunctionality can therefore also be used to diagnose the timing of association, as I discuss immediately below.

3.3.3   *Diagnosing the timing of association*

The third parameter of variation concerns the timing of association of a given UoL to the spine. In particular, for any given UoL we need to ask *when* it associates with the spine: *before* or *after* the syntactic computation. The timing of association has predictable consequences for the distributional properties of UoLs and the patterns of multifunctionality. Given the logic of association, we expect that UoLs that associate early will show effects of category-neutrality. Such effects have been used to argue for the dissociation between UoLs and their categorial identity in the domain of lexical categories (nouns and verbs). As shown in (10), the same UoL *dance* may be used as a noun (10) or as a verb (10), depending on the syntactic context.

(10)   a. *I like this **dance**.*
        b. *I know how to **dance**.*

This may be taken as an indication that the UoL *dance* is not intrinsically associated with categorial identity (*n* or *v*). Instead, words acquire categorial identities only in the context of a syntactic structure (Marantz 1997; Borer 2005). But if this is so, it implies that the sound–meaning correspondences that make up these category-neutral roots exist independently of the syntactic computation. And indeed, such roots are sometimes taken to be inserted early, at least abstractly (e.g., via an index as in Harley [2009]). In Borer's exoskeletal approach, roots are also fundamentally category-neutral and thus highly multifunctional.

But multifunctionality is not restricted to lexical categories. Function words too show multifunctionality in ways that mirror those of lexical categories, as we have already seen on the basis of the examples in (11), repeated from Chapter 1.

(11)   a. *I know **that** guy.*
        b. *I know **that** this guy is courageous.*

We observe that the same UoL (*that*) appears in different syntactic environments and consequently that it is associated with different categorial identities (demonstrative vs. complementizer, respectively).[7] Applying the same logic

---

[7] But see Kayne (2010) for the claim that *that* in (11) can still be analyzed as a demonstrative determiner (see also Davidson 1968).

that led to the postulation of category-neutral early insertion roots to such functors, we are led to the conclusion that *that* too is category-neutral and thus associated early.[8] Thus, category-neutral behavior may serve to diagnose early association UoLs. Moreover, an early association UoL will have significant impact on the identity of the grammatical category it serves to construct. In particular, the substantive content of the UoL that combines with κ to construct c will determine the substantive content of the grammatical category.

(12)   The category-neutrality diagnostic
         If a UoL displays effects of category-neutrality, it associates with κ early.

What about UoLs that associate with κ late? One of the core arguments for late insertion/spell out models is the existence of UoLs whose distribution can only be explained with recourse to syntactic derivations (such as agreement or the valuation of unvalued features). Thus late association UoLs, unlike early association UoLs, are intrinsically associated with categorial information, and this categorial information can be complex.

(13)   The categorial-complexity diagnostic
         If a UoL displays effects of categorial complexity, it associates with κ late.

3.4   Identifying grammatical categories

The purpose of this chapter is to explore the question as to how to identify grammatical categories in light of the assumption that categories are constructed, as in (14) (repeated from above).

(14) $c = \kappa + \text{UoL}$

This question is acute for linguists who seek to analyze data collected in fieldwork. But it equally applies to linguists who are interested in questions regarding universality and variation in the realm of categories. Language variation in categorial inventories has long been observed. The answer I explore here, based on the USH, is that languages differ in their inventories of grammatical categories c precisely because c is constructed. But at the same time there is a core universal basis for categorization, namely the universal spine. What sets the present approach apart from previous ones is that neither

---

[8] If indeed the timing of association cross-cuts the division between lexical and functional categories, we predict that lexical categories (i.e., roots) as well may be of the late association type. This seems to be borne out. As Armoskaite (2011) shows, Blackfoot has no category-neutral roots. That is, all roots are inherently categorized as nouns or verbs.

identification nor comparison of categories should be substance-based. Instead, what is required is a formal typology. Generative grammar provides an ideal framework for the development of such a typology, as it is fundamentally concerned with modeling the relation between sound (or more broadly, form), meaning, and categorial identities, where the latter are conceptualized as those aspects of a given UoL that are responsible for its distribution within a sentence.

Given the proposal in (14), identification of *c* requires identification of its ingredients: κ, UoL, and their association relations. Among these ingredients, only the UoL is directly observable. But crucially, UoLs come in different flavors due to several parameters of variation in the association relations. In particular, UoLs may vary in *how*, *where*, and *when* they associate with the spine. Thus, the relation between UoLs and their categorial identity is complex in ways that present us with intriguing challenges for analysis. The particular association relation has effects on essential properties of UoLs that cannot be ignored. It is therefore vital to be able to diagnose these association relations. I have introduced several such diagnostics. What many of them have in common is that they take patterns of multifunctionality of individual UoLs seriously. While this strategy has been previously exploited to identify the relation between lexical roots and their categorial identity, it is not often used in the domain of grammatical categories. One of the few exceptions is found in Leiss (2005), who explicitly endorses the significance of multifunctionality (also known as polysemy). It is worth repeating her insightful comments on this matter.

> *Before research into grammaticalization was established, morphemes with identical form were preferably classified as homonyms rather than as motivated polysemy. What was striking about this method is that the postulation of homonymy did not have to be justified whereas postulation of polysemy was not easily accepted. Polysemy not only had to appear plausible, but it had to be proven. In contrast, postulation of homonymy was acceptable even if it was implausible and counter-intuitive. Thus in older works on word formation, one can regularly find claims according to which propositions and form-identical verbal prefixes are homonyms. Such claims were never regarded as unscientific, to the contrary. They were – and still are – considered as an indication of methodical precaution. Many are not aware of this biased burden of proof. It can be made explicit if we turn the burden of proof around in a thought experiment. Nobody seems to consider this possibility. The reversal of the burden of proof would mean that from now on postulation of homonymy will have to be proven, whereas postulation of polysemy would be considered as an indication of methodical precaution. Current methodology is different: researchers dealing with grammaticalization consider it*

their task to prove the motivation for polysemy. In contrast, there is no research agenda, which considers it necessary to prove and explain postulated homophony. But the cross-linguistic frequency of homophony requires an explanation. Why is the rich potential for symbolization not utilized? Why do the same forms of inflectional and derivational morphemes recur in different functions? When specific questions are not asked it is an indication that something is axiomatically excluded. What is the axiom, which would conflict with this reversal in the burden of proof the most? It is the axiom of the arbitrariness of linguistic signs.   (Leiss 2005: 233, translation MW)

In line with Leiss 2005, I here take the multifunctionality of UoLs seriously as a heuristic in the identification of grammatical categories. Crucially, the USH predicts these patterns, and, as such has a broader range of empirical coverage than those theories that have to set them aside as instances of accidental homophony (see also Déchaine [1993]).

As for the second ingredient that plays a role in the construction of categories, namely κ, its properties can only be observed on the basis of the effects it has on c. In particular, if a given UoL appears to have different interpretations depending on its syntactic environment, we may conclude that there is a dimension of interpretation that is supplied by κ. Thus, as a consequence of the assumption that categories are constructed as in (14), we can use generalizations over the grammatical categories we discover in the languages of the world as the basis for inferences about the properties of κ. In particular, properties of κ can be gleaned by subtracting the contribution of UoL to c as in (15).

(15) $\kappa = c - \text{UoL}$

We are, however, not starting the exploration of κ from scratch. I have introduced in Chapter 1 assumptions about κ that have guided the research I report in the chapters to come. In particular, I have introduced the Universal Spine Hypothesis, which is grounded in generative insights, as discussed in Chapter 2. Based on the USH, as well as the diagnostics for association relations I have introduced in this chapter, we can now move on to explore grammatical categories across several unrelated languages. This will allow us to refine and adjust our assumptions regarding the nature of κ.

4 Anchoring categories in independent clauses

He is the past tense of you.   Rachel Ermineskin

4.1   Tense as an anchoring category

The goal of this chapter is to explore categories that are found in the anchoring domain, specifically those that can be used in independent clauses. The anchoring domain is a core grammatical domain. It is where the grammatical subject-relation is introduced and it serves to relate the reported event to the ongoing discourse. As discussed in Chapter 2, the category that is assumed (in the generative tradition) to fulfill this function is tense. For example, in English matrix declarative clauses, verbs have to be marked for tense and agreement, as shown in (1). Crucially, it is not the temporal information that is obligatory, but instead it is tense inflection. Thus, the presence of a temporal adverbial (*yesterday/today*) may modify the time of the event but it does not render tense inflection superfluous, as shown in (2).

(1)   a. *Yoshi play-**ed** ball (yesterday).*
        b. *Yoshi play-**s** ball (today).*

(2)   a. **Yoshi play ball (yesterday).*
        b. **Yoshi play ball (today).*

Thus, the use of tense is guided by grammatical principles that make the use of a tense morpheme obligatory even if the information it carries is redundant (Dahl and Vellupilai 2011). Many Indo-European languages make use of tense marking with the same set of properties: matrix indicative clauses require tense marking, often but not necessarily expressed via inflectional morphology. However, not all languages behave in this way. There are languages that lack the obligatory contrast between a past and a non-past form. For example, the *World Atlas of Language Structures* (henceforth WALS) lists 94 languages with a past/non-past contrast, 38 languages with a contrast between present tense and two to three degrees of remoteness, and four languages with a contrast between present tense and five degrees of remoteness.[1] But crucially there are 88 languages listed as lacking past tense marking (Dahl and Vellupilai 2011; see also Bybee [1985], who found that only 50% of the languages in her sample had inflectional tense).

In short, languages vary in the categorial notions they obligatorily express by morphological means (Sapir 1921). And tense is a commonly discussed example of this variation. In the generative tradition superficial differences are often taken to be just that: superficial differences that have no underlying significance. In this chapter, I will explore three languages that do not obligatorily mark past tense: Blackfoot, Halkomelem, and Upper Austrian German.[2]

I proceed as follows. Based on the diagnostics introduced in Chapter 3, I show in Section 4.2 that in none of these three languages does tense marking pattern as an obligatory morpho-syntactic category c:TENSE. This suggests that, in these languages, κ:*anchoring* does not associate with tense marking. I conclude that at least some languages without overt tense marking lack the category c:TENSE. I will refer to such languages as c:TENSE-less. But if not all languages have c:TENSE, then c:TENSE cannot be a member of C_{UG} and thus c:TENSE cannot be a universal category. At the same time, however, we will see that this does not force us to conclude that UG does not exist. To the contrary, we will see that even in c:TENSE-less languages, we can detect grammatical categories that substantiate κ:*anchoring*. This supports the conclusion that there is an underlying category, which may be manifested by c:TENSE, but which may also be manifested in different ways.

In Section 4.3, I show that the absence of c:TENSE in a given language cannot be equated with the absence of the anchoring domain, i.e., the domain where the grammatical subject relation is introduced. Rather I show that in all of the three c:TENSE-less languages we find effects that are attributable to the grammatical subject relation. This means that the potential conclusion that languages do not share the same categories, and thus that there are no universal categories, is premature. But if c:TENSE does not manifest κ:*anchoring*, what else does?

In Section 4.4, I review evidence that in the absence of the morpho-syntactic category c:TENSE, we find other obligatory morpho-syntactic categories that fulfill the same spinal function (κ:*anchoring*), but they differ in content.

---

[1] For a formal analysis of a language with degrees of remoteness see Cable (2013).

[2] I assume here that true tense-systems have a contrast between past and non-past. For languages that display an obligatory contrast between future and non-future I assume that such systems are based on modality, rather than tense.

In particular, in Blackfoot, there is an obligatory contrast between *local* participants (1st and 2nd person) and *non-local* participants (3rd person); in Halkomelem there is an obligatory contrast between *proximate* and *distal* location. And finally, in Upper Austrian German, I provide novel evidence that a contrast that can roughly be based characterized as realis/irrealis appears to associate with *κ:anchoring*. These language-specific categories (*c*:PERSON, *c*:LOCATION, and *c*:REALIS) satisfy the criteria of grammatical categories that are constructed based on *κ:anchoring* via the "*is-a*" relation.

In Section 4.5, I draw conclusions about the universal structure of *κ: anchoring*.[3] I define anchoring in a way that is independent of the substantive content associated with it. In particular, I show that the essence of an anchoring category is that it may be deictic (i.e., anchored to the utterance situation) or anaphoric (i.e., anchored to some appropriate antecedent). The former correlates mostly with matrix declarative clauses and is discussed in this chapter, while the latter corresponds to other clause-types, including dependent clauses (e.g., infinitives and subjunctives) as well as some matrix clauses that are operator dependent, such as imperatives and conditionals. This will be the topic of Chapter 5.

4.2   The Universal Base Hypothesis

As introduced in Chapter 2, one of the core functional categories of the clausal spine assumed in the generative tradition is tense, i.e., a category that is uniquely identified by its substantive content, but which also plays a crucial role in licensing the grammatical subject role. The former aspect of tense pertains to the head position. Tense marking serves – in English – to contrastively mark whether the reported event took place prior to the time of utterance (*past*) or simultaneously to the time of utterance (*present*). It is in this sense that tense is identified as an anchoring category: it anchors the reported event to the utterance situation (Enç 1987). The other important aspect of tense pertains to the argument position it introduces (what is known as the specifier position); this is the position where the grammatical subject role is licensed – via the assignment of nominative case.[4] In addition, the local (specifier–head)

---

[3] Note that much of the discussion on Blackfoot and Halkomelem is based on previous work (Wiltschko 2003, 2006a; Ritter and Wiltschko 2004, 2005, 2009, forthcoming), though I include more data and I extend their analysis to include Upper Austrian German, another *c*:TENSE-less language.

[4] For purely expository reasons I continue to use the term 'specifier' even though it does not have any theoretical status.

relation gives rise to subject–verb agreement. Finally, following work by Zagona (1990, 1995) and Demirdache and Uribe-Etxebarria (1997), the abstract utterance situation argument (arg$_{Utt-t}$) associates with SpecTP as well. Whether both arguments (the abstract argument, and the DP argument that serves as the grammatical subject (DP$_{subject}$)) occupy the same position, or whether there are multiple specifiers is a question I will ignore here.

The essential ingredients of the syntax of the functional category tense I will adopt here as a point of departure are summarized in (3).

(3)   The syntax of tense

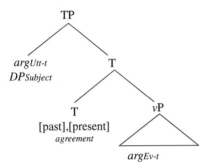

In this subsection, I show that tense marking is not universally associated with the same formal properties and I conclude that anchoring is not universally temporal. I discuss Blackfoot, which lacks dedicated tense marking, in Section 4.2.1. I then proceed to a discussion of Halkomelem, which has a past marker, but its properties are substantially different from those of Indo-European languages (Section 4.2.2). In Section 4.2.3, I explore inflectional contrasts in Upper Austrian German, which – unlike Standard German – also lacks contrastive tense marking. I conclude by discussing the possibility that tenseless languages may possess a silent tense marker.

4.2.1   Blackfoot lacks dedicated tense marking

According to the diagnostics introduced in Chapter 3, Blackfoot does not qualify as a language where tense serves as a κ-category.[5] In particular, it lacks obligatory morphological tense marking. Take for example the sentence in (4). The same surface form may be used to report an event that occurred in the past as well as one that is occurring at the time of utterance (i.e., a present event).

---

[5] According to Frantz (1991), there are some morphological means to mark past tense. However, Ritter and Wiltschko (2004) argue that these cannot be properly classified as past markers.

(4)   *Oma   píítaawa   áípaawaniwa.*
     om-wa   píítaa-wa   a-ipaawani-wa
     DEM-PROX   eagle-PROX   IMPF-fly.AI-PROX
     'That eagle is/was flying up.'

adapted from Reis Silva and Matthewson 2007: 200 (7–8)

While tense marking in Blackfoot is not obligatory, there are strategies available that disambiguate between a present and a past construal. According to Frantz (1991), *"Past tense may be realized as ... [s]imple absence of both the durative aspect and future prefixes ..."* (Frantz 1991: 35–36). According to our consultants, however, even in the absence of future or durative morphemes, a sentence may receive a present or past interpretation.

(5)   *Kitána   aasáí'niwa.*
     k-itán-wa   waasáí'ni-wa
     2-daughter-PROX cry.AI-PROX
     'Your daughter cried.'
     'Your daughter is crying.'

adapted from Frantz 1991: 36 (v)

(6)   *Nítsspiyihpinnaan.*
     nit-ihpiyi-hpinnaan
     1-dance.AI-1PL
     'We danced.'
     'We are going to dance.'

adapted from Frantz 1991: 36 (x)

To unambiguously refer to a past or present event, temporal adverbs are used.[6]

(7)   a. *Matónni   awákiiwani   pokóni.*
       matónni   a-wákiiwan-yii-wa   pokón-yi
       yesterday   IMPF-hit.TA-DIR-PROX   ball-OBV
       'He was hitting the ball yesterday.'

     b. *Annóhk   awákiiwani   pokóni.*
       annóhk   a-wákiiwan-yii-wa   pokón-yi
       now   IMPF-hit.TA-DIR-PROX   ball-OBV
       'He is hitting the ball right now.'

(8)   a. *Ná issítsimaan   annihk   áyo'kaawa.*
       ann-wa issitsimaan-wa   annihk   á-yo'kaa-wa
       DEM-PROX baby-PROX earlier   IMPF-sleep.AI-PROX
       'The baby was sleeping earlier.'

---

[6] Frantz (1991) translates all examples with the imperfective prefix as non-past, but as (7) and (8) illustrate, a past time interpretation is possible. Moreover, a past tense interpretation is obligatory in the context of *matónni* 'yesterday/the day before'.

b. *Na*   *issítsimaan*   **áyo'kaawa**   *annohk*

    ann-wa   issitsimaan-wa   **a-yo'kaa'-wa**   annohk

    DEM-PROX   baby-PROX   IMPF-sleep-PROX   right.now

    'The baby is sleeping right now.'

According to the diagnostics set up in Chapter 3, the absence of an obligatory morphological contrast between present and past suggests that tense is not a κ-category in Blackfoot. And since, according to our criteria, modifiers cannot be silent it follows that tense is not a grammatical category in the general sense.

4.2.2 *Halkomelem past marking does not pattern as a κ-category*

We now turn to Halkomelem. Here we find a morphological marker for past, but it still does not qualify as a κ-category. Rather the tense markers have the formal properties of modifiers.

Consider the data below, which establish that Halkomelem has morphological marking for past (9) and for future (10).

(9)   *í-lh* = *tsel*   *lám.*

       AUX-PST = 1SG.S   go

       'I'm gone.'   Galloway 1993: 317–319

(10)   *th'í:qw'e-th-omé* = *tsel* = **cha.**

       punch-TR-2SG.OBJ-1SG.S-FUT

       'I will punch you.'

                                              Galloway 1993: 317–319

Based on substance-based criteria, we would conclude that these markers manifest the grammatical category *c*:TENSE, just as they do in Indo-European languages. Assuming a substance-based USB this would be the default assumption. This predicts that these past and future markers have similar, if not identical, distributional properties to tense marking in English, for example. Tense markers should behave as a universal natural class. The fact of the matter is, however, that past and future markers in Halkomelem have different distributional properties than past and future markers in languages such as English or French, which have been used to develop the idea of a universal functional category tense. Recall from Chapter 3 that the characterizing property of a syntactic head is κ-contrast. Crucially, Halkomelem past and future marking does not exhibit κ-contrast. To make the point, it will suffice to focus on the properties of past marking. I show that the morphological expression of past in Halkomelem differs in its distribution and in its function from the morphological expression of past in English.

First, we observe that tense marking in Halkomelem is not obligatory and consequently not contrastive. This can be seen on the basis of the fact that in the absence of overt past marking, the reported event is not necessarily interpreted as ongoing (i.e., present tense). This is shown in (11). A sentence without past marking can be interpreted as both present and past. This contrasts with English, where in finite sentences the absence of past marking is necessarily interpreted as present.

(11)   a. *í-lh*   *qw'eyílex*   *tú-tl'ò.*
           AUX-PST   dance   DET-PRN
           'He was dancing.'

       b. *í*   *qw'eyílex*   *tú-tl'ò.*
           AUX   dance   DET-PRN
           'He is/was dancing.'

Ritter and Wiltschko forthcoming: (2)

And just like in Blackfoot, unmarked forms are compatible with adverbs of past time.

(12)   *lhith*   *lí-s*   *lheq'élexw.*
        long.ago   AUX-3S   know
        'She knew long ago.'

Galloway 1993: 317

The same pattern is also observed in embedded clauses. Past marking is possible, but it is not necessary for a past interpretation, no matter whether the matrix auxiliary is marked for past or not.

(13)   a. *i-lh*   *x̱ét'e*   *the*   *Mali* ...
           AUX-PST   say   DET.FEM   Mary ...
           ... *kw'-s-es*   *syémyem*   *kw's*   *spelwálh.*
           ... COMP-NMLZ-3S   pregnant   DET   year-PST
           'Mary said that she was pregnant last year.'

       b. *i-lh*   *x̱ét'e*   *the*   *Mali* ...
           AUX-PST   say   DET.FEM   Mary ...
           ... *kw'-s-es*   *i-lh*   *syémyem*   *kw's*   *spelwálh.*
           ... COMP-NMLZ-3S   AUX-PST   pregnant   DET   year-PST
           'Mary said that she was pregnant last year.'

       c. *x̱ét'e*   *the*   *Mali* ...
           say   DET.FEM   Mary ...
           ... *kw'-s-es*   *í-lh*   *syémyem*   *kw's*   *spelwá-lh.*
           ... COMP-NMLZ-3S   AUX-PST   pregnant   DET   year-PST
           'Mary said that she was pregnant last year.'

d. *xét'e*   *the*   *Mali* ...
   say   DET.FEM   Mary ...
   ... *kw'-s-es*   *syémyem*   *kw's*   *spelwá-lh.*
   ... COMP-NMLZ-3s   pregnant   DET   year-PST
   'Mary said that she was pregnant last year.'

Ritter and Wiltschko 2004: 356f. (37–40)

This suggests that past marking in Halkomelem has a different distribution than past marking in English. According to our criteria, this casts doubt on the assumption that the two language-specific past markers are mere instances of the same universal category. The optionality of past marking further suggests that temporal anchoring is not a linguistic universal.

This conclusion is further supported by the fact that past marking in Halkomelem does not necessarily relate an event time to the utterance time. To see this, consider the examples in (14). In Halkomelem, past marking is not restricted to verbs. Rather, the same past maker *-lh* may suffix to nouns. In this context it indicates that the property denoted by the noun *no longer* holds of an individual (Burton 1997). If an animate noun denotes a lifetime property (in the sense of Musan [1997]), then past marking indicates *death* (14a) otherwise it indicates that the individual no longer holds the relevant property (but is still alive) (14b).

(14)   a. *te-l*   *má:l-**elh***
         DET-1SG.POSS   father-**PST**
         'my late father'

Burton 1997: 67 (2)

    b. *te-l*   *stóles-**elh***
         DET-1SG.POSS   wife-**PST**
         'my ex-wife'

Similarly, when past marking attaches to inanimate nouns, it indicates that the property denoted by the noun no longer holds of the individual. This is the case if the individual was destroyed. Alternatively, past on inanimate nouns may also indicate that the individual is no longer possessed.

(15)   *te-l*   *xéltel-**elh***
     DET-1SG.POSS   pencil-**PST**
     'my former pencil'
     'my broken pencil'

Burton 1997: 67 (3)

Thus, past on nouns may be interpreted as death, destruction, or loss, subject to pragmatic constraints (Burton 1997). This pattern indicates that past marking does not necessarily indicate that an *event time* is in the past. It may either indicate that a property of an individual holds in the past or else that a possessive relation holds in the past (see Section 4.4.2 for further discussion).

Finally, there are also examples that show that the past marker *-lh* does not necessarily denote pastness relative to the utterance time. For example, the Halkomelem word for 'morning' is composed of 'night' and past marking. That is, the word for *morning* is literally 'past night,' as shown in (16).

(16)   *(s-)lat-**elh***
        (NMLZ-)night-PST
        'morning'

Galloway 1980: 61

Crucially, past marking in this context does not indicate pastness relative to the utterance situation, i.e., in Halkomelem past marking is not always interpreted deictically. Instead, even if it occurs within a future-oriented clause, past marking on the noun is still possible, as shown in (17).

(17)   *kw'ets-l-óme*   *te*   *(s)lát-**elh**.*
        see-TRANS-2SG.OBJ   DET   night-PST
        'I will see you in the morning.'

We have now established that even if a language has a marker for past, it does not have the same distributional properties across different languages. In particular, we have established the following properties of Halkomelem past marking:

(18)   Properties of Halkomelem past marking
        (i)   does not pattern as a syntactic head
        (ii) is not obligatory for anchoring
        (iii) does not always serve to anchor the event time to the utterance time

I conclude that past marking in Halkomelem is neither formally nor functionally equivalent to past marking in English. But if the different past markers do not share the same formal properties, in what sense are they instances of the same universal category? At best we would have to assume that universal categories are only defined in terms of their semantics. However, we have seen that not even their semantics is straightforwardly identical. And more crucially, under the present conceptualization of categories, they mediate between the sound–meaning relation and as such we expect them to share formal properties. I conclude that tense is not universally an obligatory grammatical category.

4.2.3   Upper Austrian German lacks dedicated tense marking

In this section I show that the Upper Austrian dialect of German also lacks a grammatical category *c*:TENSE. One piece of evidence for this comes from the

Table 4.1 *Standard German present and past*

	Strong verbs *komm* ('come')		Weak verbs *koch* ('cook')	
	Present	Simple past	Present	Simple past
1sg	*ich komm-e*	*ich kam*	*ich koch-e*	*ich koch-**te***
2sg	*du komm-st*	*du kam-st*	*du koch-st*	*du koch-**te**-st*
3sg	*er komm-t*	*er kam*	*er koch-t*	*er koch-**te***
1pl	*wir komm-en*	*wir kam-en*	*wir koch-en*	*wir koch-**te**-n*
2pl	*ihr komm-t*	*ihr kam-t*	*ihr koch-t*	*ihr koch-**te**-t*
3pl	*sie komm-en*	*sie kam-en*	*sie koch-en*	*sie koch-**te**-n*

Table 4.2 *Upper Austrian German present; past forms not attested*

	Strong verbs *kum* ('come')		Weak verbs *koch* ('cook')	
	Unmarked	*Simple past[a]	Unmarked	*Simple past
1sg	*i kum*	**i kam*	*i koch*	**i koch-**te***
2sg	*du kum-st*	**du kam-st*	*du koch-st*	**du koch-**te**-st*
3sg	*ea kum-t*	**ea kam*	*ea koch-t*	**ea koch-**te***
1pl	*mia kum-en*	**mia kam-en*	*mia koch-n*	**mia koch-**te**-n*
2pl	*ia kum-ts*	**ia kam-ts*	*ia koch-ts*	**ia koch-**te**-ts*
3pl	*si kum-en*	**si kam-en*	*si koch-n*	**si koch-**te**-n*

[a] The actual forms of the strong verbs are attested. But they are not interpreted as past but instead as subjunctive (see Section 4.4.3).

distribution of past marking. In Standard German, so-called strong verbs mark past with ablaut and so-called weak verbs do so with the suffix *-te* (Table 4.1).[7] In Upper Austrian German, neither of these morphological exponents for past are attested (Table 4.2). Thus, Upper Austrian German conforms to our first diagnostics for tenselessness: it lacks a dedicated maker for past tense.[8]

Secondly, just like in Blackfoot and Halkomelem, the unmarked verb form is compatible with present, past, and future time reference, as indicated by the use of temporal adverbials. This is shown for strong verbs in (19) and for weak verbs in (20).

---

[7] The traditional terms 'strong' and 'weak' are meant to reflect that verbs may or may not be "strong" enough to encode past on their own without a suffix.

[8] In all paradigms of German and Upper Austrian German, the word preceding the inflected verb is the personal pronoun.

(19) a. *I kum   grod   ham.*   PRESENT
         I come   now   home
         'I am coming home right now.'

      b. *I kum   gestan   ham.*   PAST[9]
         I come   yesterday home
         'I came home yesterday.'

      c. *I kum   moagn   ham.*   FUTURE
         I come   tomorrow   home
         'I will come home tomorrow.'

(20) a. *I koch   grod.*   PRESENT
         I cook   now
         'I am cooking right now.'

      b. *I koch   gestan.*   PAST
         I cook   yesterday
         'I was cooking yesterday.'

      c. *I koch   moagn.*   FUTURE
         I cook   tomorrow
         'I will cook tomorrow.'

To unambiguously establish the temporal interpretation, a periphrastic construction with an auxiliary and a non-finite verb form is used. Specifically, a past interpretation is achieved with a present perfect construal including *be* (21a) or *have* (21b), depending on the main verb, and a past participle. A present interpretation is achieved with a prepositional construction: 'I am at verb-ing' (22). And a future interpretation is achieved with the modal verb *werden* and the main verb realized as an infinitive (23).

(21) a. *I bin   ham   kuma.*   PAST (VIA PRESENT PERFECT)
         I am   home   come.PART
         'I came home yesterday.'

---

[9] In isolation, the past time interpretation is not as readily available. It is facilitated with an introductory phrase like *you know* and a locational particle in sentence-initial topic position. Furthermore, the sentence seems to require a continuation with a sentence describing what happened next.

      Wasst eh, do kumm I gestan ham . . .
      know PRT LOCV come I yesterday home . . .
      'You know. I came home yesterday. . .'

   I leave the exact conditions of use for the past use of the unmarked verb for another occasion. See Cowper (1998) for the context of use of the simple present in English.

      b. *I **hob** kocht.*
        I have   cook.PART
        'I have cooked.'

(22) a. *I **bin** am ham kuma.*   PRESENT
        I am at home come.PART
        'I am coming home.'

      b. *I **bin** am kochn.*
        I am at cook.INF
        'I am cooking.'

(23) a. *I **wead** ham kum-a.*   FUTURE (VIA MODALIZATION)
        I will home come.INF
        'I will come home.'

      b. *I **wead** koch-n.*
        I will   cook.INF
        'I will cook.'

This confirms to general patterns of temporal interpretations: a past interpretation in tenseless languages is often accomplished aspectually (see for example Lin [2006] for Chinese).

For completeness, note that there is a simple past for the auxiliary *sein* ('to be') as shown in (24). But even in the paradigm for *be* we observe a distribution different from past marking in Standard German. The evidence here has to do with the absence of a past perfect form in Upper Austrian German (25). This contrasts with Standard German, where such a form exists (26).

(24) a. *I bin*   *kronk.*
        I be.PRES.1SG sick
        'I am sick.'

      b. *I woa*   *kronk.*
        I be.PST.1SG sick
        'I was sick.'

(25) a. *I bin*   *kronk*   *gwen.*
        I be.PRES.1SG sick be PART
        'I was/have been sick.'

      b. **I woa*   *krank*   *gwen.*
        I be.PST.1SG sick   be.PART
        'I had been sick.'

(26) a. *Ich bin*   *krank* *gewesen.*
        I be.PRES.1SG. sick   be.PART
        'I was/have been sick.'

b. *I war*   *krank*   *gewesen.*
  I be.PST.1SG.   sick   be.PART
  'I had been sick.'

The tenselessness of Upper Austrian German is significant from a typological perspective. It shows that tenselessness is not restricted to non-Indo-European languages. And it also shows that even two closely related languages – in fact two dialects of the same language (German) – may differ with respect to whether or not they have a grammatical category c:TENSE. Thus, as schematized in (27), the set of grammatical categories in Standard German includes c:TENSE, but the set of grammatical categories in Upper Austrian German does not.

(27)   a. $C_{\text{Standard German}} = \{\ldots c\text{:TENSE}\ldots\}$
        b. $C_{\text{Upper Austrian German}} = \{\ldots *c\text{:TENSE}\ldots\}$

4.2.4   Silent tense?

There is a straightforward alternative available to the conclusion that tenseless languages differ from tensed languages in their categorial inventories. The absence of an overt tense marker may be interpreted as a superficial difference pertaining to morphological properties alone. Specifically, superficially tenseless languages may be analyzed as making use of silent tense marking in the form of one or more zero morphemes. Based on the distribution of morphological marking a tenseless analysis makes the same predictions as a silent tense analysis. The two analyses differ, however, in terms of the mechanism that derives the absence of an overt Unit of Language (UoL) that marks tense. Under a tenseless analysis there is no UoL marking tense (28a) whereas under the silent tense analysis there is a UoL which marks tense but which happens to be zero, as in (28b).

(28)   a. The tenseless analysis: V
        b. The silent tense analysis: V-$\emptyset_{\text{TENSE}}$

The silent tense analysis is often pursued by researchers adopting the UBH, such as the cartographic framework (Cinque 1999). On this view, UG makes available a fully articulated spine and languages differ as to which of these positions are spelled out and which ones remain silent.

A silent tense analysis has been developed for St'at'imcets (an Interior Salish language) by Matthewson (2006) and for Blackfoot by Reis Silva and Matthewson (2007). I will briefly introduce these analyses, point out some specific problems and then move on to a more general discussion of the problems it faces.

For St'at'imcets, Matthewson (2006) argues that there is a silent generalized tense morpheme, which places the event either at the utterance time (present) or prior to it (past). This analysis is intended to capture the absence of a future interpretation with predicates that lack overt tense marking.

(29)   A silent c:TENSE analysis: V-$\emptyset_{\text{NON-FUTURE}}$

This analysis predicts that superficially tenseless sentences of this sort do not allow for a future interpretation. In fact, Matthewson (2006) proposes that future is never a tense but instead must always combine with tense. Consequently, if c:TENSE were universal, we might expect that superficially tenseless languages do not allow for a future interpretation. This prediction is, however, not borne out. First, as we have seen, unmarked forms in Upper Austrian German do readily allow for a future interpretation (examples [19] and [20] above).

Similarly, as pointed out by Tonhauser (2011) in Paraguayan Guaraní, predicates unmarked for tense may receive a past time reference (30a), a present time reference (30b), and crucially also a future time reference (30c).

(30)   a. Context: Maria talks about one of her childhood summers.

                Peteĩ jey   ro-ho   la campáña-re,   che-abuéla...

                One time   1PL.EXCL-go   the countryside-for   1SG-grandmother ...

                ... o-nase-ha-gué-pe,   Kiindy´-pe.

                ... 3-be.born-NMLZ-NM.TERM-in   Kiindy-in

                'One day we went to the countryside where my grandmother was born to Kiindy.'

       b. Context: A duck offers friendship to a very sad looking frog. The frog exclaims:

                A-guereko   peteĩ   angirũ,   petĩ   angirũ   añete-te!

                1SG-have   one   friend   one   friend   true-very

                'I have a friend, a real friend!'

       c. Context: It is morning and the speaker is talking about a goose walking past her and the addressee.

                Ja'ú-ta-re   ko   gánso   ko'ẽro,   a-juka ...

                1PL.INCL-eat-PROSP-for   this   goose   tomorrow   1SG-kill ...

                ... ko   ka'arú-pe.

                ... this afternoon-at

                'Since we are going to eat this goose tomorrow, I will kill it this afternoon.'

                                                  Tonhauser 2011: 259 (4)

Thus, even in languages where the unmarked form does not allow for a future interpretation, we need not conclude that there is a silent tense marker just to exclude a future interpretation. It may simply be excluded because modalization must be encoded (Matthewson 2006).

Next we turn to Reis Silva and Matthewson's (2007) silent tense analysis for Blackfoot. They argue that Blackfoot has two silent tense morphemes, one for past and one for present, as in (31).

(31)   A silent TENSE analysis:
     a. V-Ø$_{PRESENT}$
     b. V-Ø$_{PAST}$

This is meant to capture the generalization that eventive predicates in the perfective must be interpreted as past (32a).[10] Only predicates marked for imperfective are ambiguous between a present and a past interpretation (32b).

(32)   a. *Oma*   *píítaawa*   *ípaawaniwa.*
        om-wa   píítaa-wa   ipaawani-wa
        DEM-PROX   eagle-PROX   fly.AI-PROX
        ≠ 'That eagle is flying up.'   PRESENT
        = 'That eagle flew up.'   PAST

       b. *Oma*   *píítaawa*   *áípaawaniwa.*
        om-wa   píítaa-wa   a-ipaawani-wa
        DEM-PROX   eagle-PROX   IMPF-fly.AI-PROX
        = 'That eagle is flying up.'   PRESENT
        = 'That eagle was flying up.'   PAST

              adapted from Reis Silva and Matthewson 2007: 200 (7–8)

Reis Silva and Matthewson (2007: 207) conclude that "*[i]t is therefore in the perfective that tense in Blackfoot becomes visible.*" On the silent tense analysis, the temporal interpretation of a superficially tenseless language is still regulated by tense,[11] which in this case hosts silent tense morphemes: a past interpretation arises in the presence of the silent past morpheme and a present interpretation arises in the presence of a silent present morpheme. Since the present tense morpheme, by hypothesis, encodes an instantaneous moment a "*present perfective requires the event to fit inside the speech time – but events cannot normally fit inside instantaneous moments, so present perfective eventives are ruled out*" (Reis Silva and Matthewson 2007: 203).

---

[10] Note that this generalization does not hold for all of our consultants; rather, some allow for a present interpretation of eventive predicates even in the absence of an imperfective marker. We do not know whether this is a dialectal or ideolectal difference among speakers.

[11] Though it is not clear whether semantic tense must correlate with a syntactic head.

This analysis relies on the assumption that perfective aspect places the event time inside the reference time, in contrast to imperfective aspect, which places the reference time inside the event time (Klein 1994; Kratzer 1998). This analysis of perfective aspect makes the right predictions for frame time adverbials such as *yesterday* and *last year*. With such adverbials it is indeed the case that the event is inside the reference time (33). However, it does not work for punctual temporal adverbials such as *when* clauses, as in (34). Here, the reported event does not occur inside the timeframe given by the *when*-clause since the latter is punctual.

(33)   *I danced yesterday.*

(34)   a. *My lover said I danced when I got engaged.*
        b. *My brother said I danced when he got me a new bike.*
        c. *My sister said I danced when I won a fight with her.*
        d. *My teacher said I danced when I got first mark in class.*
           www.facebook.com/permalink.php?id=146768165334402andstory_fbid=
           412882468722969

The right generalization for perfective aspect appears to be that the event is viewed from outside, which is only possible if it is over (see Chapter 7 for more discussion). If this is so, then there is no good reason why a present interpretation should not be available with perfective predicates.

There are also more general problems with the silent tense analysis. Assuming that superficially tenseless languages (i.e., languages without a morpho-syntactic category for tense) are underlyingly just the same as tensed languages would mean giving up the significance of contrast and all of its ramifications, discussed in Chapters 1 and 3. Crucially, to detect the existence of zero tense marking in the absence of contrastive marking, the universality of tense must be assumed, as stated in Matthewson (2006: 704): "*only if the child comes equipped to expect a null tense morpheme will she be prepared to expect a presupposition on that morpheme which restricts reference times to past and present.*"

If, however, we deny the existence of universal categories that are defined based on their substantive content, then the acquisition of zero contrasts becomes unlearnable. That is, on the assumption that there is a universal spine of functional categories, but that the substantive content of these categories must be learned, the child will have to rely on the presence of detectable contrasts in the form of UoLs that associate with the spine to construct the relevant categories.

In sum, the silent tense analysis is not a viable option to rescue the assumption that there are universal categories. Thus, in light of tenseless languages one might conclude that universal categories do not exist. In light of the assumptions about the functional category tense we have introduced in Chapter 2, this may indicate that tenseless languages lack the entire layer that is associated with tense in English. In the next subsection I show that this cannot be the case either.

4.3   The No Base Hypothesis

In light of tenseless languages, one may simply conclude that languages simply vary in their categorial inventories and, as a consequence, that there is nothing universal about categories. This is a version of the No Base Hypothesis. An immediate problem with this analysis is that it begs the question as to why many unrelated languages have in their categorial inventories an obligatory grammatical category *c*:TENSE. If there were not a universal basis for this, this would be a mere coincidence.

And there is another problem, namely the fact that even in tenseless languages there is evidence that grammatical relations are active. So whatever is responsible for introducing grammatical relations must be available in tenseless languages as well. A particular version of this notion of tenselessness is found in Wiltschko (2003), where it is argued that the functional category tense is absent in Halkomelem, as in (35).

(35)   tenselessness = absence of TP
        [$_{CP}$ C [$_{vP}$ ...]]

This alternative is not in fact an instance of the No Base Hypothesis. Instead Wiltschko (2003) concludes that UG provides a set of categories and that language variation reduces to selecting categories from a universal set. On this view, the absence of *c*:TENSE predicts the absence of the grammatical subject relation. The evidence Wiltschko (2003) discusses pertained mostly to absence of case (see also Ritter and Rosen [2005] for the claim that Algonquian languages lack A-positions). The situation is, however, more complicated. While I still maintain that the distribution of DPs in both Halkomelem and Blackfoot is not governed by case (see Chapter 7) there is still evidence for the existence of grammatical relations. Thus, case and grammatical relations cannot be equated. The former concerns the distribution of DPs, while the latter concerns the grammatical function of arguments.

The existence of grammatical relations however posits a problem for the conclusion that an entire layer of functional structure is missing. What we observe is that the absence of the grammatical category *c*:TENSE cannot be equated with the absence of the layer of grammar where grammatical relations are established. In this section I present evidence that Blackfoot, Halkomelem, and Upper Austrian German make use of grammatical relations despite their tenselessness. This suggests that there is another category present which is responsible for introducing the subject relation, as in (36).

(36)   Tenseless languages with grammatical relations
        [$_{CP}$ C [$_{XP}$ SUBJECT X [$_{vP}$ ...]]]

Recall the three diagnostics for grammatical relations introduced in Chapter 2 (Section 2.3.1):

(i)   Expletive subjects for grammatical relations
(ii) Mismatches between thematic and grammatical relations
(iii) Agreement which is sensitive to grammatical relations.

In what follows, I show that the existence of grammatical relations must be recognized for Blackfoot, Halkomelem, and Upper Austrian German. This suggests that the relevant layer of functional structure is in fact present, *contra* Wiltschko (2003).

We start with expletives. The tenseless languages we are investigating here all display evidence for expletive subjects. Consider the Blackfoot sentence involving a weather verb in (37). Assuming that weather verbs are not associated with a thematic subject, the fact that we nevertheless find a 3rd person prefix in this context is consistent with an analysis that posits an expletive 3rd person subject, as in (38).

(37)   *Íkssoka'piiwa*   *otáísootaahsi.*
        iik-soka'pii-wa   ot-á-sootaa-hsi
        INT-good.AI-PROX   3-IMPF-rain.II-CONJ
        'It's good that it's raining.'

                                                                    Frantz 1991: 111 (e)

(38)   [$_{CP}$ C [$_{XP}$ SUBJ$_{expletive}$ X [$_{VP}$ V]]]

The same is true for Halkomelem weather verbs. Despite the absence of a thematic role, we find 3rd person subject agreement. (Since in independent declarative clauses 3rd person subject agreement is always zero, the sentence below is negated, and negation triggers subjunctive agreement which includes and overt 3rd person agreement.)

(39)   *Éwe   i-s   lhémexw.*
        NEG   AUX-3S   rain
        'It is not raining.'

The necessity for expletive subjects in Halkomelem can also be observed in the following passive sentence. On the one hand we observe no evidence for A-movement: the thematic object is not realized as the grammatical subject, as evidenced by the fact that it triggers (passive) object agreement. However, interestingly the auxiliary is marked for 3rd person agreement despite the absence of a 3rd person argument. This is consistent with an analysis that posits a 3rd person subject triggering 3rd person agreement.

(40)   *Éwe   í-s   kw'éts-l-àlèm*
        NEG   AUX-3S   see-TR-1SG.PASS
        'I wasn't seen.'

Wiltschko 2002a: 280 (47a)

(41)   [$_{CP}$ C [$_{XP}$ SUBJ$_{expletive}$ X [$_{VP}$ V-agr THEME]]]

And finally, Upper Austrian German as well makes use of expletive subjects, just like English.[12]

(42)   *wei's   regn-t*
        since = it   rain-3SG
        'since it is raining'

Next we turn to evidence from mismatches, which again we find in all of the three tenseless languages under discussion. First consider Blackfoot, which has a construction known as *cross-clausal agreement*.[13] The crucial property to observe in this construction is that transitive verb stems agree in animacy with their object. In (43a), the matrix predicate behaves as an intransitive in that it only agrees in animacy with its subject. It is, however, also possible for the same predicate to be realized as a transitive in which case agreement is with the thematic subject of the embedded predicate (43b).

(43)   a. *Nitsíksstaa* ...
           nit-iksstaa ...
           1-want.AI ...

           ... *anna*   *mááhksinoahsi*   *amiksi*   *imitááiks.*
           ... ann-wa   m-aahk-ino-his   am-iksi   imitaa-iksi
           ... DEM-PROX   3-NONFACT-see.TA-DIR-CONJ   DEM-PL   dog-PL
           'I want him to see the dogs.'

---

[12] In German one has to use an embedded clause to control for the possibility that the neuter pronoun serves as an expletive topic to fill SpecCP (Cardinaletti 1990; Brandner 1993; Vikner 1995).

[13] See Bruening (2001) for Passamaquoddy; Branigan and MacKenzie (2002) for Innu-aimûn; and Bliss (2008) for Blackfoot.

b. *Nitsíksstaatawa ...*
nit-iksstaat-a-wa ...
1-want.TA-DIR-PROX ...

... *anna*	*mááhksinoahsi*	*anniksi*	*imitááiks.*
... ann-wa	m-aahk-ino-hsi	ann-iksi	imitaa-iksi
... DEM-PROX	3-NONFACT-see.TA-DIR-CONJ	DEM-PL	dog-PL

'I want him to see the dogs.'

adapted from Bliss 2005: 105 (81)

This is consistent with the assumption that the thematic subject of the embedded clause is realized as the grammatical object of the matrix clause. Hence it has been analyzed as a raising-to-object construction by some (see Bruening 2001).[14]

A similar construction is also found in Halkomelem. On the basis of examples like (44), it has been argued that Halkomelem has a construction that involves raising to object (see Davis [1980] for Sliammon, Mainland Comox). In particular, *te swiyeqe* ('the man') functions as the logical subject of the embedded predicate but has the distribution of a grammatical object of the matrix predicate (see Gerdts 1988). This is shown in (44), based on data from Island Halkomelem.

(44)	*i*	*cen*	*xec-t*	*te*	*swiyeqe ...*
	AUX	1s	wonder-TR	DET	man
	... *7u*	*ni-s*	*cha*	*7u*	*c'ew-et-alxw-es*
	LINK	AUX-3S	FUT	LINK	help-TR-1PL.OBJ-3S

'I'm checking out the man if he will help us.'

Gerdts 1988: 206 (31)

Next, consider Upper Austrian German, which has a passive construction just like English, as shown in (45).

(45)	a. *Da*	*Joschi*	*hod'n*	*gjogt.*
	DET	Joschi	has = him	chased.PRT

'Yoshi chased him.'

	b. *Ea*	*is*	*(vom Joschi)*	*gjogt*.PRT	*woan.*
	He	is	(from Joschi)	chased	was

'He was chased by Yoshi.'

Finally, agreement is conditioned by grammatical relations, as evidenced by the examples above.[15]

---

[14] But see Dahlstrom (1995) for an analysis of cross-clausal agreement in terms of control.

[15] In Blackfoot agreement is conditioned by a complex interaction between the person hierarchy and grammatical relations.

In sum, there is evidence that in Blackfoot, Halkomelem, and Upper Austrian German we must recognize the existence of grammatical relations despite the absence of tense. This indicates that the functional layer where grammatical relations are introduced must be present in these languages. So what is the category that introduces grammatical relations in the absence of c:TENSE?

4.4   The Universal Spine Hypothesis

We have now seen that in Blackfoot, Halkomelem, and Upper Austrian German, tense does not function as a grammatical category (not even a silent one). But at the same time we have also seen that grammatical relations are active. This suggests that the area in the spine that is constructed as c:TENSE in Indo-European languages (κ:*anchoring*) is grammatically active. In what follows, I show that in each language, a different obligatory category c is constructed from κ:*anchoring*. In Blackfoot c is substantiated by PERSON; in Halkomelem c is substantiated by LOCATION; and in Upper Austrian German c is a form of REALIS. These categories satisfy the formal diagnostics that indicate that the markers of these categories are UoLs that associate with κ:*anchoring* via the "*is-a*" relation. Furthermore, these grammatical categories also serve to anchor the event to the utterance. This suggests that there is indeed a universal basis for categorization. But the basis for categorization is not substantive content. I discuss each of these categories in turn.

4.4.1   *Blackfoot c:*PERSON

In this subsection, I show that person marking in Blackfoot can be analyzed as a UoL that associates with κ:*anchoring* via the "*is-a*" relation. The discussion is largely based on Ritter and Wiltschko (forthcoming).

Person marking is pervasive in Blackfoot. Consider the verbal template in Figure 4.1.[16]

Each of the bolded positions in Figure 4.1 encodes information about person. Ritter and Wiltschko (forthcoming) argue that the so-called *order* markers serve to anchor the event to the utterance. In the Algonquian tradition, *order* is a category that defines different types of clauses. For Blackfoot these

---

[16] For a detailed exploration of how the individual pieces in this template map onto the spine, see Bliss (2013).

Figure 4.1 *Blackfoot verbal template*

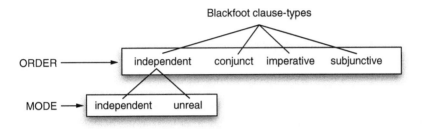

Figure 4.2 *Blackfoot clause-types (adapted from Frantz 2009)*

include the so-called *independent order*, which is restricted to matrix assertive clauses. The independent order can be of two types: unmarked and marked as *unreal*. The distinction between independent and unreal is classified as a *mode*. Other contrasts in order include the *conjunctive* (a general purpose dependent clause-type), the *subjunctive* (used in conditionals), and the *imperative*. This is schematized in Figure 4.2.

Note that at least some order markers would, in the Indo-European tradition, be classified as *mood* or *finiteness* markers. However, the clause-types classified as orders in Blackfoot behave like a natural class from a formal perspective. Based on their position in the morphological template, order may be analyzed as manifesting κ:*anchoring*.[17] It occupies the position between direct/inverse marking and person and number agreement. The former manifests κ:*point-of-view* (i.e., aspect: see Chapter 7) and the latter manifests κ:*linking* (i.e., C: see Bliss [2013]). Given the mirror principle, order must therefore be associated with κ:*anchoring*. The association of the UoLs defined by the template in Figure 4.1 and the universal spine is given in (46).

---

[17] Finiteness distinctions of this sort are often associated with INFL (Haïk 1990; Cowper 2005).

(46)   Associating Blackfoot order with the syntactic spine

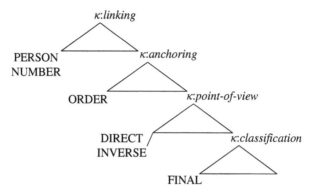

In addition to morpho-syntactic evidence there is also evidence from the function of order marking. In particular, at least in the independent order, a complementary contrast is introduced between local person (1st and 2nd person) and non-local persons (3rd person). This is illustrated in (47) below.[18]

(47)   a. *Nitáyiitsittsimaahpinnan.*
              nit-a-yiitsittsimaa-**hp**-innan
              1-IMPF-slice.meat.AI-**LOC-1PL**
              'We (excl) are thinly slicing meat (for dried meat).'

          b. *Kitáyiitsittsimaahppaawa.*
              kit-a-yiitsittsimaa-**hp**-innan
              2-IMPF-slice.meat.AI-**LOC-2PL**
              'You (pl) are thinly slicing meat (for dried meat).'

          c. *Áyiitsittsimaayaawa.*
              a-yiitsittsimaa-**Ø**-yi-aawa
              IMPF-slice.meat.AI-**NONLOC-3PL-3PL.PRN**
              'They are thinly slicing meat (for dried meat).'

                                                              Bliss 2013: 167 (4)

This contrast between local (*-hp*) and non-local (Ø) person is reminiscent of the contrast between present and past tense. Both types of contrastive marking anchor the reported event to the utterance. Specifically, local person marking signals that the event participant is identical to the utterance participant

---

[18] The morpho-syntax as well as the exponence of the order markers is further constrained by the type of verb involved as well as the plurality of the arguments involved. For detailed discussion, see Bliss (2013).

Table 4.3 *Correlation between order and person prefixes*

Order	Independent	Conjunctive	Subjunctive	Imperative
Person prefix	✓	✓	✗	✗

whereas present tense marking signals that the event time coincides with the utterance time. In contrast, non-local person marking signals that the event participant is distinct from the utterance participant whereas past tense marking signals that the event time is distinct from the utterance time. This functional equivalence between contrastive person and tense marking has been eloquently expressed by one of our Blackfoot consultants who on various occasions commented that *"he is the past tense of you"* (Rachel Ermineskin p. c.).

A final argument for the claim that order marking associates with κ: *anchoring* comes from its interaction with person prefixes (the leftmost prefix in the verbal template in Figure 4.1). The distribution of the person prefixes is sensitive to order marking: they are used in the independent and in the conjunct order, but are unattested in the subjunctive and the imperative order. This is summarized in Table 4.3.

The interaction between order and person prefixes may be interpreted as manifesting a local interaction between a head and its specifier. On the basis of this, Déchaine and Wiltschko (2012) conclude that person prefixes associate with SpecIP, i.e., the specifier associated with κ:*anchoring* (see also Ritter and Wiltschko [forthcoming] and Bliss [2013]). This is illustrated in (48).

(48)   Order and person prefixes

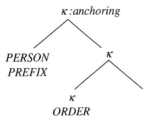

Consistent with this analysis, person prefixes cross-reference an argument role that cannot be defined in terms of thematic roles or discourse roles (topic or focus). To see this, consider the examples in (49). The 2nd person prefix *kit-* is used no matter whether the thematic role of the argument it references is the theme, as in (49a) or the agent, as in (49b).[19]

(49) a. *Kitáí'pohtoohpinnan*   *miistsííks.*
        kit-wai'poht-o-o-**hp**-innaan   miistsis-iksi
        2-haul-ta-1:2-LOC-1PL   tree-PL
        'We (excl) hauled wood for you.'

      b. *Kitáípohtookihpoaawa*   *miistsííks.*
        kit-wai'poht-o-oki-**hp**-oaawa   miistsis-iksi
        2-haul-TA-2:1-LOC-2PL   tree-PL
        'You (pl) hauled wood for me.'

                                              Bliss 2013: 167 (5)

This suggests that person prefixes do not pick out a specific thematic role and are therefore not associated with the thematic domain (i.e., *κ:classification* in our terms). Similarly, person prefixes are not sensitive to the presence of a discourse role such as focus or wh-questions (Bliss 2008). To see this, consider the sentence in (50). Even if there is a 3rd person wh-phrase or a 3rd person focus phrase, the person prefix on the verbal complex is still 2nd person (*kit*). Similarly, no matter whether the 1st person is focused (51a), or not (51b), the person prefix remains constant (*nit*).

(50) *Ááhsa*   *annííhka*   **kitohpómmatoohpihka?**
       ááhsa   annihka   **kit**-ohpómmatoo-**hp**-yihk-wa
       what   DEM   2-buy.TI-LOC-REP-PROX
       'What did you buy?'

(51) a. *Anna*   *Rosie*   *nitáísstaak* ...
        Anna   Rosie   nit-a-isstaat-ok-wa ...
        DEM   Rosie   1-IMPF-want.TA-INV-PROX ...
        ... *ninááhksspommowahsi*   *anni   Leo.*
        ... nin-aahk-sspommo-a-hsi   anni   Leo
        ... 1-NONFACT-help.TA-DIR-CONJ   DEM Leo
        'Rosie wants ME to help Leo.'
        BB: 'Nobody else but me, *nitaisstaak.*'

---

[19] The traditional Algonquianist terminology used instead of agent and theme is *actor* and *goal.*

b. *Nitáísstaata*   *anna Leo* *kitááhksinooyssi.*
nit-a-isstaat-a-wa anna Leo kit-aahk-ino-yi-his
1-IMPF-want.TA-1:3 DEM Leo 2-NONFACT-see.TA-INV-CONJ
'I want LEO to see you.'
BB: 'It's important. You only want Leo; you're picking him out.'

adapted from Bliss 2008: 5

This suggests that the role of the argument cross-referenced by the person prefix is neither a thematic role nor a discourse role. Consequently, we can conclude that the relevant role is a grammatical role.[20]

Next we turn to the diagnostics that suggest that the order marking in Blackfoot substantiates the head of *κ:anchoring* (INFL in Ritter and Wiltschko's terms). That is, the UoL marking order associates with *κ:anchoring* via the "*is-a*" relation.

One piece of evidence is that order marking is *κ*-contrastive in the sense of Chapter 3. To see this, consider Table 4.4, which illustrates the paradigm associated with order marking in independent, conjunctive, and subjunctive clause-types.

In the independent as well as in the subjunctive order there is a contrast between local (1st and 2nd) and non-local (3rd) person. Both are overt in the subjunctive (-*(mm)inniki* vs.-*(i)si*), while in the independent, local marking is overt[21] (-*hp*) and non-local marking may be Ø or -*m*, depending on the transitivity of the verb. Note that the possibility for Ø marking supports the claim that we are indeed dealing with a syntactic head: only heads but not modifiers may remain silent.

In addition to the local/non-local contrast, there is a pervasive contrast between *personal* and *impersonal* forms. While *personal* forms contain (at least one) local or non-local argument, *impersonals* do not. Instead, *impersonal* forms are commonly used for generic reference, which in turn are frequently used in nominalizations. This can be observed in the following minimal pair: the example in (52a) is a nominalization based on an impersonal form and thus translated into English with the generic pronoun *one;* in contrast, the example in (52b) is a nominalization based on a local person

---

[20] With Blackfoot being a direct/inverse system, grammatical roles have different properties than in the more familiar Indo-European languages (see Chapter 7 for discussion, as well as Bliss [2013]).

[21] This is true for plural local arguments only (see Bliss 2013).

Table 4.4 *Order paradigms*

	Independent			Conjunctive			Subjunctive		
	VAI	VTA	VTI	VAI	VTA	VTI	VAI	VTA	VTI
SUBJ									
1	*hp*	*hp*	*hp*	*hs...i*	*hs...i*	*hsi*	*iniki*	*iniki*	*mminniki*
2	*hp*	*hp*	*hp*	*hs...i*	*hs...i*	*hsi*	*iniki*	*iniki*	*mminniki*
3	Ø	Ø	*m(m)*	*hs...i*	*hs...i*	*hsi*	*si*	*isi*	*isi*
IMPERS	*o'p*	Ø	*'p*	*o'si*	*hs...i*	*hsi*	*o'*	*i'ki*	*i'ki*

form thus containing the local suffix *-hp* as well as the relevant 2nd person agreement (*-oaawa*) and 2nd person prefix (*kit-*).

(52) a. *Nitsítsooyi*   *omi*   *itáóyo'pi*
        nit-it-ioyi   om-yi   it-a-oyi-**o'p**-yi
        1-LOCV-eat.AI   DEM-INAN   LOC-IMPF-eat.AI-IMPRS-INAN.SG
        'where one eats'

     b. *Nitsítsooyi*   *omi*   *kitsítáóoyihpoaawayi*
        nit-it-ioyi   om-yi   kit-it-á-ooyi-**hp**-oaawa-yi
        1-LOCV-eat.AI   DEM-INAN   2-LOC-IMPF-eat.AI-LOC-2PL-INAN.SG
        'where you (pl) eat'

Bliss et al. 2011

Thus, the person-based contrasts across the different clause-types create a full-fledged paradigm, which is another diagnostic criterion for UoLs that associate with a syntactic head (κ) via the "*is-a*" relation. Thus, just as tense marking in English interacts with finiteness and mood distinctions (see e.g., Landau [2004] and Cowper [2005]), so does person marking in Blackfoot.

If this is on the right track, then there is an important conclusion to be drawn. The person-sensitive order markers of Blackfoot differ substantially from person marking found in the Indo-European languages. In particular, in Blackfoot, person **is** the substantive content of the clausal head. This contrasts with person marking in Indo-European languages where it is typically realized as a form of agreement rather than hosting its own projection (Chomsky 1995). The assumption that person substantiates κ:anchoring in Blackfoot has a number of empirical consequences that distinguish it from person agreement of the familiar kind. First, we have already seen that the relevant contrast is between local vs. non-local person on the one hand and personal vs. impersonal forms on the other hand. This contrasts with person agreement, which typically contrasts 1st, 2nd, and 3rd person. And impersonals are typically not marked by specialized forms but are instead recruited from either the 3rd person or the 2nd person paradigm (see Gruber [2013] for a recent overview). The necessity for a dedicated *impersonal* form in Blackfoot follows if person marking (including 3rd person) is always contentful (it asserts that the event participant is not simultaneously an utterance participant). As such 3rd person in Blackfoot is substantially different from 3rd person in many Indo-European languages where it has often been argued to be the absence of person. According to Benveniste (1971: 217) for example "*'Person' belongs only to I/you and is lacking in he*" and 3rd person is "*never reflective of the instance of discourse*" (p. 222). If 3rd person in Blackfoot is contentful, however, we expect it to be 'reflective of discourse', and indeed it is. Blackfoot 3rd person comes in two guises: proximate and obviative. The distribution of these categories is conditioned by grammatical and discourse factors alike (see Frantz 1991, 2009; Bliss 2013).

In conclusion, Blackfoot person marking has properties distinct from those of person marking in Indo-European languages. In the latter type of languages, person marking is restricted to agreement and pronominal arguments. Such agreement and pronominal forms are found in Blackfoot as well. Specifically, the right-peripheral number suffixes are instances of agreement (Bliss 2013). But the reason why person marking in Blackfoot is so pervasive is that it is not only manifested as agreement and on pronouns, but it also associates with κ:*anchoring* via the "*is-a*" relation to construct the language-specific category c:PERSON, used for anchoring instead of c:TENSE. Furthermore, as a head, c:PERSON predictably interacts with other heads in the clause, namely κ:*point-of-view* and κ:*linking*, respectively. For these heads to interact, however, they must share some of the featural content with κ:*anchoring*. We thus expect these categories to also be sensitive to person. And indeed, as we shall see in Chapter 7, the Blackfoot equivalent of temporal viewpoint aspect is person-based.

4.4.2   *Halkomelem* c: LOCATION

Halkomelem, like Blackfoot, does not make use of a morpho-syntactic category tense to anchor the event to the utterance. In Wiltschko (2003), I argue that this implies the absence of the functional category tense. But if the functional layer where tense is realized is missing in Halkomelem, we would expect that grammatical relations such as subject and object would not be realized in this language either.[22] As we have seen in Section 4.3, this is not so. There is evidence that grammatical relations are active in Halkomelem. This leads us to expect that κ:*anchoring* is an active area in the spine. So is there another grammatical category *c*, which is constructed based on κ:*anchoring*? Ritter and Wiltschko (2005, 2009, forthcoming) and Wiltschko (2006a) argue that anchoring in Halkomelem is based on location. In particular, the locative auxiliaries *í* ('be here') (53a) and *lí* ('be there') (53b) are analyzed as expressing the type of contrast we expect to find in a syntactic head that serves to anchor the event to the utterance. For example, these auxiliaries are obligatory in the context of a matrix indicative clause.[23]

(53)   a. *í*   *qw'eyílex*   *tú-tl'ò.*
          AUX.HERE   dance   DET-3PRN
          'He was dancing (here)'

       b. *lí*   *qw'eyílex*   *tú-tl'ò.*
          AUX.THERE dance   DET-3PRN
          'He was dancing (there).'

adapted from Ritter and Wiltschko 2009: 151 (3–4)

Thus the auxiliaries *í* and *lí* may be analyzed as UoLs that associate with κ:*anchoring* to construct the grammatical category *c*:LOCATION.

The idea that the locative auxiliaries are the formal and functional equivalent of tense marking in English is supported by a number of considerations. Consider first linear ordering. Locative auxiliaries obligatorily precede the verbal complex, which includes marking of transitivity and object agreement.

(54)   AUX=SUBJ.CL [$_{V\text{-stem}}$ Root-TRANS-OBJ-ERG]

Crucially, the transitivity marker simultaneously encodes information about the transitivity of the verb and aspectual information in the form of control marking. Therefore it may be analyzed as spanning across *v* and Aspect (i.e., κ:*classification* and κ:*point-of-view*). Thus, the linear ordering in the clausal template is consistent with the hypothesis that locative auxiliaries associate with κ:*anchoring*, as in (55).

---

[22] This is in fact what I argued in Wiltschko (2003), but see Matthewson (2005) for problems with this account.

[23] The obligatoriness is obscured by the fact that the proximate auxiliary *í* is in free variation with a zero form (see Wiltschko [2006a] and Ritter and Wiltschko [2009] for discussion).

(55)   Associating Halkomelem auxiliaries with the syntactic spine

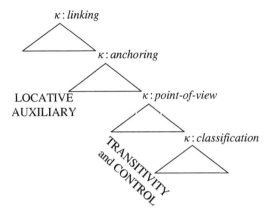

This is further supported by the fact that locative auxiliaries appear in a position lower than those elements that associate with κ:*linking* (C), such as complementizers. In terms of the linear sentential template, this is indeed the case: the complementizer *we* 'if' precedes the locative auxiliaries (56).

(56)   a.   *we*   **lí-s**   *thét*   *ta*   *sqwálewel* ...
                if   AUX-3S   say   DET.2SG   thought
                'if you think that ...'
                lit.: 'if your mind says so ...'

Galloway 2009: 886

        b.   *x̲élh*   *cha*   *te-l*   *sqwálewel* ...
                sad   FUT   DET-1SG.POSS thought ...
                ... *we*   **lí-s**   *lhémexw.*
                ... COMP AUX-3SS rain
                'I'll be sad (lit.: 'My thoughts will be sad') if it rains.'

Wiltschko 2006b: 291 (8b)

In sum, the linear position of locative auxiliaries is consistent with the claim that they associate with κ:*anchoring*.

The examples in (56) also provide support for the claim that locative auxiliaries associate with the area in the spine where the grammatical subject role is deployed. Specifically, Halkomelem conditionals trigger a form of subjunctive agreement, which indexes the grammatical subject role (Wiltschko 2003). Again, this is consistent with the claim that locative auxiliaries associate with κ:*anchoring*.

Table 4.5 *Distribution of auxiliaries across clause-types*

	Independent clause	Nominalized clause	Imperative	Subjunctive
Locative auxiliary	✓	Some	✗	✓

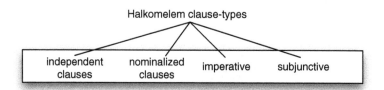

Figure 4.3 *Halkomelem clause-types*

Another argument has to do with the fact that locative auxiliaries are sensitive to clause-type. As shown in Figure 4.3, Halkomelem has four clause-types: *independent* (matrix) clauses, *nominalized* clauses, *imperatives*, and *subjunctives*, each associated with a characteristic set of properties.

Locative auxiliaries are unrestricted in independent clauses and subjunctives, they may not occur in imperatives, and they are restricted to only a subset of nominalized clauses. This is summarized in Table 4.5.

The distribution of locative auxiliaries across clause-types is particularly revealing. First, the ban on auxiliaries in imperatives (Wiltschko 2006a), as shown in (57), is reminiscent of the fact that tense marking in English is banned from imperatives.

(57)   a. *qw'eyílex-lha!*
dance-IMP
'Dance!'

b. **lí   qw'eyílex-lha!*
AUX   dance-IMP
intended: 'Dance (there)!'

Ritter and Wiltschko 2009: 171 (40)

Similarly, the restriction on auxiliaries in nominalized clauses is reminiscent of the contrast between non-finite and finite embedded clauses in English. In particular, whenever an embedded clause is interpreted as a property, rather than a proposition, the auxiliary is ungrammatical (58). This effect resembles the distinction between non-finite and finite embedded clauses in English, which in turn supports the conclusion that locative auxiliaries are the formal and functional equivalent of English tense marking.

(58) a. *l-stl'í*   *kw-el-s*   *qw'eyílex.*
          1SG.POSS-want DET-1SG.POSS-NMLZ dance
          'I want to dance.'

      b. *l-stl'í*   *kw-el-s*   **lí**   *qw'eyílex.*
          1SG.POSS-want DET-1SG.POSS-NMLZ AUX dance
          'I like it when I used to dance.'

Wiltschko 2006b: 293 (15)

And finally, locative auxiliaries serve the same function as tense marking in English and person marking in Blackfoot – namely that of anchoring. That is, in matrix declarative clauses, locative auxiliaries order the event situation relative to the utterance situation by virtue of asserting whether or not the location of the former is the same as the location of the latter. The proximate auxiliary (*í*) asserts that the event location is the same as the utterance location, while the distal auxiliary (*lí*) asserts that the event location is not the same as the utterance location (i.e., the event took place elsewhere). This is reflected in the description found in the two major grammars for Halkomelem:

> *The choice between ʔi and niʔ[24] depends on the **location of the speaker** relative to whatever the predicate refers to.*   Suttles (2004: 35) (emphasis MW)

> *The choice between í and lí is governed by considerations having to do with the **location of the event**. In particular, locative auxiliaries encode the semantic oppositions of emplacement ('here' ...) and displacement ('there' ...).*   Galloway (1993: 359) (emphasis MW)

In sum, if we ask whether Halkomelem has a grammatical category c:TENSE, the answer is *No!* But if we ask whether Halkomelem has a grammatical category that serves to anchor the event and which occupies a position within the domain of κ:*anchoring* the answer is *Yes!* In particular, the Halkomelem-specific category constructed from κ:*anchoring* is c:LOCATION and the UoLs used in the construction of this category are the locative auxiliaries *í* and *lí*. If this analysis is on the right track, it indicates that universal categories cannot be defined by their content. Rather, the substantive content is added to the universal categorizer on a languages-specific basis.

---

[24] Suttles (2004) describes the Island dialect of Halkomelem in which the auxiliary *li* is pronounced as *ni*.

And moreover, we must conclude that we cannot use substantive content as the proper heuristic to identify which language-specific categories associate with particular positions in the universal spine. If we were to do so, we would have to conclude that Halkomelem past marking associates with κ:*anchoring* and that the locative auxiliaries instantiate some form of locative adverbials. But neither conclusion would lead to a proper understanding of the distributional properties of these elements. As we have seen in Section 4.2.2, past marking in Halkomelem behaves like a modifier, and we have now seen that the locative auxiliaries behave like a syntactic head in the domain of κ:*anchoring*. They are obligatory, contrastive, and serve as the host for subject agreement.

4.4.3   *Upper Austrian German* c:REALIS

We have now seen that κ:*anchoring* may serve as the basis to construct c:TENSE, c:PERSON, and c:LOCATION. Thus, the existence of tenseless languages does not imply that universal categories do not exist. Different language-specific categories can be constructed from the same universal category κ:*anchoring*. In Section 4.2.3, we saw yet another tenseless language, namely Upper Austrian German. We now predict that in this language, too, there is a category constructed based on κ:*anchoring*. But what is it?

The main inflectional contrast we find in Upper Austrian German matrix declarative clauses is between what is typically classified as *present tense indicative* and *subjunctive*.[25] It is perhaps somewhat unexpected that a value from the category tense (present) contrasts with a value from the category mood (subjunctive). In particular, tense is typically an independent category (used in matrix clauses) while subjunctive is typically a dependent category (restricted to embedded clauses). But the contrast between present tense and subjunctive mood is only unexpected if we assume that the traditional descriptive categories tense and mood map onto functional categories of the spine in a one-to-one fashion. What I propose instead is that the contrast between present tense and subjunctive mood can be analyzed as a contrast between *realis* and *irrealis*, where both are independent categories. Accordingly, Upper Austrian German uses c:REALIS rather than c:TENSE to anchor the event. Thus c:REALIS is another language-specific substantiation of κ:*anchoring*.[26] This is supported

---

[25] In the German grammatical tradition, this category is known as Konjunktiv 2, though, as we will see, its distribution differs in the Upper Austrian dialect.

[26] This is not to say that c:REALIS manifests κ:*anchoring* in all languages that make use of this category. In line with the main gist of the present proposal, we cannot determine the language-specific association relations on the basis of meaning alone.

by the fact that (at least in Upper Austrian German) *c*:REALIS is functionally similar to *c*:TENSE in that it allows speakers to anchor the event to the ongoing utterance (by stating whether or not the state of affairs holds in the utterance world). This conclusion is supported by the fact that Upper Austrian German subjunctive marking differs significantly from subjunctive marking in languages where *c*:TENSE substantiates *κ:anchoring*. This suggests that subjunctive is not a homogeneous category, as expected given the assumption that all grammatical categories are constructed (see Chapter 5 for evidence that this is indeed so).

4.4.3.1   A *κ*-contrast between subjunctive and present

Upper Austrian German lacks the morphological marking for simple past (Section 4.2.3, Table 4.1). This holds for strong and weak verbs, which, in Standard German, use different allomorphs for past. Weak verbs are marked by *-te* suffixation, whereas strong verbs are marked by ablaut. Both of these morphological processes are available in Upper Austrian German as well. But instead of marking past tense, they mark subjunctive. Specifically, as illustrated in Table 4.6, in weak verbs *-at* suffixation marks subjunctive. This is reminiscent of Standard German *-et* suffixation.

For strong verbs, the morphological properties of Upper Austrian German subjunctive marking differ from Standard German past. Specifically, as illustrated in Table 4.7, there are three morphological strategies to mark subjunctive. First, just like Standard German past, Upper Austrian German subjunctive may be marked by ablaut. The second strategy is *-at* suffixation (just as with weak verbs). And finally, the third strategy is for ablaut and *-at* suffixation to co-occur. The distribution of these forms has not yet been explored.

Table 4.6 *Subjunctive marking in Upper Austrian German weak verbs*

| | Weak verb: *koch* 'cook' | |
	Unmarked	Subjunctive
1SG	*i koch*	*i koch-**at***
2SG	*du koch-st*	*du koch-**at**-st*
3SG	*ea koch-t*	*ea koch-**at**-t*
1PL	*mia koch-n*	*mia koch-**at**-n*
2PL	*ia koch-ts*	*ia koch-**at**-ts*
3PL	*si koch-n*	*si koch-**at**-n*

Table 4.7 *Subjunctive marking in Upper Austrian German strong verbs*

		Strong verb: *kum* 'come'		
	Unmarked	Subjunctive: ablaut	Subjunctive: unmarked -at	Subjunctive: ablaut -at
1SG	*i kum*	*i kam*	*i kum-**at***	*i kam-**at***
2SG	*du kum-st*	*du kam-st*	*du kum-**at**-st*	*du kam-**at**-st*
3SG	*ea kum-t*	*ea kam*	*ea kum-**at**-t*	*ea kam-**at***
1PL	*mia kum-en*	*?mia kam-en*	*mia kum-**at**-n*	*mia kam-**at**-n*
2PL	*ia kum-ts*	*ia kam-ts*	*ia kum-**at**-ts*	*ia kam-**at**-ts*
3PL	*si kum-en*	*?si kam-en*	*si kum-**at**-en*	*si kam-**at**-n*

Table 4.8 *Subjunctive marking in Standard German weak verbs*

		Weak verb: *koch* 'cook'		
	Present	Past: -te	Konjunktiv 1: -e	Konjuntiv 2: -te
1sg	*ich koch-e*	*ich koch-te*	*ich koch-e*	*ich koch-te*
2sg	*du koch-st*	*du koch-te-st*	*du koch-e-st*	*du koch-te-st*
3sg	*er koch-t*	*er koch-te*	*er koch e*	*er koch-te*
1pl	*wir koch-en*	*wir koch-te-n*	*wir koch-en*	*wir koch-te-n*
2pl	*ihr koch-t*	*ihr koch-te-t*	*ihr koch-e-t*	*ihr koch-te-t*
3pl	*sie koch-en*	*sie koch-te-n*	*sie koch-en*	*sie koch-te-en*

The subjunctive in Standard German differs in form from its Upper Austrian counterpart. Specifically, Standard German has two types of subjunctives known as *Konjunktiv 1* and *Konjunktiv 2* with different distributional properties. As illustrated in Table 4.8, in weak verbs Konjunktiv 1 is marked with a suffix *-e* while Konjunktiv 2 is identical in form with past tense marking.

The homophony between past tense and Konjunktiv 2 has been argued to be responsible for the decline in the use of the synthetic subjunctive in favor of a periphrastic construction (Fabricius-Hansen and Sæbø 2004). As illustrated in Table 4.9, for strong verbs, Konjunktiv 1 is formed based on the form for the present tense with an additional suffix *-e*, whereas Konjunktiv 2 is formed by means of the subjunctive *-e* suffix in combination with ablaut, albeit a different type of ablaut than past tense. Thus, in the case of strong verbs, past and subjunctive marking are not homophonous (though in colloquial German the periphrastic construction is still preferred).

Table 4.9 *Subjunctive marking in Standard German strong verbs*

| | Strong verb: *komm* 'come' | | | |
	Present	Past: ablaut	Konjunktiv 1: -e	Konjuntiv 2: ablaut -e
1sg	*ich komm-e*	*ich kam*	*ich komm-e*	*ich käm-e*
2sg	*du komm-st*	*du kam-st*	*du komm-e-st*	*du käm-e-st*
3sg	*er komm-t*	*er kam*	*er komm-e*	*er käm-e*
1pl	*wir komm-en*	*wir kam-en*	*wir komm en*	*wir käm-en*
2pl	*ihr komm-t*	*ihr kam-t*	*ihr komm-e-t*	*ihr käm-e-t*
3pl	*sie komm-en*	*sie kam-en*	*sie komm-en*	*sie käm-en*

In sum, we have seen that the form of subjunctive marking in Upper Austrian German is more similar to past tense marking in Standard German than it is to subjunctive marking. This is consistent with the claim that Upper Austrian German subjunctive and Standard German past associate with the same universal category κ:*anchoring*. This is despite the fact that they are classified as different categories according to traditional grammatical analysis (mood vs. tense, respectively).

4.4.3.2   Upper Austrian German subjunctive marking associates
             with κ:anchoring

The claim that subjunctive marking in Upper Austrian German associates with κ:*anchoring* is consistent with its morpho-syntactic distribution. Based on the paradigms illustrated in Table 4.6 and Table 4.7, we observe that the subjunctive suffix -*at* precedes subject agreement suffixes. Assuming that subject agreement suffixes attach to whatever UoL associates with κ:*anchoring* (INFL), we may conclude that subjunctive marking associates with κ:*anchoring*. Further evidence comes from the distribution of complementizer agreement. In particular, Upper Austrian German displays complementizer agreement with 2nd person singular and plural (Bayer 1984). That is, in the presence of a complementizer, the same subject agreement marker is associated with both the verb and the complementizers, as in (59).

(59) a. *Wonn-st   nua   du   kumm-st* ...
          if-2SG   only   you   come-2SG
          'If only you would come ...'

     b. *Wonn-ts   nua   es   kumm-ts*...
          if-2PL   only   you.2PL come-2PL
          'If only you guys would come ...'

Crucially, as shown in (60), subjunctive marking is restricted to verbs and cannot attach to complementizers.

(60) a. *Wonn-st   nua   du   kumm-at-st* ...
          if-2SG   only   you   come-SUBJ-2SG
          'If only you would come ...'

      b. * *Wonn-at-st   nua   es   kumm-at-ts* ...
          if-SUBJ-2SG   only   you.PL come-SUBJ-2SG
          'If only you guys would come ...'

      c. * *Wonn-at-st   nua   es   kumm-ts* ...
          if-SUBJ-2SG   only   you.PL come.SUBJ-2SG
          'If only you guys would come ...'

This suggests that subjunctive marking associates with a position that is lower than that where complementizers occur.

At the same time, there is evidence that subjunctive marking associates with a position that is higher than that of viewpoint aspect (κ:*point-of-view*). We know this because the two may co-occur. In particular, subjunctive marking is compatible with both imperfective (unmarked) and perfective (marked).[27] And crucially it associates with the finite auxiliary verb rather than with the verbal participle. This holds for both strong and weak verbs (61)–(62).

(61) a. *Ea   kam-at*   *eh.*
          he   come.SUBJ-SUBJ   PRT
          'He would come anyhow.'

      b. *Ea   war-at*   *eh*   *kumma.*
          he   was.SUBJ-SUBJ PRT   come.PART
          'He would have come anyhow.'

(62) a. *Ea   koch-at*   *eh.*
          he   cook-SUBJ   PRT
          'He would cook anyhow.'

      b. *Ea   hed-at*   *eh*   *kocht.*
          he   has-SUBJ   PRT   cook.PART
          'He would have cooked anyhow.'

---

[27] There is of course the possibility that (im)perfective marking in Upper Austrian does not associate with aspect. That is, given the main thesis developed here, substantive content cannot be taken as a criterion to determine categorial identity. In order for this argument to really go through we would have to investigate the formal properties of Upper Austrian German aspect.

This pattern is reminiscent of tense marking, which in English is associated with κ:*anchoring*. Thus, the morpho-syntactic distribution of subjunctive marking is consistent with the claim that it associates with κ:*anchoring*.

4.4.3.3 Dependent and independent subjunctives

κ:*anchoring* is universally responsible for anchoring the reported event to the utterance situation. In a tense-based system, anchoring proceeds via times; in a location-based system, anchoring proceeds via places; in a person-based system, anchoring proceeds via participants. But which aspect of the event and utterance situation does a realis-based system utilize for anchoring? I propose that anchoring to the utterance proceeds via the evaluation world. In the present, the event is part of the evaluation world, which is itself based on the utterance world; in the subjunctive, the event is asserted not to be part of the evaluation world and an irrealis interpretation arises (see Section 4.5 for a formal implementation). In this respect, the Upper Austrian German subjunctive is predicted to pattern with independent clauses rather than with the dependent subjunctives of the Romance and Balkan type. This is indeed the case, as I will now show.

The Upper Austrian German subjunctive differs substantially from the more familiar subjunctives found in the Romance and Balkan languages (see Quer [2006, 2009] for a recent overview). In these languages, the subjunctive is a dependent clause-type. It requires licensing from an appropriate matrix predicate or a higher operator. In contrast, if the Upper Austrian German subjunctive contrasts with indicative past marking, then by hypothesis it cannot be intrinsically dependent and should be able to occur in a matrix clause. This prediction is borne out as shown in (63) (see also [62] above).

(63)   a. *Ea   ruaf-at   õ*.
             He   call-SUBJ PRT
             'He (would) call.'

        b. *Es   regn-at*.
             it   rain-SUBJ
             'It would rain.'

This contrasts with the more familiar type of subjunctive marking. As shown in (64), Spanish matrix clauses do not allow for subjunctive marking.

(64)   a. **Daniel   haya   llamado*.
             Daniel   call   CALLSUBJ.PERF.3SG
             'Daniel has called.'

b. * *Ahir   plogués.*
    Yesterday   rain.SUBJ.IMPF.3SG
    'Yesterday it rained.'

Quer 2006: 667 (3)

But even when it occurs in embedded clauses, the Upper Austrian German subjunctive differs. It does not display any of the dependency effects associated with the more familiar subjunctives. For example, in Catalan the temporal specification of the embedded subjunctive clause depends on the temporal specification of the embedding clause (65a). This differs from embedded indicative clauses, whose temporal specification is independent of that of the matrix clause (65b).

(65)   a. *Desitja   que telefoni/*telefonés.*
            Desire.PRS.3SG   that phone.**SUBJ.PRES**.3sg/phone.**SUBJ.IMPF**.3SG
            'S/he wishes that s/he calls/called.'

        b. *Sabia   que telefona/telefonava.*
            Know.IMPF.1SG   that phone.**IND.PRES.3SG**/phone.**IND.IMPF.3SG**
            'I knew that s/he calls/that she used to call.'

Quer 2006: 663 (2)

In contrast, in Upper Austrian German the temporal specification of embedded subjunctive clause is independent of the temporal specification in the embedding clause. In this respect, the Upper Austrian German subjunctive patterns with the Catalan indicative, rather than with the Catalan subjunctive. As illustrated in (66), the embedded clause may be (periphrastically) specified as present, perfect, or future even though the matrix clause is specified as perfect.

(66)   a. *Ea hot gsogt,   du   kumm-at-st.*
            He has said.PART   you   come-SUBJ-2SG
            'He said you would come.'

        b. *Ea hot gsogt,   du   war-at-st   kumma.*
            He has said.PART   you   was-SUBJ-2SG   come.PART
            'He said you would have come.'

        c. *Ea hot gsogt,   du   wuat-at-st   kumma.*
            He has said.PART   you   will-SUBJ-2SG   come.PART
            'He said you would come.'

The next criterion has to do with the fact that a dependent subjunctive does not allow for independent temporal reference. As a consequence, no temporal adverb can modify the predicate in the subjunctive clause. This is illustrated in (67) for Greek.

(67) | * O | eaftos | to | arxizi ... |
|---|---|---|---|
| The | self | his-NOM | begin-3SG ... |
| ... **na** | ton | anisixi | **avrio.** |
| ... SUBJ | CL.ACC | worry.3SG.PST | tomorrow |

'He started being worried about himself tomorrow.'

Alexiadou and Anagnostopoulou 1999: 26 (31b)

In contrast, the Upper Austrian German subjunctive allows for independent temporal reference, as shown in (68).

(68) | *Ea hot gestan* | *gsogt* | *dass* | *a* | *moagn* | *ham* | *gang-**at**.* |
|---|---|---|---|---|---|---|
| He has yesterday | said.PART | that | he | tomorrow | home | go-SUBJ |

'He said yesterday that he would go home tomorrow.'

In addition, in languages with dependent subjunctives, syntactic transparency often goes along with the dependency. That is, relations that are clause-bound with indicatives become cross-clausal in the subjunctive. For example, in Spanish the subjunctive displays obviation effects. The embedded subject may not be co-referent with the matrix subject (69a). This contrasts with the indicative in which the two subjects may co-refer (69b).

(69) a. | **Queremos$_i$* | *que* | *ganemos$_i$.* |
|---|---|---|
| Want.1PL | that | win.SUBJ.PRES.1PL |

'We want to win.'

  b. | *Queremos$_i$* | *que* | *ganen$_k$.* |
|---|---|---|
| Want.1PL | that | win.SUBJ.PRES.3PL |

'We want them to win.'

Quer 2006: 677 (29)

Again, this contrasts with the independent SUBJUNCTIVE in Upper Austrian German, which does not trigger obviation effects (70).

(70) | *Ea vasuach-(at)t* | *(eh) dass* | *a* | *gwinn-at.* |
|---|---|---|---|
| He try-SUBJ | PRT that | he | win-SUBJ |

'He is trying to win.'

Another transparency effect is found in Icelandic, where dependent subjunctives allow for long-distance reflexive binding. This is illustrated in (71): embedded subjunctives, but not embedded indicatives, allow for long-distance reflexives.

(71) a. | *Jón$_i$* | *segir* | *að* | *Pétur$_j$* | *raki* | *sig$_{i/j}$.* |
|---|---|---|---|---|---|
| Jón | say.3SG | that | Pétur | shave.**SUBJ.3SG** | **REFL** |

'Jón says that Pétur shaves himself.'

b. *Jón$_i$ veit   að   Pétur$_j$ rakar   sig*$_{*i/j}$.
Jón   know.3SG   that   Pétur   shave.**IND.3SG**   REFL
'Jón knows that Pétur shaves himself.'

Quer 2006: 679 (35–36)

And again, the Upper Austrian German subjunctive does not allow for long distance reflexives, as shown in (72).

(72)   a. *Da Hons$_j$ hot gsagt   dass da   Peda$_i$ si$_{i/*j}$ rasiert.*
DET Hans has said.PART   that DET   Peter   REFL   shave
'Hans said that Peter shaved himself.'

b. *Da Hons$_j$ hot gsagt   dass da   Peda$_i$ si$_{i/*j}$ rasier-at.*
DET Hans has said.PART   that DET   Peter   REFL   shave-SUBJ
'Hans said that Peter would shave himself.'

We have now established that the Upper Austrian German subjunctive does not pattern with the dependent subjunctives of the Romance or Balkan type. Instead, relative to some common characteristics of the subjunctive, it behaves just like an indicative. In other words, the Upper Austrian German subjunctive forms a natural class with the indicative rather than with the dependent subjunctive, as indicated by shaded cells in Table 4.10.

If the independent subjunctive does indeed pattern with the indicative, then in what sense is it a subjunctive? In a way this question is moot under the present proposal, since all categories are constructed. Traditional labels are here used as convenient cover terms only, with no theoretical status. The reason we want to compare the Upper Austrian German subjunctive marking with those of other languages, however, has to do with the fact that it occurs in similar contexts of use as the Standard German subjunctive. That is, the Upper

Table 4.10 *Distribution of independent subjunctives*

	Independent subjunctive (Upper Austrian German)		Dependent subjunctive (Romance, Balkan, Icelandic)	
	IND	SUBJ	IND	SUB
Possible in matrix clause	✓	✓	✓	✗
Independent temporal specification	✓	✓	✓	✗
Allows for long distance reflexives	✗	✗	✗	✓
Triggers obviation effects	✗	✗	✗	✓

Austrian German subjunctive is for the most part interpreted as an irrealis construction, just like the Standard German subjunctive.[28]

We have now established that the Upper Austrian German subjunctive is an independent clause-type that contrasts with the matrix indicative clause in the present tense. This is consistent with the analysis that it substantiates *κ:anchoring*. Thus, Upper Austrian German presents us with another language-specific guise of the anchoring category, namely *c*:REALIS.

4.5   The universal structure of the anchoring category

Let us take stock. We have seen that in the three tenseless languages introduced in Section 4.2 grammatical relations are active (Section 4.3). This suggests that the domain where *c*:TENSE is found in English is grammatically active. We have furthermore seen that all three languages have a distinct grammatical category that shares essential properties with *c*:TENSE in English. Thus, relative to the following core properties these categories form a natural class:

(i)   **Contrastiveness** They are *κ*-contrastive in the sense defined in Chapter 3 (Section 3.3). The UoLs that express them have the distribution of UoLs that associate with *κ* via the "*is-a*" relation.

(ii)   **Domain effects** They are located between the domain of event structure (*κ:classification*) and the area of discourse roles and clause-typing (*κ:linking*). Thus, they pattern as categories in the domain of grammatical relations (*κ:anchoring*).

(iii)   **Spinal function** All three categories serve the function of anchoring events. Blackfoot *c*:PERSON establishes a relation to the utterance by asserting that the event participant is or is not the same as the utterance participant; Halkomelem *c*:LOCATION establishes this relation by asserting that the event location is or is not the same as the utterance location; and *c*:REALIS in Upper Austrian German codes this relation by asserting that the state of affairs does or does not hold in the utterance world.

In sum, English *c*:TENSE, Blackfoot *c*:PERSON, Halkomelem *c*:LOCATION, and Upper Austrian German *c*:REALIS have the same formal and functional properties but their substantive content differs. It is for this reason that we need

---

[28] The question as to how independent subjunctives are interpreted is addressed in Section 5.4.5.

a formal typology that is not based on substantive content. We need to keep track of the formal properties of categories where *formal* refers to the patterns of the sound–meaning associations rather than patterns of meanings alone.

The main insight behind the Universal Spine Hypothesis is that identity in function goes along with identity in formal characteristics. This points to the existence of an underlying categorizer κ that mediates between event structure and discourse structure. Given that its core function is that of anchoring, we call it the anchoring category (κ:*anchoring*). The picture that emerges, then, is that there are (thus far) four language-specific categories that may instantiate the anchoring category, as in (73).

(73) κ:*anchoring* = {c:TENSE, c:PERSON, c:LOCATION, c:REALIS}

Consequently, the data we have seen thus far are compatible with the Universal Spine Hypothesis. On the syntactic spine, the anchoring domain mediates between the event and the utterance. But how is this relation established? How is anchoring formalized? As introduced in Chapter 1 (Section 1.4.3) κ is intrinsically transitive. Thus we expect that all grammatical categories that are constructed based on κ via the "*is-a*" relation are also transitive. Specifically, such categories involve heads that mediate between two arguments, one in the position that is known as the complement position (sister to κ), and the other in the position that is known as the specifier position (sister to the head–complement complex).

Moreover, following Ritter and Wiltschko (2009, forthcoming), I implement the anchoring relation by means of a coincidence feature that is intrinsically associated with all instances of κ [$u$coin]. In particular, this feature establishes whether or not the two arguments coincide (in time, space, participancy, or reality). That coincidence is a central universal characteristic of a variety of grammatical categories was first observed by Hale (1986).[29]

Building on work by Demirdache and Uribe Etxebarria (1997) (and subsequent work) the central proposal of Ritter and Wiltschko (forthcoming) is that this coincidence feature is inherently unvalued. In line with much recent work within the minimalist program, Ritter and Wiltschko further assume that this unvalued feature must be valued as either [+coin] or [−coin]. At least in indicative clauses it is the substantive content of the UoL that associates with κ:*anchoring* which serves to value [$u$coin], regardless of whether its content is

---

[29] See Chapter 8 (Subsection 8.6.2.1) for further discussion.

temporal, spatial, participant-based, or realis-based. We refer to this type of valuation as *m(orphological)-valuation*.

But what are the arguments that categories based on κ:*anchoring* relate? For tense-based languages, these arguments are abstract time arguments (Demirdache and Uribe-Etxebarria 1997). To accommodate for tenseless languages, Ritter and Wiltschko (forthcoming) modify this proposal. Along with the content associated with κ:*anchoring*, the flavor of the abstract arguments changes as well. To capture this, they assume that the arguments associated with κ:*anchoring* are *situation arguments* (*arg$_{sit}$*). This is reminiscent of Percus (2000) who assumes that worlds are explicitly represented in the syntax as pronouns (situation pronouns in his framework).[30] By hypothesis, these situation arguments contain temporal coordinates (*t*) and spatial coordinates (*loc*) as well as participants (*part*). Thus the universal structure of κ:*anchoring* is given in (74).

(74)   Formalizing anchoring

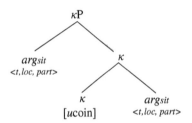

This structure captures the universal characteristics of the anchoring function on the one hand, while at the same time allowing for language-specific variation in substantive content on the other. In particular, as schematized in (75), the substantive content of language-specific categories values [*u*coin], regardless of whether it is temporal, spatial, or participant-based (we turn to realis-based systems below).[31] It will thus always be the substantive content of κ:*anchoring* that establishes a direct relation to the utterance context. The highest argument picks out the utterance situation and is therefore responsible for relating the event to the utterance (what we might refer to as the property of *contextuality*).[32]

---

[30] See also Hacquard (2010).
[31] This departs from existing minimalist accounts according to which an unvalued feature [uF] is valued by an interpretable feature [iF] via the operation AGREE.
[32] See Chapter 5 for further modification.

Moreover, the substantive content also determines the flavor of the two arguments being ordered: temporal content orders times, spatial content orders places, and person orders participant roles. Specifically, present tense asserts that the event time coincides with the utterance time, proximate location asserts that the event location coincides with the utterance location, and local participant asserts that the designated event participant coincides with an utterance participant. This is shown in (75).

(75)

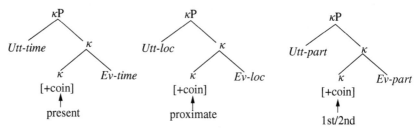

Conversely, past tense, distal location and non-local person value [*u*coin] as [−coin], thereby asserting that the time, location, or designated participant of the event situation does not coincide with that of the utterance situation. This is shown in (76).

(76)

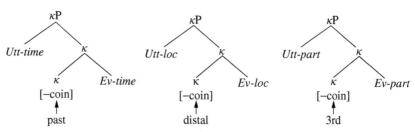

Thus, substantive content, such as past, is not universally associated with *κ:anchoring* and consequently, substance cannot be the basis for comparison.[33] Rather it is the formal and functional similarity between categories which allows for comparison. Identifying universal categories based on content does not

---

[33] Recall that Halkomelem has a past marker, which has the distribution of a modifier. I submit that, when it adjoins to *κ:anchoring*, it places the coincidence relation in the past.

lead to the discovery of natural classes; identifying them on the basis of their formal and functional properties does.

But what about the third tenseless language introduced in Section 4.2.3? How does Upper Austrian German *c*:REALIS fit into this analysis? If *c*:REALIS is constructed based on *κ*:*anchoring* we predict that it also anchors the event to the utterance. This is indeed the case. To see why, consider the examples below. The unmarked conditional in (77) receives a temporal interpretation. It describes real events in the past. In contrast, the subjunctive-marked conditional in (78) receives a counterfactual interpretation. The event in the antecedent clause is contrary to fact, and so is the consequent.

(77)   Conditional
        Wonn   *I*   *gwunna*   *hob* ...
        If   I   win.PART   have ...
        ... *donn*   *hob*   *I ma*   *wos*   *kaufn*   *kinna.*
        ... then   have   I myself   something   buy   can
        'When I won then I was able to buy myself something.'

(78)   Counterfactual conditional
        Wonn   *I*   *gwunna*   *hed-**at** ...
        If   I   win.PART   have.SUBJ-SUBJ ...
        ... *donn hed-**at***   *I ma*   *wos*   *kaufn kinna.*
        ... then   have.SUBJ-SUBJ   I myself   something buy   can
        'If I had won, then I could have bought myself something.'

According to Iatridou (2000), counterfactual marking in English denotes an abstract exclusion feature that ranges over worlds. Translated into the representation of categories adopted here, this means that the abstract argument in the specifier position is the evaluation world. Thus, realis marks that the event situation coincides with the evaluation world (79a), whereas irrealis (including subjunctive) marks that the event situation does not coincide with the evaluation world (79b).

(79)   a. Realis ('present')   b. Irrealis (subjunctive)

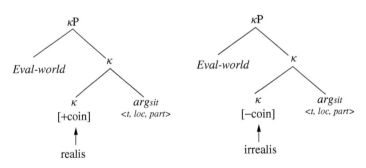

In English, as in many other languages, counterfactual marking is homophonous with past marking (James 1982), and thus sometimes referred to as *fake past*. However, in Upper Austrian German subjunctive marking is not a form of past marking. In fact, Upper Austrian German lacks past tense. Nevertheless, we may still analyze it as a [−coin] construction. The difference from English is that it is never valued by tense whereas in English it is. What remains to be explained though is why the abstract argument corresponds to the evaluation world, rather than the utterance situation, as it does in other instances of *κ:anchoring*.

I hypothesize that this has to do with the fact that Upper Austrian German, like Standard German, is a Verb-second (V2) language. On most analyses of V2, the verb targets C and thus the CP layer is present in every declarative clause. This means that in this language *κ:anchoring* is always embedded into a larger structure such as CP. We therefore have to explore the properties of embedded TPs in more detail. This is the topic of investigation in Chapter 5, where I develop an analysis for Upper Austrian German subjunctives and a typology of subjunctives more generally. Crucially, the basis for this typology is the structure of *κ:anchoring* as introduced above. We will show that the assumption of this universal structure of anchoring provides us with the right tools for comparison, as well as discovery not only for the anchoring in embedded clauses but also for nominal anchoring. The conceptualization of categories as being constructed out of a universal categorizer *κ* and language-specific Units of Language ($c = κ + \text{UoL}$) allows us to come to terms with categories that have been elusive in analyses that are based on the premise that categories are defined by their meanings, such as the subjunctive (discussed in Chapter 5), case (discussed in Chapter 6), and direct/inverse marking (discussed in Chapter 7).

5 Anchoring categories in dependent clauses

You can't believe a word he says since he invented the subjunctive.

Baloo Rex May

5.1 Introduction

In Chapter 4, I argued that κ:*anchoring* is universal. However, unlike what is commonly assumed in the generative tradition, we have seen that κ:*anchoring* is not universally associated with temporal content. Thus the content of a given category is not intrinsically associated with it; instead the category–content association is language-specific. This follows from the claim that language-specific categories are constructed from a universal categorizer combined with a Unit of Language (UoL), as in (1).

(1) $c = \kappa + \text{UoL}$

On this view, it comes as no surprise that not all languages have c:TENSE. In this chapter, I extend the investigation of κ:*anchoring* from independent clauses to clauses that are embedded in a larger syntactic structure. I show that the dissociation of categories from their substantive content allows for a novel typology of embedded clauses.

In languages where c:TENSE instantiates κ:*anchoring*, embedded clauses may lack an overt manifestation of this grammatical category (that is, they may be tenseless). Alternatively, in such contexts c:TENSE may be defective and behave differently from its manifestation in independent clauses. On the assumption that c:TENSE arises when [$u$coin] is valued via morphological marking with temporal content (m-valuation), we expect that in the absence of morphological tense marking something else will have to value [$u$coin]. Building on Ritter and Wiltschko (forthcoming), I will show that valuation proceeds via a higher head. I refer to this as *external valuation*. There are two ways in which a clause headed by κ:*anchoring* may be embedded. It may either be embedded by a matrix predicate via *pred(icate)-complementation* as

145

in (2a), or else by a higher functional head via *f(unction)-complementation*, as in (2b), defining different patterns of dependence.

(2)   a. *pred-complementation:*   [predicate [κ:*anchoring*. . .]]

        b. *f-complementation:*   [f-head [κ: *anchoring*. . .]]

Clauses embedded via pred-complementation are often realized as infinitives, or as subjunctives of a sort. Clauses embedded via f-complementation are found in clause-types such as imperatives, hypotheticals, and counterfactuals. These are sometimes realized with dedicated morphological marking (such as special imperative morphology, for example), but sometimes they are realized just like clauses embedded via pred-complementation (via subjunctive marking, for example). The question I address in this chapter is about the status of such categories that are found in dependent clauses. Are they universal, and if so, what is the range of variation we observe? I will focus on the subjunctive, as it is an ideal category to make the point that categories cannot be defined based on their content.

In Section 5.2, I start by testing the predictions of the Universal Base Hypothesis (UBH) and I identify two problems in light of the categories found in dependent clauses. First, it is hard even to define categories such as the subjunctive in a way that allows for comparison across languages. Second, and more crucially, categories like the subjunctive do not behave like a natural class, neither within a given language nor across different languages. At first sight, these findings seem to support the conclusion that universal categories do not exist, as in the No Base Hypothesis (NBH). In Section 5.3, however, I show that this conclusion is not empirically supported either. In particular, there are generalizations to be made about categories like the subjunctive within and across languages. What we cannot do is generalize over their formal properties AND their substantive content or morphological realization.

So once again we end up with this seemingly contradictory result that on the one hand it looks as if the subjunctive is not a universal category, but on the other hand if we draw this conclusion we miss important generalizations. I then turn to an analysis within the Universal Spine Hypothesis (USH) in Section 5.4. I adopt the formal analysis that Ritter and Wiltschko (forthcoming) develop for embedded infinitives as well as imperatives and counterfactuals and extend it to subjunctives. This formal analysis will provide us with a straightforward way to capture the variation we observe with subjunctives, while still maintaining a universal core in the form of κ:*anchoring*. The crucial difference between κ:*anchoring* in dependent and independent clauses has to do with the nature of the situation argument in its specifier. In independent clauses, this is the utterance situation, accounting for the deictic properties of matrix anchoring categories. In dependent clauses this argument is inherently anaphoric, as in (3).

(3)   The essence of anchoring

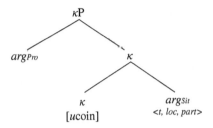

In the absence of an accessible antecedent, the anaphoric argument is necessarily linked to the utterance and therefore in matrix independent clauses the anchoring category receives a deictic interpretation (see also Percus 2000). In contrast, when the anchoring category is embedded, the anaphoric situation argument is dependent on a higher argument made available by the embedding structure. Therefore, in embedded clauses, the anchoring category is no longer directly deictic. As a result, if anchoring is otherwise temporal (i.e., *c*:TENSE), the same category suddenly appears defective or dependent.

5.2   The Universal Base Hypothesis

To test the UBH, I examine the subjunctive, which is itself traditionally classified as a particular value of *mood*. The reason for focusing on the subjunctive is that it is a category that has long defied a unified analysis in terms of its interpretation; thus, it makes an ideal testing ground for formal approaches. Moreover, it is relatively uncontroversial that mood is located in the same general domain as tense (Haïk 1990; Cowper 2005).

Mood is commonly considered to be a *universal* functional category, both in the generative tradition (Cinque 1999) as well as in typological linguistics (Bybee 1985; Palmer 2001). It is often treated as a modal category in the semantic literature (Palmer 2001; Matthewson 2010).

The types of values associated with mood differ between authors. For example Comrie (1976) considers mood to include the values *realis/irrealis* (see also Palmer 2001); Palmer (2001) associates mood with an *indicative/subjunctive* contrast; and Greenberg (1963) associates with it an *indicative/hypothetical* contrast. Rather than reflecting a real empirical difference between languages, Palmer (2001) takes it to reflect different scholarly traditions associated with specific language families. If so, we may collapse the realis/irrealis distinction with the indicative/subjunctive distinction. Both notions instantiate a contrast associated with mood. An obvious question then concerns the substantive content of this contrast. This question arises on the view that universal categories are defined by the substantive content associated with them, as in the version of the UBH we are considering here. The indicative/subjunctive distinction appears (roughly) to correlate with the difference between making an assertion (indicative) and not making an assertion (subjunctive), but the exact content that correlates with this contrast is hard to pin down. The following semantic features are exemplary for the kinds of meanings proposed to associate with the subjunctive: *assertion* (Bybee and Fleischmann 1995), *factuality* (Palmer 2001; Noonan 2007), *actualization* (Mithun 1995), *(speaker) certainty* (Siegel 2009), and *modal weakening* (Matthewson 2010). It is well known, however, that a meaning-based account for the subjunctive runs into problems: the range of meanings encompassed by it varies considerably from one language to another (Diekhoff 1911: 625; Plungian 2005: 137) but also within a single language (Nordström 2010: 5). But if categories are defined based on their meaning, and if at the same time they differ in meaning across languages, then how do we even compare such categories across languages?

For example, the notions of *factuality* or *unreal* cannot capture the fact that, in many languages factive emotive predicates (Kiparsky and Kiparsky 1970) require that their complements be marked with subjunctive, despite the fact that they presuppose the truth of their complement. This is illustrated with data from French in (4) below.

(4) a. *Nous somme   désolés   que   notre president   soit   un   idiot.*
        We are   sorry   that our   president   be3SG.SUBJ an   idiot.
        'We are sorry that our president is an idiot.'

                                                                    Siegel 2009: 1861 (4)

     b. **Nous somme   désolés   que   notre president est   un   idiot.*
        We   are   sorry   that our   president be3SG.IND   an   idiot.

                                                                    Ileana Paul (p. c.)

The grammaticality of (4a) is unexpected if the subjunctive were a category that expresses non-factuality, non-actualization, or non-speaker certainty. In this respect, the proposal that the relevant contrast is based on *assertion* fares better: since complements of factive predicates are presupposed, they cannot be asserted. So if subjunctives differ from indicatives in lacking the ability to make assertions, the contrast in (4) is expected. However, the analysis in terms of *assertiveness* also runs into problems. For example in Spanish, complements of causative verbs have to be marked for subjunctive, as in (5).

(5) a. *Le   hice   que   saliera.*
        Him   make.PST.1SG that   leave.PST.3SG.SUBJ
        'I made him leave.'

                                            Siegel 2009: 1861 (9)

      b. **Le   hice   que   salió.*
         him   make.PST.1SG that   leave.PST.3SG.IND

                                            Adriana Osa Gomez (p. c.)

These types of realis subjunctives do not fit into a meaning-based analysis according to which subjunctives express irrealis or non-asserted propositions.

More generally, meaning-based analyses run into problems in cases where the subjunctive is obligatory and appears to have no semantic import. A recent example of this sort is found in Matthewson's (2010) investigation into St'at'imcets (Northern Interior Salish). In particular, Matthewson proposes that the core contribution of the subjunctive in St'at'imcets is to weaken the force of a governing modal. This analysis not only accounts for the observed cross-linguistic variation in a systematic way, but it also successfully accounts for a variety of apparently disparate semantic effects subjunctive marking has within this language. In particular, the semantic effects of the subjunctive differ depending on the construction it appears in. By way of illustration, consider an example with the deontic modal (*ka*), as in (6). Here the use of the subjunctive has the effect of weakening the strength of the modal force (*should* vs. *hope*). Similarly, in the context of an adhortative (*malh*), as in (7), the subjunctive weakens the strength of the imperative (*you better* vs. *you could*).

(6) a. *gúy't = Ø = ka   ti = sk'úk'wm'it = a.*
        sleep = 3IND = DEON   DET = child = EXIS
        'The child should sleep.'

      b. *guy't = ás = ka   ti = sk'úk'wm'it = a.*
         sleep = 3SUBJ = DEON   DET = child = EXIS
         'I hope the child sleeps.'

                                            Matthewson 2010: 9:3 (4)

(7) a. *nás = malh   áku   7 pankúph = a.*
        go = ADHORT DEIC Vancouver = EXIS
        'You'd better go to Vancouver.'

b. *nás = acw = malh*   *áku7 pankúph = a.*
  go = 2SG.SUBJ = ADHORT   DEIC Vancouver = EXIS
  'You could go to Vancouver.'

                                          Matthewson 2010: 9:8 (14)

Crucially, however, Matthewson's analysis runs into the same problem as all meaning-based analyses: there is a residue of cases in which the subjunctive is syntactically obligatory (grammaticalized) while being without "semantic import" (Matthewson 2010: 9:2). This is the case in matrix clauses marked by a so-called 'perceived evidential'.

(8)   a. **táyt = kacw = an'.*
        hungry = 2SG.IND = PERC.EVID
        'You must be hungry.'

     b. *táyt = acw = an'.*
        hungry = 2SG.SUBJ = PERC.EVID
        'You must be hungry.'

                                     Matthewson 2010: 9:16 (31)

(9)   a. **nílh = Ø = an'*   *s = Sylvia*   *ku = xílh-tal'i.*
        FOC = 3IND = PERC.EVID   NMLZ = Sylvia DET = do(CAUS)-TOP
        'Apparently it was Sylvia who did it.'

     b. *nílh = as = an'*   *s = Sylvia*   *ku = xílh-tal'i.*
        FOC = 3SUBJ = PERC.EVID NMLZ = Sylvia DET = do(CAUS)-TOP
        'Apparently it was Sylvia who did it.'

                                   Matthewson *et al.* 2007: 208 (13)

So again, a semantically based definition of the subjunctive cannot account for all of its uses – instead what unifies the construction is its morpho-syntax. It is uniquely identifiable on the basis of a certain agreement pattern, which differs in form and distribution from those of independent clause-types on the one hand and nominalized dependent clauses on the other.

There are several proposals available that attempt to deal with these mismatches between form and meaning of the subjunctive: (i) the subjunctive is treated as the elsewhere case; (ii) its grammatical space depends on the availability of other clause-types; (iii) it is treated as a constructed category. I briefly discuss each of these in turn.

First, we may take indicative as the marked form and subjunctive as the elsewhere (default) case (Portner 1997; Schlenker 2005; Siegel 2009). This has the advantage that we do not need to identify a core semantics for the subjunctive. However, the burden is now to define a meaning for the indicative. For example, Siegel (2009) argues that in Romance languages, indicative is associated with a supposition that the speaker believes in the truth of the embedded proposition, while in the Balkan languages indicative is used to express certainty on the part of the matrix subject. This not only accounts for the observed cross-linguistic variation but also for the fact that the subjunctive does not appear to be definable on the basis of its semantics. However, as Quer (2009) observes, it also cannot fully account for the distribution of the indicative and subjunctive within a single language. For example, according to Siegel (2009), in the Balkan languages there is no speaker presupposition attached to the indicative mood, and it should therefore be possible to be embedded under factive emotive verbs like *manage*. This is contrary to fact. In Greek the indicative is prohibited in such contexts, as shown in (10).

(10)   a. *Katafere*   *na*   *ton*   *voithisi.*
           manage.PST.3SG   SUBJ   him   help.PNP.3SG
           'S/he managed to help him.'

   b. **Katafere*   *{pu / oti}*   *ton voithise.*
           manage.PST.3SG   that   him help. PST.PERF.3SG

Quer 2009: 1911 (1)

A second suggestion to deal with the problems of a meaning-based analysis is to pay attention to the range of grammatical constructions available in the language, i.e., the grammatical landscape of a given language. For example, Giorgi (2009) suggests that at least some cross-linguistic differences in the properties of subjunctives can be understood by appealing to the lack of infinitives in some languages (e.g., Greek and Romanian). However, this cannot explain the full range of differences among subjunctives; as we shall see neither Blackfoot nor Halkomelem has an infinitive, but the distribution of the subjunctives in both these languages differs.

A third proposal to deal with the form–meaning mismatches observed in the subjunctives of the world is to say that the subjunctive is constructed, and individual pieces of this construction contribute to the overall meaning (Quer 2009). If indeed the subjunctive were constructed, then it would not be expected to be constructed in the same way across different languages. But if it can be constructed in different ways, we expect to find different results. This is precisely the approach the Universal Spine Hypothesis (USH) will lead us to adopt (see Section 5.4). The problem with existing versions of a deconstructionist approach is that they are not explicit enough to identify the ingredients that would allow us to derive the properties of all of the subjunctives that we explore here. In particular, many formal analyses of the subjunctive treat it as instantiating a form of defective tense (Picallo 1985; Landau 2004) or as introducing a dependency (Giannakidou 2009). The defective tense analyses run into problems in light of the fact that a subjunctive category is not restricted to tensed languages, but is also found in the tenseless languages we introduced in Chapter 4: Blackfoot (11), Halkomelem (12), and Upper Austrian German (13).

(11)   *Ikkamáyo'kainoainiki,*   *nitáakahkayi.*
        ikkam-á-yo'kaa-inoa-**iniki**   nit-yáak-wa:hkayi
        if-IMPF-sleep.AI-2PL-SUBJ   1-FUT-go.home.AI
        'If you are sleeping, I'll go home.'   Frantz 1991: 113 (l)

(12)   *we-lám-àl* . . .
        if-go-1SG.SUBJ
        'If I go . . .'   Galloway 1993: 184

(13)   *Wonn*   *a*   *nua*   *ham*   *gang-at!*
        If   he   only   home   go-SUBJ
        'If only he went home!'

In the 'subjunctive-as-dependent tense' analysis, it is not immediately clear what the predictions for tenseless languages are. It would appear that in the absence of tense, there cannot be a defective tense, by definition.

Furthermore, the 'subjunctive-as-dependent' analysis runs into problems in light of the fact that the Upper Austrian German subjunctive may be realized in independent clauses without an obvious candidate for a category it would be dependent on, as in (14).

(14)   *Dei*   *Ex*   *ruaf-at*   ŏ.
        your   ex   call-SUBJ   PRT
        'Your ex is calling.'

Note also that this construction is a problem for approaches which seek to identify the subjunctive with an irrealis, non-actual, or hypothetical construal: the sentence can felicitously be uttered if the addressee's ex is indeed calling at the time of utterance (see Section 5.4.5 for discussion).

Of course, we could conclude that these subjunctives are not really subjunctives, and thus that they do not constitute counter-examples. However, this presents a problem: if the subjunctive is not a primitive but instead composed, then the question as to what counts as a subjunctive becomes difficult, if not impossible, to answer. This problem is highlighted by Matthewson's (2010) treatment of the St'at'imcets subjunctive, which at first sight does not behave like a semantically defined class. One of her goals, however, is to show that this subjunctive is indeed a subjunctive and not an irrealis. While this requires the assumption of some notion of subjunctive that can be identified across languages (i.e., some kind of 'universal subjunctive'), it nevertheless leads to the problem of identifying the comparison set. But if the subjunctive is decomposable, then it is not immediately clear what about it is universal. That is, it requires a formal typology that allows us to identify the universals as well as the potential sources of variation.

Mithun (1995: 368) arrives at a similar conclusion:

> *Given this variation, the utility of the labels 'Irrealis' and 'Realis' for cross-linguistic comparison is open to question. If there is no common semantic or pragmatic basis for the terminology, its application to such diverse phenomena could lead to unnecessary confusion. In what follows, the Irrealis and Realis categories of several languages will be compared. It will be suggested that despite the apparent heterogeneity of the categories to which the distinction is applied, indeed perhaps because of it, the Irrealis/Realis terminology can prompt fruitful cross-linguistic comparisons with potential for furthering our understanding of certain processes of grammaticization.*

We have now seen that the subjunctive is especially hard to define based on its meaning. This makes it difficult to identify the properties that would serve to demarcate this category. The absence of categorical diagnostics is sometimes used to conclude that categories never behave in a categorical way but instead that one needs to analyze them along a continuum. This is the position I discuss in the next subsection.

5.3   The No Base Hypothesis

As introduced in Chapter 1, the assumption that there are universal categories is not universally accepted. Interestingly, despite the fact that, when it comes to the subjunctive, it is in fact really hard to identify its universal properties, especially on a meaning-based definition, there is nevertheless no explicit claim that the subjunctive is not a linguistic universal. Instead, within the typological tradition it is often assumed that it is (see Palmer 2001). The fact that it is not attested in the same way across all languages is consistent with the widespread view in the functional typology literature, according to which linguistic universals must always be seen as being prototypes with fuzzy boundaries (Comrie 1989; see Chapter 1). A prototype is defined by a set of features, but peripheral members of a particular category may not be associated with all of the features of the prototypical one (Croft 2003). For the subjunctive, this is explicitly argued for by Plungian (2005: 138), who describes the irrealis as a continuum, as in (15): different construction types are more or less likely to be marked with irrealis marking (which includes subjunctive).[1]

(15)   The irrealis continuum (adapted from Plungian 2005: 138)

always	most often	less often	never
counterfactual	future	indirect evidential	past perfective
optative	prospective	negative	immediate past
conjunctive	conditional	interrogative	resultative past
intentional	concessive	imperative	present progressive
volitional	purposive	prohibitive	
probabilitive		habitual	
dubitative		past imperfective	
		remote past	

This view of grammatical categories, with specific reference to irrealis, is summarized as follows by Plungian (2005: 137):[2]

> *Probably, the most interesting property of irrealis as a cross-linguistic category is that the range of "irreal" domains varies considerably from language to language, so what is called irrealis in one language may – at first glance – have only a remote resemblance to what is called irrealis in another language. This cross-linguistic variation is, in principle, typical for most grammatical categories (cf. for example, the extent of what is called perfect, or conjunctive, in different languages), and irrealis is not very specific in this respect.*

I take the prototype theory of grammatical categories as an instantiation of the No Base Hypothesis (NBH). It denies the existence of categorical universal categories. However, assuming that there is no universal basis underlying the subjunctive misses a number of important generalizations.

First, a clause-type like the subjunctive is pervasive across typologically and geographically unrelated languages (such as, for example, Blackfoot, Halkomelem, and Upper Austrian German, along with the more widely discussed Romance and Balkan languages). So even if the subjunctive defines a non-categorical continuum, there is something universal about this continuum.

---

[1] This classification is based on the typological studies of Roberts (1990), Bugenhagen (1993), Givón (1994), Mithun (1995), Elliott (2000), among others.

[2] See also Bybee *et al.* (1994) and Mithun (1995).

Denying its universal status misses this generalization. In particular, in most cases the subjunctive is a dependent category that cannot be used in main clauses. And if it is, it receives a modal interpretation (we return to an exception to this in Section 5.4.5). The modal interpretation itself may be seen as a form of dependence on a higher modal operator. Thus, we may conclude that the subjunctive is always embedded, either by a higher predicate or by a higher functional head or operator.

Second, as already discussed above, what unifies most (if not all) of the contexts in which the subjunctive appears is the fact that no assertion can be made, either because the state of affairs does not hold or because it is presupposed (Bybee *et al.*, 1994: 236). Thus, it may be understood as a type of clause that contrasts with the independent clause-type used for assertions, i.e., the indicative. As a result, the subjunctive is typically used in exclamatives, desideratives, optatives, hypotheticals, counterfactuals, and imperatives. Again, if there were nothing universal about the subjunctive, this would be an unexpected coincidence.

Third, at least in tensed languages, the substantive content that defines the indicative (i.e., tense) is either absent or defective in the subjunctive. This is true for Romance and Balkan languages, but also for Japanese (Uchibori 2000). The absence or defectiveness of tense unites the subjunctive with other types of clauses, such as the infinitive and the imperative. As shown in (16) for English, in an indicative matrix clause the verb is inflected for tense (16a); this contrasts with infinitive (16b) and imperative (16c) clauses where the verb is used in its bare, untensed form.

(16)   a. *I left.*   INDICATIVE

        b. *I wanted to leave.*   INFINITIVE

        c. *Leave!*   IMPERATIVE

Interestingly, not all languages have infinitives or dedicated imperatives however and often these clause-types are realized in the subjunctive. This suggests that the absence or defectiveness of tense marking is not a coincidence. But if we conclude that there is no universal base, we miss this generalization.

Finally, another property often found in subjunctives across unrelated languages has to do with the fact that it appears to be associated with the area in the clause where grammatical roles are introduced, as opposed to the area where thematic roles are introduced. This conclusion is in turn consistent with the interpretive contrasts it may introduce. While we have seen that the subjunctive is not easily defined in terms of its content, it is nevertheless the case that all of the semantic features proposed to be associated with it have in common that they denote a propositional-level modality (Bybee and Fleischman 1995; Nordström 2010). This is consistent with the assumption that the indicative/subjunctive distinction is a phenomenon associated with the anchoring domain. In the next section I shall argue that this is indeed what is universal about the subjunctive: it is a manifestation of κ: *anchoring*.

5.4   The Universal Spine Hypothesis

The core claim which defines the Universal Spine Hypothesis (USH) is the assumption that grammatical categories are not intrinsically associated with substantive content, i.e., content which is interpreted with reference to the extra-linguistic context (such as present or past tense, for example). In Chapter 4, we saw evidence for this based on language variation. Ritter and Wiltschko (forthcoming) have shown that the same category of the spine (κ) may be associated with different substantive content (Σ), deriving different language-specific categories (c). This conclusion is supported by distributional evidence. All of the categories investigated occupy the same relative position: above the thematic domain and below the linking domain. The conclusion that they occupy the same absolute position in a universal spine is supported by the fact that all of these categories are associated with the same core syntactic function, namely *anchoring*, which is defined as relating the reported event to the utterance. The empirical ground leading to this conclusion was exclusively based on independent (matrix) clauses, however. It thus remains to be seen if and how anchoring is established in dependent contexts, i.e., contexts where the category κ:*anchoring* is embedded in a larger structure, either via predicate complementation or via function-complementation as in (17), repeated from (2) above.

(17)   a. *pred-complementation:*   [predicate [κ:*anchoring*. . .]]

       b. *f-complementation:*   [f-head [κ:*anchoring*. . .]]

It turns out that such contexts are often tenseless, even in languages that are otherwise tensed. Ritter and Wiltschko (forthcoming) interpret the tenselessness of such embedded contexts as further evidence for the claim that functional categories are not to be identified by their substantive content. In particular, just as tenseless languages still display evidence for the presence of the area in the spine that introduces grammatical relations, so do tenseless clauses. In Section 5.4.1, I introduce and adopt the formal analysis for dependent anchoring developed in Ritter and Wiltschko (forthcoming) for infinitives, imperatives, and counterfactuals. In Section 5.4.2, I extend this analysis to develop a formal typology for the subjunctive. In particular, I shall argue that the subjunctive (in most languages) may be understood as a manifestation of κ:*anchoring*. It differs crucially from language-specific categories manifesting κ:*anchoring* in independent clauses in that it lacks substantive content.[3] Thus, it supports the view that function and content are dissociated. The subjunctive is a grammatical category which is associated with a grammatical function (anchoring), but not with substantive content. From this perspective, it is not surprising that meaning-based definitions have failed. The formal typology I develop here allows us to come to terms with the puzzling properties of the subjunctive. Within and across languages, it is not defined based on substantive content and it does not pattern as a natural class. Its universal properties are purely formal: it realizes a particular syntactically defined configuration, namely embedded κ:*anchoring*. At the same time we can understand why the subjunctive may give the impression that it is definable in terms of its meaning. It is a clause-type that contrasts with independent clauses, which in turn are used for assertions. Thus it appears that subjunctive clauses are definable as being non-assertive or irrealis.

5.4.1   *Formalizing dependent anchoring*

In Chapter 4, Section 4.5, I introduced and adopted the formal implementation of anchoring developed in Ritter and Wiltschko (forthcoming). In particular, κ: *anchoring* (commonly known as INFL) is assumed to be intrinsically (i.e., via UG) associated with an unvalued coincidence feature [*u*coin] which establishes a relation between two abstract situation arguments: the event situation in vP and the utterance situation associated with the specifier of κ:*anchoring*. The unvalued coincidence feature must be valued for the derivation to converge. As we have seen, in independent clauses [*u*coin] is valued by the substantive content of the UoL that associates with κ:*anchoring*, i.e., via *m-valuation*. In the languages under consideration, the relevant substantive

---

[3] The Upper Austrian subjunctive is an exception to this generalization. While it still manifests κ:*anchoring*, it does not remain without substantive content (see Section 4.4.3).

content is tense-based, location-based, person-based, or realis-based. This derives a number of distinct language-specific categories, which are all reducible to a common universal core, namely κ:*anchoring*. The gist of this analysis is schematized in (18).

(18)   Constructing anchoring categories in independent clauses

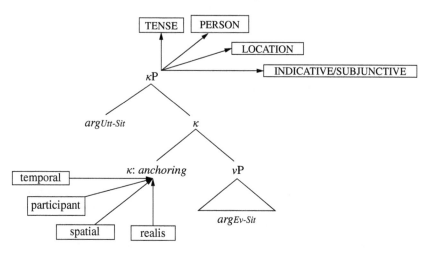

This formalization captures the universal properties of independent clauses as well as the variation in content we observe. However, it cannot immediately derive the properties of all clause-types. Consider for example English embedded infinitives, as in (19).

(19)   *I wanna be loved by you.*

Bert Kalmar

From the present perspective, there are two properties of this sentence that we need to pay attention to. First, there is no tense morphology. And second, the event of *being loved* is not directly related to the utterance. Rather, it is ordered relative to the matrix event of *wanting*. In particular, if the event of *being loved by you* occurs at all, it must occur after the *wanting* event. For this reason this type of infinitive is sometimes referred to as a *future irrealis infinitive;*[4] *future* because the embedded event will take place in the future relative to the matrix predicate and *irrealis* because it may never take place. But in light of tenseless embedded constructions, the universal structure of

---

[4] The term *future* is not intended to invoke the presence of grammatical *tense*. As such the term *anterior* may be more appropriate.

κ:anchoring introduced in Section 4.5, repeated below as (20), faces the two problems in (i) and (ii).

(20)   Formalizing anchoring

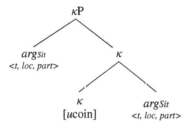

(i)   In the absence of tense marking, what serves to value [*u*coin]?
(ii) Why is the embedded event ordered relative to the matrix event and not relative to the utterance?

For completeness, note that the tenselessness of this construction does not result from the absence of an entire layer of structure. Specifically, there is evidence that the area of the spine where grammatical relations are introduced is present in (at least some) infinitives (Wurmbrand 2001; Landau 2004). To see this, consider again (19) where the embedded predicate is passivized. Passivization is only possible in the presence of the layer where grammatical relations are introduced. Even though – for reasons of abstract case – the grammatical subject cannot be spelled out in this context, it is still interpreted. This is represented in the form of PRO, as in (21).

(21)   *I wanna* PRO *be loved by you.*

In this context, the matrix subject controls the interpretation of the embedded subject: PRO must be interpreted as being co-referent with the matrix subject. Crucially, in this case, the matrix subject is co-referent with the embedded theme, which, via passivization, becomes the embedded subject.

But if *κ:anchoring* is indeed present, the questions in (i) and (ii) above become rather pressing. The answer Ritter and Wiltschko (forthcoming) develop is as follows: [*u*coin] may not only be valued by the substantive content of the morphological marking that associates with *κ:anchoring* directly. It may also be valued by the substantive content associated with the head of the embedding structure. In the context of pred-complementation, this is the higher predicate; in the context of f-complementation, this is the higher functional head. Thus in infinitives, the embedding predicate serves to value [*u*coin], depending on its substantive content. Ritter and Wiltschko (forthcoming) refer to this as *pred(icate)-valuation*. As for the question of how the embedded event is ordered relative to the matrix predicate, Ritter and Wiltschko (forthcoming) propose that the abstract argument associated with the anchoring category is pronominal in nature, as in (22).

(22)   Formalizing dependent anchoring

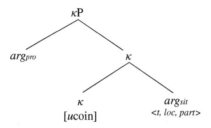

In the absence of an appropriate antecedent, i.e., in independent clauses, this pronominal situation argument is by default interpreted deictically, resulting in deictic anchoring (as discussed in Chapter 4). However, if an antecedent for this pronominal situation argument is available, it will be interpreted as being co-referent with that antecedent. The relevant antecedent is the event argument associated with the embedding verb, i.e., the matrix event. Thus, the embedded event is first ordered relative to the pronominal situation argument in the specifier of κ:*anchoring*, which is in turn co-referent with the next higher argument, i.e., the matrix event situation. This is schematized in (23).

(23)   predicate valuation

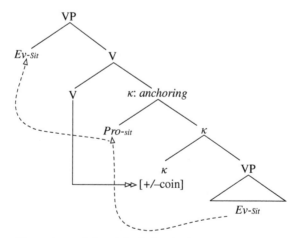

The specific value of [*u*coin] derived via pred-valuation depends on the substantive content of the valuing verb. In particular, two types of infinitives are correctly predicted to exist: those where [$u$coin] is valued as [+coin], and those where it is valued as [−coin]. Future-oriented predicates such as *want* derive the [−coin] value, thereby asserting that the embedded event does not coincide with the matrix event. In contrast, aspectual verbs such as *start* derive the [+coin] value, thereby asserting that the embedded event coincides with the matrix event. The difference between the two types of predicates is illustrated by the examples in (24). The possibility for two temporal adverbs – one modifying the matrix VP, the other modifying the embedded VP, is restricted to future irrealis infinitives (24a), but excluded in simultaneous infinitives (24b). This supports the claim that simultaneous infinitives assert that the two events coincide and therefore they cannot be taking place at two different times.

(24)   a. *Yesterday, Yoshi wanted to play (tomorrow).*
        b. *Yesterday, Yoshi started to play (*tomorrow).*

Inasmuch as this analysis of infinitives is successful, it provides further support for the claim that functional categories are not intrinsically associated with substantive content. If the anchoring category were indeed universally defined by its substantive content (e.g., tense), then the tenselessness of this construction would be unexpected. It does, however, follow from the claim that substantive content is associated with functional categories on a language-specific basis.

   There are two other tenseless constructions Ritter and Wiltschko (forthcoming) analyze within this framework: imperatives (25a) and counterfactuals (25b).

(25)   a. *Catch the ball!*
        b. *If he had caught the ball, he would have run off.*

These are clauses that are embedded via f-complementation: κ:*anchoring* is dominated by higher structure known as CP, and here conceptualized as κ: *linking*, to reflect its function of linking the clause to a higher structure or the discourse. As with m-valuation and pred-valuation, Ritter and Wiltschko (forthcoming) argue that it is the substantive content associated with the higher head which values [$u$coin]. I refer to this as *f-valuation*.[5] Specifically, the directive force of imperatives values it as [+coin], whereas counterfactuality values it as [−coin]. In the case of f-valuation, the pronominal argument associated with the anchoring category is anaphoric to the abstract argument associated with the higher structure. For imperatives, this argument is the *plan set* (in the sense of Han [2000, 2001]) or the *to-do list* (in the sense of Portner

---

[5] Ritter and Wiltschko (forthcoming) use the label C-valuation.

[2004]). Thus, the imperative functions as an instruction to the addressee to make the event situation coincide with the plan set, as illustrated in (26).

(26)   F-valuation in imperatives

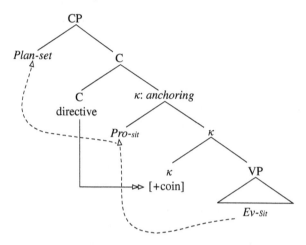

In counterfactual conditionals, the relevant argument in SpecCP is the evaluation situation (Mezhevich 2008: also Zagona 2003). Thus, counterfactuals assert that the event situation does not coincide with the evaluation situation and is therefore not real. This is schematized in (27).

(27)   F-valuation in counterfactuals

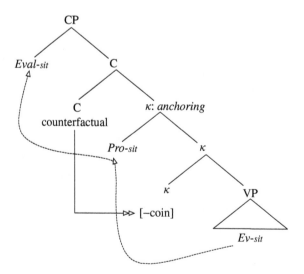

The tenselessness of counterfactuals in English presents itself with an interesting twist. As is evident from the example in (25), tense morphology is present, but it lacks temporal force. This can be seen in the examples in (28). The temporal adverbial of present tense (*now*) is compatible with past morphology in the context of counterfactuals (28a), but it is incompatible with past morphology in an independent clause where tense marking has temporal force (28b).

(28)   a. *If I had a car right now I would drive.*
        b. *I had a car (*right now).*

The absence of temporal force in tense morphology is a pervasive phenomenon and is often referred to as *fake past* (Steele 1975; James 1982; Iatridou 2000). In Ritter and Wiltschko's (forthcoming) approach, fake past results from the use of tense marking in contexts where it does not serve to value [*u*coin], but instead something else does (namely the higher head). Thus, tense morphology itself cannot be equated with the grammatical category tense. Instead, *c*:TENSE is composed from *κ*:*anchoring* and the UoL that serves to value it. The interpretation of tense morphology is mediated by the syntactic spine. Thus, on the assumption that the relation between a UoL and its interpretation is mediated by *κ*, such patterns of fakeness are expected: they are exactly the type of mismatches we expect when postulating mediating structure.

To sum up, Ritter and Wiltschko (forthcoming) develop a typology that seeks to account for the differences between anchoring in dependent clauses and anchoring in independent clauses. There are two key ingredients. First, the anchoring category hosts an intrinsically anaphoric abstract situation argument (*pro-sit*) that is specific to *κ*:*anchoring*. It allows for deictic anchoring in the absence of an available antecedent, as well as anaphoric anchoring to the next available argument. The second key ingredient is the unvalued coincidence feature universally associated with all categories along the spine. In Chapter 4, we saw that this feature may be valued by the substantive content of the morphological marking associated with *κ*:*anchoring* (i.e., m-valuation). This framework allows us to understand the morpho-syntactic characteristics of superficially tenseless languages; while they lack *c*:TENSE, they still have evidence for the structural layer occupied by *c*:TENSE in, e.g., English. Instead, morphological marking with different substantive content may value [*u*coin] in such languages. But morphological marking that serves to m-value *κ*:*anchoring* is not present across all clause-types. For example, in languages where *κ*:*anchoring* is tense-based in independent clauses, a variety of clause-types still remain tenseless. This includes infinitives, imperatives, and counterfactuals. In such contexts [*u*coin] is valued by the substantive content associated with the next available head: the matrix predicate in the case of infinitives (pred-valuation) or a higher functor in the case of imperatives and counterfactuals (f-valuation). This derives the typology for English clause-types summarized in (29).

(29)   Valuation typology: English

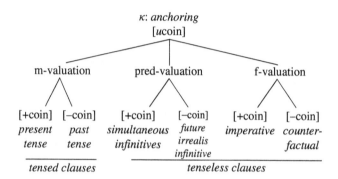

The core of Ritter and Wiltschko's (forthcoming) article is dedicated to testing one of the predictions of this typology. In particular, the substantive content of morphological marking does not play a role across all clause-types. Consequently, the differences between tense-, location-, and participant-based *κ: anchoring* are predicted to disappear in contexts of pred- and f-valuation. They show that this prediction is indeed borne out. Thus, in contexts of pred- and f-complementation the universal properties of *κ:anchoring* emerge.

In what follows I use and extend the valuation typology in (29) to develop a formal typology for subjunctives. In particular, I discuss four unrelated languages: Cypriot Greek (a tense-based language) as well as Halkomelem, Blackfoot, and Upper Austrian German, all three tenseless. I show that the valuation typology in (29) allows for a novel way to analyze subjunctives. In particular, subjunctives are language-specific categories (*c*) that are constructed out of *κ:anchoring* and a Unit of Language (UoL).

(30)   *c*:SUBJUNCTIVE = *κ:anchoring* + UoL

The UoLs that define clause-types that are typically classified as subjunctive are (in most instances) not associated with substantive content (Σ), but instead they realize a particular instantiation of the coincidence feature. This includes the unvalued coincidence feature [*u*coin] (in Cypriot Greek), as well as the [−coin] feature derived via f-valuation (Halkomelem and Blackfoot). In addition, I show that Blackfoot has a second clause-type which may be classified as a subjunctive, and which is constructed by modifying the independent clause-type as an unreal. As for the Upper Austrian German subjunctive, I have argued in Chapter 4 that the UoL that serves to construct it is in fact defined by its substantive content (a form of *irrealis*) deriving [−coin] via m-valuation. While these subjunctives are all constructed in different ways, they share in common that they all manifest κ:*anchoring* and that they contrast with the independent clause-type used for assertions.

5.4.2   Cypriot Greek subjunctive marks [ucoin]

In this subsection, I discuss the subjunctive of Cypriot Greek. It has many of the typical subjunctive properties that have been widely discussed in the literature.[6]

In terms of its form, Cypriot Greek subjunctive marking is characterized by the use of an invariant particle *na* in clause-initial position. This particle has been independently argued to associate with INFL (our κ:*anchoring*) (see Philippaki-Warburton and Veloudis 1984; Philippaki-Warburton 1987; Malagardi 1994; Rivero 1994; Kyriakaki (2006).[7]

In terms of its syntactic distribution I show that the Cypriot Greek subjunctive falls squarely into the prototypical use identified in (15). In terms of the valuation typology in (29), the contexts are precisely those that are realized as tenseless constructions in English, i.e., contexts of pred- and f-valuation, as schematized in (31).

(31)   Contexts of subjunctive marking in Cypriot Greek

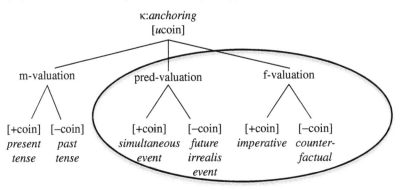

---

[6] This discussion is based on Christodoulou and Wiltschko (2012).

[7] The assumption that *na* is associated with INFL is not uncontroversial, however. In particular, Agouraki (1991), Dobrovie-Sorin (1994), and Tsoulas (1995) argue that it occupies C. For our purpose here, we simply assume that *na* is associated with INFL. We note that the empirical evidence suggesting *na*'s association with C may be reconciled with our view, if we assume that I moves to C (see Pesetsky and Torrego 2001).

First, *na* is used in the context of pred-valuation. Aspectual verbs, such as *arxis-* ('start') (32a) and *katafer-* ('manage') (32b) embed complement clauses introduced by *na*.

(32)   a. *O*   *Kostas*   *arxis-e* ...
         DET   Costas   start.PERF-PST.3.SG ...
         ... *na*   *pez-I*   *kithara.*
         ... SUBJ   play.IMPF-PRES.3.SG   guitar
         'Costa has started playing the guitar.'

       b. *Katafer -a* ...
         manage.PERF-PST.1.SG ...
         ... *na*   *parados-o*   *ti*   *diatrivi*   *mu.*
         ... SUBJ   submit.PERF-DEP.1.SG   DET   dissertation   1SG.GEN
         'I managed to submit my dissertation.'
                                       Christodoulou and Wiltschko 2012: 128 (17)

These *na* clauses are interpreted like simultaneous infinitives in English; the embedded event is interpreted as occurring simultaneously with the matrix event, consistent with the analysis according to which the matrix predicate values [*u*coin] in *κ:anchoring* as [+coin].

Second, future-oriented verbs like *thel-* also embed complement clauses introduced by *na*, as in (33).

(33)   a. *thel-is* ...
         want.IMPF-PRES.2.SG ...
         ... *na par-ume*   *liga*   *frut -a?*
         ... SUBJ take.PERF-DEP.1.PL   little   fruit-NEUT.PL.ACC
         'Would you like us to get some fruit?'

       b. *i-thel-a* ...
         PAST-want.IMPF-PST.1.SG
         ... *na*   *pernus-ame*   *ap'*   *ti*   *vivliothiki.*
         ... SUBJ   pass.IMPF-PST.1.PL   from   DET   library
         'I wanted us to pass by the library.'
                                       Christodoulou and Wiltschko 2012: 128 (18)

The *na* clauses in (33) are interpreted just like future irrealis infinitives in English; the embedded event is interpreted as being non-coincidental with the matrix predicate. It necessarily follows the matrix event, consistent with the analysis according to which the matrix predicate values *κ:anchoring* as [−coin].

Third, *na* may be used in the context of f-valuation. Both imperatives (34) and counterfactuals (35) are marked as subjunctive by means of *na*.

(34) **na**   mas   *grap-s-ete.*
     SUBJ   1.PL.GEN   write-PERF-DEP.2.PL
     '(Do) write to us!'

                            Christodoulou and Wiltschko 2012: 128 (19)

(35) *An*   *kerdiz-es*   *to*   *laxio ...*
     if   win.IMPF-PST.2.SG   DET   lottery ...
     ... na   *anakeniz -es*   *to*   *spiti.*
     ... SUBJ   renovate.IMPF-PST.2.SG   DET   house
     'If you had won the lottery, you would have been able to renovate the house.'

                            Christodoulou and Wiltschko 2012: 129 (20)

This establishes that *na* is used in all of those contexts where [*u*coin] is valued from a higher head: via pred-valuation by the embedding verb or via f-valuation by the substantive content associated with C (directive force or counterfactuality). Conversely, *na* cannot be used in the context of m-valuation (i.e., in independent clause-types with present or past marking). This is shown in (36)–(38).

(36) a. *O*   *Petr-os*   *kolimb-ai*   *kaθe proi.*
        DET   Petr-NOM   swim.IMPF-PRES.3.SG   every morning
        'Peter swims every morning.'

     b. *O*   *Petros*   *kolimb-ai*   *tora.*
        DET   Petr-NOM   swim.IMPF-PRES.3.SG   now
        'Peter is swimming right now.'

                            Christodoulou and Wiltschko 2012: 129 (22)

(37) a. *O*   *Petr-os*   *kolimb-use*   *kaθe proi.*
        DET   Petr-NOM   swim.IMPF-PST.3.SG   every morning
        'Peter was swimming/used to swim every morning.'

     b. *O*   *Petr-os*   *kolimb-is-e*   *xθes*   *to*   *proi.*
        DET   Petr-NOM   swim-PERF-PRES.3.SG   yesterday DET morning
        'Peter swam yesterday morning.'

                            Christodoulou and Wiltschko 2012: 129 (23)

(38) a. *O   *Petr-os*   *na*   *kolimb-ai*   *tora.*[8]
        DET   Petros-NOM   SUBJ   swim.IMPF-PRES.3.SG   now

---

[8] The example in (38) is grammatical when the main focus of the utterance falls on the subject *o Petr-os*. However, in this case the sentence receives a modal interpretation, such that 'Petros should (be the one to) swim now,' or an imperative reading where Petros is indirectly instructed to swim. Therefore, we can analyze these cases as involving a modal force which values [*u*coin].

b. */??O   Petr-os   na   kolimb-is-i   tora.
   DET   Petros-NOM   SUBJ   swim-PERF-DEP.3.SG   now
   'Peter should swim right now.'

Christiana Christodoulou (p. c.)

Note that the contexts of subjunctive marking in Cypriot Greek do not form a natural class in terms of traditional grammatical categories. They are, however, straightforward to define within the valuation typology. Specifically, *na*-marked clauses manifest κ:*anchoring* unless it is derived via m-valuation. This distribution can be understood if we analyze the UoL that derives c:SUBJUNCTIVE as spelling out a syntactic constellation, rather than a particular meaning (Σ). This accounts for the absence of a unified meaning associated with the subjunctive, even within a given language. Specifically, Christodoulou and Wiltschko (2012) propose that *na* spells out [$u$coin]. Thus, c:SUBJUNCTIVE in Cypriot Greek is constructed as in (39).

(39) c:SUBJUNCTIVE = κ:*anchoring* + UoL: $<\pi$:*na* [κ:*anchoring*, $u$coin]$>$

Since *na* realizes [$u$coin], it follows that *na* must be associated with κ: *anchoring* early, indicated by its initial position in the ordered pair in (39). This is because otherwise an unvalued feature would be present in the interpretive component (see Section 5.5).

    In this way, the characteristic properties of Cypriot Greek subjunctive are derived. First, none of the ingredients of the c:SUBJUNCTIVE are defined by their substantive content. κ:*anchoring* is part of the universal spine, and is itself defined by the presence of an abstract anaphoric argument as well as an unvalued coincidence feature [$u$coin]. This derives the anchoring function that we have observed with independent clauses (in the form of deictic anchoring), and also with dependent clauses (in the form of anaphoric anchoring). In the latter, the event situation is not ordered relative to the utterance situation but instead to either a higher event situation (in the case of pred-valuation) or else an abstract argument introduced in the discourse domain. This may be the plan set in imperatives or the evaluation world in counterfactuals.

    Second, the assumption that *na* realizes [$u$coin] derives its obligatory dependency. Since [$u$coin] must be valued as per UG, realizing [$u$coin] signals that valuation has yet to take place, namely in the form of either pred- or f-valuation. Thus, the dependent character of *na* is not directly

Table 5.1 *Halkomelem agreement paradigm*

	Independent	Subjunctive	Ergative
1SG	*tsel*	*-l*	–
2SG	*chexw*	*-xw*	–
3SG	–	*-s*	*-es*
1PL	*tset*	*-t*	–
2PL	*chap*	*-p*	–
3PL	–	*-s*	*-es*

Source: Galloway (1993).

encoded in its lexical entry, but rather it is a matter of UG: unvalued features must be licensed.

5.4.3   Halkomelem subjunctive is derived via f-valuation

We now turn to the subjunctive in Halkomelem, a tenseless language. In terms of form, it is realized as a special form of agreement, which contrasts with the agreement found in independent clauses on the one hand and so-called ergative agreement on the other. This is summarized in Table 5.1. Specifically, subjunctive agreement is a truncated form of independent agreement, except in the 3rd person where independent agreement is not overtly realized. Conversely, ergative agreement is restricted to 3rd person.

In terms of its place of association, there is evidence that subjunctive agreement associates with κ:*anchoring*. This may be gleaned from the fact that it interacts with the subject role. In this respect, subjunctive agreement contrasts with ergative agreement, which cross-references the thematic subject (i.e., the agent). In Wiltschko (2006b, 2006c; see also Elouazizi and Wiltschko 2006), I argue that, while ergative agreement associates with *v* (the locus of transitivity), subjunctive agreement associates with INFL. As a consequence, the former is restricted to transitive verbs (40), and the latter is used irrespective of the verb's transitivity (41). Moreover, ergative agreement always attaches to the verb irrespective of the presence of an auxiliary (42), whereas subjunctive agreement attaches to verbs only in the absence of an auxiliary (43).

(40)   a. *q'ó:y-t-es*   *te*   *Strang*   *te*   *qwá:l.*
         kill- TR-3ERG   DET   Strang   DET   mosquito
         'Strang killed the mosquito.'

b. *í:mex   te   Strang.*
walking   DET   Strang
'Strang is walking.'

Wiltschko 2006b: 242 (1)

(41)   a. *éwe   lí-s   í:mex.*
NEG   AUX-3S   walking
'He is not walking.'

b. *éwe   lí-s   tl'ils-th-óx-es.*
NEG   AUX-3S   want-TR-1SG.O-3ERG
'He doesn't like me.'

Galloway 1993: 186

(42)   a. *i-lh   q'ó:y-t-es   te   Strang   te   qwá:l.*
AUX-PST   kill-TR-3ERG   DET   Strang   DET   mosquito
'Strang killed the mosquito.'

Elouazizi and Wiltschko 2006: 155 (27b)

b. * *li-lh-es   q'ó:y-t te   Strang   te   qwá:l.*
AUX-3ERG   kill-TR DET   Strang   DET   mosquito
'Strang killed the mosquito.'

(43)   a. *éwe   í:mex-es.*
NEG   walking-3ERG
'He is not walking.'

b. *éwe   tl'ils-th-óx-es.*
NEG   want-TR-1SG.OBJ-3ERG
'He doesn't like me.'

Galloway 1993: 186

The patterns of subjunctive agreement are consistent with the claim that *c:* SUBJUNCTIVE is constructed from κ:*anchoring*, the area where grammatical relations are introduced.

In terms of its distribution, Halkomelem subjunctive marking is more restricted than its counterpart in Cypriot Greek. In particular, it is used in the context of negation as well as conditionals (both realis and irrealis conditionals). In terms of the valuation typology, this means that it is restricted to contexts of f-valuation that derives [−coin] (henceforth [f-val:−coin]) as schematized in (44). Specifically, both the conditional complementizer *we* as well as the negative marker *éwe* value [*u*coin].

(44)　　Valuation typology: Halkomelem

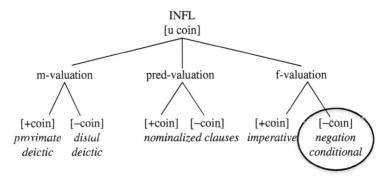

Examples of subjunctive marking in the context of negation have already been given in (41) and (43) above. An example of subjunctive marking in the context of conditionals is given in (45), repeated from Chapter 4 (Section 4.4.2).

(45)　x̲élh　　cha　　te-l　　　sqwálewel . . .
　　　sad　　FUT　　DET-1SG.POSS　thought . . .
　　　. . .we　lí-s　　lhémexw.
　　　. . .COMP AUX-3S rain
　　　'I'll be sad (lit.: 'My thoughts will be sad') if it rains.'

Wiltschko 2006b: 291 (8b)

These are common contexts where clause-types are classified as subjunctives cross-linguistically. In terms of our analysis, it suggests that both derive a [−coin] value in *κ:anchoring*. Note that the fact that subjunctive is used in the context of negation implies that both the conditional complementizer *we* and the negative marker *éwe* are associated with the spine in a position higher than *κ:anchoring*. For the conditional complementizer, this is uncontroversial, since complementizers are typically associated with the C-domain. As for negation, on independent grounds Wiltschko (2002a) argues that negation in Halkomelem associates with C; this is compatible with the claim that it may f-value [*u*coin] in *κ:anchoring*.[9] That both the conditional complementizer and the negative marker are associated with the head above *κ:anchoring* receives independent support from the fact that they appear to be transparently related to each other (*éwe* vs. *we*).

---

[9] But see Davis (2005) for arguments that negation is a predicate. If so, this would imply that subjunctive agreement under negation realizes a context of pred-valuation.

Note that compared to Cypriot Greek, the grammatical landscape for subjunctive marking is much more restricted in Halkomelem. The subjunctive is not used in imperatives, nor in clauses embedded under verbal predicates. Instead, imperatives are either marked with a dedicated imperative marker -*lha* (46a), or with the independent subject clitic (46b).

(46)   a. *omet = lha.*
            sit.down = IMP
            '(You) sit down.'

Galloway 1993: 310

        b. *xó:lh-met-thet = chexw.*
            look.after-TR-REFL = 2SG.SUBJ
            '(You) take care of yourself.'

Galloway 1993: 311

This means that Halkomelem subjunctive marking does not realize [f-val:+coin].

Furthermore, the subjunctive is also not found in clauses embedded under verbal predicates. Instead, in such contexts embedded clauses are always nominalized (Galloway 1993; Thompson 2012). Relevant examples are given in (47) below.

(47)   a. *tsel   t'át-et   kw'-el-s   xwemxál-ém*
            1SG.S   try-3OBJ   COMP-1SG.POSS-NMLZ   run-MID
            'I tried to run.'

Thompson 2012: 158 (24)

        b. *tsel   iyó:-thet   kw'-el-s   xwemxál-ém*
            1SG.S   start-REFL   COMP-1SG.POSS-NMLZ   run-MID
            'I started to run.'

Thompson 2012: 159 (25)

This suggests that Halkomelem subjunctive marking does not realize contexts of pred-valuation. Thus, the Halkomelem subjunctive is constructed as in (48).

(48)   *c*:SUBJUNCTIVE = *κ*:*anchoring* + UoL: [f-val:-coin]

This constellation is realized in the form of subjunctive agreement, which simultaneously realizes person features. Thus the paradigm of UoLs that defines subjunctive marking in Halkomelem is summarized in (49). Note that, because the form realizes a syntactic configuration, derived by f-valuation, this must be a late association UoL, indicated by the fact that π is the second

Table 5.2 *Blackfoot subjunctive marking*

Subject	Subjunctive		
	VAI	VTA	VTI
1	... *iniki*	*-iniki*	... *mminn*
2	... *iniki*	*-iniki*	... *mminn*
21 = x	... *o'*	*-'ki/hki*	... *'ki/hki*
3	... *si*	*-si*	... *si*

member in the ordered pair. Note that I here analyze the person features as modificational, hence the curly brackets.

(49)   a. $<\{[\kappa\text{:}anchoring, \text{f-val:}-\text{coin}], 1\text{SG}\}\ \pi\text{:-}l>$
       b. $<\{[\kappa\text{:}anchoring, \text{f-val:}-\text{coin}], 1\text{PL}\},\ \pi\text{:-}t>$
       c. $<\{[\kappa\text{:}anchoring, \text{f-val:}-\text{coin}], 2\text{SG}\},\ \pi\text{:-}xw>$
       d. $<\{[\kappa\text{:}anchoring, \text{f-val:}-\text{coin}], 2\text{PL}\},\ \pi\text{:-}p>$
       e. $<\{[\kappa\text{:}anchoring, \text{f-val:}-\text{coin}], 3\text{rd}\},\ \pi\text{:-}s>$

5.4.4   *Blackfoot subjunctive is derived via f-valuation*

We now turn to Blackfoot, which has a clause-type classified as subjunctive in the reference grammar (Frantz 1991, 2009). In terms of form, it is realized by means of a suffix that varies according to verb class and participant, as shown in Table 5.2.

Its place of association has been independently argued to be INFL (i.e., κ: *anchoring*) in Déchaine and Wiltschko (2012; see also Bliss [2013] and Ritter and Wiltschko [forthcoming]). Evidence for this place of association comes from the fact that it is sensitive to verbal classification (associated with the domain below κ:*anchoring*) as well as to the person of the subject (see Table 5.2) (associated with SpecIP).

In terms of its distribution, Blackfoot subjunctive is even more restricted than its Halkomelem counterpart. In particular, it is used in the context of present time and future-oriented conditionals (usually with the prefix *ikkam-* 'if') as well as future-oriented or generic "when" clauses.[10]

---

[10] While not listed in Galloway (1993), Thompson (2012) also found generic temporal clauses in Halkomelem.

    i) *cəl*   *xex-els [lhi = l*   *la*   *elhtel].*
        1SG.S write-ACT [when = 1SG.S AUX   eat]
        'I write when I go and eat.'
                               Thompson 2012: 46 (47)

(50)   *Ikkamáyo'kainoainiki,*   *nitáakahkayi.*
       ikkam-á-yo'kaa-inoa-**iniki**   nit-yáak-wa:hkayi
       if-IMPF-sleep.AI-2PL-SUBJ   1-FUT-go.home.AI
       'If you are sleeping, I'll go home.'

Frantz 1991: 113 (l)

(51)   a. *Áótooyiniki*   *áakitsoyo'pa.*
          a'-o'too-iniki   yáák-it-Ioyi-o'pa
          INCH-arrive.AI-LOC.SUBJ   FUT-then-eat.AI-INCL
          'When you/I arrive, then we'll eat.'

       b. *Aisóótaasi,*   *áakitsipiuimmiaawa.*
          a'-sootaa-si   yáak-it-IpiiM:-yi-aawa
          INCH-rain.II-INAN.SG.SUBJ FUT-then-enter.AI-3PL-PRN
          'When it rains, they will go in.'

       c. *Kanáísootaasi,*   *itáípiimma.*
          kana-á-isootaa-si   it-á-IpiiM:-wa
          all-IMPF-rain.II-3SG.SUBJ then-IMPF-enter.AI-PROX
          'Whenever it rains, he goes in.'

adapted from Frantz 1991: 113 (o–q)

The distribution of subjunctive clause-types in Blackfoot suggests that, like in Halkomelem, it manifests an instance of [−coin] derived via f-valuation. If so, the Blackfoot subjunctive is constructed as in (52).

(52) c:SUBJUNCTIVE $= \kappa$:*anchoring* $+$ UoL: [f-val:−coin]

Subjunctive marking in Blackfoot enters into a relation of complementary κ-contrast with three other clause-types known as *orders* in the Algonquianist tradition: independent, conjunct, and imperative (Frantz 1991, 2009). Furthermore, orders may be subdivided into *modes*. In Blackfoot, this is only true for the independent, which comes in two guises, the unmarked and the *unreal*. This is illustrated in Figure 5.1 (repeated from Figure 4.2 above) and the morpho-syntactic marking associate with this classification is summarized in Table 5.3.

How does this system of clause-typing map onto the universal spine? Assuming that κ-contrast diagnoses UoLs that associate to the same position on the spine, we may conclude that all four orders substantiate κ:*anchoring* (Déchaine and Wiltschko 2012). In particular, I propose the following analysis. First, the independent order was analyzed in Chapter 4 as an instance of m-valuation: local participant marking gives a positive value to [$u$coin] (53a); non-local participant marking gives it a negative value (53b).

Table 5.3 *Clause-type paradigms*

Order					
	Independent				
	Independent	Unreal	Conjunctive	Subjunctive	Imperative
MARKING	**{...*hp*, ...Ø}**	**...*htopi***	**...*hs***	**...*iniki***	**...*t***
PROCLITIC AGR	✓	✓	✓	✗	✗

Source: adapted from Déchaine and Wiltschko (2012).

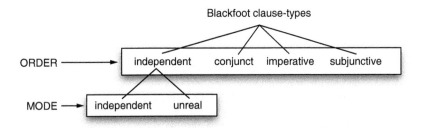

Figure 5.1 *Blackfoot clause-types (adapted from Frantz 2009)*

(53)   a. *c*:INDEP (LOCAL) = *κ:anchoring* + UoL: $<\pi$:-*hp*, [m-val: +coin]$>$
        b. *c*:INDEP (NON-LOCAL) = *κ:anchoring* + UoL:$<\pi$:-*m*/Ø[m-val: −coin]$>$

As for conjunct order, it serves as the elsewhere category (similar to the subjunctive in Cypriot Greek). It marks [*u*coin] by means of the suffix -*hsi*, as in (54).[11] By marking [*u*coin], it encodes a dependency because it signals that *κ:anchoring* has yet to be valued. It is the clause-type defining most embedded clauses such as complements embedded under future-oriented verbs (55) and complements of verbs of thinking or saying (56), as well as various adjunct clauses (57).

(54)   *c:* CONJUNCT = *κ:anchoring* +UoL $<\pi$:-*hsi*,[*u*coin]$>$

---

[11] The conjunct suffix -*hsi* is itself complex consisting of -*hs* and the proximate suffix -*yi* (Frantz 1991, 2009). See Bliss (2013) for a detailed analysis.

(55)   a. *Nitsíksstaa*   *nááhksoy'ssi.*
        nit-iik-sst-aa   n-ááhk-ooyi-hsi
        1-INT-want-AI   1-NON.FACT-eat-CONJ
        'I want to eat.'

                                        adapted from Frantz 1991: 112 (i)

        b. *Nitaanista*   *oomaahkootooyakstsissi.*
        nit-waanist-a   ot-ááhk-go-yáakihtsiiyi-hsi
        1- say.TA-DIR   3-NONFACT-go-go to bed.AI-CONJ
        'I told him to go to bed.'

(56)   a. *Nitsikannistsikssimmsta*   *nitssisstsiikoohsi.*
        nit-iik-annist-ikssimmstaa   nit-sistsikoo-his
        1-INT-MANNER-think.AI   1-tired.AI-CONJ
        'I think I am tired.'

        b. *Anii*   *otaissistsikoohsi.*
        wanii-wa   ot-a-sistsikoo-his
        say.AI-PROX   3-IMPF-tired.AI-CONJ
        'He said he was tired now.'
        ('They were working, and he said he's tired.')

(57)   *Nomohtó'too*   *kááhksspommookssoaayi.*
        n-omoht-o'too   k-ááhk-sspommo-o:k-i-hs-oaa-yi
        1-SOURCE-arrive.AI   2-NONFACT-help.TA-INV-1-CONJ-2PL-CONJ
        'I came for you(pl) to help me.'

                                        adapted from Frantz 1991: 111

The fourth order is the imperative, which, like in English, may be analyzed as instantiating the positive value derived via f-valuation (58). It is marked by the suffix -*t* (59).

(58)   *c*:IMPERATIVE = <κ:*anchoring*>+ UoL: <[f-val:+coin], π:-*t*>

(59)   *Ooyí-t!*
        eat.AI- IMP
        'Eat!'   Frantz 1991: 114, ex (r)

As for mode marking, in Blackfoot it is non-contrastive: the UNREAL mode is a special form of the independent. According to our criteria this suggests that it associates as a modifier. I propose that the UoL that serves to construct *c*: UNREAL (-*htopi*) modifies the independent clause-type. As a modifier, its lexical entry is a simple sound meaning correspondence <π,Σ>, as in (60).

(60)   *c*:UNREAL = [κ:*anchoring*:m-val] + UoL: <π:-*htopi*, Σ:UNREAL>

The resulting valuation typology of Blackfoot clause-types is summarized in (61).[12]

(61)   Valuation typology: Blackfoot

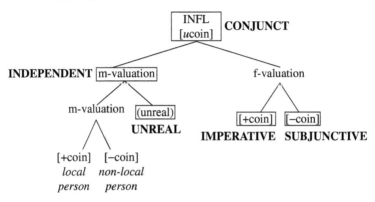

Despite the fact that the Blackfoot subjunctive occupies the same space in the valuation typology as the Halkomelem subjunctive, it does not have the same distribution. Most notably, it is not triggered by negation, and it is not used in counterfactual conditionals.[13] This difference between the two languages reduces to independent factors. Consider first negation. Blackfoot has two negative markers: *maat-* and *sa-*. *maat-* is restricted to independent clauses (62a). As such it cannot co-occur with the subjunctive (62b). The other negative marker *sa-* is compatible with subjunctive (63a), but crucially does not require it (63b).[14] (See Louie [2008] for a more complete discussion of the interaction between negation and clause-type.)

(62)   a. *Nimaatsinowawaatsiks.*
          nit-**maat**-ino-a-wa-atsiks
          1-NEG-see.TA-DIR-PROX-NONAFF
          'I didn't see him/her.'

                                                                  Louie 2008: 1 (2a)

---

[12] Blackfoot lacks clauses derived via pred-valuation (Ritter and Wiltschko forthcoming). Whether there is a principled reason for this gap or whether it is purely coincidental is unclear at this point.

[13] See Louie (forthcoming) for a detailed discussion of Blackfoot conditionals.

[14] *sa* negation in independent clause-types is restricted to modal contexts (see Louie [2008] for discussion).

b. **Nitaaksayinakoyi*   *kammaatooyiniki.*
nit-áak-sa-inakoyi   kam-**maat**-ooyii-**iniki**
1-FUT-NEG-be.visible.AI   if-NEG-eat.AI-SUBJ.1SG
'I will be invisible if I don't eat.'

Louie 2008: 29 (57b)

(63)   a. *Kikaahkamapsayinowa.*
kit-aahkamap-**sa**-ino-a-wa
2-might-NEG-see.TA-DIR-PROX
'You might not see him.'

Louie 2008: 31 (62a)

b. *Nitaaksayinakoyi*   *kamsooyiniki.*
nit-áak-sa-inakoyi   kam-**sa**-ooyi-**iniki**
1-FUT-NEG-be.visible.AI   if-NEG-eat.AI-SUBJ.1SG
'I will be invisible if I don't eat'.

Louie 2008: 28 (57a)

Since *sa-* negation is associated with the spine in a position lower than *κ:anchoring* it can therefore not be used to value [*u*coin] via f-valuation. And *maat-* negation cannot be used to f-value [*u*coin] because m-valuation via person marking takes place before f-valuation.

Next we turn to counterfactual conditionals. In Blackfoot, counterfactual conditionals are necessarily realized by the unreal mode.

(64)   *Nitsíísaykamo'saata'ohtopi*   *oma*   *apasstaaminaam.*
nit-ii-sa-ikamo'saat-a-**ohtopi**   om-wa   apasstaaminaam-wa
1-IC-NEG-steal.TA-DIR-UNREAL   DEM-PROX   apple-PROX
... *nókowaan*   *áakitomatapohtako.*
... n-okowaan-wa   yáak-it-omatap-ohtako-wa
...1-stomach-PROX   FUT-then-start-sound.AI-PROX
'If I hadn't stolen that apple, my stomach would have started sounding.'

Louie forthcoming

This may be understood as blocking effect. Since there is a more specialized form available to realize counterfactuality, the subjunctive is blocked (see Louie, [forthcoming] for a semantic analysis).

5.4.5   Upper Austrian German subjunctive m-values κ:anchoring

As discussed in Chapter 4, in Upper Austrian German subjunctive marking in the form of *-at* and ablaut associates with *κ:anchoring*. We have seen that – unlike other subjunctives – it is not dependent. Rather, based on several

Table 5.4 *Distribution of independent subjunctives*

	Independent subjunctive (Upper Austrian German)		Dependent subjunctive (Romance, Balkan, Icelandic)	
	Ind	Subj	Ind	Subj
Possible in matrix clause	✓	✓	✓	✗
Independent temporal specification	✓	✓	✓	✗
Allows for long distance reflexives	✗	✗	✗	✓
Triggers obviation effects	✗	✗	✗	✓

diagnostics it patterns with independent clause-types. This is summarized in Table 5.4 repeated from Chapter 4.

The analysis developed in Chapter 4 accounts for this pattern. In particular, I proposed that Upper Austrian German subjunctive marking derives a negative value for [*u*coin] in κ:*anchoring* via m-valuation. Thus, in terms of the valuation typology, the subjunctive occupies a different space than the subjunctives discussed thus far. This is shown in (65).

(65)   Upper Austrian German m-valuation

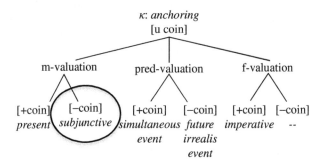

I have further proposed that the substantive content associated with the subjunctive marker in Upper Austrian German can be characterized as irrealis. Thus, the upper Austrian German subjunctive is constructed as in (66).

(66) c:SUBJUNCTIVE $= \kappa$:*anchoring* $+$ UoL $<\{\pi$:-*at*, Σ:IRREALIS$\}$, [m-val: $-$coin]$>$

In terms of its distribution, we have observed that it is used in several of the familiar subjunctive environments, including, for example, conditionals. Thus, to account for its interpretation, the event situation must be ordered relative to the evaluation world as in (67).

(67)   a. "indicative"   b. "subjunctive"

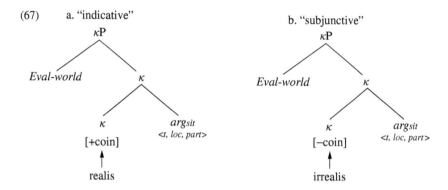

The question we were left with in Chapter 4 was how the argument, relative to which the event situation is ordered, came to be the evaluation world. In particular, in all other contexts of m-valuation in independent clauses, the highest argument was the utterance situation deriving deictic anchoring. As mentioned there, the key to understanding the special property of Upper Austrian German subjunctives is the fact that matrix independent clauses are always embedded within another functional layer. That is, Upper Austrian German, like Standard German is a verb-second language where the verb moves to C (our κ:*linking*) in independent clauses.

As we have seen in this chapter (Section 5.4.1), SpecCP may host a variety of abstract arguments including the evaluation world (or situation). Moreover, according to Ritter and Wiltschko (forthcoming) the argument associated with κ:*anchoring* is not intrinsically deictic. Rather it is intrinsically anaphoric (Pro_{sit}) and only interpreted relative to the utterance in the absence of an antecedent. With these ingredients in place, the interpretation of Upper Austrian German subjunctive can now be explained. As schematized in (68), subjunctive marking derives [−coin] via m-valuation thereby asserting that the event situation does not coincide with the anaphoric situation associated with κ:*anchoring*. The interpretation of this anaphoric argument in turn is dependent on the abstract argument in SpecCP, which corresponds to the evaluation situation.

(68)   Upper Austrian German subjunctive

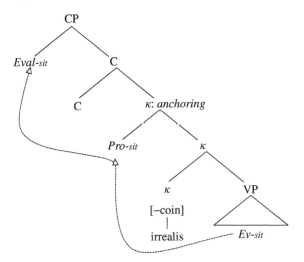

This analysis straightforwardly derives the properties of the independent subjunctive. It is used in typical irrealis/subjunctive contexts like dependent subjunctives. This follows from the substantive content associated with m-valuation (Σ:irrealis). However, it differs from the other subjunctives we have discussed in this chapter in that the valuation of [*u*coin] is not dependent on a higher head. Instead it is an instance of m-valuation.

There is, however, one apparent exception to the claim that the Upper Austrian German subjunctive receives an irrealis interpretation. Consider the examples in (69) and (70). Here the subjunctive is used despite the fact that the event situation does in fact hold in the real world. In (69), Strang is in fact coming and in (70) the weather is in fact beautiful.

(69)   Context: Strang (Martina's husband) is not at home. Sonja and Martina are at Martina and Strang's house talking about whether Strang could help out with some drawings. Martina suddenly hears Strang's footsteps and says to Sonja:

> *Du, da   Strang   kam-**at**   eh   grod ...*
> you, DET   Strang   come.SUBJ-SUBJ   PRT   just.now ...
> *... do   kunnt-st = n   glei frogn.*
> ... PRT   could.SUBJ.2SG = him   PRT   ask
> 'You know, he is coming just now ... so you could ask him.'

(70)   Context: Strang and Martina have been planning to go on a bike tour for a while. But it has been raining for days now. Sunday morning Martina gets up and notices that it's nice out:

Ma schau!			*Heit*	*war-at = s*		*sche ...*	
oh look			today	would-SUBJ-it		beautiful ...	
... do	*kunnt*	*ma jo*	*endlich*	*ral*		*foan*	*geh.*
... PART	could	we PRT	finally	bike		drive	go

'Oh look! It's nice out today. So we could go for a bike ride.'

The contexts in which such subjunctives are well formed have two things in common. On the one hand, the addressee does not know that the event situation holds in the real world. On the other hand, the speaker knows that if the addressee knew that the event were to hold, then they would act on this event. That is, the speaker knows that the addressee has a plan that is conditional on the event situation.

Evidence for the first precondition comes from the fact that if the addressee is obviously aware that the event situation holds in the real world then subjunctive marking is ruled out. This can be gleaned from the fact that the subjunctive is incompatible with the discourse particle *jo* (71). Just as its Standard German counterpart *ja*, this particle indicates that the proposition is taken to be uncontroversial at the time of the utterance (Lindner 1991: 173).

(71) a. *Ea* *komt* **jo** *grod.*
he   come   PRT   just.now
'He is coming just now (as you know).'

b. **Ea* *kam-at* *jo* *grod.*
he   come.SUBJ-SUBJ   PRT   just.now
'He is coming just now.'

Evidence for the second precondition comes from the fact that subjunctive is ungrammatical if it occurs in a sentence that, out of the blue, expresses a surprising proposition.

(72) Context: out of the blue. The possibility of the Pope dying has not been mentioned before and there is no contextually salient event that depends on the Pope having died.

#*Ma stö* *da* *voa, da* *pobst* *war-at* *gstoam.*
Gee, imagine   yourself   PRT   DET   Pope   would-SUBJ   died
'Gee, imagine that. The Pope died.'

A detailed semantic and pragmatic analysis of this unusual subjunctive must await future research. I tentatively suggest that what is responsible for the effect just described is the possibility of relativizing the evaluation world to the addressee's, as in (73). The event situation is asserted to not coincide with the addressee's evaluation world.

(73)   Relativizing the evaluation world to the addressee

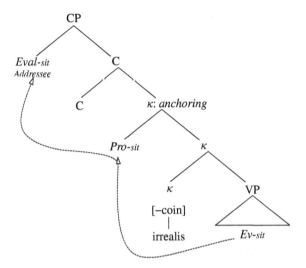

This analysis receives some support from the fact that this interpretation is facilitated if the utterance starts with a vocative 2nd person pronoun or an imperative. This suggests that the addressee's evaluation situation must be triggered by other addressee-oriented categories inside the clause.

5.5   Towards a formal typology of subjunctives

We have seen that within the four languages investigated here, the subjunctive does not form a natural class, either in terms of its form or in its distribution. Regarding its form, subjunctives may be marked by a dedicated person-sensitive paradigm (Halkomelem or Blackfoot) or by an invariant particle (Cypriot Greek) or suffix (Upper Austrian German). In terms of its distribution, each language uses the subjunctive in a different set of clause-types. This is summarized in Table 5.5.

What all subjunctives have in common is the fact that they construct a language-specific category, which contrasts with independent clauses used for assertions. This gives the impression that the subjunctive is in fact a natural class, at least in terms of its function. But crucially, this apparent function (the contrast with independent assertive clauses) may be constructed in

Table 5.5 *Formal and distributional properties of subjunctives*

	Form	Context
Cypriot Greek	Invariant particle	Conditional
		Imperative
		Dependent future irrealis
		Dependent simultaneous
Halkomelem	Variant agreement	Conditional
		Negation
Blackfoot	SUBJUNCTIVE:	Conditional (realis)
	Variant agreement	When clause
	UNREAL:	Conditional (irrealis)
	Invariant suffix	Reportative
Upper Austrian German	Invariant suffix/Ablaut	Matrix
		Conditional
		Hypothetical
		Reportative

different ways. As a consequence, the subjunctive is not among the set of universal categories, but is instead always a language-specific category (c), and as such constructed.

If subjunctive is not a universal category, then mood cannot be a primitive category either, because the subjunctive is typically conceived of as a sub-category of mood. So if the subjunctive is not a universal category, there cannot be a universal hyper-category that includes it. This excludes the possibility for a position dedicated to mood on the universal spine (*contra* Cinque [1999]). Again, this highlights the need for a formal typology for categories that is not based on substantive content or traditional grammatical categories. The USH provides the basis for such a typology. Specifically, there are three key ingredients that derive the formal properties of these subjunctives:

(i)   the universal anchoring category κ:*anchoring*
(ii) the coincidence feature [$u$coin] associated with κ:*anchoring* and
(iii) the valuation strategy for [$u$coin].

The valuation typology developed in Ritter and Wiltschko (forthcoming) allowed us to analyze the clause-types classified as subjunctives in the four languages under investigation, both with respect to their common properties, as well as their differences. The result of this analysis is summarized in (74).

(74)   A typology of subjunctives in four languages

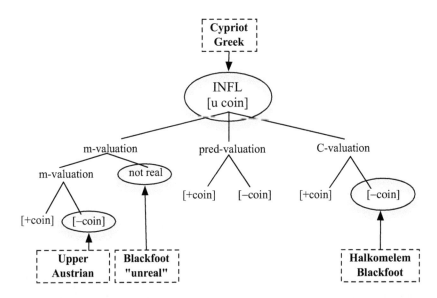

In Cypriot Greek, the subjunctive marker *na* is analyzed as an instance of
[*u*coin]. As a consequence, this subjunctive is found in several unrelated
constructions. This is because it is compatible with both the positive and the
negative value of the coincidence feature. The reason that it is not compatible
with contexts of m-valuation is that, at this point in the derivation, valuation
will have to take place from a higher head. The subjunctive in Halkomelem
and one of the Blackfoot subjunctives are both instantiations of [f-val:−coin].
The reason that subjunctive marking is found in different types of constructions in the two languages has to do with other language-specific properties
(the syntax of negation and the availability of a dedicated unreal in Blackfoot).
Finally, the Upper Austrian German subjunctive instantiates [m-val: −coin].
This is the only way to derive an independent subjunctive, i.e., one that may be
used in independent clauses. A similar subjunctive is also found in Blackfoot,
the second clause-type with "subjunctive type" properties, namely the unreal.
It is here analyzed as a modified instance of m-valuation.

In sum, the USH allows us to identify the universal basis for the subjunctive:
it instantiates the universally available anchoring category, though the
specific syntactic constellations in which it is found differ significantly. It is
these syntactic constellations (m-valuation, pred-valuation, or f-valuation)
which place restrictions on the types of constructions that allow for or require

Table 5.6 *A typology for UoLs used to construct subjunctives*

Cypriot Greek	
c:SUBJUNCTIVE =	<π:*na*, [κ:*anchoring, u*coin]>
Halkomelem	
c:SUBJUNCTIVE =	<{[κ:*anchoring*, f-val:−coin], 1st}, π:*-l*>
	<{[κ:*anchoring*, f-val:−coin], 2nd}, π:*-xw*>
	<{[κ:*anchoring*, f-val:−coin], 3rd}, π:*-s*>
	…
Blackfoot	
c:SUBJUNCTIVE =	<{[κ:*anchoring*, f-val:−coin], ANIM}, π:*-iniki*>
	<{[κ:*anchoring*, f-val:−coin], INANIM}, π:*-mminn*>
	…
Blackfoot	
c:UNREAL =	{{π:*-htopi*, Σ:UNREAL}, [κ:anchoring, m-val: ±coin]}
Upper Austrian German	
c:SUBJUNCTIVE =	<{π:*-at*, Σ:UNREAL}, [κ:*anchoring*, m-val:−coin]>

subjunctive marking. Furthermore, these syntactic constellations provide the underpinnings for interpretation in a universal way. These include the coincidence feature and the abstract arguments that are being ordered by κ: *anchoring*. It is the substantive content of the valuing category that determines whether it receives a positive or negative value. There are two general strategies: (i) valuation may be derived via a dedicated morphological marker, deriving anchoring in independent categories, or (ii) valuation may be derived via external valuation by a higher head (either an embedding predicate or a higher functor).

Finally, the valuation typology makes predictions about possible lexicalization patterns for the UoLs involved. Consider the different subjunctives summarized in Table 5.6. Two of the UoLs used to construct the category are intrinsically associated with substantive content: the Blackfoot unreal marker (*-htopi*) and the Upper Austrian German subjunctive marker (*-at*). The Blackfoot unreal marker modifies an m-valued instance of κ:*anchoring*. Since, by hypothesis, modifiers are {π,Σ} pairs, it follows that the Blackfoot unreal must be defined by its meaning. This correctly predicts that there are no expletive occurrences of Blackfoot unreal marking. The Upper Austrian German subjunctive marker is also defined as a {π,Σ} pair. But it differs from the Blackfoot unreal in that it serves to m-value [κ:*anchoring*, *u*coin]. As an m-valuing UoL it must be part of the pre-syntactic lexicon.

The other three UoLs used to construct subjunctives are defined solely by the syntactic constellations they realize. They are not themselves associated with substantive content (Σ). Two types of syntactic constellations must be distinguished. If a UoL manifests [$u$coin] it must be associated with the spine pre-syntactically; if a UoL realizes an externally valued κ, it must be associated with the spine post-syntactically. Consistent with this claim is the fact that those UoLs that are predicted to be post-syntactic are paradigmatic: they are also sensitive to other features, such as person, animacy, or transitivity.

Thus, the formal typology makes predictions about correlations between form, meaning, and syntactic context. Moreover, the seemingly erratic behavior of subjunctives, both within and across languages, is no longer surprising. First, its existence across so many languages results from two factors: (i) there is a functional need to talk about states of affairs that do not hold in the real world, and (ii) the universal anchoring category provides the right ingredients to fulfill this need. It allows for the event situation to be ordered relative to the evaluation world.

Second, the observation that the subjunctive does not behave as a natural class across languages follows from the assumption that it is a language-specific category and as such, necessarily constructed. I submit that an adequate analysis for c:SUBJUNCTIVE is only possible if we recognize that neither language-specific categories (c) nor the UoLs that realize them are necessarily definable in terms of their meaning.[15]

The formal typology developed here allows us to derive some of the common properties of the subjunctive. Many subjunctives appear to be dependent and/or defective because they require valuation from a higher head.

As we have seen, the subjunctive provides us with a unique window into the syntax of categorization. It has served as an example of a category that resists a characterization in terms of its meaning. Though, because it contrasts with the clause-type used for assertions, it sometimes appears to be definable by its meaning. The lesson here is, once again, that we cannot compare language-specific categories such as subjunctive and irrealis directly to each other. Instead, they must be compared via a more abstract set of categories, which is precisely what the USH provides.

---

[15] Other candidates for functors that are definable only in terms of their function, but not in terms of their meaning, are linkers and relators in the sense of Den Dikken (2006).

6   *Nominal anchoring categories*

> *Time is the enemy of identity.*   Michael Moorcock

6.1   Introduction

In the last two chapters I have argued that κ:*anchoring* is universal and that it plays a key role in the construction of categories. Crucially, it cannot be defined on the basis of its substantive content. We saw in Chapter 4 that the language-specific substantive content that it associates with in the construction of language-specific categories differs across languages. And in Chapter 5 we saw that it may remain without content. Despite these different instantiations of κ:*anchoring*, it can be identified by its formal and functional properties. It is located in the area of the spine that relates the event to the utterance. As such, it does not itself constitute an interface category, but instead it mediates between two interface domains. It serves as the basis for the construction of quintessential grammatical categories, such as, for example, the subjunctive, and it is sensitive to argument roles that are purely grammatical (such as subject and object).

Given the well-established parallelism between clausal and nominal hierarchies, we expect that κ:*anchoring* has a nominal instantiation as well. And indeed the two core manifestations of anchoring, *anaphoricity* and *deixis*, are essential qualities of the nominal domain. In this chapter, I explore several instances of anaphoric and deictic nominal categories, including *pronouns*, *demonstratives*, and *case*. The inclusion of case in this set of categories is perhaps a bit unexpected, in that it is not typically assumed to be a member of the set of deictic or anaphoric categories (see however Pesetsky [2011]). Here I argue that case can be successfully analyzed as an instance of κ:*anchoring*. In particular, it is the nominal instantiation of dependent anchoring, similar to subjunctives in the clausal domain. Just like subjunctives, case has remained elusive for any approach that seeks to define grammatical categories in terms of their meaning. This highlights the fundamental premise of this monograph: we cannot define universal categories on the basis of their content. The association

188

of a particular category with content in this sense is necessarily language-specific, but it is based on universal constraints on categorization. As a consequence, categories like pronoun, determiner, or demonstrative are necessarily language-specific, with regularities derived from the universal spine.

As in the preceding two chapters, I will develop the argument as follows. I first explicitly compare two opposing views regarding the existence of universal categories in light of nominal deixis and anaphora. We shall see that both views face empirical problems.

In Section 6.2, I explore the Universal Base Hypothesis (UBH). On this view, one might expect that pronouns, demonstratives, and case are universally attested, and that at the very least they have the same properties across languages. This is, however, not the case, suggesting that such categories are not universal.

In Section 6.3, I explore the No Base Hypothesis (NBH), which also faces problems. If there were nothing universal about pronouns, demonstratives, and case, then it would be a surprising result that they are attested in many of the worlds' languages, including genetically and geographically unrelated ones.

The Universal Spine Hypothesis (USH) will again allow us to reconcile this seemingly contradictory result, as I show in Section 6.4. Just like in the clausal hierarchy, there are two main ingredients that are used to derive deictic and anaphoric categories. First, the abstract argument associated with the nominal version of κ:*anchoring* (i.e., D) is intrinsically anaphoric. However, instead of referring to a situation, it refers to an individual. Second, the intrinsic unvalued feature associated with the head of κ:*anchoring* is not [coin(cidence)], but instead [ident(ity)].

Applying the valuation typology developed in Chapter 5, some demonstratives manifest [+ident] or [−ident] derived via m-valuation. In contrast, some case marking manifests [+ident] or [−ident] derived via pred- or f-valuation. In this way, case marking is analyzed as the nominal equivalent of subjunctive marking, namely dependent anchoring. This similarity between subjunctive and case has already been pointed out by Diekhoff (1911: 625) who claims that "*the subjunctive and in general the phenomena of one language will often be quite different from apparently the same phenomena of other languages both as to origin and as to function. What is true of the moods is equally true of the cases.*"

6.2   The Universal Base Hypothesis

In this section, we test the hypothesis that pronouns, demonstratives, and case are among the set of universal categories as in (1).

(1) $C_{UG} = \{c{:}\text{PRONOUN}, c{:}\text{DEMONSTRATIVE}, c{:}\text{CASE} \dots\}$

The first problem for this view is the fact that not all languages make use of all of these categories. But even if this is so, we could assume a version of the parametric base hypothesis, according to which the language-specific categories belong to a set of universal categories from which languages choose. The problem for this view comes from the fact that these categories (pronouns, demonstratives, and case) do not share the same formal properties across languages. I start by investigating pronouns in Section 6.2.1 where I review evidence that they do not form a natural class cross-linguistically. In Section 6.2.2 I explore demonstratives showing that they too vary across languages in a way that casts doubt on the idea that they instantiate a universal category. Finally, in Section 6.2.3, I consider case and I show that it is not universally attested, either as a morphological category or as an abstract syntactic category. Furthermore, even in languages where case is attested, it does not behave in a unified way. This is problematic for the assumption that case belongs to the set of universal categories that languages chose from.

6.2.1   *Pronouns are not a natural class universally*
According to Greenberg (1963: 96), pronouns are universal.

(2)   Greenberg's Universal 42
       All languages have pronominal categories involving at least three persons and two numbers.

This is not surprising. In fact, how would a language get by without pronouns? It appears that there is a functional need to make available a set of deictic expressions that allow for reference to the speaker and addressee (1st and 2nd person: Siewierska 2004: 8–13), alongside some reference tracking devices (3rd person).

For 3rd person pronouns, it has, however, been shown that pronouns are not universal. For example, Evans and Levinson (2009: 431) state that Southeast Asian languages "*lack clear personal pronouns, using titles (of the kind 'honorable sir') instead*" (see also Cysouw 2001; Siewierska 2004).

However, even if we only consider languages with pronouns, we observe that they do not show the same distributional properties within and across languages. As shown in Chapter 1 (Section 1.2.3), English pronouns may be interpreted as bound variables, while Halkomelem pronouns may not. One might think that in polysynthetic languages such as Halkomelem, pronouns behave differently because they are never necessary for the sentence to be grammatical. As a consequence, pronouns are more likely to be used contrastively. This may in fact be the reason that they cannot serve as bound variables. However, polysynthesis is neither a necessary nor a sufficient condition for the pronouns of a language to resist a bound variable interpretation. On the one hand, in Blackfoot, another polysynthetic language, pronouns allow for a bound variable interpretation just like English pronouns (Wiltschko *et al.* forthcoming). This is shown in (3), where *nistoo* allows for the sloppy (bound variable) interpretation of the elided VP. On the other hand, in German there is a set of pronouns known as d-pronouns, which coexist with the regular personal pronoun paradigm. Such pronouns resist the bound variable interpretation (Wiltschko 1998), as shown in (4).

(3)   *Nitoo'ohtsipoyi*   *nistoo*   *kistoo*   *ni'toyi.*
     nit-oht-i'poyi   **n-iistoo**   k-iistoo   ni'toyi
     1-about-speak.AI   1-PRN   2-PRN   be.same.II
     'I talked about myself and you too.'
     = (i) and you also talked about yourself
     ≠ (ii) and you talked about me

                                                  Wiltschko *et al.* forthcoming

(4)   *Jeder*   *Mann*   *ist*   *fröhlich*   *wenn*   ***der***   *singt.*
     Every   man   is   joyful   when   PRN   sings.
     = (i) 'Every man is joyful when he (= someone else) sings.'
     ≠ (ii) 'Every man is joyful when he sings.'

There are several other distributional characteristics that distinguish pronouns that allow for a bound variable interpretation from those that do not (see Déchaine and Wiltschko [2002] for discussion and analysis). Thus, from the point of view of their distribution, pronouns do not behave like a natural class. But if distributional differences are indicative of categorical differences, then we are led to the conclusion that pronouns are not a uniform category, and consequently, that they cannot simply be among a universal repository of categories that languages chose from.

This conclusion is supported by functional considerations as well. In particular, pronouns serve a different function in polysynthetic languages than they do in inflectional languages. In polysynthetic languages, core arguments are indexed in the verbal complex. Thus the use of pronouns, which encode phi-features only, is semantically redundant. And indeed, in polysynthetic languages, pronouns are often used to establish emphasis (Dahlstrom 1988). Compare this to languages where arguments must be overtly expressed. In such languages pronouns are commonly used for reference tracking and as such they appear to be a functional necessity. However in principle, languages may get by without a word class dedicated to reference tracking. There are other means by which anaphoric reference can be established. In polysynthetic languages the relevant strategy may be zero marking. For example in Salish languages, an ongoing topic in a discourse tends to be zero (Roberts 1994; Kroeber 1995; Beck 2000; Gerdts and Hukari 2008). A second strategy consists of copying, as for example in San Lucas Quiaviní Zapotec (Oto-Manguean) where the same form (a name) is copied in a reflexive construction.

(5)   *R-yu'làaa'z*   *Gye'eihlly*   *Gye'eihlly*.
       HAB-like   Mike   Mike
       'Mike likes himself.'

Lee 2003: 84 (1)

The existence of alternative strategies for reference tracking points to the conclusion that we need not expect the universality of pronouns even from a functional perspective.

6.2.2   *Demonstratives are not a natural class universally*

We now turn to demonstratives, another closed word class whose main function is deictic reference and which is therefore likely to instantiate the nominal anchoring category. Indeed, Diessel (1999) suggests that all languages have demonstratives, making them a good candidate for a language universal. But at the same time, he maintains that *"their form, meaning and use vary tremendously across the languages of the world"* (Diessel 1999: 1). These differences include, most notably, their feature composition. According to WALS, out of a sample of 234 languages, the majority of languages express a two-way contrast in distance: *here* vs. *there* (127 languages), followed by those that express a three-way contrast (88 languages). Eight languages display a four-way contrast and four express a five(or more)-way contrast.

Languages with a three-way contrast divide into two groups, according to Diessel's (2005) WALS chapter. There are those languages that are purely distance-oriented, encoding the relative distance between the referent and the deictic center (proximal, medial, distal), and there are those languages that are person-oriented, encoding distance relative to the speaker (PROX 1), relative to the hearer (PROX 2), and away from speaker and hearer (DISTAL). An example of the former language type is Squamish (Gillon 2006, 2009), as shown in Table 6.1, while an example of the latter is Blackfoot, as shown in Table 6.2 (this paradigm constitutes only a small subset of Blackfoot demonstratives; see discussion immediately below).

In addition to the basic contrast in distance, demonstratives may encode further dimensions of location: visibility, high or low elevation, upriver or

Table 6.1 *The Squamish demonstrative system*

	Neutral, invisible	Proximal	Medial	Distal Unmarked	Invisible
Gender-neutral					
Number-neutral	*kwíya*	*tí, tíwa*	*táy'*	*kwétsi*	
Plural	*kwiyáwit*	*iyá(wit)*	*ítsi(wit)*	*kwétsiwit*	*kwáwit*
Feminine	*kwsá*	*tsíwa*	*álhi*	*kwélhi*	

Source: From Gillon (2009: 8, Figure 6).

Table 6.2 *The Blackfoot demonstrative system*

	Prox1	Prox2	Distal
Singular			
Animate	*amo*	*anna*	*oma*
Inanimate	*amo*	*anni*	*omi*
Plural			
Animate	*amoksi*	*anniksi*	*oomiksi*
Inanimate	*amostsi*	*annistsi*	*omistsi*

Source: Data from Frantz (1991: 63).

downriver, moving towards or away from the deictic center, etc. (see Diessel 1999: ch. 3). As shown in table Table 6.1, Squamish demonstratives mark whether or not the referent is visible from the utterance location.

Blackfoot is particularly prolific in the distinctions marked by the full set of the morphologically complex demonstratives.[1] In particular, the forms in Table 6.2 belong to the three demonstrative roots that may be suffixed by a series of up to five optional suffixes (Frantz 2009: 64–66; see Bliss [2013] for discussion). There are six positions available in the demonstrative template (6). These include diminutive marking, a "restricting" vowel, inflection for number and animacy, post-inflectional affixes encoding movement and directionality, and a final position for two suffixes (*-o'ka*, and *-ayi*), whose status is still unclear. They are classified as *verbalizers* in Uhlenbeck (1938) and Frantz (2009) because they form equative or existential predicates. However, depending on the morphological composition

---

[1] The discussion of Blackfoot demonstratives is based on joint work with Heather Bliss.

Table 6.3 *Derived Blackfoot demonstratives*

		Prox 1	Prox 2	Remote
I	Singular (animate)	*anna*	*ama*	*oma*
II	Non-visible singular	*annahk*	*amahk*	*omahk*
III	Derived non-visible singular	*annahkayi*	*amahkayi*	*omahkayi*

of the base to which it attaches, *-ayi* does not consistently have this function.

(6)   Demonstrative template.
        Root + (diminutive) + (restricted) + (inflection) + (post-inflection) +
        (?? suffix)

On the basis of the morphological template in (6), one would expect about 900 distinct demonstrative forms. Taylor (1969: 212) notes:

> The number of individual forms of demonstratives is enormous. A detailed study of Uhlenbeck's texts was made during the analysis of the morphology of demonstrative pronouns, and between Uhlenbeck's and the author's texts, almost all predictable forms are attested. [...] the completely random pattern of the unattested forms rules out the likelihood that there are real gaps in the morphological pattern.

Thus, in terms of their internal composition, Blackfoot demonstratives are strikingly different from demonstratives in English, which has a simple contrast between proximate and distal. And moreover, their internal composition affects their syntactic distribution. In particular, demonstratives suffixed with *-ayi* have a distribution distinct from other demonstratives. To see this, consider the sub-paradigm of demonstratives in Table 6.3, which consists of simple singular (animate) demonstratives (series I), (singular) demonstratives used for invisible referents (suffixed by *-ahk*) (series II), and finally, the demonstratives suffixed by *-ayi* (series III).

In terms of their syntactic distribution, these demonstratives differ in a number of respects. First, series I and II demonstratives can function as nominal modifiers (7), as pronouns (i.e., without an overt NP) (8), or as predicates (9); series III demonstratives can only function as modifiers.

(7)   a. *anna*   *ninaawa*   SERIES I
           ann-wa   ninaa-wa
           DEM-PROX   man-PROX
           'this man'

b. *annahk*   *ninaawa*   SERIES II
   ann-wa-hk   ninaa-wa
   DEM-PROX-NV   man-PROX
   'this man'

c. *annahkayi*   *ninaawa*   SERIES III
   ann-wa-hk-ayi   ninaa-wa
   DEM-PROX-NV-ayi man-PROX
   'this one certain man'

(8) a. *Nitsíínoawa*   *anna.*   SERIES I
   nit-iino-a-wa   ann-wa
   1-see-DIR-3S   DEM-3S
   'I saw him/her.'

b. *Nitsíínoawa*   *annáhk.*   SERIES II
   nit-iino-a-wa   ann-wa-hk
   1-see-DIR-3S   DEM-3S-NV
   'I saw him/her.'

c. **Nitsíínoawa*   *annáhkayi.*   SERIES III
   nit-iino-a-wa   ann-wa-hk-ayi
   1-see-DIR-3S   DEM-3S-NV-*ayi*
   intended: 'I saw him/her.'

(9) a. *Anná*   *nínssta.*   SERIES I
   ann-wa   n-insst-wa
   DEM-3S   1-sister-3S
   'She is my sister.'

b. *Annáhk*   *nínssta.*   SERIES II
   ann-wa-hk   n-insst-wa
   DEM-3S-NV   1-sister-3S
   'She is my sister.'

c. **Annáhkayi*   *nínssta.*   SERIES III
   ann-wa-hk-ayi   n-insst-wa
   DEM-3S-NV-*ayi* 1-sister-3S
   intended: 'She is my sister.'

Moreover, these demonstratives also differ in the way they combine with verbal predicates. Series I and II are restricted to nominal complements of morphologically transitive verbs, such as the TI verb in (10a). They cannot co-occur with morphologically intransitive verbs, such as the AI verb in (10b). In contrast, series III demonstratives derived by *-ayi* are compatible with both morphologically transitive and intransitive verbs, as in (11).

(10) a. *Oma   imitááwa   imsstsíma   omi   nápayini.*
      om-wa   imitaa-wa   imsstsi-m-wa   om-yi   napayin-yi
      DEM-3S   dog-3S   steal.TI-3:INAN-3S DEM-INAN   bread-INAN
      'That dog stole the bread.'

      b. **Oma   imitááwa   imsstákiwa   omi   nápayini.*
      om-wa   imitaa-wa   imsstaki-wa   om-yi   napayin-yi
      DEM-3S   dog-3S   steal.AI-3S   DEM-INAN   bread-INAN
      intended: 'That dog stole the bread.'

(11) a. *Oma   imitááwa   imsstsíma   anníhkayi   nápayini.*
      om-wa   imitaa-wa   imsstsi-m-wa   ann-yi-hk-ayi   napayin-yi
      DEM-3S   dog-3S   steal.TI-3:INAN-3S DEM-INAN-NV-*ayi* bread-INAN
      'That dog stole that one certain (piece of) bread.'

      b. *Oma   imitááwa   imsstákiwa   anníhkayi   nápayini.*
      om-wa   imitaa-wa   imsstaki-wa   ann-yi-hk-ayi   napayin-yi
      DEM-3S   dog-3S   steal.AI -3S   DEM-INAN-NV-*ayi* bread-INAN
      'That dog stole that one certain (piece of) bread.'

And finally, in terms of their context of use, series III demonstratives differ
from others in two respects. First, they are not compatible with a pointing
gesture. And second, they are not compatible with nouns denoting unique
individuals, as shown in (12).

(12) a. *Nitsíínoawa   annahkayi   kisíssa.*
      nit-iin-o-a-wa   ann-wa-hk-ayi   k-isiss-wa
      1-see-TA-DIR-PROX   DEM-PROX-NV-*ayi* 2-sister-PROX
      'I saw that one certain sister of yours.'
      (only felicitous if you have more than one sister)

      b. *Nitsíínoawa   annahkayi   kiksíssta.*
      nit-iin-o-a-wa   ann-wa-hk-ayi   k-iksisst-wa
      1-see-AI-DIR-PROX   DEM-PROX-NV-*ayi* 2-mother-PROX
      'I saw that one certain mother of yours.'
      (only felicitous if you have more than one mother, e.g., a stepmother)

      c. **Nitsíínoawa   annahkayi   ki'sómma / naató'si.*
      nit-iin-o-a-wa   ann-wa-hk-ayi   ki'somm-wa / naato'si-wa
      1-see-TA-DIR-PROX   DEM-PROX-NV-*ayi* moon-PROX / sun-PROX
      intended: 'I saw that one certain moon/sun.'

In light of the morphological, syntactic, and semantic differences observed, we
can conclude that despite their paradigmatic organization, Blackfoot demonstratives do not form a natural class. This is in line with one of the core theses
of this book: universals cannot be based on word classes such as demonstratives or pronouns because these notions are intrinsically language-specific.

Table 6.4 *Morphological case is not a homogeneous category*

	Number of languages
No morphological case	100
2 case categories	23
3 case categories	9
4 case categories	9
5 case categories	12
6–7 case categories	37
8–9 case categories	23
10 or more	24
Exclusively borderline	24
Total	261

6.2.3   Case is not universal

I now turn to the question of whether case is a language universal. As a working definition, I take case to be a system of marking dependent nouns for the type of relationship they bear to their heads (see Blake 1994). The reason it is included in this chapter on nominal anchoring is because of this core characteristic: to mark a dependency. In this way it parallels the dependent verbal anchoring category, often instantiated as the subjunctive.

Problems for the assumption that case is a universal category are, however not hard to come by. Consider first morphological case. Out of the 261 languages surveyed by WALS, 100 do not mark case morphologically. And even in those languages that mark case, it does not appear to be a homogeneous category. The number of contrasts expressed in these languages differ. The distribution is summarized in Table 6.4.

Next we turn to syntactic case. In particular, within the generative tradition there is a notion of case that is not defined based on morphological marking. This is known as *abstract case*. Abstract case is generally assumed to be attested across all languages as a matter of UG. In particular, it is a standard assumption within the generative tradition that an integral part of UG is *case theory* (Chomsky 1980, 1981; Rouveret and Vergnaud 1980; Vergnaud 1982). The ingredients of case theory conspire to ensure that all nominal arguments receive case. Within the Government and Binding framework, case was conceived of as a filter, which rules out caseless NPs, as in (13).[2]

---

[2] More recently, case is often conceptualized as a feature associated with NPs or their functional superstructure (see fn. 20).

(13)   *[NP]$_{[-case]}$

Case theory regulates at least two aspects of the distribution of nominal arguments: (i) the (im)possibility for overt nominal arguments, and (ii) their linear ordering, which in turn is dependent on (iii) their structural position.

As for the first property, we observe that grammatical relations cannot always be realized by an overt DP. For example, (nominative) subjects are not attested when the verb is in its infinitival form.

(14)   a. *He wanted (*he) to play.*
         b. *He played.*

In terms of their linear ordering, in some languages at least, a particular case value (nominative vs. accusative) is associated with a specific syntactic position, which may in turn translate into a linearization effect. Thus in English, nominative subjects must linearly precede accusative objects.

(15)   a. **saw he him*
         b. **him saw he*

The assumption that case theory is an integral part of UG stems from the fact that even in English we can observe the workings of case theory, despite the fact that case is only morphologically realized on pronouns and not on full DPs. The former use different forms, depending on whether they realize the grammatical subject or object relation, as in (16). This contrasts with full DPs, which realize the subject and object role with identical forms, as in (16).

(16)   a. *He saw him.*
         b. *The woman saw the man.*

While many languages lack evidence for morphological case (as we have seen in Table 6.4), this is not sufficient to show that they lack abstract case. In fact, morphological case has been explicitly argued to not be directly correlated with abstract case (McFadden 2004). Instead, to show that a language lacks case, one needs to show that the distribution of DPs is not regulated by case theory. And indeed, neither in Blackfoot nor in Halkomelem do we find case effects of this type (Wiltschko 2011). While we have seen in Chapter 4 (Section 4.3) that grammatical relations play a role in both languages, they do not play a role in regulating the distribution of full DPs.

First, we observe that – like in English – full DPs in Blackfoot (17) and Halkomelem (18) are not morphologically case-marked.[3]

(17)   a. *Ikakomimmííwa*   *nohkówa*   *kitáni.*
       ik-akomimm-ii-wa   n-ohkó-wa   k-itan-yi
       INT-love.TA-DIR-PROX   1-son-PROX   2-daughter-OBV
       'My son loves your daughter.'

Frantz 1991: 53 (l)

      b. *Otsikákomimmokwa*   *nohkówa*   *otáni*
       ot-ik-ákomimm-ok-wa   n-ohkó-wa   ot-itán-yi
       3-INT-love.TA-INV-PROX   1-son-PROX   3-daughter-OBV
       'Her daughter loves my son.'

Frantz 1991: 56 (k)

(18)   a. *títelem*   [*te*   *swíyeqe*].
       sing   DET   man
       'The man is singing.'

      b. *kw'éts-l-exw-es*   [*te*   *swíyeqe*] [*te*   *spá:th*].
       see-TRANS-3OBJ-3S   DET man   DET bear
       'The man sees a bear.'

Galloway 1993: 41

However, unlike in English, the distribution of full DPs is not regulated by case theory. First, the overt manifestation of full DPs is not restricted in the same way as it is in Indo-European languages. A case in point is the absence of the infinitive effect in both Halkomelem and Blackfoot. That is, the realization of subject DPs is allowed across all types of embedded clauses, including those that are dependent on intensional verbs. These are often realized as infinitival complements in Indo-European languages. Relevant examples are given for Halkomelem[4] in (19) and for Blackfoot in (20).

(19)   a. s-*tl'i'-s*   *kw'-s*   *nem'-s*   *toqw'*
       NMLZ-want-3POSS   COMP-NMLZ go-3POSS return.home
       ... *tthe* *se'wey'qe*   *'e*   *te-n'a*   *sneyt.*
       DET   man.PL   OBL   DET-DEM   night
       'The man wants to go home tonight.'

---

[3] The absence of morphological case marking is even more pervasive than it is in English. Neither in Halkomelem nor in Blackfoot are pronouns marked for case.

[4] I am grateful to James Thompson for providing the data. They come from the Isand dialect of Halkomelem.

b. *s-tl'i'-s*   *kw'-s*   *nem'-s*   *toqw'*
   NMLZ-want-3POSS   COMP-NMLZ   go-3POSS   return.home
   ... *tthe   Tully   'e   te-n'a   sneyt.*
   DET   Tully   OBL   DET-DEM   night
   'He wants Tully to go home tonight.'

(20)   a. *Kistoo   kammayiniki   kitaakomai'to.*
          k-istoo   kam-waani-iniki   kit-aak-omai'to-o
          2-PRN   if-say.AI-1SG.SUBJ   2-FUT-believe.TA-1:2
          'If you say so, I will take your word for it.'

       b. *Nitsikkst   kistoo   kitaahkaa'po'takssi.*
          nit-ikkstaa   **k-istoo**   kit-aahk-áa'po'taki-hsi
          1-want.AI   2-PRN   2-NONFACT-work.AI-CONJ
          'I want you to get a job.'

Second, the linear order of full DPs in Halkomelem and Blackfoot is not restricted by case theory either: word order is not determined by grammatical relations as shown for Halkomelem in (21) and for Blackfoot in (22).

(21)   SVO   *te*   *swíyeqe*   *kw'éts-l-exw-es*   *te*   *spáth.*
             DET   man   see-TR-3O-3S   DET   bear
             'The man saw the bear.'

       VSO   *kw'éts-l-exw-es*   *te*   *spá:th*   *te*   *swíyeqe.*
             see-TR-3OBJ-3S   DET   bear   DET   man
             'The man sees a bear.'

       VOS   *kw'éts-l-exw-es*   *te*   *swíyeqe*   *te*   *spá:th.*
             see-TRANS-3O-3S   DET   bear   DET   man
             'The man sees a bear.'

                                              adapted from Galloway 1993: 41

(22)   SVO   *Ooma*   *saahkomapi*   *ihpookoowa'(w)aahkami*
             ooma   saahkomapi-wa   ii-ohpok-a-waahkaa-m-yii-wa
             DEM   boy-PROX   IC-ACCOM-IMPF-play.AI-TA-
                                               3:4-PROX ...

             ... *omi*   *otoomitam.*
             ... omi   ot-omitaa-m-yi
             ... DEM   3-dog-POSS-OBV
             'The boy is playing with his dog.'

       OVS   *Omi*   *otoomitam*   *ihpookoowa'(w)aahkami* ...
             omi   ot-omitaa-m-yi   ii-ohpok-a-waahkaa-m-yii-wa ...
             DEM   3-dog-POSS-OBV   IC-ACCOM-IMPF-play.AI-TA-
                                               3:4-PROX ...

             ... *ooma*   *saahkomapi*
             ... ooma   saahkomapi-wa
             ... DEM   boy-PROX

VOS *Ihpookoowa'(w)aahkami*   *omi   otoomitam* . . .
ii-ohpok-a-waahkaa-m-yii-wa   omi   ot-omitaa-m-yi . . .
IC-ACCOM-IMPF-play.AI-TA-3:4-PROX DEM 3-dog-POSS-OBV . . .
. . . *ooma saahkomapi.*
. . . ooma saahkomapi-wa
. . . DEM boy-PROX

VSO *Ihpookoowa'(w)aahkami*   *ooma   saahkomapi* . . .
ii ohpok-a-waahkaa-m-yii-wa   ooma   saahkomapi-wa . . .
IC-ACCOM-IMPF-play.AI-TA-3.4-PROX DEM   boy-PROX . . .
. . . *omi   otoomitam.*
. . . omi   ot-omitaa-m-yi
. . . DEM 3-dog-POSS-OBV

SOV *Ooma saahkomapi*   *omi*   *otoomitam.* . .
ooma saahkomapi-wa   omi   ot-omitaa-m-yi . . .
DEM boy-PROX   DEM   3-dog-POSS-OBV . . .
. . . *ihpookoowa'(w)aahkami.*
. . . ii-ohpok-a-waahkaa-m-yii-wa
. . . IC-ACCOM-IMPF-play.AI-TA-3:4-PROX

OSV *Omi*   *otoomitam*   *ooma saahkomapi.* . .
omi   ot-omitaa-m-yi   ooma saahkomapi-wa . . .
DEM   3-dog-POSS-OBV   DEM boy-PROX . . .
. . . *ihpookoowa'(w)aahkami.*
. . . ii-ohpok-a-waahkaa-m-yii-wa
. . . IC-ACCOM-IMPF-play.AI-TA-3:4-PROX

The overt manifestation of a given full DP, as well as its linear order, is not regulated by case theory, but instead by considerations having to do with (ill-understood) constraints on discourse structure and information packaging (see Gerdts and Hukari [2004, 2008] for Halkomelem, and Bliss [2013] for Blackfoot). This suggests that case plays no role in either Blackfoot or Halkomelem. Similar conclusions have been drawn for Bantu languages (see Diercks [2012], among others).

We have now seen that there are reasons to doubt that either pronouns, demonstratives, or case are manifestations of a universal category. On the one hand, none of these nominal categories are attested across all languages, and where they are attested, they have different formal properties. Thus, it is hardly meaningful to talk about a universal category without it becoming vacuous. Once again, this seems to lead to the conclusion that there are no universal categories. But as I will show, this conclusion also faces problems.

6.3   The No Base Hypothesis

Suppose there are no universal categories. What does this hypothesis predict? And how can it be falsified? In this section, I explore this question relative to the three phenomena under consideration: pronouns, demonstratives, and case.

6.3.1   *A common pattern of multifunctionality in pronouns*

In the last section we saw that not all languages use pronouns, and even if they do, they do not form a natural class across all languages. But the potential conclusion that there are no language universals (Evans and Levinson 2009) is also not tenable. Despite much variance, pronouns are also strikingly similar. That is, at least some subsets of pronouns do in fact form natural classes across unrelated languages. There are many ways in which pronouns pattern alike in surprising and unexpected ways. If there were no universal principles underlying the construction of language-specific pronouns, then these similarities would be coincidental.

In Section 6.2.1 we mainly explored the properties of 3rd person pronouns, which are not universally available. The situation is different for 1st and 2nd person pronouns, which appear to be universally available (Siewierska 2004; Finegan 2008). In light of this fact, a proponent of the NBH might argue that this universal is due to a functional need. One needs to be able to address the addressee, and that is what 2nd person pronouns do. If so, the universal availability of 2nd person pronouns does not bear on the question as to whether there is a universal grammar.

This type of functional explanation, however, does not make any predictions about the formal properties of 2nd person pronouns. But there are certain generalizations to be made which do not fall out from a functional explanation. Here, I discuss one characteristic of 2nd person pronouns that is shared across several unrelated languages. Second person pronouns are often multifunctional. In particular, they are often used as *impersonal* or *generic* pronouns (Malamud 2012; Gruber 2013). Consider the examples in (23) and (24) from English and Standard German respectively. Even though the 2nd person pronoun is used, this is not a statement about the addressee, but instead a generic statement about people in general.

(23)   a. ***You** add the eggs to the butter not the other way round.*

        b. ***Du** gibst   die   Eier   zur   Butter, ...*
           You give-2SG   DET   eggs   to.DET   butter ...
           ... und nicht die   Butter zu den   Eiern.
           ...and   not   DET butter to   DET eggs
           'You add the eggs to the butter and not the butter to the eggs.'

                                         Siewierska 2004: 11 (13b)

(24) a. *In Holland **you** learn to ride a bike before **you** even learn to walk.*

  b. *In Holland lern-st   **du**   Fahrrad   fahren, ...*
  In Holland learn-2SG you bike   drive
  *... noch   bevor   **du**   gehen   lern-st.*
  ... PRT before you walk learn-2SG

Gruber 2013: 10

And this is not a quirk about English and German. The use of 2nd person pronouns as impersonals is attested across a range of unrelated languages.[5]

In this way, the 2nd person pronoun has a use similar to that of impersonal pronouns, such as English *one* and German *man*. And indeed, there are contexts in which both types of pronouns can be used with an impersonal interpretation. This is shown in (25), which minimally contrasts with (24) above in that the impersonal pronoun is not formally identical to the 2nd person pronoun, but is instead a different pronoun (English *one* and German *man*).

(25) a. *In Holland **one** learns to ride a bike before **one** even learns to walk.*

Gruber 2013: 119 (6)

  b. *In Holland lernt   **man**   Fahrrad fahren, ...*
  In Holland learn-3SG IMPERS bike   drive ...
  *... noch bevor **man**   gehen   lern-t.*
  ... PART before IMPERS walk learn-3SG

However, 2nd person pronouns do not have an impersonal interpretation in all contexts. For example, in contrast to the generic contexts in (24)–(25) above, in episodic contexts 2nd person pronouns can no longer be interpreted impersonally (26) even though the dedicated impersonal pronoun is still well formed.

(26) *Immer wenn ich länger als   drei   Wochen in Holland bin, ...*
  always when I longer than three weeks in Holland be.1SG ...
  *... stiehlst **du**   mir   mein   Rad.*
  ... steal you me my bike
  'Whenever I spend more than three weeks in Holland, you steal my bike.'

Gruber 2013: 129 (19)

  ✓ Addressee-oriented
  ✗ Generic

---

[5] Siewierska (2004: 212) lists Godi, Gulf Arabic, Hindi, Kashmiri, Koromfe, Koyra Chin, Kurdish, Mandarin, Marathi, Mauwake, Maybrat, Macushi, Modern Hebrew, Mundani, Nkore-Kiga, and Tuvuluan; and Gruber (forthcoming: 158) adds Afrikaans, English, Italian, Romanian, Spanish, Greek, Mandarin Chinese, Indonesian, and Plains Cree.

(27)   *Immer   wenn   ich   länger   als   drei   Wochen   in   Holland   bin,* ...
       always   when   I   longer   than   three   weeks   in   Holland   am ...
       ... *stiehlt   **man**   mir   mein   Rad.*
       ... steal   one   me   my   bike
       'Whenever I spend more than three weeks in Holland, someone steals
       my bike.'

Gruber 2013: 127 (17)

The cross-linguistic stability of the impersonal use of 2nd person pronouns, and the equally cross-linguistic validity of the restriction that comes with it requires an explanation (see Gruber 2013). Furthermore, there are also generalizations to be made about the formal properties of the 2nd person/impersonal connection, which are unexpected from a functional perspective. In particular, Gruber 2010 shows that (i) if a language has the option of dropping the (2nd person) subject pronoun it will always do so in the generic use. And (ii), if a language has more than one set of (2nd person) pronouns, it will always use the weakest form available in the generic use (Gruber 2013). These cross-linguistically valid generalizations about the use of 2nd person pronouns cast doubt on the assumption that there is no universal base. In the absence of a universal base that is responsible for these patterns, these generalizations would be coincidental.

The NBH also faces problems in light of 3rd person pronouns. In particular, we have seen in Section 6.2.1 that dedicated pronominal forms are not necessary for establishing anaphoric dependencies and reference tracking; languages can get by without them. Other strategies exist to establish dependencies (i.e., copying and deletion). Thus, it is surprising that pronouns are nevertheless a pervasive phenomenon across many unrelated languages. This suggests once again that a universal base governs the construction of pronominal forms across languages.

6.3.2   A common grammaticalization path based on demonstratives

We now explore the NBH in light of demonstratives. Demonstratives have in fact been argued to be universally attested (see Himmelmann 1997; Diessel 1999, 2005; Dixon 2003). If so, this poses an immediate problem for the NBH.

It also appears to contradict one of the main theses developed here, namely that language universals cannot be defined in terms of *word class*. It turns out, however, that in order to maintain that demonstratives are universal, one has to define them broadly, including several types of word classes such as determiners, pronouns, particles, verbs, and adverbs (Diessel 1999).

Again, one may take a functional approach. For example, Diessel (2006: 266) argues that demonstratives comprise a third word class alongside grammatical and lexical categories and that, universally, this class serves two functions. (i) Demonstratives locate the referent relative to the deictic center on the basis of spatial coordinates. (ii) Demonstratives coordinate the interlocutors' joint attentional focus. Suppose that there is indeed a functional need for speakers to do both these things. Is this an explanation for their universality? Maybe. But a function-based explanation does not make any predictions about the similarities of their formal properties nor about the range of variation we expect. Some of the recurring formal properties in the realm of demonstrative determiners includes the fact that they can be used not only deictically but also anaphorically. And successively, many demonstratives develop into grammatical markers such as definite determiners (Diessel 1999: 109–113; see also Brugmann 1904: 7–8; Bühler 1934: 390; Levinson 2004). While definite determiners are not universal, their grammaticalization paths are remarkably similar (Carlier and de Mulder 2010: 1), suggesting a universal underlying core. Thus, the common pattern of grammaticalization (DEMONSTRATIVE >> DEFINITE DETERMINER) across unrelated languages is unexpected unless there is something universal about the connection between the two. And indeed the DEMONSTRATIVE >> DEFINITE DETERMINER path mirrors what we have seen in the clausal anchoring area: deixis and anaphoricity are known to pattern together.

6.3.3   Common patterns of case marking

As we have seen in Section 6.2.3, case is not an absolute language universal: not all languages make use of case. No matter whether we identify case by virtue of its morphological marking (m-case) or by its syntactic effects (abstract case), not all languages seem to make use of it. This has been pointed out in the typological literature (Gil 2001; Evans and Levinson 2009) and also in the generative tradition (Danon 2006; Diercks 2012). However, the fact that case is not found in all of the languages of the world does not automatically lead to the conclusion that there is not something universal about case.

First, if there were nothing universal about the construction of case, it would be surprising that so many unrelated languages use case to mark the grammatical relations of nominal arguments. Thus in the language sample of WALS, case marking is found in 161 out of 261 languages (see Table 6.4 above). A functional explanation for the frequent marking of case across unrelated languages is hard to conceive of. In particular, among the grammatical categories that are difficult, if not impossible, to define in terms of their meaning, case is perhaps the most notorious one. Traditionally, cases are described as having a number of functions or meanings (Jakobson 1936; Fillmore 1968; Anderson 1971). Its function is often defined purely in terms of grammatical relations. This highlights the absence of meaning, since grammatical relations (*subject* and *object*) themselves cannot be defined in terms of their meaning. Moreover, the meaning of case is sometimes equated with the kinds of meaningful relations it may express, such as extent in place or time (Blake 1994). Given the heterogeneity of case functions beyond the marking of subject and object roles, a functional explanation for its widespread occurrence seems unlikely.

In addition to the unexpected frequency of case across unrelated languages, there are also universal generalizations to be made about case, which cast doubt on the assumption that there is nothing universal about it. To mention but one example, consider the following implicational universal.

(28)   If a language uses a non-zero case marking for a P argument on the animacy/
definiteness hierarchies, then it uses a non-zero case marking for P arguments
higher on the hierarchies.

Croft 1990: 166

As discussed in Croft (1990), this type of interaction is instantiated in Punjabi (Shackle 1972: 69). In this language, object pronouns are overtly coded using the dative suffix *-nũ*. Animate object common nouns also use *nũ*, but an inanimate direct object uses *nũ* only if it is definite.

(29)   *Mɛ*   *tɛɛ-nũ*   *pəɽávaŋga.*
        1SG 2SG   OBJ   will.teach
        'I will teach you.'

Croft 1990: 166 (3)

(30)   *O*   *nili*   *ketab*   *nu*   *mez*   *te*   *rako.*
        that   blue   book   **to** table   on   put
        'Put that blue book on the table.'

Croft 1990: 166 (4)

(31)   *Ko*   *kitab*   *mez*   *te*   *rako.*
        Some   book   table   on   put
        'Put some book on the table.'

Croft 1990: 166 (5)

If there were no underlying mechanism governing the deployment of case and its interaction with definiteness and animacy marking, then this pattern would be coincidental.

We have again arrived at a dilemma. Pronouns, determiners, and case are not universally attested and if they are attested they do not share the same formal or functional properties across languages. This suggests that they do not instantiate universal categories. At the same time however, we have also seen that there are some common formal patterns associated with these categories. That is, many unrelated languages do in fact have instantiations of pronouns, demonstratives, and case and there are some striking generalizations to be made. As in previous chapters, I argue that this dilemma can be resolved if we assume that language-specific categories are constructed and moreover that this construction is guided by the universal spine.

6.4   The Universal Spine Hypothesis

I now test the USH in light of pronouns, demonstratives, and case. In particular, I shall argue that (at least some) language-specific instantiations of these categories can be analyzed as being constructed based on κ:*anchoring* in its nominal instantiation.[6] The relevant functional category to explore is D, which is commonly taken to be the nominal counterpart of INFL (see Section 2.3.4 for detailed discussion).

On the basis of several case studies, I will show that demonstratives, pronouns, and case may all be analyzed as being constructed via κ:*anchoring*. If so, our task is to discover the language-specific Units of Language (UoLs), which are used to construct these categories. This section is organized as follows.

I first introduce my assumptions regarding the formal underpinnings of nominal anchoring in Section 6.4.1. The main difference to verbal κ:*anchoring* lies in the content of its intrinsic feature. In particular, instead of a coincidence feature, I suggest that nominals are defined by an unvalued *identity* feature. I then proceed to an analysis of Standard German personal pronouns in Section 6.4.2. I show that the USH allows for a straightforward analysis of a surprising pattern of multifunctionality. I then proceed to analyze deictic determiners in Squamish and Blackfoot (Section 6.4.3). I argue that they manifest a pattern of m-valuation. This will allow us to develop a novel analysis for DP arguments in pronominal argument languages. In Subsection 6.4.3.2, I analyze the demonstratives of Squamish and Blackfoot, and I show how they differ from the so-called deictic determiners. I show that the formal typology developed here allows for a principled way to distinguish these categories. What

---

[6] This does not preclude the possibility that there are also pronouns, demonstratives, and instances of case that associate with the spine in a position above or below κ:*anchoring*. But for reasons of exposition, I will here focus on those constructed with κ:*anchoring*. For a typology of pronouns that focuses on differences in their categorial identity see Déchaine and Wiltschko (2002).

distinguishes pronouns and demonstratives on the one hand from case on the other is the fact that the former are derived via m-valuation whereas the latter are derived via external valuation (i.e., pred- or f-valuation). Thus, as I show in Section 6.4.4, the existence of case is predicted by the valuation typology developed thus far. In Section 6.5 I conclude.

6.4.1 Formalizing nominal anchoring

Recall from Chapters 4 and 5 that the essence of κ:*anchoring* is that it relates an eventuality to the utterance context, either deictically or anaphorically. The relational characteristic arises via the coincidence feature in κ:*anchoring*, while contextualization arises via the pronominal situation argument in its specifier position, as schematized in (32).

(32)   Clausal anchoring

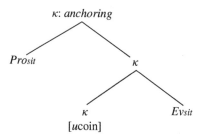

As we have see in Chapter 4, in the absence of an appropriate antecedent for Pro-sit (i.e., in independent clauses), the abstract pronominal argument is deictically anchored. If, however, κ:*anchoring* is embedded in a larger structure, then it is the immediate linguistic environment which provides the relevant context for the interpretation of Pro-sit.

In what follows, I show that the nominal anchoring category (also known as D) is almost identical to its verbal counterpart (INFL). In particular, it has the same fundamental characteristics: relationality (introduced by its intrinsic feature) and contextuality (introduced by the abstract arguments that it orders). But both relationality and contextuality differ in verbal and nominal anchoring categories in predictable ways.

Following Baker (2003), I assume that the defining features of nominality is *identity*. That is, according to Geach (1962) nouns carry, as part of their meaning, *criteria of identity* (see also Gupta 1980; Carlson 1982; Barker 1998, 1999). These are criteria that determine whether the individual denoted by one instance of a noun is the same as the individual denoted by another instance of that noun (Geach 1962: 39, 154). For example, as Geach notes, the sentence in (33a) may be true in a context where the sentence in (33b) may be false.

(33) a. *Heraclitus bathed in some river yesterday, and bathed in the same river today.*
      b. *Heraclitus bathed in some water yesterday, and bathed in the same water today.*

It makes a difference whether we conceive of the fluid Heraclitus bathed in as a river or as water. The river remains the same but the water that defines the river changes. And according to Geach, to know a noun is to be able to identify the individual that it denotes (but see Barker [2010] for a different view).

Thus, I shall assume that the identity feature distinguishes nominality from verbality, which is defined by the coincidence feature.

The second difference between nominal and verbal categories (across the spine) has to do with the abstract arguments. Nominality is fundamentally concerned with individuals, rather than with situations. I thus assume that the arguments that are being related to each other are *individual* arguments, rather than situation arguments. That is, in the unmarked case, the nominal anchoring category takes a nominal complement, which denotes an individual.[7] As shown in (34), the nominal equivalent of the abstract situation argument in VP is an abstract individual argument (arg_{ind}) in the nominal complement of D. Similarly, the abstract argument in SpecDP relative to which the NP-internal argument is ordered is a variable (represented as Pro_{ind}). This is how contextuality is established.

(34)   Nominal anchoring

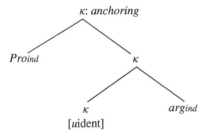

Other than that, the syntax of κ:*anchoring* is predicted to be identical in the nominal and the verbal domain. In particular, we expect the same strategies for

---

[7] For a discussion of nominalization within the USH see Wiltschko (2014).

valuation to be available for [κ:anchoring, *u*ident]. We should find instances of *κ:anchoring* derived via m-valuation. This is instantiated by some pronouns (Section 6.4.2) and demonstratives (Section 6.4.3.) Furthermore, we also expect that [*u*ident] may be externally valued by a higher head. This is instantiated by case (Section 6.4.4).

Since m-valued categories are by hypothesis independent from any embedding structure, they are expected to be the nominal equivalent of independent clauses. I propose that DPs in polysynthetic languages are best analyzed as m-valued nominal constituents. This explains the fact that their distribution does not appear to be regulated by case theory. Case, by definition, involves a dependency and must therefore instantiate external valuation by a higher head. Thus, independent DPs are caseless.

6.4.2   Pronominal anchoring

Pronouns are not a homogeneous class, either within or across languages (Section 6.2.1). From the present perspective, this does not come as a surprise: the notion of a pronoun refers to a word class, and word classes are constructed, rather than being primitives of UG. It is thus expected that pronouns can be constructed in different ways, which is indeed what we find – though I cannot do justice here to the various ways in which they can be constructed (this would warrant another monograph). For example as shown in Déchaine and Wiltschko (2002), pronouns can associate with different layers in the syntactic spine. I will restrict the discussion here to a particular set of pronouns that associate with *κ*: *anchoring*, namely German personal pronouns (Table 6.5). In particular, what I wish to demonstrate here is that the USH allows for a straightforward analysis of a peculiar pattern of multifunctionality which has, to date, largely been ignored in the literature (with the exception of Leiss [2005]).

What is intriguing about this pattern is that the same UoL that is used for 1st person pronouns (*ich* – dark gray shading) reappears in other cells of the

Table 6.5 *German personal pronouns*

	1	2	3 Masc	Fem	Neut
NOM	*ich*	*du*	*er*	*sie*	*es*
ACC	*mich*	*dich*	*ihn*	*sie*	*es*
REFL			*sich*		
DAT	*mir*	*dir*	*ihm*	*ihr*	*ihm*
POSS	*mein*	*dein*	*sein*	*ihr*	*sein*

paradigm (indicated by lighter gray shading). In particular, the accusative forms of 1st and 2nd person (*mich* and *dich*), as well as the reflexive form for 3rd person (*sich*), all contain *ich*. In most analyses of the paradigm (with the exception of Leiss [2005]), this is not considered a pattern and does therefore not constitute an analytical challenge. This is not surprising under the standard assumption that the interpretation of a UoL is determined by its lexical entry alone. So suppose we take *mich, dich,* and *sich* to be decomposable. We would not want to say that they contain an instance of the 1st person pronoun. After all, why would there be a morpheme denoting 1st person inside the 3rd person reflexive? As a consequence, *mich, dich,* and *sich* are usually considered to be simplex forms and the fact that the string *ich* reappears in all three forms is then (implicitly) considered an accident.

It is one of the methodological goals of the formal typology I develop here to exploit systematic patterns of grammatical multifunctionality. Apparent loss or change in meaning is a systematic pattern of natural languages and need not lead us to the postulation of accidental homophony. I argue that *ich* can be analyzed as an *identity predicate*, as in (35).

(35)   {π:*ich*,Σ:identity}

Given this substantive content, I further argue that it values [*u*ident] as [+ident]. Thus, when it is associated with the syntactic spine, as in (36), it asserts identity between the referent of the NP and an utterance individual, which in the absence of further marking is interpreted as the speaker.

(36)   The syntax of German 1st person pronoun

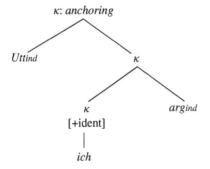

According to this analysis, the 1st person pronoun is in fact constructed. It consists of a UoL that does not itself encode a 1st person feature. Instead, it instantiates the identity predicate, which in turn serves to value the unvalued identity feature, as in (37).

(37)   *c: 1st person pronoun* $= <\{\pi\text{:}ich, \Sigma\text{:identity}\}, [\kappa\text{:}anchoring, \text{m-val:}+\text{ident}]>$

The 1st person interpretation comes about by virtue of being associated with a syntactic configuration, which contains the utterance participant as its external argument. The fact that the relevant utterance participant is the speaker, rather than the addressee, suggests that the speaker is the default participant (Harley and Ritter 2002) while the addressee is marked and thus must be licensed in some way.[8]

If *ich* associates with the spine when the abstract argument is not the speaker, then it will no longer function as a 1st person pronoun, but its substantive content (Σ:identity) will remain constant. This is the case when *ich* occurs in the context of the reflexive pronoun *sich*. Here, the identity predicate *ich* is prefixed by *s-*, which is restricted to 3rd person antecedents.

(38)   Sie   hat   sich   rasiert.
         She   has   REFL   shaved.
         'She shaved.'

In this context, *sich* is not dependent on an utterance participant. This means that the abstract argument that is asserted to be identical with the referent must be anaphoric. The anaphoric character of this abstract argument correlates with the presence of the 3rd person prefix *s-* on *ich*. Thus, *sich* patterns with dependent clauses in that its abstract argument is interpreted relative to a (local) antecedent.

(39)   The syntax of reflexives

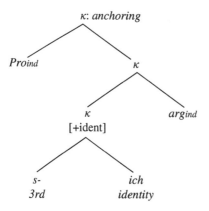

In its occurrence within the reflexive pronoun *sich*, *ich* still functions as the identity predicate. This is in accordance with analyses that treat reflexive pronouns as identity predicates (Cresswell 1973; Keenan 1988; Gast 2006; among others). Thus the 3rd person reflexive pronoun in German is constructed as in (40).

(40) c:3REFL $= <<\{\pi{:}s\text{-},\Sigma{:}3\},\{\pi{:}ich,\Sigma{:}identity\}>,[\kappa{:}anchoring$, m-val:+ident]$>$

Thus, to account for the formal correspondence between *ich* and *sich*, it is essential that some components of interpretation be contributed by the syntactic context. This type of syntactically conditioned multifunctionality is predicted under the USH.

But is there independent evidence that *ich* in *s-ich* is indeed the same form as *ich* when used as a 1st person pronoun? Consider the alternative hypothesis: sameness in form (*ich*) might be purely accidental. There are a number of problems with this. First, the use of *ich* in all of these contexts is somewhat related: it is always part of the pronominal paradigm. Second, this particular pattern of multifunctionality is not restricted to German. Leiss (2005) reports a number of other Germanic languages, as well as Russian, which show the same pattern. This is shown in Table 6.6.

Thus, the occurrence of *ich* in *sich* is not a coincidental quirk about German. If *sich* can indeed be decomposed as proposed in (39), then we further predict that *s-*, too, should be independently attested. This is indeed the case.

Consider first the fact that *ich* is found not only in 3rd person reflexive *sich* but also in 1st and 2nd person accusative *mich* and *dich* respectively as shown in (41).

Table 6.6 *Reflexives and 1st person across languages*

Language	Reflexive pronoun (3rd acc)	1st sg pronoun
Russian	*sebja*	*ja*
German	*sich*	*ich*
Old High German	*sih*	*ich*
Old Icelandic	*sik*	*ik/ek*
Gothic	*sik*	*ik*
Modern Icelandic	*sig*	*eg/ég*
Norwegian	*seg*	*jeg*

Source: Adapted from Leiss (2005).

(41)   Accusative/reflexive pronouns
    a. $\{\pi{:}m,\Sigma{:}1\}{-}\{\pi{:}ich,\Sigma{:}\text{identity}\}$
    b. $\{\pi{:}d,\Sigma{:}2\}{-}\{\pi{:}ich,\Sigma{:}\text{identity}\}$
    c. $\{\pi{:}s,\Sigma{:}3\}{-}\{\pi{:}ich,\Sigma{:}\text{identity}\}$

This decomposition is motivated by consideration of other paradigms. The UoLs remaining under this decomposition (*m-*, *d-*, and *s-*) are attested elsewhere. In particular, as shown in (42), possessive pronouns *mein, dein*, and *sein* invite a similar decomposition yielding the same initial UoLs (*m-*, *d-*, *s-*) attaching to *ein*. The latter exists independently as the indefinite determiner, whose core meaning Σ has yet to be determined.

(42)   Possessive pronouns
    a. $\{\pi{:}m,\Sigma{:}1\}{-}\{\pi{:}ein,\Sigma{:}?\}$
    b. $\{\pi{:}d,\Sigma{:}2\}{-}\{\pi{:}ein,\Sigma{:}?\}$
    c. $\{\pi{:}s,\Sigma{:}3\}{-}\{\pi{:}ein,\Sigma{:}?\}$[9]

Similarly, the dative series also allows decomposition, at least in 1st and 2nd person where we find – once again – the initial UoLs *m-* and *d-*. In this case, the remainder of the form *ir* is identical in form to the 3rd person feminine dative *ihr* (abstracting away from spelling differences).

(43)   Dative pronouns
    a. $\{\pi{:}m,\Sigma{:}1\}{-}\{\pi{:}ir,\Sigma{:}?\}$
    b. $\{\pi{:}d,\Sigma{:}2\}{-}\{\pi{:}ir,\Sigma{:}?\}$

According to this decomposition then, we can isolate *m-*, *d-*, and *s-* as person prefixes as in (44).

(44)   a. $\{\pi{:}m{-},\Sigma{:}1\}$
    b. $\{\pi{:}d{-},\Sigma{:}2\}$
    c. $\{\pi{:}s{-},\Sigma{:}3\}$

The fact that we can isolate the person prefixes supports the decomposition of *mich, dich*, and *sich*. Without this decomposition, i.e., on the assumption that we are dealing with homophony, we would miss a generalization about the form–meaning correspondences in the pronominal paradigms of German.

    In addition, we also find cross-linguistic evidence for this decomposition. Consider the French pronominal paradigm in table Table 6.7.

    We observe nearly identical initial consonants (*m-*, *t-*, *s-*) which share the same function as their German cognates, as illustrated in (45) (see Kayne 2000).

---

[9] The feminine pronoun is an exception to this generalization. Here the possessive pronoun is syncretic with the dative pronoun *ihr*.

Table 6.7 *French pronouns*

	1	2	3 Masc	Fem
NOM	*je*	*tu*	*il*	*elle*
ACC	*me*	*te*	*le*	*la*
REFL			*se*	
DAT	*me*	*te*	*lui*	*elle*
POSS	*mon*	*ton*	*son*	*leur*

Table 6.8 *Blackfoot pronoun paradigm*

	Independent pronoun
1	*n-iistó*
2	*k-iistó*
3	*o-(ii)stó*
1p	*n-iistó-nnaan*
21	*k-iistó-nnoon*
2p	*k-iistó-waaw*
3p	*o-(ii)stó-waaw*

Source: From Frantz (2009).
Note: Frantz (2009) lists these pronouns
with proximate and obviative suffixes.
I have so far not been able to identify the
discourse conditions of these markers in the
context of pronouns (see Wiltschko *et al.*
[forthcoming] for some discussion).

(45)   a. {π:*m*-,Σ:1}
       b. {π:*t*-,Σ:2}
       c. {π:*s*-,Σ:3}

The French pattern supports the morphological decomposition of the German accusative/reflexive forms in (41). That is, in the construction of 1st person pronominal forms, German combines the identity predicate (*ich*) with person prefixes, which are cognate to French person prefixes. The same way of constructing pronouns is also found in Blackfoot. Here, independent pronouns (Table 6.8) are constructed from the stem *iistó* and independently attested person prefixes (46). Plural pronouns are further constructed by number suffixes.

(46)   a. {π:*n*-,Σ:1}
       b. {π:*k*-,Σ:2}
       c. {π:*o*-,Σ:3}

Table 6.9 *Blackfoot possessor constructions*

	Inalienably possessed nouns *mo'tsís* ('hand')	Alienably possessed nouns *omitaa* ('dog')
1	*n-o'tsís*	**nit**-*omitaa*
2	*k-o'tsís*	**kit**-*omitaa*
3	*w-o'tsís*	**ot**-*omitaa*
1p	*n-o'tsís-innaan*	**nit**-*omitaa-innaan*
21	*k-o'tsís-innoon*	**kit**-*omitaa-innoon*
2p	*k-o'tsís-oaawa*	**kit**-*omitaa-oaawa*
3p	*w-o'tsís-oaawa*	**ot**-*omitaa-oaawa*

Source: From Wiltschko *et al.* (forthcoming).

The person prefixes are independently attested on lexical nouns and verbs. Combined with nouns, they index the possessor; combined with verbs they index the subject relation. Note that the person prefixes come in two forms: a short form and a long form. As indicated in Table 6.9, the short form is used with inalienably possessed nouns, while the long forms are used otherwise.[10]

As for the pronominal stem *iistó*, it is listed as a dedicated pronominal form in Frantz and Russell (1995). Wiltschko *et al.* (forthcoming) analyze it as an identity predicate. If so, *iistó* is a UoL that values [$u$ident] as [+ident] via m-valuation as in (47).[11]

(47)　　*c:*1st person pronoun
　　　　= <{{π:*n-*,Σ:1} {π:*iistó*,Σ:identity}}, [κ:*anchoring*, m-val:+ident]>

Incidentally, English reflexive and logophoric pronouns (Table 6.10) are constructed in similar ways (48). The identity predicate *self* (Reinhart and Reuland 1991) combines with person-sensitive possessive prefixes.

(48)　　*c:*1st person pronoun
　　　　= <{{π:*my-*,Σ:1} {π:*self*,Σ:identity}}, [κ:*anchoring*, m-val:+ident]>

In sum, German patterns with French, Blackfoot, and English in that (at least) some of its pronouns are constructed by means of a person prefix and the identity predicate. Alternatively, the 1st person interpretation may come about

---

[10] Similar distributional restrictions on the long and short person prefix are also found when they attach to verbs (see Bliss and Gruber 2011; Bliss 2013; Gruber 2013).

[11] Whether or not the pronominal stem *iistó* associates directly with κ:*anchoring* (i.e., via external merge) or whether it associates in a lower position (i.e., as a light noun *n*) and then associates with κ:*anchoring* via internal merge is an open question.

Table 6.10 *English reflexive pronouns*

	Singular	Plural
1	*myself*	*ourselves*
2	*yourself*	*yourselves*
3	*himself, herself, itself*	*themselves*

Table 6.11 *Halkomelem pronoun paradigm*

	Singular	Plural
1	*te'élthe/te á'elthe*	*telhlímelh*
2	*teléwe*	*telhwélep*
3	*túl'ò/thútl'ò*	*tutl'ó:lem/thutl'ó:lem/yutl'ó:lem*

Source: Wiltschko (2002b: 159, Table 1).

by default (in the unmarked case *ich*). In this construction, the pronominal stem is person-neutral (i.e., the identity predicate). This person-neutral stem may come in the form of a body-part noun or else as a contrastive (focus) marker.[12] In this case, person-sensitivity is introduced by an independently attested functor (such, as for example, a possessive prefix).

(49)   [Person [identity]]

For completeness, note that there is another general strategy available for natural languages to construct pronouns. For example in Halkomelem, the pronominal stem itself is person-sensitive, while the functor that introduces it is a UoL which otherwise is used as a determiner. This is shown in table Table 6.11.

As shown in Wiltschko (2002b), all of the independent pronouns are preceded by a syntactically active determiner *te/tu*. Evidence for the assumption that the determiner is syntactically active comes from the fact that it is obligatorily present if the pronoun is used as an argument (50a), but obligatorily dropped if the pronoun is used as a predicate (50b).

(50)   a. *í:mex = tsel   te-'á'elthe.*
           walk-1SG.S   DET-1SG.PRN
           'I am walking.'

                              Wiltschko 2002b: 165 (11a)

---

[12] See Eckardt (2002) for an analysis of the German focus marker *selbst* as an identity predicate.

b. *[élthe]*$_{pred}$ te   í:mex.
1SG.PRN   DET   walking
'That's me that's walking.'

Wiltschko 2002b: 163 (7a)

This establishes that there are different ways in which pronouns can be built. As shown by Déchaine and Wiltschko (2002), the external syntax of a given pronoun, as well as its semantic properties, depend on its internal syntax. Here we have seen that at least a subset of pronouns can be analyzed as instantiating the identity predicate that we have postulated to be at the core of the nominal anchoring category.[13]

Finally, recall the multifunctionality of 2nd person pronouns we discussed in Section 6.3.1. In many languages, 2nd person pronouns appear to be constructed in a way that allows – at least in certain environments – for a non-indexical interpretation, namely an impersonal or generic interpretation (Gruber 2010). According to the logic of the USH, this pattern suggests that the difference in interpretation must come about via differences in the abstract arguments in the spine. This is the general idea that Gruber (2013) pursues. Her main idea is that the grammatical category *c*:PERSON is constructed by means of time and location. The generic interpretation comes about in the absence of a temporal argument.

6.4.3   *Deictic anchoring: demonstratives and their kin*

In this subsection I turn to a discussion of demonstratives. In particular, I analyze two sets of demonstratives found in Squamish. One of these sets is classified as *deictic determiners*, the other as *demonstratives* (Gillon 2006, 2009). A word of terminological caution is in order, however. The notion *determiner* is sometimes used to refer to a grammatical function, similar to that of subject in the clausal domain. This reflects the fact that different word classes as well as phrases may fulfill this function: articles (51a), demonstratives (51b), and possessors, including pronominal (51c) as well as phrasal possessors (51d).

(51)   a. *the dog*
       b. *this cat*
       c. *his dog*
       d. *the boy's dog*

---

[13] This analysis predicts that there should be pronominal forms that manifest a negative value for the nominal identity predicate as in (i).

(i)   <Σ:non-identity, [κ:*anchoring*, m-val:−coin]>

I submit that this may be instantiated by disjoint anaphors in the sense of Saxon (1984).

Thus, within this tradition, definite articles and demonstratives are both considered *determiners*. However, the notion *determiner* has a different use as well. In particular, with the introduction of D as a position within the nominal extended projection (Abney 1987), *determiner* is sometimes used to refer to the word class that associates with D (i.e., definite and indefinite determiners). On this view *determiners* are restricted to those UoLs that associate with the functional head D. Since demonstratives are often phrasal and therefore cannot be directly associated with D, they would not be classified as determiners. This lies behind Gillon's classification of the Squamish determiner/demonstrative system. I will continue using Gillon's terminological conventions.

Within the context of the USH, neither determiners nor demonstratives in the latter sense can be thought of as language universals. Word classes are necessarily language-specific constructs. For Gillon (2006), the term *deictic determiner* is used for a word class that associates with the syntactic head D (our κ:*anchoring*), while the term *demonstrative* is used for a word class that associates with the spine as a phrase. What is interesting about Squamish is that both the determiners and the demonstratives are deictic, whereas in many Indo-European languages, the word class identified as determiners is not deictic, but instead encodes a distinction in *definiteness*.

6.4.3.1 Squamish deictic determiners

The deictic determiners of Squamish are marked for location and visibility relative to the utterance location, as well as gender (Gillon 2006, 2009). The classification in Table 6.12 is taken from Gillon (2006) and will serve as the basis for my (re-)analysis.

Consider the gender-neutral determiners (*ta, ti, kwa*, and *kwi*). *ti* is used for referents near the speaker (52a), *kwa* is used for referents away from the speaker (52b).

Table 6.12 *The Squamish deictic determiner paradigm*

	Deictic			Non-deictic
	Neutral	Proximal	Distal, invisible	
GENDER-NEUTRAL	*ta*	*ti*	*kwa*	*kwi*
FEMININE	*lha*	*tsi*	*kwelha*	*kwes*

Source: Gillon (2006: 15, Table 2.2).

(52)   a. *Chen*   *kw'ách-nexw*   *ti*   *swí7ka.*
        1SG.S   look-TR(LC)   DET   man
        'I see the man' (near speaker).

                                                     Gillon 2009: 16 (31a)

        b. *Kw'áy'*   *kwa*   *Bill.*
        hungry   DET   Bill
        'Bill is hungry' (Bill is not in room).

                                                     Gillon 2009: 12 (18a)

This is a location-based κ-contrast: PROXIMAL versus DISTAL. Within the valuation typology for κ:*anchoring*, we can analyze these determiners as manifesting the [±ident] contrast derived via m-valuation. The proximate determiner *ti* m-values κ:*anchoring* as [+ident] (53a), the distal determiner *kwa* m-values it as [−ident] (53b).

(53)   a. *c*:proximate deictic determiner = <{π:*ti*,Σ:proximal}, [κ:*anchoring*,
        m-val:+ident]>
        b. *c*:distal deictic determiner = <{π:*kwa*,Σ:distal}, [κ:*anchoring*,
        m-val:−ident]>

Given that the context of use of these determiners correlates with the location of their referent, we have to conclude that the abstract arguments they relate are location-based, as in (54). Thus, as we have already seen, the substantive content of the valuing UoL has an effect on the interpretation of the abstract argument.

    In particular, the use of the proximate determiner marks the referent location as being identical to the utterance location (54a), while the use of the distal determiner marks the referent location as being not-identical to the utterance location (54b).

(54)   a. Proximal determiner   b. Distal determiner

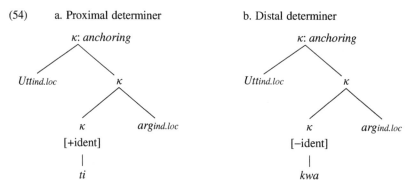

How did the abstract argument turn into a locative argument? Recall that we have seen a similar shift in the interpretation of the abstract arguments in Chapter 4 with the verbal manifestation of κ:*anchoring*. There, we assumed

that the universal spine contains situation arguments, which in turn are complex in that they contain the spatio-temporal coordinates of the utterance, as in (55) repeated from Chapter 4.

(55)   Clausal anchoring

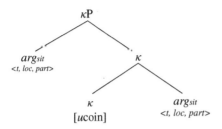

The substantive content of the UoL that m-values [*u*coin] in κ:*anchoring* determines which aspect of the argument is ordered (the temporal or spatial coordinates or the participant arguments). The interpretation of deictic determiners invites a similar analysis. Suppose the abstract individual argument, just like the situation arguments, contains spatio-temporal co-ordinates (Gruber 2010, 2013).

Thus we can assume that the substantive content of *ti* and *kwa* (PROXIMATE vs. DISTAL) determines which aspect of the arguments is considered. In this case, the interpretation is location-based.

Not all of the determiners in the paradigm in Table 6.12, are location-based, however. In particular *ta* is classified as a *neutral deictic determiner* while *kwi* is classified as a *non-deictic* determiner (Gillon 2006, 2009). Consider first the basis for Gillon's classification of *ta* as *neutral deictic*. In terms of its context of use, it differs from the other deictic determiners (*ti* and *kwa*) in that it is compatible with any referent, no matter how close or distant to the speaker in terms of location. For example, in (56a) *ta* is used when the referent is close to the utterance location, a context where *ti* can also be used (56b). But *ta* is also felicitous in a context where the referent is far from the speaker (57a), a context where *ti* is not possible (57b).

(56)   a. *Chen takw-an*   *ta*   *stakw.*
               1SG.S drink-TR   DET   water
               'I drank the water.' (water near speaker)

           b. *Chen takw-an*   *ti*   *stakw.*
               1SG.S drink-TR   DET   water
               'I drank the water.' (water near speaker)

                                                           Gillon 2006: 40 (60)

(57)   a. *Chen takw-an*   **ta**   *stakw.*
          1SG.S drink-TR   DET   water
          'I drank the water.' (water far from speaker and hearer)

    b. **Chen takw-an*   **ti**   *stakw*
          1SG.S drink-TR   DET   water
          'I drank the water.'(water far from speaker and hearer)

Gillon 2006: 41 (62)

Thus, while the use of *ti* is conditioned by the location of the referent relative to the utterance situation, the use of *ta* is not regulated by location. Instead, suppose that *ta* is anchored to an abstract utterance individual Utt_{ind}, as defined in (58).

(58) $Utt_{ind} =_{def}$ an individual associated with a file-card at the utterance situation[14]

If so, *ta*, like *ti*, derives [κ:*anchoring: +ident*] via m-valuation but, unlike *ti*, its content is not explicitly spatial. Consequently, the arguments it relates are also not spatial (59). Instead, *ta* asserts that the referent is identical to the utterance individual.

(59)   Neutral determiner

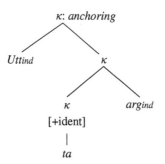

This analysis correctly predicts that *ta* is compatible with three contexts of use: (i) deictic, (ii) novel, and (iii) familiar. In the deictic context, the referent qualifies as Utt_{ind} by virtue of being present in the utterance situation, as in (60). In the novel context, the referent qualifies as Utt_{ind} by virtue of being introduced as a new discourse referent in the utterance situtation, as in (61). And thirdly, in the familiar context, the referent qualifies as Utt_{ind} by virtue of having already been introduced in discourse, prior to the utterance situation, as in (62).

---

[14] The notion of file-card here is in the sense of Heim (1988).

(60)   Deictic context of use
    a. *Kw'áy'*   *ta*   *Bill.*
        hungry   DET   Bill
        'Bill is hungry' (Bill in room).

Gillon 2006: 43 (66b)

    b. *Na7-kw*   *hem'í*   *ta*   *Tám.*
        RL-already   approach   DET   Tom
        'Tom is coming' (said when Tom is seen approaching).

Gillon 2009: 3 (2a)

(61)   Novel context of use
    Chen-t   *wa*   *í-7imesh.*   *Chen*   *kw'ách-nexw*   *ta*   *míxalh.*
    1SG.S-PST   IMPF   REDUP-walk   1SG.S   look-LC.TR   DET   bear.
    'I was walking. I saw a bear.'

Gillon 2006: 84 (7)

(62)   Familiar context of use
    ... Ta   *míxalh*   *na*   *mi*   *ch'i-ch'áy-s-t-ts-as.*
    ... DET   bear   RL   come   REDUP-follow-CAUS-TR-1SG.OBJ-3ERG
    'The bear followed me.'

Gillon 2006: 84 (7)

On this analysis, the fourth determiner, classified as a non-deictic determiner by Gillon, may be analyzed as contrasting with *ta*. Suppose *kwi* derives [−ident] via m-valuation, as in (63).

(63)   The non-deictic determiner

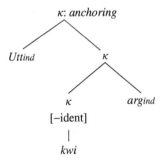

Accordingly, *kwi* asserts that the referent is not an utterance individual. One way of not qualifying as Utt$_{ind}$ is simply by not being referential at all. And indeed, *kwi* is typically used in non-referential contexts such as (64) (see Gillon [2006] for detailed discussion).

Table 6.13 *English and Squamish determiners*

	English	Squamish
Familiar	*the*	*ta*
Novel	*a*	*ta*
Non-referential	*a*	*kwi*

(64)   a. *N-s-tl'i7*   *kwi-n-s*   *yeltx* *kwi* *kwtams.*
        1SG.POSS-NMLZ-want   COMP-1SG.POSS-NMLZ   find   DET   husband
        'I want to find a husband.'

                                                        Gillon 2006: 135 (40d)

        b. *Yuu*   *chaxw,* ...
           take.care   2SG.EMPH ...
           ... *iw'ayti*   *na wa*   *lesiw'ilh*   *t-ta*   *smant* *kwi* *elhkay'.*
           ... maybe   RL IMPF   under   OBL-DET   stone   DET   snake
           'Careful, there may be a snake under the stone.'

                                                        Kuipers 1967: 138

Note that the contrast between *ta* and *kwi* is similar to, but not identical with, definiteness marking familiar from English. In particular in English, a non-referential interpretation is typically associated with the indefinite determiner, while the familiar context of use is typically associated with the definite determiner. In this respect, *kwi* behaves like an indefinite, while *ta* behaves like a definite. Where Squamish and English differ is in the novel context. While in English, novel referents are marked with indefinite determiners, thus patterning with the otherwise non-referential use, in Squamish they are marked with *ta* thus patterning with the determiner which marks the familiar context, as seen in Table 6.13.[15]

Note that if definiteness is defined in terms of discourse novelty and familiarity, then we are led to the conclusion that Squamish does not encode this distinction (Matthewson 1998).[16]

We have now seen that with the ingredients in place for the valuation typology in the clausal domain, we can also describe the properties of Squamish deictic determiners. In what follows, I show that such an analysis is not only

---

[15] *kwi* is also used in partitive contexts as well as referring to a dead person (Gillon 2006). Why these do not count as Utt$_{ind}$ has yet to be explored.

[16] The difference between English definite determiners, which are not compatible with the novel context of use, and Squamish deictic determiners, which are, is reminiscent of the difference between states and inchoative states.

possible, but is also superior to previous analyses of the Squamish determiner system. In particular, it allows us to capture certain formal properties of the Squamish determiner system that remain puzzling under previous analyses.

According to Gillon the features proximal/distal/neuter are associated with the UoLs themselves and are thus directly responsible for the interpretation of the DPs they head. As such, it is the lexical entry itself that restricts the context of use of the DP it heads. Gillon's (2006) analysis is given in (65).

(65) Gillon's analysis of deictic determiners

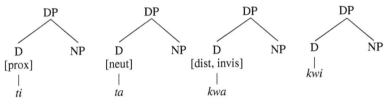

Gillon 2006: 118 (1)

This direct mapping approach contrasts with the USH, according to which much of the form–meaning relation is mediated by syntactic structure. Concretely, the proximal/distal contrast is decomposable into the identity feature (valued either as + or −), as well as the abstract arguments that it relates. On this approach then, it is not the determiners *ti* and *kwa* alone that are responsible for the interpretation, rather the determiners are interpreted relative to a particular syntactic context.

What sets apart the analysis in terms of the universal spine from previous analyses is that it captures the systematic formal contrast between *t*-forms and *kw*-forms. Under this analysis, the former value [uident] as [+ident], while the latter value it as [−ident]. Neither of the existing classifications of the Squamish determiner system captures this contrast. There are, to date, three such classifications available: Kuipers (1967), Currie (1997) (based on Jacobs p.c.), and Gillon (2006, 2009). For ease of exposition, I have translated the feature specifications of existing analyses into a feature-geometric representation in (66).[17] What is striking is that in all these classifications the *t*-forms form a natural class, in that there is a single node in the geometry that picks out all *t*-forms. This is, however, not the case for the *kw*-forms. This is shown for

---

[17] These hierarchies are based on how the paradigms in each of the existing analyses are partitioned. For example, Kuipers (1967) recognizes a contrast between definites and indefinites. But indefinites do not partition further while definites partition into present and non-present. For ease of exposition I represent these partitions as hierarchies, reminiscent of feature geometries.

Kuipers' (1967) classification in (66a), for Currie's (1997) classification in (66b), and for Gillon's (2006) classification in (66c).

(66)   a. Kuipers' classification

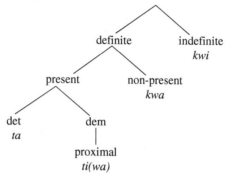

b. Currie's classification

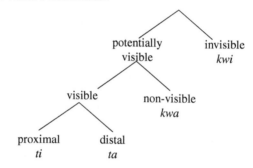

c. Gillon's classification

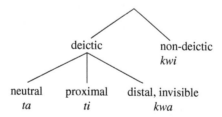

The failure to capture formal natural classes is due to a failure to recognize formal correspondences in the paradigmatic organization. For example, Gillon's (2006, 2009) goal is to identify the conditions on the context of use, based on the assumption that they can be unified by a certain meaning. This assumes the type of direct correspondence between a UoL and its interpretation that I have rejected here. Interestingly, even such direct mapping analyses must assume the existence of an abstract category that underlies the organization of the paradigm. Notably, in the classifications summarized in (66), the absence of a particular feature is defined relative to a well-defined set of other features. For example, the non-deictic determiner *kwi* contrasts with all other determiners (non-deictic *kwi* vs. deictic *ta, ti, kwa*). In contrast, the neutral determiner *ta* is neutral relative to, and thus contrasts with, proximate and distal determiners but not relative to the non-deictic determiner *kwi*. Thus, patterns of markedness require the recognition of certain 'overarching features'. On the present analysis, these overarching features are defined by means of a κ-contrast and are therefore indicative of the presence of κ, which in turn mediates the form–meaning correspondence.

6.4.3.2 Demonstratives
In addition to the deictic determiners, Squamish also has a set of determiners classified as demonstratives. They are summarized in Table 6.14, based on the paradigmatic organization assumed by Gillon (2006).

The demonstratives differ from the deictic determiners in several respects. First, demonstratives may be used either with or without an overt NP, as shown in (67). This contrasts with deictic determiners, which have to be followed by an overt NP, as shown in (68).

(67) a. *Chen kw'ach-nexw*   *tay'/kwetsi/alhi/kwelhi/ti mixalh.*
         1SG.S look- LC.TR   DEM bear
         'I saw that/this bear.'

      b. *Chen kw'ach-nexw*   *tay'/kwetsi/alhi/kwelhi/ti.*
         1SG.S look- LC.TR   DEM
         'I saw that/this.'

Gillon 2006: 34 (50)

Table 6.14 *Squamish demonstratives*

	Neutral, invisible	Proximal	Medial	Distal Unmarked	Distal Invisible
GENDER-NEUTRAL					
NUMBER-NEUTRAL	*kwíya*	*tí, tíwa*	*táy'*	*kwétsi*	
PLURAL	*kwiyáwit*	*iyáwit*	*ítsi(wit)*	*kwétsiwit*	*kwáwit*
FEMININE		*tsíwa*	*álhi*	*kwélhi*	

Source: From Gillon (2006: 39, Table 3.8).

(68)   a. *Chen kw'ach-nexw*   *ta/ti/kwa/lha/tsi/kwelha mixalh.*
          1SG.S look- LC.TR   DET bear
          'I saw the bear.'

       b. **Chen kw'ach-nexw*   *ta/ti/kwa/lha/tsi/kwelha.*
          1SG.S look- LC.TR   DET

                                                    Gillon 2006: 34 (51)

Second, the Squamish demonstratives are morphologically more complex than the deictic determiners. Specifically, while both are composed of the demonstrative roots *tV* and *kwV*, the demonstratives are composed with additional suffixes, namely *ya*, contrasting with *wa*, as well as the plural suffix *-wit*. This defines another difference between deictic determiners and demonstratives. According to Gillon (2006), only the latter (and not the former) may be marked for plurality. The relevant templates are given in (69).

(69)   Determiner template   Demonstrative template
       Root-D   Root-D-DEM-PL
       {kw,t}-V   {kw,t}-V-{ya,wa}-wit

In terms of their context of use, determiners and demonstratives also differ in various ways (see Gillon [2009] for detailed discussion). What is of relevance in the present context is the fact that the demonstratives do not allow for a non-locative use. That is, unlike the determiners *ta* and *kwi*, whose use is determined either by location or by the status of the referent as an utterance individual, the use of Squamish demonstratives is always conditioned by the spatial coordinates of the referent relative to the utterance. Under the analysis developed here, this suggests that demonstratives must always order the referent relative to the utterance location (Utt_{loc}) and not relative to the utterance individual (Utt_{ind}). The differences between deictic determiners and demonstratives are summarized in Table 6.15.

Properties (i)–(iii) are indicative of a difference in the way demonstratives and deictic determiners associate with the spine, i.e., their manner of

Table 6.15 *Differences between determiners and demonstratives*

		Determiner	Demonstrative
I	Pronominal	No	Yes
ii	Nominal modifier	Yes	Yes
iii	Plural *-wit*	No	Yes
iv	Can relate to Utt_{loc}	Yes	Yes
v	Can relate to Utt_{ind}	Yes	No

association. Demonstratives associate with the spine as phrases, while deictic determiners associate with the spine as heads.

Properties (iv) and (v) indicate that the abstract arguments of demonstratives must be locative arguments. The morpho-syntactic properties summarized in (69) suggest that the relevant UoLs that force the locative interpretation for the Squamish demonstratives are *yi* and *wa*. That is, we may analyse the demonstrative roots as before (as manifesting the m-valuing distal and proximal heads). In addition, I tentatively suggest that *yi* and *wa* are overt manifestations of Leu's (2008) silent adjectives (HERE and THERE). Specifically, for Leu demonstratives are analyzed as adjective phrases with a demonstrative root and a silent adjective as in (70).

(70)   Leu's analysis of demonstratives

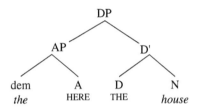

adapted from Leu 2008: 11 (12)

The locative modifiers force the locative interpretation, i.e., the referent is ordered to the utterance via spatial coordinates. Accordingly, the Squamish distal demonstrative can be analyzed as in (71), where Σ:there differs from Σ: distal in that it is obligatorily associated with a locative interpretation.

(71)   *c*:DEMONSTRATIVE
        $= <\{\pi{:}kwi,\Sigma{:}\text{distal}\}\{\pi{:}\text{-}ya,\Sigma{:}\text{there}\},[\kappa{:}anchoring, \text{m-val}{:}-\text{ident}]>$

I submit that it is the affinity between Σ:there and Σ:distal which allows for a reanalysis of demonstratives as (definite) determiners, which defines a common grammaticalization path (see Section 6.3.2). The former requires a locative interpretation while the latter allows for a non-locative interpretation.

We have now seen two types of language-specific categories that are based on κ:*anchoring*: pronominal anchors relating a referent to the utterance participant, as well as deictic anchors relating a referent to the utterance location or the utterance referent. These categories have in common that they are derived via m-valuation and therefore encode a form of deictic anchoring.

But if κ:*anchoring* is indeed fully parallel in the nominal and in the verbal domains, we expect that there are also cases of dependent anchoring, just like there are categories which manifest dependent anchoring in the verbal domain (such as, for example, *c*:SUBJUNCTIVE). In the next subsection I argue that case may indeed be analyzed as manifesting pred- and f-valuation of [*u*ident] in *κ:anchoring*.

6.4.4   Case as dependent anchoring

Recall from Chapter 5 that, in addition to m-valuation, *κ*-anchoring in the verbal domain may also be valued externally, either via a higher predicate (pred-valuation) or by a higher functor within the same extended projection (f-valuation). Here, I show that at least certain instantiations of case may be analyzed as manifesting [*κ:anchoring*, ±ident], derived via external valuation.[18] To abstract away from the content of the valuing head, I simply represent it as *κ* in (72).

(72)   External valuation of *κ:anchoring*

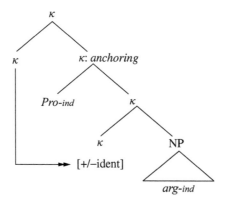

In Subsection 6.4.4.1, I explore the syntax of case under this analysis in more detail, exploring the logical possibilities predicted by the valuation typology. One of the crucial predictions that sets this analysis apart from other approaches to case is the fact that it not only predicts the existence of case, but it also predicts the existence of caseless DPs (Subsection 6.4.4.2). In particular, if case is viewed as an instance of external valuation, then internally valued DPs may remain caseless. This will allow for a novel approach towards polysynthetic languages, in which (at least some) DPs are indeed caseless. In addition, the typology of valuation, along with the lexicalization patterns it derives, allows

---

[18] See also Giusti (1995) for the assumption that case associates with D. Note however that, as with pronouns and demonstratives, this does not preclude the possibility that there are certain forms that are labeled as *case* which associate with a higher position (K) or a lower position (Asp).

for a fresh look at the interaction between morphological case (*m-case*) and abstract syntactic case (*s-case*), as I will show in Subsection 6.4.4.3.

6.4.4.1 The syntax of case

Case has played an important role in the theory of grammar, both within and without the generative tradition. This is despite, or perhaps because of, its elusive character. It defies straightforward definitions in terms of meaning and presents us with a grammatical category par excellence. I cannot do justice here to the rich empirical or theoretical literature on case (see Malchukov and Spencer [2008] for a recent detailed overview). My focus here is on outlining the core ingredients of the case theory that emerges within the formal valuation typology based on the USH. In so doing, we will develop a generalized theory of nominal licensing, according to which case is but one instance of a more general licensing requirement that follows from the necessity of [*u*ident] to be valued.

Maybe one of the most important virtues of the present approach is the fact that it predicts the existence of case in the first place. This sets it apart from most current minimalist analyses, according to which the existence of case is unexpected, if not inexplicable. For example Pesetsky and Torrego (2011: 13) pose the question:

> [W]hy [should] languages show "case phenomena" in the first place. This question is particularly urgent in the context of a Minimalist Program that seeks to attribute syntactic properties that do not arise directly from the action of Merge to properties of the interfaces between syntactic computations and adjacent systems (or else to language external factors).

I will now show that under the USH the existence of *c:*CASE, a category that is defined by its function (anchoring), but not by its content is straightforwardly predicted. This is because content is dissociated from function.

Let us first consider the core cases in a nominative/accusative system. What all descriptions and analyses of case have in common is that they view it as marking the case-marked nominal as dependent. In particular, according to Blake (1994), case is a system of marking dependent nouns for the type of relationship they bear to their heads. I propose that this marking of a dependency is an instance of predicate valuation, as in (73).

(73)   *c:*NOMINATIVE/ACCUSATIVE CASE = UoL+[*κ:anchoring*,pred-val:+ident]

As an instance of f-valuation, case establishes a relation between the DP it values and the argument position associated with the specifier of the valuing head. As discussed in Chapter 2 (Section 2.3), nominative is the case that defines the argument associated with the specifier position of the verbal anchoring category (also known as SpecIP). This position is, in the generative tradition, taken to define the grammatical subject role. In contrast, accusative is the case that defines the argument associated with the specifier position of *κ:point-of-view* (also known as SpecAspP). This position is often taken to define the grammatical object role. Thus, as illustrated in (74a), if [*κ:anchoring,u*ident] is valued by INFL as [+ident], then the DP is dependent on the grammatical subject relation. This is what we call nominative case. And as illustrated in (74b), if [*κ:anchoring, u*ident] is valued by Asp as [+ident] then the DP is dependent on the grammatical object relation. This is what we call accusative case.[19] For ease of exposition, I use below the traditional labels INFL and Asp.

(74)   a. Nominative case   b. Accusative case

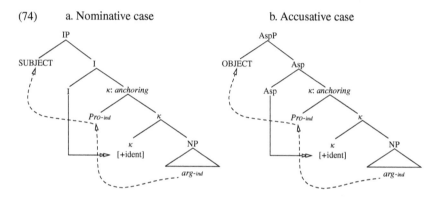

The assumption that *κ:anchoring* (INFL) and *κ:point-of-view* (Asp) value [*κ: anchoring, u*ident] (D), thereby identifying the DP as the subject or object respectively, is a variation on a familiar theme. The difference with the present approach is the fact that – in line with minimalist requirements – no case-specific features had to be introduced. This contrasts with analyses according to which case is a dedicated uninterpretable feature, such as [*u*case], as in Diercks (2012) for example.[20] In addition, the typology derived in this manner makes available a new framework for analyzing different case systems.

---

[19] In (71) I simplified the representation in that DP is represented as a complement to INFL and Asp, respectively. More accurately, according to standard assumptions, these DPs should be in the specifier of IP and AspP. The key assumption is that the valuing head (INFL or Asp) must be able to access the head of the case-bearing DP.

[20] Following Williams (1994), Pesetsky and Torrego (2001) analyze case as an uninterpretable categorical feature. Specifically a tense feature (T) on a nominal category is considered intrinsically uninterpretable and results in the configuration we refer to as case. A problem with this approach is that in some languages temporal features are in fact interpretable on D, but they nevertheless show evidence for case. This is true for Somali (Lecarme 2004; see also Alexiadou 2008; Wiltschko 2011).

Consider first the question of whether there are instances of case that can be analyzed as the manifestation of INFL and Asp valuation, deriving a negative value for the identity feature (i.e., [κ:*anchoring*, −ident]). Ergative and partitive case are amenable to such an analysis, schematized in (75).

(75)   *c*:ERGATIVE/PARTITIVE CASE = UoL+ [κ:*anchoring*,pred-val:−ident]

Consider first ergative case. Suppose INFL values κ:*anchoring* as [−ident], asserting that the referent of the nominal constituent is not identical to the subject relation introduced in SpecIP. This accords with the properties of ergative case in Halkomelem, for example. As shown in (76), in Halkomelem, transitive subjects, but not intransitive subjects or transitive objects, may be preceded by a dedicated oblique determiner *tl'*.[21]

(76)   Halkomelem ergative case

a. *q'ó:y-t-es*   **te/tl'**   *Strang*   *te*   *sqelá:w.*
   kill-TR-3S   DET/DET.OBL   Strang   DET   beaver
   'Strang killed the beaver.'

b. *í:mex*   **te/*tl'**   *Strang.*
   walk   DET/DET.OBL   Strang
   'Strang is walking.'

c. *q'ó:y-t-es*   *te*   *spá:th*   **te/*tl'**   *Strang.*
   kill-TR-3S   DET   bear   DET/DET.OBL   Strang
   'The bear killed Strang.'

Wiltschko 2000b: 262 (52–54)

The analysis according to which Halkomelem ergative case can be analyzed as instantiating [κ:*anchoring*,−ident] is consistent with the fact that it is not associated with SpecIP. In particular, as argued in Wiltschko (2005, 2006), ergative case and ergative agreement mark transitive subjects because, unlike nominative in Indo-European languages, they are associated with *v*, rather than INFL. Consequently, the relevant relation is encoded in Spec*v*P, not SpecIP. Evidence that ergative agreement in Halkomelem associates with the thematic domain comes from the fact that, unlike subject agreement in English, ergative agreement is always realized on the verb, even in the presence of an auxiliary (see Section 5.4.3.). This distribution is accounted for under the assumption that ergative agreement associates with *v*, whereas subject agreement in English associates with INFL (see Wiltschko [2005, 2006c] for further arguments and discussion). The fact that the ergative

---

[21] This determiner is restricted to names.

subject is identified by *v* is consistent with the assumption that INFL values the corresponding *κ:anchoring* as [−ident]. Thus, it is not identified with the role introduced in SpecIP.

Another type of case that may be analyzed in this way is the possessive (genitive) case. Here valuation may stem from the UoL itself, i.e., it may be a form of m-valuation. Assuming that this case asserts that the referent is not identical to the abstract argument in the Specifier of the valuing head is consistent with the fact that the referent is, in fact, not identical to its possessor. In this way, the possessor relation is the converse of the identity relation (i.e., [−ident]).

(77)   *c*:POSSESSIVE/GENITIVE CASE = UoL+ [*κ:anchoring*,m-val:−ident]

This analysis is consistent with the fact that, in many languages, ergative and possessive (genitive) case are identical in form (Baerman 2009: 224). Under this analysis this syncretism is a matter of the [−ident] value in *κ:anchoring*.

Next we turn to partitive case, which I analyze as instantiating [*κ:anchoring*,−ident] valued by Asp via pred-valuation. Accordingly, in this context, the nominal referent is asserted not to be identical with the grammatical object role, which in turn is sometimes equated with the participant that *measures out the event* (Tenny 1987, 1994). We can observe this effect in Finnish (Kiparsky 1998). If the object is interpreted as delimiting the event (the bear is shot), it receives accusative case (78a); if it is interpreted as not delimiting the event, it receives partitive case (78b).

(78)   a. *Ammu-i-n* *karhu-a /* *kah-ta* *karhu-a /* *karhu-j-a.*
   shoot-PST-1SG bear-PRTV / two-PRTV bear-PRTV / bear-PL-PRTV
   'I shot at the (a) bear / at (the) two bears / at (the) bears.'

  b. *Ammu-i-n* *karhu-n /* *kaksi* *karhu-a /* *karhu-t.*
   shoot–PST-1SG bear-ACC / two-ACC bear-PRTV / bear-PL.ACC
   'I shot the (a) bear / two bears / the bears.'

Thus, partitive case may be analyzed in the same way as ergative case: it instantiates [*κ:anchoring*,−ident]. The difference is that the valuing head is Asp, rather than INFL. In this context [*κ:anchoring*,−ident] indicates that the referent of the nominal constituent is not dependent on SpecAsp (i.e., the object relation). This is consistent with the fact that DPs bearing partitive case are often structurally lower than their accusative counterparts (Belletti 1988).

Thus far we have seen cases that are derived via the valuation of *κ:anchoring* via a verbal licensing head, i.e., by means of pred-valuation, as in (79).

(79)   *c*:STRUCTURAL CASE = UoL + [*κ:anchoring*,pred-val:±ident]

Everything else being equal, the valuation typology developed for *κ:anchoring* in the verbal domain predicts that we should also find cases derived via f-valuation, where the valuing head is a functional head that is higher on the nominal spine. Case-assigning prepositions lend themselves to be analyzed in precisely this way. And in fact, it has been argued that there is a functional category above D responsible for case-assignment, namely K (Lamontagne and Travis 1987). In this constellation, the relation between verbs and the nominal constituent is mediated by a preposition (Blake 1994). The flavor of the abstract argument relative to which the referent is ordered is affected by the content of K. The coexistence of K- and D-case may explain systems that involve case-stacking (Gerdts and Youn 1999; Schütze 2001; Richards 2012). I leave a detailed analysis of K-case for future research.

What is relevant for now is that the valuation typology we have developed based on the verbal anchoring category (INFL) may equally be used to analyze case systems. In particular, the dependent character of case is a characteristic of external valuation. The typology that emerges is summarized in (80).

(80)   Valuation typology for nominal anchoring

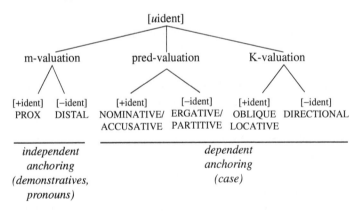

Crucially, the USH not only predicts the existence of case, it also predicts the existence of languages with no manifestation of case. In particular, we have seen that, with the same ingredients ([*u*ident] and abstract reference arguments) and elementary operations (association and valuation), we can analyze deictic anchoring (demonstratives and pronouns) as well as the system of case. These two seemingly different phenomena are thus viewed as two sides of the same coin: they have the same formal underpinnings. Consequently, the absence of case in a given language is no longer to be viewed as a counter-example to the existence of universal category. Rather it is the abstract anchoring category that is universal, but it may be instantiated in different ways.

6.4.4.2   The syntax of caselessness

According to (77), caselessness may arise in two ways: (i) in the absence of κ:*anchoring* (i.e., for nominal constituents that do not project all the way to DP), or (ii) if [κ:*anchoring*,±ident] is derived via m-valuation, in which case the DP is deictically anchored. I discuss each of these strategies in turn.

Since case reduces to a manifestation of κ:*anchoring*, we predict that, in the absence of this category, the nominal constituent will remain caseless. This prediction is borne out in Hebrew. Danon (2002, 2006) argues that bare NPs in Hebrew lack case. This is evidenced by the fact that a nominal argument preceded by the definite determiner *ha* must be case-marked by the object marker *et* (81a). In contrast, a nominal argument not preceded by the definite determiner cannot be so case-marked (81b).

(81) a. *Dan kara*   *(*et*)   *ha-itonim.*
          Dan read   OBJ   DET-newspapers
          'Dan read the newspapers.'

      b. *Dan kara*   (*et)   (*kama*) *itonim.*
          Dan read   OBJ   (some) newspapers
          'Dan read (some) newspapers.'

Danon 2006: 979 (1)

The second way in which DPs may remain caseless is if [κ:*anchoring*,±ident] is derived via m-valuation. As we have seen in Section 6.4.3, [κ:*anchoring*, *u*ident] may be internally valued. The UoLs that manifest this configuration are known as demonstratives. Accordingly, the valuation typology predicts that case marking (i.e., dependent anchoring) is in complementary distribution with demonstrative determiners (independent anchoring). We have seen that this prediction is indeed borne out for Squamish and Blackfoot. In particular, in neither of these two languages is the distribution of DPs governed by case (Section 6.2.3). And at the same time, in both languages nominal arguments are obligatorily introduced by deictic determiners.

Thus, the case theory derived from the valuation typology not only predicts the existence of case, it also predicts the existence of caseless arguments, as long as they are deictically anchored. In this respect, the current proposal differs from previous approaches in several respects. First, there is no need for a macro-parameter to distinguish between languages in which the distribution of nominal arguments is regulated by case and languages where this is not

Table 6.16 *Halkomelem determiner paradigm*

	Gender-neutral	Feminine	Oblique
VISIBLE	*te*	*the*	*tl'*
INVISIBLE	*kwthe*	*kwse*	
REMOTE	*kw'e*	*kw'se*	

Source: Adapted from Galloway (1993: 387).

so (i.e., pronominal argument languages; see for example Baker [1996] and Diercks [2012]). But on the present approach, caselessness need not define an entire language. Instead, even within a given language, we may expect that some DPs are deictically anchored while other DPs are dependent (i.e., have case). We see the coexistence of case-marked and deictically anchored arguments in Halkomelem. In particular, the determiner paradigm is organized in a way that shows that deictic features and case features can coexist in a single language, while at the same time supporting the prediction that they are in complementary distribution. As shown in Table 6.16, determiners are equipped with deictic features except for the oblique determiner *tl'*, which is not sensitive to the location of the referent.

The organization of the determiner paradigm follows straightforwardly from the valuation typology: deictic features and case features should be in complementary distribution. Whether this prediction holds up against a larger set of languages remains to be seen, however.

For completeness, note that the predictions based on this formal typology cannot simply be tested against surface features. In particular, not all demonstratives are constructed in the same way. For example, Wiltschko (2009) argues that the deictic features of German demonstratives do not define a κ-contrast. As a consequence, they cannot be analyzed as m-valuing [$u$ident]. Instead, the deictic features of German demonstratives behave as modifying features. Thus, demonstratives coexist with non-deictic definite determiners. But if demonstratives are not constructed by m-valuation, we predict that they should be compatible with case. This is indeed the case, as shown in Table 6.17.

Finally, the case theory based on the valuation typology for κ:*anchoring* allows us to come to terms with the elusive character of case: it cannot be defined in terms of its substantive content. In this respect, case behaves similarly to subjunctives. Language-specific categories that are not derived via m-valuation cannot be identified by their content. Instead, they will always appear to encode a dependency.

Table 6.17 *German demonstratives inflect for case*

Det	Masc	Fem	Neut
NOM	*dies-er*	*dies-e*	*dies-es*
ACC	*dies-en*	*dies-e*	*dies-es*
DAT	*dies-em*	*dies-er*	*dies-em*
GEN	*dess-en*	*dies-er*	*die-es*

Under the present approach, the absence of content is predicted: categories generally are not intrinsically (i.e., via UG) associated with content. But nevertheless there is no need for an abstract dedicated case feature (such as, for example, in Chomsky [1995]). Rather, abstract structural case reduces to anchoring. On the current proposal the feature [uident] is responsible for case. It is, however, not a dedicated case feature. First, the *identity* feature is key in distinguishing nominal categories from verbal categories. As such, it is responsible for nominality (see also Baker 2003). Moreover [uident] can also be valued by dedicated morphological marking deriving independent DPs that are interpreted deictically. This derives the types of caseless DPs we observe in some polysynthetic languages resulting in the appearance of non-configurationality.[22] Thus, case is a special instance of nominal anchoring.

In sum, if we ask whether all languages have case, the answer is *No!* In many languages (including Halkomelem and Blackfoot) the distribution of nominal arguments is not regulated by the notion of case. Thus, case is not a universal category. But this does not imply that there is not a universal category that is responsible for the construction of case. And indeed, if we ask instead whether languages that lack case have a nominal anchoring category, the answer is *Yes!* Both Halkomelem and Blackfoot have obligatory deictic (demonstrative) determiners. To the best of my knowledge, the valuation typology is the only formal analysis of case that predicts, on principled grounds, the existence of case as well as caselessness.

6.4.4.3   The status of morphological case
We have thus far considered the syntactic constellations that make up the language-specific categories we refer to as case. For example, we have

---

[22] But note that non-configurationality does not always come about in the same way. As Hale (1989: 294) puts it *"nonconfigurationality is not a global property of languages; rather, it is a **property of constructions**."*

Table 6.18 *The nominative/accusative determiner*
paradigm of Standard German

	Singular			Plural
	Masc	Fem	Neut	
NOMINATIVE	*der*	*die*	*das*	*die*
ACCUSATIVE	*den*	*die*	*das*	*die*

analyzed structural case as manifesting the valued identity feature derived via predicate valuation, as in (82), repeated below for convenience.

(82)   *c*:STRUCTURAL CASE $= $ UoL $+$ [κ:*anchoring*,pred-val:$\pm$ident]

However, language-specific categories are not only comprised of syntactic constellations; they are also overtly realized in the form of function words or morphological markers, i.e., UoLs. In this subsection, I briefly explore the properties of the UoLs that participate in the construction of *c*:CASE.

There is in fact a long tradition of distinguishing between the syntactic constellation of case (s-case) and the morphology that marks it (m-case).[23] What is the relation between the two? In what follows, I explore this question in light of USH and the valuation typology in (80).

Given the logic of the system, *c*:STRUCTURAL CASE must be realized by a UoL from the post-syntactic lexicon. This is because the value of the identity feature is determined by a higher head. And indeed, many m-case markers have the properties typically associated with post-syntactic UoLs. For example in German, m-case is realized on determiners (consistent with the assumption that it manifests κ:*anchoring*), and it takes the form of fusional inflection. This can be seen in the example in (83), which contains a nominative, an accusative, and a dative argument. The relevant determiner paradigm is given in Table 6.18.

(83)   *Der*   *Hund*   *fängt*   *den*   *Ball mit*   *dem*   *Maul.*
        DET.NOM dog   catches   DET.ACC   ball with   DET.DAT   muzzle
        'The dog catches the ball with the muzzle.'

Thus, the full analysis of *c*:NOMINATIVE including the post-syntactic UoL that realizes it is given in (84).

---

[23] The distinction between m- and s-case is sometimes indicated as case and Case, respectively (see, e.g., McFadden 2004).

(84) a. *c*:NOMINATIVE = <{[κ:*anchoring*,pred-val(I):+ident], MASC}, π:*der*>
      b. *c*:NOMINATIVE = <{[κ:*anchoring*,pred-val(I):+ident], FEM}, π:*die*>
      c. *c*:NOMINATIVE = <{[κ:*anchoring*,pred-val(I):+ident], NEUT}, π:*das*>

The assumption that this type of m-case is post-syntactic is consistent with recent work in the generative literature, according to which m-case is a post-spell-out phenomenon (McFadden 2004; Legate 2008; Baker and Vinokurova 2010, among others). As usual, the post-syntactic character of the UoL that realizes case implies that the UoL is somewhat independent of the syntactic constellation that it realizes. That is, we do not expect that s-case and m-case stand in a one-to-one relation to each other. And indeed, it has long been known that there are significant mismatches between m-case and s-case, suggesting that the two cannot be equated (see Yip *et al.* 1987; Falk 1991; Marantz 1991; Sigurðsson 1991, 2001; Harley 1995; Bittner and Hale 1996; Schütze 1997).

Note further that the UoL that realizes *c*:CASE consists of form (π) only. Thus *c*:CASE is not definable based on meaning. Neither the syntactic constellation nor the UoL that realizes it is based on meaning Σ. As a consequence, case, just like the subjunctive, is a category that defies straightforward analysis in a framework where UoLs are strictly defined by their meaning. Under the USH, however, the relation between UoLs and their interpretation is mediated by the syntactic spine.

One of the parameters of variation within the USH has to do with the timing of Associate. In addition to the realizational, post-syntactic UoLs, the USH makes available another type of UoL, one that is associated with the spine before the syntactic computation. Within the valuation typology, there are two types of pre-syntactic UoLs: those that serve to m-value [*u*ident] and those that realize the unvalued identity feature [*u*ident]. I discuss each of them in turn.

Consider first whether *c*:CASE may also be constructed via m-valuation. If so, we predict that it is associated with substantive content and that it is a pre-syntactic UoL. There are indeed cases that behave in exactly this way, such as, for example, certain locative cases. They are meaningful in that they express particular spatial relations. While in some languages such case are realized by prepositions, which may or may not themselves govern nominal cases, this is not necessarily so. Several languages appear to have dedicated locative case endings (see Creissels [2008] for an overview). Under the USH, such cases can be analyzed as instantiating the head that serves to m-value [*u*ident].

A case in point is found in Blackfoot. In this language spatio-temporal adjuncts must be licensed by the prefix *it-* which is realized within the verbal complex, as in (85) and (86) (data are from Bliss and Gruber [2011]).

(85)   a. *Ááksitsipssstsooyiwa*   *omi*   *ksikóókooyiss*
          aak-**it**-ipsst-iooyi-wa   om-yi   ksikookooyiss
          FUT-LOCV-inside-eat-PROX   DEM-OBV   tent
          'S/he will eat in that tent.'

       b. **Ááksipsstsooyiwa   omi   ksikóókooyiss*

                                             Bliss and Gruber 2011: 6 (27)

(86)   a. *Matónni*   *nitsítsinoowaw*   *kiksíssta*
          matonni   nit-**it**-inoo-a-wa   k-iksisst-wa
          yesterday   1-LOCV-see-DIR-PROX   2-mother-PROX
          'Yesterday I saw your mother.'

       b. **Matónni   nitsinoowaw   kiksíssta*

                                             Bliss and Gruber 2011: 6 (28)

This use of *it-* can be analyzed as instantiating the UoL responsible for m-valuing the anchoring category, as in (87).[24] For evidence that *it-* associates with D, see Bliss and Gruber (2011); Bliss (2013); Gruber (2013).

(87)   *c*:SPATIO-TEMPORAL CASE = $<\{\pi{:}it\text{-},\Sigma{:}\text{HERE}\},[\kappa{:}anchoring,\text{m-val}{:}+$
          ident]>

Evidence that *it-* is part of the pre-syntactic lexicon comes from the patterns of multifunctionality. In particular, the use of *it-* is pervasive in the grammar of Blackfoot in ways that are indicative of the pre-syntactic lexicon. The pre-syntactic lexicon is characterized by the absence of a categorical identity and therefore defines the multifunctionality heuristic. Its pervasiveness can be gleaned from the sentence in (88), in which *it-* appears three times: as part of the person prefix (*nit*), as a verbal prefix licensing a locative adjunct (*nitsitooyi*), and as part of the nominalization (*itáísooyo'pi*).

(88)   *Nitsítsooyi*   *anni*   *itáísooyo'pi.*
          n-it-it-ooyi   ann-yi   it-a-iso-ooyi-o'p-i
          1-LOCV-LOCV-eat   DEM-INAN   LOCV-IMPF-HORIZ-eat-IMPRS-INAN
          'I ate at the table.'

                                             Bliss 2013: 41 (31)

This pattern of multifunctionality is characterized by the identity of the $\{\pi,\Sigma\}$ bundle, and at the same time by a difference in categorical identity derived via the association relation. This correlates with a difference in syntactic distribution with predictable differences in meaning.

---

[24] Note that Blackfoot *it-* is not linearized in a position immediately preceding the noun phrase it licenses, but rather inside the verbal complex (see Bliss *et al.* [2013] for discussion; see also Baker [1988] for an analysis of applicatives in terms of preposition incorporation).

M-case markers of the realizational type, i.e., post-syntactic UoLs, differ. Since they are part of the post-syntactic lexicon they must be associated with categorical identity and can no longer acquire their category during the syntactic computation. Instead, they realize a particular syntactic configuration.

Nevertheless, post-syntactic UoLs may also be multifunctional, albeit in different ways. In fact, a recurrent topic in the literature on m-case concerns patterns of *syncretism*. Case syncretism refers to the "combination of multiple distinct case values in a single form" (Baerman 2009: 219). Thus, syncretism is a special case of multifunctionality. It provides us with a window into the internal structure of UoLs. The valuation typology for the nominal anchoring category in (80) makes predictions about the patterns of syncretism that we may expect. For example, the realizational (post-syntactic) UoLs may be fully specified for their value ([+ident] or [−ident]), as well as for the source of valuation (pred- or f-valuation), as in (89).

(89)   *c*:CASE = UoL + <[*κ:anchoring*,pred-val(I):+ident]>

UoLs that are so specified are predicted not to be syncretic. And indeed there are languages where case forms are never syncretic. According to WALS, out of 198 languages, 35 are such that inflectional case marking is never syncretic.

It is, however, also possible for a given UoL to spell out the valued identity feature without specifying the source of valuation, as in (90).

(90)   *c*:CASE = UoL + <[*κ:anchoring*,+ident]>

This predicts a pattern of syncretism in which several [+ident] or [−ident] cases are realized with the same UoL respectively. This is indeed the case. While I cannot do justice to the full range of syncretic patterns found across the languages of the world, I will here introduce a few cases that exemplify some of the predictions of the valuation typology.

First, a common pattern of syncretism is one where the core structural cases (nominative and accusative) are realized by the same UoL. In fact, this is the most frequent type of syncretism (Baerman 2009: 222). It is illustrated in Table 6.19 on the basis of Classical Armenian, where the nominative and accusative forms are identical for singular nouns (Meillet 1936: 81–2, 91 cited from Baerman [2009: 220 (2)]).

This type of syncretism can be understood if we assume that the UoL is specified for the value of the identity feature only (namely [+ident]) but does not restrict the source of the valuation (it could be valued by INFL or Asp).

Table 6.19 *Classical Armenian:* NOM/ACC *syncretism*

	Father	Fathers
NOM	*hayr*	*hark'*
ACC	*hayr*	*hars*
LOC	*hawr*	*hars*
GEN	*hawr*	*harc'*
DAT	*hawr*	*harc'*
ABL	*hawrē*	*harc'*
INS	*harb*	*harbk'*

Table 6.20 *Lak:* ERG/GEN *syncretism*

	Noun 'house'
ABS	*k'atta*
ERG	*k'atlu-l*
GEN	*k'atlu-l*
DAT	*k'atlu-n*

(91)   The nominative/accusative syncretism:
         [κ:*anchoring*,pred-val:+ident]

Another common pattern of syncretism is the one between ergative and genitive case as illustrated in Table 6.20, for Lak (Žirkov 1955: 36, 64–6, cited from Baerman [2009: 225 (13)]).

This type of syncretism can be understood if we assume that the UoL is specified for the negative value of the identity feature but does not restrict the source of valuation (it could be I [ergative] or K [genitive]).

(92)   The ergative/genitive syncretism:
         [κ:*anchoring*,pred-val:−ident]

Another common syncretism, however less commonly discussed, is that between nominative and vocative. For example, in Latin nominative and vocative are identical for all inflection classes in the plural, and for all but one in the singular (Blake 1994: 5; Albright and Fuss 2012: 240). Many analyses of the vocative treat it as an m-case rather than an s-case. Consequently, it is difficult to understand this syncretism: if the input for nominative and vocative is so different, then how is the syncretism derived? This difficulty is reflected by the fact that the vocative is excluded from Caha's (2009) generative analysis of patterns of syncretism. More generally, the vocative has not received much attention within the generative tradition, presumably because within this tradition it is s-case which is the phenomenon of interest (a notable exception is the discussion in Bernstein [2008], see below).

The valuation typology for κ:*anchoring* allows us to capture this syncretism. Consider how. Vocative case can be understood as an instance of [+ident] derived by f-valuation from the higher functional head (K), as in (93).

(93)   *c:*VOCATIVE CASE = <[κ:*anchoring*,f-val(K):+ident]>

But how does this analysis derive the context of use for vocatives? Suppose that one of the key ingredients of the vocative is an addressee-oriented valuing head K. Note that an addressee-oriented head has been proposed in the verbal domain (Speas and Tenny 2003; Lam *et al.* 2013). Under the assumption that the nominal spine parallels the verbal spine, we expect such an addressee-oriented head above DP as well. See also Section 5.4.5 for an addressee-oriented head in Upper Austrian subjunctives

If indeed vocative K is addressee-oriented, it will restrict the individual denoted by the abstract argument in SpecKP to the addressee. Consequently, the pronominal argument of the anchoring category is interpreted as the addressee as well.

(94)   The syntax of VOCATIVE

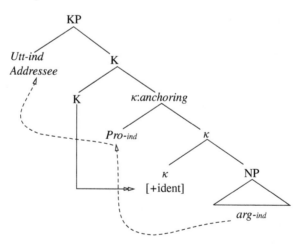

The analysis in (94) captures the descriptive generalization that the vocative is a form of address, just like the imperative is. In particular, it asserts that the referent of the NP is identical to the addressee. While the vocative is not a case in the sense that it expresses a dependency on a particular verb, it still is dependent on a functional head: the addressee-oriented functor values [κ:*anchoring,u*ident] as [+ident].

Independent support for the claim that the vocative is licensed by an addressee-oriented functional head comes from the fact that, in some languages, vocatives are preceded by a 2nd person pronoun. In fact, Bernstein (2008) argues that vocatives are always constructed with an abstract (unpronounced) 2nd person pronoun YOU. This pronoun is overtly realized in Upper Austrian German, as shown in (95).

(95)   *Du, Maria, kummst   du   moagn?*[25]
        You Mary, come-2SG   you   tomorrow
        'Mary? Are you coming tomorrow?'

In sum, under the analysis sketched in (94), nominative and vocative form a natural class. They both manifest [+ident] derived by external valuation as in (96).

(96)   The nominative/vocative syncretism:
        [κ:*anchoring*,+ident]

To the best of my knowledge, this is the first principled account for the nominative/vocative syncretism. At the same time, it makes it possible to understand the fact that vocative is realized as an m-case, despite not functioning as an s-case (i.e., it is not dependent on a verbal predicate). In fact, from the present perspective, the question as to whether or not a given UoL is to be categorized as case is meaningless. Case is necessarily a language-specific category and as such cannot be universal. But the formal underpinnings that are used to construct case are universal. And in this respect, vocative patterns with other cases in that it realizes the externally valued identity feature of κ:*anchoring*. In other words, vocative, like case, is an instance of nominal anchoring.

This concludes our discussion of patterns of syncretism in the domain of case. We have seen that the valuation typology allows for a new way of analyzing such patterns. In conclusion, observe that case syncretism is not

---

[25] Vocative *du* is only felicitous in sentence-initial position:

(i)   *Kummst du moagn (*du) Maria?*
       Come-2SG you tomorrow, (you) Mary?
       'Are you coming tomorrow, Mary?'

This is in line with Zwicky's (1974) observation that there are two types of vocatives: *calls* and *addresses*. The former are used to attract the addressee's attention, while the latter are used to maintain or emphasize the contact between speaker and addressee (Zwicky 1974: 787).

the only pattern of multifunctionality we predict to occur. In particular, since case is not defined based on meaning, and is instead defined by its syntactic constellation, we may expect that UoLs which realize valued features only without specifying the source of valuation display systematic multifunctionality. This is indeed the case.

For example, according to Blake (1994: 184), there is a common homophony between case marking and *switch-reference* marking. Strikingly, this is observed in several unrelated languages such as the Muskogean, Yuman, and Uto-Aztecan languages (Jacobson 1983: 151) as well as Australian languages (Austin 1981). Blake illustrates this multifunctionality on the basis of an example from the Yuman language Diegueño.

(97)　　a.　*Sin^y-c*　　　　　　*Pəcwəyu-w-m*　　　*Pəyip-s.*
　　　　　　woman-**NOM**　　　3SG.sing-DS　　　1SG&3SG.hear-ASSERT
　　　　　　'I heard the woman sing.'

　　　　b.　*Pamp*　　　　*n^{y}a-taPam-c*　　　　　　*Pəwu-w-s.*
　　　　　　1SG.walk　　　when-1SG.be.around-SS　　　1SG&3SG.saw-ASSERT
　　　　　　'As I was walking, I saw him.'
　　　　　　　　　　　　Langdon 1970: 150–4, cited from Blake 1994: 184 (25–26)

According to Blake (1994: 185), there is general agreement that switch-reference markers derive from case markers. From the present perspective, this is not surprising: nominative marking is analyzed as realizing [+ident]. Since same-subject marking encodes an identity relation between two subjects, it does not come as a surprise that it may also be realized with the same marker [+ident]. Thus, we can identify the formal similarities even between categories that appear – on the surface – quite different from each other.

In sum, the USH allows for a novel approach to m-case as well as patterns of syncretism. By recognizing that case realizes the valued identity feature in D, we are able to analyze not only patterns of case syncretism, but also other patterns of multifunctionality, including the nominative/same-subject multifunctionality. It remains to be seen whether other patterns of multifunctionality are amenable to a similar analysis.

6.5　　The essence of nominal anchoring

The goal of this chapter was to extend the analysis of anchoring to the nominal anchoring category (i.e., the category standardly labeled as D).

I have argued that both nominal and verbal anchoring are subject to the same valuation typology: their unvalued feature may be valued via morphological marking (m-valuation), or else by a higher head (pred- or f-valuation). Since m-valued phrases are by hypothesis independent of an external licensor, they may surface as independent constituents. In the verbal domain, this derives independent matrix clauses and in the nominal domain it derives argument expressions that are not licensed by the verbal spine (i.e., caseless arguments). This allows for a new way to understand pronominal argument languages, which are characterized by the relative independence of nominal expressions from the verbal complex. The proposal predicts that such internally valued Ds must be deictically anchored. Thus, it is predicted that nominal expressions in caseless languages are all deictically anchored.

In contrast, external valuation introduces a dependency, either to a higher head in the same extended projection (f-valuation), or else to a predicate or functional head of a different extended projection (pred-valuation). In the verbal domain, this derives dependent clauses such as infinitives and subjunctives; in the nominal domain, this derives case, a form of dependent marking. On this view then, case-licensed DPs are to dependent clauses what deictically anchored DPs are to matrix clauses. As such, the present approach makes available a novel understanding of case, one that allows us to understand the fact that case has a function (encoding dependency) without being associated with a particular semantic content (see also Manzini and Savoia 2010).

Thus, the essence of nominal anchoring is similar to that of its verbal equivalent. Its core function is derived by virtue of its position in the universal spine: it occupies the anchoring domain. This differs from previous approaches towards D, according to which D is inherently defined by some substantive content such as definiteness (Lyons 1999), or person (Bernstein 2008). While these notions may be part of the make-up of the language-specific categories that are constructed from κ:*anchoring*, they do not define them universally.

As for the difference between nominal and verbal anchoring, I have put forth the proposal that the difference lies in the feature that is intrinsically associated with each of them. While verbal anchoring is defined by a *coincidence* feature, nominal anchoring is defined by an *identity* feature. Thus, one of the core differences between verbs and nouns is that the former introduce a dimension of dynamicity. In particular, *identity* is a special case of coincidence, namely perfect coincidence, which requires a complete overlap, but coincidence allows for partial overlap and is thus compatible with dynamicity.

The assumption that nominal categories are characterized by identity, which is itself a special case of coincidence, predicts that verbs are basic, while nouns are special. That this may in fact be on the right track is supported by the fact that patterns of nominalization are attested across many languages of the world, while patterns of verbalization are much less frequent (Baker 2002).

The dynamic aspect of verbal categories introduced by the coincidence feature will become crucial in the next chapter, where we explore the syntax of aspect.

7 Categories that introduce a point of view

> Man is pre-eminently endowed
> with the power of voluntarily and consciously
> determining his own point of view.
>
> Ernst Mach

7.1 Introduction

This chapter is concerned with categories that serve to introduce a *point of view* (henceforth PoV). In particular, I have four goals. **(i)** First, I introduce the category most commonly assumed to fulfill this function, namely (viewpoint) aspect (henceforth aspect), which, in Indo-European languages, is based on temporality. **(ii)** Second, I will test the Universal Base Hypothesis (UBH) as well as the No Base Hypothesis (NBH) in light of aspect. We shall see that – as with the other categories discussed in previous chapters – neither of these hypotheses can come to terms with the empirical findings. Aspect does not behave like a universal category, in that it is not attested across all languages, and if a language has such a category, it does not necessarily share the same formal properties. Thus, aspect does not behave like a universal natural class. But at the same time there seem to be universal characteristics associated with aspect marking. **(iii)** I will then introduce an analysis of aspect based on the Universal Spine Hypothesis (USH). As predicted, there are categories in the general domain where we would expect to find aspect which express different notions, while still introducing a PoV. This defines the last goal of this chapter. **(iv)** In particular, I argue that Blackfoot direct/inverse marking, as well as Squamish control marking, can be analyzed as language-specific instantiations of the category responsible for introducing PoV. Recall that these were the two main categories introduced in Chapter 1 that presented us with the main challenge for the hypothesis that categories are universal. Specifically, it was not clear how to treat these typologically rare categories under a universalist approach towards categories.

7.1.1   *What is viewpoint aspect?*

Within the generative tradition, aspect is commonly associated with a functional category Asp, which is located above *v*P but below IP.

In Indo-European languages such as English, PoV is substantiated with temporal content.[1] In this respect, it parallels the anchoring category INFL, which is also substantiated by temporal content in most Indo-European languages, resulting in the functional category tense (see Chapter 4). This parallel also manifests itself in the fact that, like tense, viewpoint aspect is a category that mediates between the reported event and the utterance. It does so by introducing the PoV from which to report the event (see the discussion immediately below). As such, it functions as one of the core grammatical categories, one that does not directly interface with another module. This correlates with the fact that (in many analyses) aspect is responsible for the assignment of accusative case (see Chapter 6).

As for their specific substantive content, both tense and aspect deal with times. They nevertheless differ. Tense is a deictic category and as such is concerned with locating the event time relative to the utterance time. In contrast, viewpoint aspect provides a temporal perspective on events; it locates events relative to a PoV time, which is also known as the *reference time* (Reichenbach 1947). Roughly, this can be done in two ways, such that the PoV can either be within the event or outside of the event (Comrie 1976: 16). Consider first a scenario where the reference time is during the runtime of the event. In this case a PoV is established inside the event, as in (1a). This is often realized by means of imperfective aspect, marked in English by means of progressive *-ing* as in (1b). In this example, the relevant event consists of Yoshi's looking for the ball, while the reference time is introduced by the temporal clause (*when the burglar broke into the house*). In this case, the event is ongoing from the point of view of the break-in.

(1)   a. PoV is inside the event

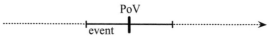

b. *Yoshi was looking for the ball when the burglar broke into the house.*

---

[1] Generally, there are two notions of aspect recognized in the literature. The type of aspect we are concerned with in this chapter is known as *viewpoint aspect* (Smith 1991/1997), *grammatical aspect* or *outer aspect* (Travis 2010). The other type of aspect is concerned with the internal make-up of the event. This type of aspect is also known as *situation aspect* (Smith 1991/1997), *lexical aspect*, or *inner aspect* (Travis 2010).

The alternative is to place the reference time after the runtime of the event, thereby establishing a PoV that lies outside of the event, as in (2a). This is often realized by the perfective aspect, which in English is unmarked (2b). In this example, the relevant event consists of Yoshi's finding the ball and the reference time is again introduced by the temporal clause (*before he chased away the burglar*). In this case, the event is over from the point of view of the chasing event. Thus, the event is viewed as a whole.

(2)   a. PoV is outside the event

        b. *Yoshi found the ball before he chased away the burglar.*

In this way, aspect functions like the lens of a camera, in that it allows us to view the event from within its own bounds or else from outside (Smith 1997).

A note on the difference between *perfective* and *perfect aspect* is in order here. As noted above, perfective aspect is generally assumed to be a way of marking that the event is viewed from outside (as a whole). A given aspectual contrast is generally viewed as perfect aspect if the event still has relevance at the time of utterance. For example, in English the difference between a simple past (3a) and a present perfect (3b) has to do with whether or not the ball is still lost.

(3)   a. *Yoshi lost the ball.*
        b. *Yoshi has lost the ball.*

The use of the present perfect implies that the ball is still lost but no such implication arises with the simple past (Comrie 1976: 52). Thus, while both simple past and present perfect are perfective, only the present perfect is a perfect.[2]

Crucially, current theories view temporal aspect as being intrinsically linked to the viewpoint category. But as I will show, this is not a necessary assumption.

7.1.2   Aspect beyond times

A PoV can be established in ways other than introducing a reference time. Instead, the PoV may simply be equated with one of the sub-events defined by the event itself. That is, events typically have an initial sub-event (*ie*) and a final sub-event (*fe*), as illustrated in (4).

---

[2] Since the perfect is a special form of the perfective it comes as no surprise that there is a common diachronic path whereby a perfective form develops from a perfect, which in turn often develops from a resultative (Dahl 1985; Bybee *et al.* 1994).

(4)   The makeup of an event

The presence of a grammatically relevant final sub-event is commonly assumed in the literature, mainly in order to account for *telicity* effects (see for example Krifka [1998] for an overview). That is, aspectual predicates can be distinguished based on whether or not the events they denote are defined by an intrinsic endpoint. For example, *writing a book* is a telic event (aka bounded event) in that it is over when the book is finished. It has an intrinsic endpoint. In contrast *running* is an *atelic* event in that it has no intrinsic endpoint. I can potentially run forever, so the endpoint of a running event occurs at an arbitrary bound rather than a natural endpoint.

In contrast, the presence of a grammatically relevant initial sub-event is assumed less commonly. For example, Smith (1997) suggests that the initial sub-event of an event distinguishes activities and accomplishments on the one hand from activities, and states on the other.[3] However, she assumes that initial sub-events, in contrast to final sub-events, always occur at an arbitrary, rather than a natural bound. On the basis of data from Squamish, Bar-el (2005) argues for the equal status of initial and final sub-events: both are grammatically relevant (see also Jacobs 2011).[4]

Since initial and final sub-events are known to be grammatically active, we may hypothesize that they can introduce a PoV instead of introducing a separate reference time. Thus, PoV can be defined by the makeup of the event itself: it may be equated with the initial sub-event or else with the final sub-event, as in (5). I will show that this is the way a PoV is introduced in Squamish. It derives the language-specific category known as control marking.

(5)   Establishing a PoV without introducing a reference time

    a. PoV = initial sub-event

---

[3] Following Vendler (1967), verbal predicates are commonly assumed to partition into several aspectual classes. Whether these classes are sufficient and how to analyse and/or derive them has generated a vast literature (see MacDonald [2008], Travis [2010], and Filip [2011, 2012] for recent discussion and overviews).

[4] Bar-el's (2005) diagnostics for the presence of a grammatically relevant initial sub-event in Squamish include readings available for punctual clauses and adverbials as well as the readings induced by the auxiliary *mi* ('come').

b. PoV = final sub-event

Once we recognize that a PoV can be equated with a situation already defined by the event (*ie* or *fe*), we may expect that facets of the internal constituency of a situation may play a role. We have assumed throughout that situations consist of spatio-temporal coordinates as well as participants. And indeed, I show that participants may also be utilized in establishing a PoV. That is, one may take the PoV of the event participant that initiates an event. Alternatively one may take the PoV of the event participant that defines the endpoint of the event. Thus in a participant-based system, introducing a PoV is about identifying with a particular PoV holder. Unsurprisingly, this participant-based way of introducing a PoV is attested in Blackfoot, a language that also anchors events via participants rather than times. Since aspect mediates the relation between the event and the utterance, it is expected that, if this relation is based on participants, then the mediating relation must also be participant-based. I show that the direct/inverse system of Blackfoot can be analyzed as a participant-based version of viewpoint aspect (Bliss *et al.* 2011). The analysis of aspectual systems that are not based on times has implications for the analysis of those systems that have been analyzed in terms of a reference time, as I will show.

In sum, I shall argue that the domain in the spine which has been assumed to be dedicated to a temporally based viewpoint aspect is in fact more general. In particular, as shown in (6), we may conclude that it is an area that is dedicated to the introduction of a PoV from which the event is presented. This area is located below the anchoring area (discussed in Chapters 4–6) and the area of classification (not discussed here).

(6)   The areas in the spine

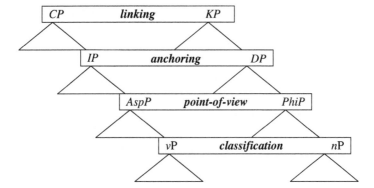

254   *Categories that introduce a point of view*

A note on terminology is in order. Because the term aspect has always been associated with temporal aspect, I shall continue to use it in this way. But it should be kept in mind that it refers to a language-specific category, which is constructed based on the universal category κ:PoV and temporal content, as in (7).

(7)   *c*:ASPECT = UoL{Σ:time,π} + κ:PoV

7.2   The Universal Base Hypothesis

Aspect is commonly assumed to be a universal category. It is often discussed in combination with the two other categories that, in many Indo-European languages, are realized as verbal inflection: tense and mood. These are known as the TAM categories. In this section, I begin by showing that not all languages use a grammatical category viewpoint aspect (Section 7.2.1). I then turn to problems with the most explicit version of the UBH, namely the cartographic approach (Section 7.2.2). Next I discuss general problems with the assumption that temporally based aspect is a universal category. In particular, I show that temporally based aspectual categories have different formal properties across languages, making it unlikely that we are dealing with a universal category (Section 7.2.3). And finally, in Section 7.2.4, I show that in the general domain where we expect to find aspect, Blackfoot and Squamish realize categories that are not based on reference time.

7.2.1   *Not all languages use viewpoint aspect*
The first problem to note is that not all languages seem to make use of a temporally based viewpoint aspect category. In particular, according to WALS, 121 out of 222 languages do not have any grammatical marking for the perfective/imperfective distinction. This is more than half of the languages, suggesting that aspect may not in fact be a language universal.

For example, in the Upper Austrian dialect of German, a tenseless language, there is no grammatical category aspect. This can be gleaned from the fact that viewing the event from inside or from outside does not yield a contrast in form. Both may be expressed with the construction that, in Standard German, is known as the *present perfect*, i.e., an auxiliary construed with the participle form of the verb. This is illustrated in (8).

(8)   a. *Da   Joschi hot n 'Boi*   *gsuacht . . .*
        DET Joschi has DET=ball   search.PART
        . . . wia   da   Einbrecha   ins   Haus   kumma   is.
        . . . as   DET   burglar   in.DET   house   come.PART   is
        'Joschi was searching for the ball when the burglar entered the house.'

        b. *Da   Joschi hot n' Boi*   *gfundn . . .*
        DET Joschi has DET = ball   found.PART
        . . . bevoa   a   den Einbrecha   vajogt   hot.
        . . . before he DET burglar   chased.away.PART   has
        'Joschi found the ball before he chased away the burglar.'

Thus, there is no aspectual κ-contrast between perfective and imperfective aspect. Note, however, that there is a construction which unambiguously triggers an imperfective interpretation, namely in the form of a nominalization which is preceded by a preposition (literally *to be at verbing*). This is illustrated in (9).

(9) *Da   Joschi woa grod*   *am*   *Boi*   *suachn . . .*
    DET Joschi was PRT   at.DET   ball   search.INF
    . . . wia   da   Einbrecha   ins   Haus   kumma   is.
    . . . as   DET   burglar   in.DET   house   come.PART   is
    'Joschi was searching for the ball when the burglar entered the house.'

This establishes that aspect cannot be viewed as a universal category, in the sense that not all languages mark a temporal aspectual contrast. Of course, this does not necessarily lead to the conclusion that aspect so construed is not among the set of universal categories. For example, in the cartographic approach towards variation, we would say that this category is simply not overtly expressed in Upper Austrian German. There are however other problems with the cartographic version of the UBH to which I turn next.

7.2.2   Problems with the cartographic approach

According to Cinque (1999), the universality of aspect is a matter of its presence in the universal hierarchy of functional categories. Moreover, the interrelatedness of aspect, tense, and mood is reflected by the fact that there are several positions for each of them, as shown in (10).

(10)   Cinque's hierarchy of functional categories: the TAM categories
        [$Mood_{speech-act}$ [$Mood_{evaluative}$ [$Mood_{evidential}$ [$Mode_{pistemic}$ [T_{past} [T_{future}
        [$Mod_{irrealis}$ [$Mod_{necessity}$ [$Mod_{possibility}$ [$Asp_{habitual}$ [$Asp_{repetitive}$
        [$Asp_{frequentative(I)}$ [$Mod_{volitional}$ [$Asp_{celerative(I)}$ [$T_{anterior}$ [$Asp_{terminative}$
        [$Asp_{continuative}$ [$Asp_{perfect(?)}$ [$Asp_{retrospective}$ [$Asp_{proximative}$ [$Asp_{durative}$
        [$Asp_{generic/progressive}$ [$Asp_{prospective}$ [$Asp_{sg.completive(I)}$ [$Asp_{pl.completive}$ [Voice

[Asp$_{celerative(II)}$ [Asp$_{repetetive(II)}$ [Asp$_{frequentative(II)}$
[Asp$_{sg.completive(II)}$]]]]]]]]]]]]]]]]]]]]]]]]]]]]]]]]]]]

Cinque 1999: 106

In the structure in (10), a series of aspectual heads, all hierarchically organized, represent different aspectual values, such as *habitual, repetitive, frequentative, continuative, perfect*, etc. According to the cartographic model, variation in the inventory of grammatical category arises because languages differ according to which of these categories are realized.

There are problems with this approach, however. First, we have seen that the presence of a grammatical category entails a κ-contrast, implemented as a bivalent feature. In the cartographic structure in (10), each aspectual value is associated with its own head. If so, the significance of contrast cannot be captured. To see this, consider the cross-linguistically common contrast between perfective and imperfective aspect (Jakobson 1932; Smith 1991). According to the diagnostics introduced in Chapter 3, the presence of a κ-contrast is indicative of the presence of a grammatical category (i.e., a category that is constructed based on κ via the "*is-a*" relation). And indeed, it is often assumed that viewpoint aspect instantiates a single syntactic head (Asp), immediately above the verb phrase (i.e., vP) and immediately below INFL (Travis 2010, among others).

In addition to its contrastive nature, there are several other criteria that support the view that aspect functions as a syntactic head. For example, as we have already seen, aspect interacts with case in a way that is indicative of a syntactically active head. That is, as a syntactic head, aspect must support a phrasal position (i.e., its specifier). For example, in Finnish, different aspectual properties of a predicate correlate with different case-assigning properties (Kiparsky 1998, among others). In particular, predicates in the perfective aspect assign accusative case to the internal argument, whereas predicates in the imperfective aspect assign partitive case (see Chapter 6).

(11)   a. *hän   luki   kirjan.*
          he   read   book-ACC
          'He read the book.'

        b. *hän   luki   kirjaa.*
          he   read   book-PRTV
          'He was reading the book.'

Svenonius 2002: 3 (2)

Note that in Finnish, the verb itself is not marked for aspect; instead the aspectual properties are purely read off the nominal case. This contrasts with

Russian where the opposite holds: the verb is marked for aspect, while nominal case remains unchanged, as illustrated in (12).

(12) a. *Rita   prochitala   knigu.*
         Rita   read.PERF   book
         'Rita read the book.'

      b. *Rita   chitala   knigu.*
         Rita   read.PERF   book
         'Rita was reading the/a book.'

                                                    Svenonius 2002. 3 (3)

Another common case-related correlate of aspect is found in Hindi. Here we find an aspectually driven split between a nominative/accusative case system and an absolutive/ergative case system (Dixon 1994). In particular, the imperfective is associated with a nominative/accusative alignment, as in (13a). In this case, the verb agrees in gender with the nominative argument. In contrast, the perfective aspect is associated with an ergative/absolutive alignment, as in (13b). In this case, the verb agrees in gender with the absolutive argument.

(13) a. *raam*   *roTii*   *khaataa*   *thaa.*
         Ram.MASC   bread.FEM   eat.IMP.MASC   be.PST.MASC
         'Ram (habitually) ate bread.'

      b. *raam-ne*   *roTii*   *khaayii*   *thii.*
         Ram.MASC-ERG bread.FEM   eat.PERF.FEM   be.PST.FEM
         'Ram had eaten bread.'

                                                    Mahajan 1990: 76, 78

The postulation of a series of aspectual heads, each corresponding to a different value, does not allow for a straightforward analysis of these aspectually driven patterns.

Another problem with the hypothesis that aspectual distinctions are the result of a series of aspectual heads has to do with morphological markedness relations. If a language marks aspectual distinctions, then it may do so in various ways: (i) both values are m(orphologically)-marked; (ii) perfective is m-marked but imperfective is not; (iii) imperfective is m-marked but perfective is not, as summarized in Table 7.1.

The absence of overt marking for a particular value follows straightforwardly if we assume that aspect is associated with a categorical head κ. In fact, it is the hallmark of a κ-contrast. In the absence of overt marking the head is still interpreted. Conversely, this pattern of contrast it is not as straightforward to analyze within the cartographic approach sketched in (10).

Table 7.1 *Morphological markedness in aspectual contrasts*

Imperfective	Perfective
✓	✓
✓	✗
✗	✓

The syntactic and morphological correlates of aspect suggest that aspectual contrasts are associated with a single aspectual head. But if this head, Asp, were indeed a universal category, then the question arises as to why it is not universally attested. However, absence of marking is not the only problem that the assumption that aspect is a universal category faces. Another problem has to do with its formal properties: aspectual contrasts do not have identical formal properties across different languages, as I will now show.

7.2.3   *Aspectual categories have different formal properties*

In this section I discuss one way in which aspectual marking differs formally across languages. In particular, it appears to be associated with different positions in the hierarchical organization of morphemes.

Consider, for example, Blackfoot, which has the following markers of temporal aspectuality: (i) an imperfective marker (*á* in [14], Frantz 1991, 2009; Dunham 2007) and (ii) a perfect marker (*akaa* in [15], Bliss 2013).[5]

(14)   Blackfoot imperfective marking
       a. *Nitáó'tsisi.*
          nit-á-o'tsisi
          1-IMPF-smoke
          i.   'I smoke.'
          ii. 'I am smoking.'

b. *Nitáístsitso'tatsimasii*	*annahk*	*Martina …*
nit-a'-isttsitsa-o'táaatsiim-aa-hsi	annahka	Martina …
1-INCH-first.time-meet.TA-DIR-CONJ	DEM	Martina …
… *áótsisi.*		
… á-o'tsisii-wa		
… IMPF-smoke.AI-PROX		

---

[5] Frantz (1991) labels *á* as a durative marker but acknowledges that it is an imperfective in Frantz (2009). Seok Koon (2007) analyzes *akaa* as a perfective while Bliss (2013) analyzes it as a perfect. And finally, Armoskaite (2008) argues that bare stems are perfective in Blackfoot.

i. 'When I first met Martina, she was a smoker.'
ii. 'When I first met Martina, she was smoking.'

adapted from Dunham 2007: 1 (1–2)

(15) Blackfoot perfective marking
a. *Anna   Rafa   ihpiyi.*
   Anna   Rafa   hpiyi
   DET   Rafa   dance
   'Rafa danced.'

b. *Anna   Rafa   akaaihpiyi*
   Anna   Rafa   akaa-hpiyi
   DET   Rafa   PERF-dance
   'Rafa has already danced (now).'

Seok Koon 2007: 4 (8)

On the surface, these aspectual markers look just like perfective and imperfective markers. Even the fact that the imperfective marker *á-* is compatible
with both an in-progress and a habitual interpretation is familiar from Indo-
European languages. For example, the Italian imperfective marker also allows
for a habitual interpretation, as shown in (16).

(16) *Leo gioca-va   a   golf.*
      Leo play-IMPF   PREP   golf
      'Leo used to play golf.'

Bonomi 1997: 485

If all aspectual markers associated with a universal category aspect, we would
expect that the Blackfoot aspectual prefixes too should associate with the spine
above *v*P but below IP. This prediction is however not borne out. In particular,
patterns of nominalization in Blackfoot reveal that both aspectual markers must be
associated with the spine inside of the classifying category *v*P. In particular, there
is Blackfoot internal evidence that the so-called abstract nominalizer (*-hsin/-n*)
attaches below *v*P, namely at the level of inner aspect (see Ritter [2014] for
details). Thus, if the aspectual markers *á-* and *akaa-* were instances of viewpoint
aspect, then we would expect them to be banned from these abstract nominalizations. This is, however, contrary to fact. Both aspectual markers productively
occur inside abstract nominalizations, as shown in (17) and (18).

(17) Imperfective inside low nominalization
a. *A'páíksikka'yissin   iksoka'pi.*
   a'p-**á**-iksika'yi-hsin   ik-sok-a'pii-wa
   around-IMPF-walk-NMLZ   INT-good-be.AI-PROX
   'Walking is good.'

b. *Kitáwawaahkaani*   *iksoka'pii.*
kit-**á**-wawaahk-aa-n-yi   ik-sok-a'pii-wa
2-IMPF-play-AI-NMLZ-INAN.SG INT-good-be.AI-PROX
'Your playing is good.'

Bliss *et al.* 2012: 8 (22)

(18)   Perfective inside low nominalization
        Annihkayi   nitsíkaaisttokimaan   nitsístapihkahto'p.
        annihkayi   nit-**ikaa**-isttokimaa-n   nit-ista'pihkahtoo-hp-wa
        DEM   1-PERF-drum-NMLZ   1-give.away-1:INAN-PROX
        'This one drum I've had, I gave it away.'

Ritter 2014: (23)

This establishes that the aspectual markers of the temporal kind occupy an unexpected position in the hierarchical organization of the clause, namely much lower than the hypothesized universal aspectual category. This is schematized in (19) where the higher arrow points to the position expected for aspectual marking and the lower arrow points towards its actual position in Blackfoot.

(19)   Perfective inside low nominalization

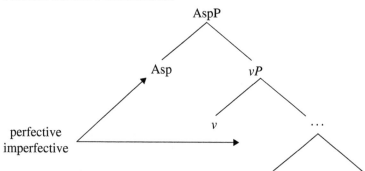

Thus even if two languages share the same substantive categories, the language-specific instantiations of these categories do not behave like a natural class. Again, this casts doubts on the assumption that aspect instantiates a universal category.

7.2.4   Unexpected categories in the aspectual domain

Above we saw that categories, if defined on the basis of their substantive content (such as temporal aspect) do not form a natural class across languages, at least when it comes to their formal properties. At the same time, however, there are categories that appear to be associated with the general area where we

| Person-(Prefix(es))- | Root-(Noun)-Final | -Direct/Inverse-Order-Person/Number-Number-Clitic(s) |
| | Stem | |

Figure 7.1 *Blackfoot verbal template*

would expect aspect. Specifically, the Blackfoot system of direct/inverse marking and the Squamish system of control marking associate with this domain in the clausal hierarchy. This is schematized in (20).

(20)   Different categories in aspect

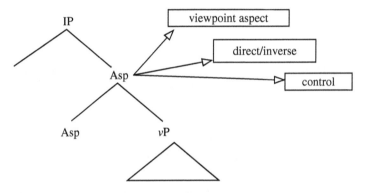

I discuss each of these language-specific categories in turn.

7.2.4.1 Blackfoot direct/inverse marking

As briefly mentioned in Chapter 1, Blackfoot, like other Algonquian languages, has a system of direct/inverse marking which occupies the position following the verb stem in the verbal template, repeated in Figure 7.1. Direct and inverse markers are both known as the *theme* markers in the Algonquianist tradition.

Crucially, direct/inverse marking is sandwiched between the order markers and the finals. I have shown in Chapter 4 that order markers associate with κ: *anchoring*. Thus, given the mirror principle, direct/inverse marking must associate with the spine in a position lower than the anchoring category. Furthermore, direct/inverse marking follows the so-called final suffixes. These are suffixes which subcategorize verbs based on transitivity and animacy of an argument. Given this function, I assume that finals associate with the classifying layer of the spine (see Ritter and Rosen 2010). If so, then we can conclude – again based on the mirror principle – that direct/inverse marking associates with the spine above κ:*classification*, namely with κ:*PoV*. It turns out that this is indeed consistent with its function. Consider again the logic of direct/inverse marking. In (21), we observe that the verb is prefixed with the 1st person prefix *nit-*, independent of whether the speaker functions as the subject or the object.[6] Direct/inverse marking is used to signal which role *nit-* does in fact index. If the speaker is the subject, direct marking is used (*-aa*); if the speaker is the object, inverse marking (*-ok*) is used.

(21)   a. *Nitsinóáwa.*   b. *Nitsinóóka.*

        nit-ino-**aa**-wa   nit-ino-**ok**-wa

        1-see.TA-**DIR**-3SG   1-see.TA-**INV**

        'I see him/her.'   'S/he sees me.'

                                                        Bliss *et al.* 2011: (2)

The terms *direct* and *inverse* reflect a particular conceptualization of this category, which is based on the alignment between two hierarchies.[7] On the one hand, on the hierarchy of argument relations, subject is ranked above object. On the other hand, on the person hierarchy, local participants (1st and 2nd) are ranked above non-local participants (3rd person). If these two hierarchies are directly aligned such that the local participant serves as the subject and the non-local participant serves as the object, the sentence is marked as direct. Conversely, if the hierarchies are inversely aligned, such that the non-local participant serves as the subject and the local participant serves as the object, the sentence is marked as inverse.

(22)   a. Direct mapping   b. Inverse mapping

        1 / 2 > 3   1 / 2 > 3

        subject > object   object < subject

A grammatical category of this kind, while typologically rare, is attested in several unrelated languages, including Tibeto Burman languages (DeLancey 1981), Chukotko-Kamchatkan (Comrie 1980), Wakashan (Whistler 1985), and Tupi Guarani (Payne 1990), among others.

---

[6] Here I use classical labels for grammatical roles (subject and object). Note that in the Algonquianist tradition, the relevant labels are *actor* and *goal*, respectively. See Bliss, (forthcoming) for a discussion of the status of traditional grammatical roles in Blackfoot.

[7] I here use these hierarchies as descriptive tools only without ascribing theoretical significance to them. See Wiltschko and Burton (2004) on possible sources of hierarchy effects.

What is the relation between direct/inverse marking and the hypothesized set of universal categories? There is no obvious position in the cartographic structure in (10) where direct/inverse marking would be located. So what type of category are we dealing with? These questions have received different answers in the relevant literature. Some have tried to reduce direct/inverse marking to an independently attested category. Let us refer to this family of analyses as *reductionist*. According to one line of thought, direct/inverse systems reduce to **agreement** (Rhodes 1976;[8] Brittain 1999; McGinnis 1999; Bejar and Rezac 2009). Another line of research suggests that it is a form of **ergativity** (DeLancey 1981; Hewson 1985; Déchaine and Reinholtz 2008). Of course, both these treatments push the question regarding the universality of categories to a different level. Neither agreement nor ergativity behave as uniform categories across languages.

In addition to these reductionist approaches, there are also analyses according to which the direct/inverse system instantiates a category in its own right. For example, Thompson (1990) and Grimes (1985) suggest that direct/inverse is a system that marks the topicality of non-agents relative to agents. And in a similar vein, Aissen (1997) and Zúñiga (2006) argue that it is a grammatical category that marks the alignment of the person hierarchy relative to a hierarchy of grammatical roles as in (22). The problem with this approach is that the status of these hierarchies as a primitive has been questioned (see Newmeyer 2002; Jelinek and Carnie 2003).

An analysis that explicitly locates direct/inverse marking on the syntactic spine is found in the work of Bruening. In particular, Bruening (2001) suggests that it associates with a position above *v*P, which he does not identify with an existing category, simply labeling it as HP. In later work, he seeks to identify HP with an existing category in the clausal spine: IP in Bruening (2005; see also Quinn 2006) and TP in Bruening (2009). The particular function of this head is identical, no matter what label he assumes: in the context of direct marking, it is the higher argument which moves to the specifier position of HP/IP/TP, while in the context of inverse marking, it is the lower argument which moves. What is lacking from his proposal, however, is a general theory that regulates the association of language-specific categories to the universal spine.

---

[8] More precisely, Rhodes (1976) argues that direct marking is a form of object agreement while inverse is a form of passive marking. The problem with the passive analysis is that, in some Algonquian languages, passive marking co-exists with inverse marking (see for example Dahlstrom [1991] for Plains Cree).

Finally, there are also approaches which reduce direct/inverse marking to a form of marking **perspectival information** (Mühlbauer 2008) or **point of view** (DeLancey 1981). Specifically, DeLancey (1981: 641) suggests that direct/inverse marking is *"a mechanism for marking the identity or non-identity of natural viewpoint and natural starting-point."*

That there are numerous accounts for direct/inverse marking is not surprising. Given that the grammatical categories we find in the languages of the world are constructed, it is not surprising that they may be constructed in different ways while arriving at similar effects. Thus, the various analyses available for direct/inverse systems may in fact all be on the right track for the particular direct/inverse system in the language under investigation. That is, direct/inverse systems are not expected to be the same across languages. In fact, Bliss *et al.* (2012) show that, even within a given language (Blackfoot), direct/inverse marking is not a homogeneous phenomenon. If only non-local (3rd person) participants are involved, direct/inverse marking patterns as an agreement marker (as in Rhodes 1976; Brittain 1999; McGinnis 1999; Bejar and Rezac 2009). Conversely, if local participants are involved direct/inverse marking patterns as an intrinsically relational category which identifies the relative semantic or syntactic prominence of the event participants (as in Grimes 1985; Thompson 1994; Aissen 1997; Bruening 2001, 2005, 2009; Quinn 2006; Zúñiga 2006).

Summing up, on the one hand the formal properties of temporal aspectual marking (perfective/imperfective) differ from their English equivalent. On the other hand, there is a morpho-syntactic category (direct/inverse) that English lacks, and it is located in the area where we might expect aspect marking. Interestingly, this category is also used to encode a point of view, just not from a temporal perspective. In Section 7.4.3, I develop a formal analysis that takes this constellation of facts to be significant.

7.2.4.2   Squamish control marking

Squamish Salish has another grammatical category in the general domain where we might expect temporal aspect, namely the so-called control markers. This is a system of markers which are often described in terms of the amount of control the agent has over the event. Consider the examples in (23). The bare root *kw'elh* ('spill') is interpreted as an unaccusative verb, i.e., without an agent. To introduce an agent, Squamish deploys a system of transitivizing suffixes. For the present purpose, two are significant: *-at* (23b) and *-nexw* (23c).

(23)   a. *na   kw'elh   ta   tiy.*
          RL   spill   DET   tea
          'The tea spilt.'

Jacobs 2011: 2 (2)

        b. *chen   kw'lh-**at**   ta   tiy.*
          1SG.S   pour-TR   DET   tea
          'I poured the tea.' (on purpose)

Jacobs 2011: 1 (1b)

        c. *chen   kw'élh-**nexw**   ta   tiy.*
          1SG.S   spill-LC.TR   DET   tea
          'I spilt the tea.' (accidentally)

Jacobs 2011: 1 (1b)

In this case, each of the derived forms has a bare root equivalent in English: *pour* vs. *spill*. But this is not a systematic property of the English lexicon: not all verbs come in such pairs. And if they don't, then the difference between the two transitivizers is sometimes rendered into English by means of a modifier such as *'on purpose'* and *'accidentally'* as shown in (24).

(24)   a. *chen   kwélash-t   ta   nkw'ekw'chústn.*
          1SG.S   shoot-TR   DET   window
          'I shot the window.'(on purpose)

        b. *chen   kwélash-nexw   ta   nkw'ekw'chústn.*
          1SG.S   shoot-LC.TR   DET   window
          'I shot the window.'(accidentally)

Jacobs 2011: 10 (17)

This may suggest that the Squamish transitivizers not only introduce the agent but also encode whether the agent performed volitionally (Kuipers 1967). Thus, we may hypothesize that the transitivizer comes with a modifier, which specifies volition. But this does not capture the facts adequately. Volition is neither a necessary nor a sufficient condition for the use of the supposedly volitional transitivizer *-at*. As shown below, *-at* may be used when the agent is non-volitional as in (25a), and conversely *-nexw* may be used when the agent is fully volitional as in (25b).

(25)   a. *na   kp'-ét-Ø-as   ta   spahím'   ta   shewálh.*
          RL   shoot-TR-3OBJ-3S   DET   wind   DET   door
          'The wind shut the door.'

Jacobs 2011: 3 (3)

        b. Context: the speaker is practicing shooting bottles
          *chen   kwélash-**nexw**   ta   nexwlámay.*
          1SG.S   shoot-LC.TR   DET   bottle
          'I *managed to* shoot the bottle.'

Jacobs 2011: 3 (4)

Thompson (1979) introduces the notion of *control* to account for the distribution of these transitivizers. Thompson and Thompson (1992) define control events as in (26a) and non-control events as in (26b).

(26)   a. Control events:
            the agent functions with usual average capacities in keeping things under control.

        b. Non-control events
            (i)   natural spontaneous happening without the intervention of any agent
            (ii)   unintentional accidental acts
            (iii) intentional premeditated events which are carried out to excess, or are accomplished only with difficulty, or by means of much time special effort and/or patience and perhaps a little luck.

                                                Thompson and Thompson 1992: 52

While this definition of control captures the interpretation of the control markers across a range of contexts, it still does not adequately describe the whole system. Consider the examples in (27). None of the conditions for the use of non-control marking given in (26b) are met in (27), and nevertheless the limited control marker is used in this context.

(27)   a. *chen   cháy-n-t-umi*
            1SG.S   chase-TR-TR-2S.OBJ
            'I chased you.'

        b. *chen   cháy-n-umi*
            1SG.S   chase-LC.TR-2S.OBJ
            'I caught up to you.'

                                                Jacobs 2011: 12 (20)

Thus the contrast introduce by control marking does not (always) express the expected interpretation. This is further illustrated in Table 7.2, with examples that have in common that they cannot be defined in terms of control.

Thus, none of the attempts that seek to define the difference between the two transitivizers in terms of their meaning are able to account for the full range of facts. This is of course the hallmark of a grammatical category: it is not definable based on meaning. Note further that control marking is not only a pervasive category across the Salish family; it has also been reported for Malagasy and Tagalog (Travis 2000) as well as Ilokano (Gerdts 1979). This suggests that control marking is construed in a universally constrained fashion. But how? And what is its relation to the hypothesized set of universal categories? Again, based on its meaning, there is no obvious position in the cartographic structure in (10) where it would be located.

Table 7.2 *Control marking without a contrast in control*

Control-marked predicate	Limited control marked predicate
kw'ach-t 'to look at it'	*kw'ách-nexw* 'to see it'
p'i7-t 'to take/grab it'	*p'i7-nexw* 'to have/hold/receive it'
yelx-t 'to search for it'	*yélx-nexw* 'to have found it'
ta7l-t 'to study it'	*tél'-nexw* 'to have learnt it, to realize it, to have found it out, to discover'
kw'úy-ut 'to beat (a person)', 'to kill (game)'	*kw'úy-nexw* 'to have beaten (a person) up', 'to have killed (game)'
húy-ut 'to create it'	*húy-nexw* 'to finish it'
kw'e'n-á'n 'to pour it'	*kw'e'n-á'n* 'to spill it, to have poured it'

Source: From Jacobs (2013: 18, Table 3).

As with direct/inverse marking, there are also reductionist analyses available for control marking. For example, Davis *et al.* (2009) analyze control marking in St'at'imcets as a type of circumstantial modality (see also Rivero *et al.* 2009 for Polish); and Siraj (2010) analyzes the accidental marker in Malay as an *anti-bouletic* modifier. However, this cannot account for the aspectual contrast we have observed above. As Jacobs (2011) shows, the core contrast of the control system revolves around event completion. This is exemplified by the data in (28).

(28)   a. *chen*   *ts'its'áp'-nexw.*
         1SG.S   work-LC.TR
         'I finished my work.'

      b. *na míkw'-nexw-as*   *ta*   *snexwílh.*
         RL clean-LC.TR-3S   DET   canoe
         'He finished washing his canoe.'

      c. *chen*   *tséxw-nexw* *ta*   *swíwlus*   *t-kwetsi* *smant.*
         1SG.S   hit-LC.TR   DET   young.man O-DEM   rock
         'I hit the young man with a rock.'
         Speaker's comment: 'already happened'   Jacobs 2011: 227 (47)

Jacobs' (2011) analysis of control marking in terms of aspect is interesting in the present context. Its morpho-syntactic distribution is certainly compatible with an analysis in terms of aspectual marker. But why would its interpretation differ so drastically from its English counterpart? We turn to answering this question in Section 7.4.4.

We have now seen that viewpoint aspect is not universally attested as a grammatical category; the most immediate consequence is that it is not marked in all languages. However, even if it is marked in a given language, it is not associated with the same formal properties. First, languages differ in which of the values of aspect is overtly marked and which is unmarked. Second, not all of the markers of aspect are associated with the spine in the same domain. Third, we have seen a grammatical category (direct/inverse), which appears to introduce a point of view, but not along a temporal dimension. And finally, we have seen a grammatical category (control) which is reminiscent of an aspectual category, but which still is not straightforwardly analyzable in terms of common aspectual distinctions.

If we postulate the existence of universal grammatical categories, this state of affairs is unexpected. If aspect were indeed a universal grammatical category, we would expect it to be attested in all languages. And even if it were a universally available category, but one which does not have to be realized in all languages, we would expect it to have the same formal properties where it is attested, contrary to fact. And finally, we have seen two typologically less common categories which appear to be in the same general domain as aspect marking and which appear to have similar functions, but which are nevertheless substantively different. It is precisely this state of affairs which has led some to conclude that universal categories simply do not exist. We turn to this position in the next section.

7.3   The No Base Hypothesis

On the one hand, the diversity of aspect marking we have seen above might lead us to conclude that aspect is not a universal category. This is the position of Evans and Levinson (2009), who argue that universal categories do not exist. But this position runs into problems as well. First and foremost, while it is true that not all languages have aspect marking, at the same time it is also the case that aspect marking is attested in many unrelated languages. Out of the 222 languages surveyed for WALS, 101 have a grammatical perfective/imperfective distinction. And even if they do not all share the same formal properties, the fact of the matter is that it is a widespread distinction. Denying the existence of some universal property responsible for the construction of this type of aspect marking would miss a generalization.

One may argue that this pervasiveness is due to a functional need. It is, after all, useful to be able to talk about the relative ordering of events and situations.

And in addition to saying whether a given event precedes or follows another event, it is sometimes necessary to talk about events that occur inside of each other. This is precisely what aspect marking allows us to do: we can view an event from inside by means of the imperfective, or from outside by means of the perfective.

This functional need, however, is not sufficient to explain the pervasiveness of aspect. If there were indeed a functional need, then all languages should have such marking, contrary to fact. It must be possible to get by without it. Moreover, the functional need fulfilled by viewpoint aspect in English can also be fulfilled in other ways (e.g., by means of modifiers).

The second problem that comes with denying the existence of universal categories in general, and aspect in particular, has to do with generalizations that we can make about aspect markers across a range of unrelated languages. For example, Bybee (1985) discusses the fact that, cross-linguistically, aspect marking occupies a position that is closer to the verb than tense marking or mood marking. This is a generalization about the formal properties of aspect marking which suggests some universal characteristics of aspect (despite the fact that it does not apply to all languages, as we have seen based on Blackfoot).

Another common property of aspectual marking is that it is often recruited from the language of space. For example in Ewe (Niger Congo) progressive marking takes the form of a locative marker, as in (29).

(29)   *é-le*   *mɔli*   *du-m*.
        3-be.at rice   eat-**LOCV**
        'She is eating rice.'

                                                        Schmidtke 2006: 9 (21)

The same is true for Standard German, where the progressive is expressed by means of a prepositional construction typically used for locative marking, as in (30).

(30)   *Sie*   *ist*   *am*   *Essen*.
        she   is   at.DET eating
        'She is eating.'

This suggests that there are some core ingredients that are recurrent in the construction of aspect marking. If there were no universal basis for this construction, this would be unexpected. Finally, we have seen that there are other categories, in the same general domain, which differ superficially but have in common that they introduce a point of view. It thus seems that, universally, languages use the same formal mechanism that allows for the introduction of a point of view. However, this may be achieved in different ways. And this is precisely what the USH is designed to capture.

7.4 The Universal Spine Hypothesis

The essence of the USH is that it recognizes a distinction between language-specific categories and universal categories. Specifically, language-specific categories are constructed from the universal spine and language-specific Units of Language (UoLs) as in (31).

(31) $c = \kappa + \text{UoL}$

On this view, universal categories are not intrinsically associated with substantive content. Instead, the substantive content that (in some cases) defines a language-specific category is introduced by the UoLs. The universal categorizer itself is defined by its hierarchical position and by its function but not by its substantive content.

In the domain of *κ:anchoring* discussed in Chapters 4–6, we have seen that there are several suitable types of substantive content that may lead to language-specific anchoring categories (tense, location, participants, realis). In English (and other tense-based languages) aspectual marking is based on temporal content as well. This is not surprising, as there is a close interaction between tense and aspect, which is due to the fact that both categories relate times to each other. I introduce the formal analysis for aspect that captures this insight in Section 7.4.1. But according to the USH, categories are not defined based on their substantive content. We expect this to hold for aspectual categories as well. In Section 7.4.2, I introduce the idea that the core and universal property of aspect is to introduce a point of view. However, a PoV may be introduced in different ways. A temporally based PoV is only one of several possibilities. In particular, in section 7.4.3, I review the analysis developed in Bliss *et al.* (2012), according to which direct/inverse marking is a participant-based form of aspect marking. And in Section 7.4.4, I develop an analysis of Squamish control marking based on Jacobs (2011), according to which control marking is a form of generalized aspect marking not defined based on content. The construction of the point of view categories in different languages is schematized in (32).

(32)   Constructing language-specific PoV categories:

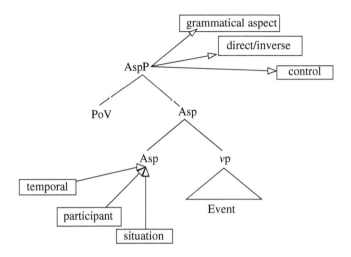

7.4.1   *Formalizing viewpoint aspect*

We now turn to the formal underpinnings for constructing viewpoint aspect. I follow the basic insights of Demirdache and Uribe-Etxebarria (1997, 2007) in the assumption that tense and aspect make use of essentially the same building blocks: they both establish topological relations between temporal arguments. In particular, aspect relates the *event time* to the *reference time* while tense relates the *reference time* to the *utterance time*. As with other grammatical categories, the relational character of aspect is introduced by virtue of the unvalued coincidence feature intrinsically associated with the head position. In this respect, aspect is identical to tense. Where it differs is in the type of abstract argument introduced in the specifier position. In Chapters 4 and 5, we saw that for tense this argument is a pronominal argument, which, in the absence of an antecedent, is interpreted deictically as the utterance time. In contrast, aspect introduces a *reference time* (in the sense of Reichenbach [1947]), which serves as the time from which the event is viewed. Hence I shall call it a *point-of-view (PoV) time*. Note that this time is also known as *topic time* (Klein 1994) and *assertion time* (Klein 1995). Translated into the USH as perceived here, this analysis is represented in (33).

(33)   Tense and aspect

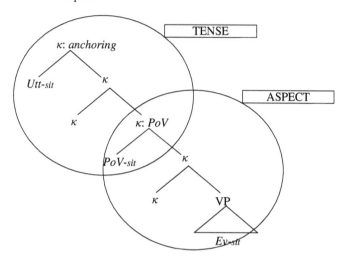

Note that Demirdache and Uribe-Etxebarria (1997) assume that the spatio-temporal ordering predicates that relate the abstract temporal arguments are *within*, *before*, and *after*. I depart from this particular implementation and assume that the ordering predicate is universally [coincidence]. If valued as [+coin] it results in the within interpretation; if valued as [−coin] it results in either a before or after interpretation (see below; see also Mezhevich [2008] for a similar proposal).

On the analysis schematized in (33), the computation of aspect is as follows: a present progressive, as in (34a), is characterized by both tense and aspect being valued as [+coin] as in (34b). This captures the fact that the event time coincides with the reference time, which in turn coincides with the utterance time, as schematized in (34c). (I adopt the convention of representing the timeline and event line following the utterance as a lighter shade of grey. The timeline is represented as a dotted line, while the event run time is represented by an unbroken line with bounds at both ends.)

(34)   present progressive
        a. *Kim is eating lunch.*

        b. [TP Utt-time [T [+coin] [AspP PoV-time [Asp [+coin] [VP Ev-time V]

        c.
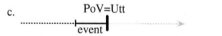

A past progressive, as in (35a), is characterized by tense being valued as [−coin] but aspect being valued as [+coin], as in (35b). This reflects the fact that the event time coincides with the reference time, which in turn does not coincide with the utterance time, as schematized in (35c).

(35)   Past progressive
       a. *Kim was eating lunch.*

       b. [$_{TP}$ Utt-time [$_T$ [−coin] [$_{AspP}$ PoV-time [$_{Asp}$ [+coin] [$_{VP}$ Ev-time V]]]]]

       c.
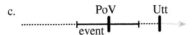

The present perfect, as in (36a), is derived by the converse valuation, with tense being valued as [+coin] and aspect being valued as [−coin], as in (36b). This reflects the fact that the event does not coincide with the reference time, which in turn coincides with the utterance time (36c).

(36)   Present perfect
       a. *Kim has eaten lunch*

       b. [$_{TP}$ Utt-time [$_T$ [+coin] [$_{AspP}$ PoV-time [$_{Asp}$ [−coin] [$_{VP}$ Ev-time V]]]]]

       c.

Finally, the past perfect, as in (37a), is characterized by both tense and aspect being valued as [−coin], as in (37b). This reflects the fact that the event does not coincide with the reference time, which in turn does not coincide with the utterance time (37c). It is in this context that we really see the need for a third time beside event and utterance time, since all three times are distinct.

(37)   Past perfect
       a. *Kim had eaten lunch.*

       b. [$_{TP}$ Utt-time [$_T$ [−coin] [$_{AspP}$ PoV-time [$_{Asp}$ [−coin] [$_{VP}$ Ev-time V]]]]]

       c.
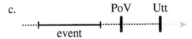

Aspect is concerned with the relation between the event and the PoV. To assert that they coincide means that the PoV time overlaps with the event time. One way in which this is the case is if the PoV time is located inside the event time as in (38).

(38)   Viewing the event from inside (imperfective)

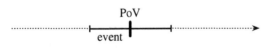

In contrast, asserting that the two times do not coincide means that they refer to two distinct times, as in (39).

(39)   Viewing the event from outside (perfective)

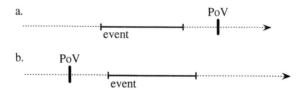

Note that this view of perfective differs from one that is currently found in the relevant literature. In particular, perfective is typically conceptualized such that the event time occurs inside the reference time (Klein 1994; Kratzer 1998), as in (40).

(40)   Events inside the reference time

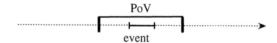

While this way of conceptualizing the perfective aspect works if the reference time is provided by a time-frame adverbial such a *yesterday*, as in (41a), it does not capture the interpretation of perfectives when other time adverbials are considered. For example, in (41b), the reference time provided by the time adverb is *the minute I arrived*. Here the event time is not included in the reference time, but is instead consecutive: at the time of my arrival, the event of Kim's leaving started.

(41)   a. *Kim left yesterday.*

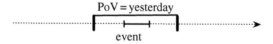

        b. *Kim left the minute I arrived*

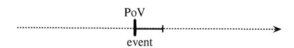

As will become clear below, for the purpose of generalizing aspect to non-temporal systems, this conceptualization of aspect is essential. In essence, while we can conceive of a PoV holder as being non-identical to an event participant, we cannot conceive of an event participant as being placed "inside of" a PoV holder. (See also Kiyota [2008] for a similar adaptation of the analysis of perfective aspect for different reasons.)

With this formalization of aspect in place, we can now turn to extending this analysis to systems that are not based on times. I proceed in two steps. First I establish how to abstract away from content (Section 7.4.2) and then I develop an analysis for Blackfoot direct/inverse marking (Section 7.4.3) and Squamish control marking (Section 7.4.4) in terms of marking point of view.

7.4.2   Abstracting away from content

Analyses of aspectual categories across different languages have long been concerned with determining universals of aspect, as well as its range of variation (Smith 1991, 1997; Kiyota 2008). In the context of the USH, according to which categories are not intrinsically (i.e., via UG) associated with substantive content, we add a novel spin to the question regarding the range of variation associated with aspect. In particular, we may expect that temporal aspect as discussed above is only one possible substantiation of $<\kappa\text{:PoV}>$. But what does it take to remove the temporal content from aspect? To explore this question, it is essential to establish the function of aspect that is independent of its content. There are two essential properties that are relevant. First, aspect serves to mediate between the event and the utterance. Second, aspect introduces a PoV relative to which the event is evaluated. Crucially, neither of these functions is intrinsically linked to times.

The reason that the category aspect appears to be so tied to temporal arguments is that it has been studied mainly in languages where anchoring is based on tense. But note that the notion *aspect* itself is not intrinsically temporal. It is a loan translation of the Slavic term *vid*, cognate with 'view' and 'vision', and related to the Latin word *aspectus* translated as 'view,' '(the act of) seeing, looking at' (see Binnick [1991: 135–214] for a terminological overview).

Similarly to what we have done for the anchoring category (κ: *anchoring*), we can abstract away from the substantive content of aspect by recognizing that the abstract arguments that are being ordered are not times, but rather situations (which contain times, along with locations and participants). Thus I propose that aspect is a language-specific instantiation of the universal category that is responsible for introducing a PoV, as in (42). Crucially the UoL that serves to construct c:ASPECT will be intrinsically temporal.

(42) c:ASPECT = UoL + κ:*PoV*

The abstract representations with all the relevant arguments, before they are categorized as temporal or otherwise, is given in (43).

(43)

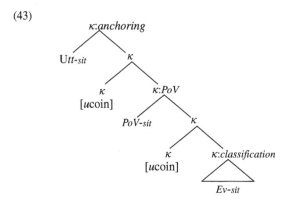

This is the first step we need to generalize aspect to languages that are not organized around times.

There is, however, a second step that is required. This has to do with the interpretation of [−coin]. There are in principle two ways in which the event time may not coincide with the PoV time. As schematized in (44), the PoV time may either follow (44a) or precede (44b) the utterance time.

(44)   a.

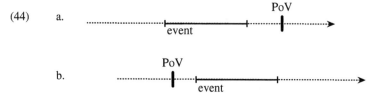

         b.

In most cases, perfective marking is interpreted such that the PoV time follows the event time, as in (44a). I argue that this has to do with the fact that reference is made to the *endpoint* of the event. This is consistent with the fact that in many theories of aspect, the calculation of the aspectual interpretation is sensitive to either initial or final sub-events, or both. Consequently, in work on the syntax–semantics interface, these sub-events are both represented in the syntactic representation (see for example Borer 2005; MacDonald 2008; Ramchand 2008). In what follows, I will follow this tradition and represent the complexity of events as in (45).

(45)   Introducing initial and final events

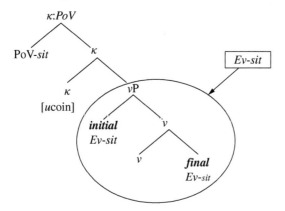

In what follows, I assume that if [*u*coin] is valued as [+coin], the result is that the PoV situation is ordered relative to the closest argument. This can be the entire event situation as in (46a) or else the initial event situation only, as in (46b).

(46)   a.

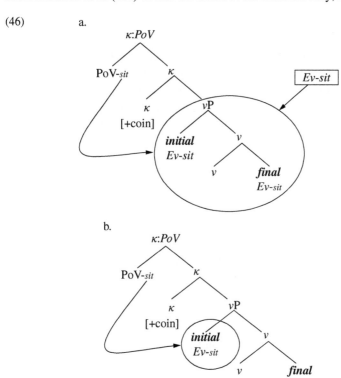

         b.

In contrast, if [*u*coin] is valued as [−coin], the resulting interpretation is that the PoV situation does not coincide with the closest event situation. Suppose, however, that there has to be a PoV. If so, asserting that the PoV situation does not coincide with the closest event situation is still compatible with an interpretation according to which it coincides with the final event situation, as in (47).

(47)

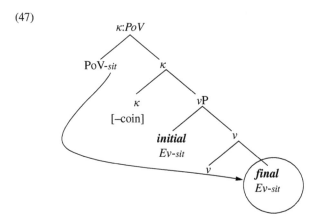

In this way, we capture the original insight of Hale (1986: 238), according to whom the main contrast based on *coincidence* is that between *central coincidence* and *terminal coincidence*. Under the present conceptualization of this insight, central coincidence correlates with [+coin] while terminal coincidence correlates with [−coin] (see Chapter 8, Subsection 8.6.2.1 for further discussion).

   In what follows, I show two language-specific instantiations of aspect that are readily understood within this schema. We start with a discussion of Blackfoot direct/inverse marking.

7.4.3   Blackfoot direct/inverse system as participant-based aspect

The first thing we need to establish is that direct/inverse marking does indeed associate with *κ* via the "*is-a*" relation. Using the diagnostics introduced in Chapter 3, we can show that this is indeed so. Direct/inverse marking is obligatory, unique, paradigmatic, and it introduces a *κ*-contrast. I discuss each of these properties in turn.

7.4.3.1 Direct/inverse marking is obligatory

One of the hallmarks of a grammatical category is obligatoriness. Direct/ inverse marking in Blackfoot fulfills this property. However, it is not the case that all sentences in Blackfoot are marked for direct or inverse. Instead, only those sentences with the right constellation of facts are so marked. But if the right constellation holds, they have to be so marked, conforming to the obligatoriness criterion. So what is the relevant constellation of facts? Direct/inverse marking is intrinsically relational: it establishes which of two participants serves as the subject. Consequently it is not surprising that direct/inverse marking applies to transitive predicates only, but in this context it must apply. This is shown in (48)–(49) where the absence of a direct marker leads to ungrammaticality, and in (50)–(51), where the absence of an inverse marker leads to ungrammaticality.

(48) a. *Anna*   *Beth* *á'psstoyiiwa*   *anni*   *ohsíssi.*
         ann-wa   Beth   a'psst-o-yii-wa   ann-yi   w-isiss-yi
         DEM-PROX   Beth   wave-TA-3:4-PROX   DEM-OBV   3-sister-OBV
         'Beth waved to her sister.'

      b. **Anna*   *Beth* *á'psstowa*   *anni*   *ohsísi.*
         ann-wa   Beth   a'psst-o-yii-wa   ann-yi   w-isiss-yi
         DEM-PROX   Beth   wave-TA-PROX   DEM-OBV   3-sister-OBV
         intended: 'Beth waved to her sister.'

(49) a. *Anna*   *nitá'paisstoawa.*
         ann-wa   nit-a'p-a-isst-o-a-wa
         DEM-PROX   1-around-IMPF-wave-TA-DIR-PROX
         'I am waving to him.'

      b. **Anna*   *nitá'paisstowa.*
         ann-wa   nit-a'p-a-isst-o-wa
         DEM-PROX   1-around-IMPF-wave-TA-PROX
         intended: 'I am waving to him.'

(50) a. *Anna*   *Beth* *anni*   *ohsíssi*   *otá'psstookáyi.*
         ann-wa   Beth ann-yi   w-isiss-yi   ot-a'psst-o-ok-wa-áyi
         DEM-PROX B   DEM-OBV 3-sister-OBV 3-wave-TA-INV-PROX-3SG.PRN
         'Beth's sister waved to her.'

      b. **Anna*   *Beth*   *anni*   *ohsísi*   *otá'psstowáyi.*
         ann-wa   Beth   ann-yi   w-isiss-yi ot-a'psst-o-wa-áyi
         DEM-PROX B   DEM-OBV 3-sister-OBV 3-wave-TA-PROX-3SG.PRN
         intended: 'Beth's sister waved to her.'

(51) a. *Anna*   *nitá'paisstooka.*
         ann-wa   nit-a'p-a-isst-o-ok-wa
         DEM-PROX   1-around-IMPF-wave-TA-INV-PROX
         'He is waving to me.'

b. **Anna   nitá'paisstowa.*
ann-wa   nit-a'p-a-isst-o-wa
DEM-PROX   1-around-IMPF-wave-TA-PROX
intended: 'He is waving to me.'

Thus with transitive animate predicates, direct/inverse marking is obligatory. This contrasts with intransitive predicates on the one hand, and transitive inanimate predicates on the other. As for intransitive predicates, they are not marked for direct/inverse, as shown in (52). This is not surprising, as in the context of only one argument, it need not be established which of them corresponds to the PoV holder.

(52)   *Ááhksa'paisstakiwa.*
aahksa-a'p-a-isst-aki-wa
always-around-IMPF-wave-AI-PROX
'He's always waving.'

Interestingly, it is not enough that there be two event participants. Rather, these event participants must be realized as grammatical arguments that are licensed by formally transitive predicates. To see this, consider the example in (53) where a formally intransitive predicate co-occurs with an internal argument ('beavers'). Syntactically, objects of formally intransitive predicates behave as if they were incorporated (Glougie 2001; Bliss 2013). Crucially, in such contexts, direct/inverse marking is not attested.

(53)   *Annáhk   Carmelle   ááhksikkamaapi   ksísskstakiks.*
Ann-wa-hk   Carmelle   aahk-ikkam-yaapi   ksisskstaki-iksi
DEM-PROX-NV   Carmelle   NONFACT-if-see.AI   beaver-PL
'Carmelle might see (some) beavers.'

Bliss 2013: 117 (89)

Next consider transitive inanimate predicates. They also cannot be marked for direct/inverse, despite the fact that there are two participants (54). Inanimate individuals can never be PoV holders, and therefore they do not participate in the direct/inverse system.

(54)   a. *Áíhkssima   omistsi   í'ksisakoists.*
a-ihkssi-m-wa   om-istsi   i'ksisako-istsi
IMPF-dry.TI-3:INAN-PROX   DEM-PL   meat-PL
'She is drying those meats.'

b. **Áíhkssiwa   omistsi   í'ksisakoists.*
a-ihkssi-wa   om-istsi   i'ksisako-istsi
IMPF-dry.TI-PROX   DEM-PL   meat-PL
intended: 'She is drying those meats.'

c. **Áíhkssiyiiwa*   *omistsi*   *í'ksisakoists.*
   a-ihkssi-yii-wa   om-istsi   i'ksisako-istsi
   IMPF-dry.TI-3:4-PROX   DEM-PL   meat-PL
   intended: 'She is drying those meats.'

d. **Áíhkssioka*   *omistsi*   *í'ksisakoists.*
   a-ihkssi-ok-wa   om-istsi   i'ksisako-istsi
   IMPF-dry.TI-NV-PROX   DEM-PL   meat-PL
   intended: 'She is drying those meats.'

Thus, while it is not the case that all Blackfoot sentences are marked for direct or inverse, it is the case that a certain class of sentences, namely those that are transitive with an animate object, obligatorily require direct or inverse marking. This establishes that direct/inverse marking is obligatory, which is in turn consistent with the assumption that it associates with a syntactic head *κ*, via the "*is-a*" relation.

7.4.3.2 Direct/inverse marking is unique
Another diagnostic for grammatical categories is *uniqueness*. There can only be one instance of a given grammatical category in a given sentence. This is true for direct/inverse marking as well, as shown in (55)–(56).

(55)   a. *Anna*   *nohkówa*   *nitsskotohpommaattsaaawa ...*
        ann-wa   n-ohko-wa   nit-ssk-oto-ohpommaa-attsi-a-wa
        DEM-PROX   1-son-PROX   1-back-go-buy.AI-CAUS.TA-DIR-PROX
        ... omiksi apótskinaiks.
        om-iksi aapotskina-iksi
        DEM-PL cow-PL
        'I made my son buy those cows.'
                                    Frantz 2009: 101 (e)

     b. **Anna*   *nohkówa*   *nitsskotohpommaattsaaawa ...*
        ann-wa   n-ohko-wa   nit-ssk-oto-ohpommaa-attsi-a-a-wa
        DEM-PROX   1-son-PROX   1-back-go-buy.AI-CAUS.TA-DIR-DIR-PROX
        ... omiksi apótskinaiks.
        om-iksi aapotskina-iksi
        DEM-PL cow-PL
        intended: 'I made my son buy those cattle.'

(56)   a. *Anna*   *nohkówa*   *nitsskotohpommaattsooka ...*
        ann-wa   n-ohko-wa   nit-ssk-oto-ohpommaa-attsi-ok-wa
        DEM-PROX 1-son-PROX   1-back-go-buy.AI-CAUS.TA-INV-PROX

> ... *omiksi apótskinaiks.*
> om-iksi aapotskina-iksi
> DEM-PL cow-PL

'My son made me buy those cattle.'

b. **Anna*   *nohkówa*   *nitsskotohpommaattsookoka...*
   ann-wa   n-ohko-wa   nit-ssk-oto-ohpommaa-attsi-ok-ok-wa
   DEM-PROX   1-son-PROX   1-back-go-buy.AI-CAUS.TA-INV-INV-
                                                    PROX
   ... *omiksi   apótskinaiks.*
   om-iksi aapotskina-iksi
   DEM-PL cow-PL

intended: 'My son made me buy those cattle.'
(two inverse theme suffixes)

Note that these examples are causative and hence involve three event participants (me, my son, and the cattle). So there is no obvious reason as to
why there should not be two direct markers or two inverse markers, or
one of each. You could imagine that there might be one direct or inverse
marker per participant pair. Nevertheless, only one marker is possible. This
means that direct/inverse marking is unique, which in turn is consistent
with the claim that it functions as a grammatical category that is constructed
based on κ.

7.4.3.3 Direct/inverse marking defines a paradigm

A third criterion that serves to diagnose grammatical categories is that of
paradigmaticity. In particular, grammatical categories are characterized by
the fact that more than one UoL may associate with a given head on the spine,
and thus these UoLs enter into paradigmatic relations. In particular, we might
expect there to be two UoLs; one that realizes the [+coin] value and another
one that realizes the [−coin] value. Interestingly, this is not the case. The
direct/inverse system of Blackfoot is not a simple binary opposition. Instead,
as shown in Table 7.3, there are five UoLs, which serve to mark the 12 logically
possible combinations of transitive predicates. For direct marking there are three
UoLs: *-o,-a,* and *-yii;* for inverse marking there are two UoLs: *-oki* and *-ok.*

Despite the appearance of a uniform paradigm however, Bliss *et al.* (2012)
argue that there are in fact several sub-paradigms that make up the system of
direct/inverse marking. Specifically, according to their analysis, the core
direct/inverse contrast is encoded by *-aa* and *-ok,* respectively. These forms
are restricted to sentences where local participants interact with non-local ones

Table 7.3 *The paradigm of direct inverse marking in matrix clauses*

Goal	1	2	3	3′
1	n/a	-oki	-ok	-ok
2	-o	n/a	-ok	-ok
3	-aa	-aa	n/a	-ok
3′	-aa	-aa	-yii	n/a

Source: From Louie (2008: 17 (22)).

(shaded cells). In this domain, direct/inverse marking is indeed relational, in that it marks the relative ranking between the two participants. They assert that the closest argument coincides or does not coincide with the PoV holder. This is represented in (57).

(57) a. *c*:DIRECT = <{π:-aa,Σ:local}, [κ:PoV,+coin] >
      b. *c*:INVERSE = <{π:-ok, Σ:non-local}, [κ:PoV,−coin]>

But what about the other UoLs in the paradigm of direct/inverse markers? Bliss *et al.* (2012) argue that they are best analyzed as agreement suffixes: *-yii* is a 3rd person subject agreement (58a), while *-o* is a 2nd person object agreement (58b) and *-oki* is a 1st person object agreement (58c).

(58) a. <[κ:v], {π:-yii,Σ:3}>
      b. <[κ:V], {π:-o,Σ:2}>
      c. <[κ:V], {π:-oki,Σ:1}>

As schematized in (59), under the Bliss *et al.* (2012) analysis, the direct/inverse markers do not associate with the spine in a uniform fashion.[9] The core markers associate with κ:PoV, subject agreement associates with *v* and object agreement associates with inner aspect.[10]

---

[9] For ease of exposition, I use the standard labels to distinguish between different layers in the articulated *v*P.

[10] Everything else being equal, this analysis predicts that, in some contexts, more than one UoL could be realized. However, this is not the case. Bliss *et al.* (2012) propose a morphological constraint according to which there is only one position in the morphological template of Blackfoot. A series of spell-out restrictions determines which of the positions is spelled out. The status of such templates and spell-out restrictions has yet to be explored within the USH.

(59)   The distribution of direct/inverse marking

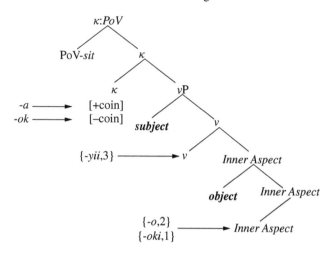

Thus under this analysis, there are only two relevant UoLs that manifest what we might call the core of direct/inverse marking (*-aa* and *-ok*). They are intrinsically relational. This provides us with the required binary contrast: *-aa* encodes the direct relation [*κ:PoV*, +coin], whereas *-ok* encodes the inverse relation [*κ:PoV*,−coin].

This supports the claim that direct/inverse marking associates with *κ* via the "*is-a*" relation. It is obligatory, unique, paradigmatic and introduces a *κ*-contrast. The lesson to learn from this example is that, even in light of a seemingly uniform paradigm, we cannot conclude that all of the forms associate with the spine in the same way.

Next we turn to evidence that direct/inverse marking associates with *κ:PoV*. This evidence comes from its relative position, as well as its function. Consider first its relative position based on the morphological template, repeated here as Figure 7.2.

Observe that direct/inverse marking immediately follows the position of finals (the rightmost member of the verb stem) and immediately precedes the order markers. Based on Ritter and Wiltschko (forthcoming), order markers are analyzed as associating with *κ:anchoring* (INFL). On the other hand, Ritter and Rosen (2010) argue that finals are best analyzed as light verbs, associating with *v*. Given the mirror principle, it follows that direct/inverse marking must be lower than *κ:anchoring* but higher than *κ:classification* (*v*). This is precisely the position we have identified as *κ:PoV* (Aspect).

Next we turn to the core function of direct/inverse marking. At an abstract level, it serves the same function as temporal aspect: it marks point of view

Person-(Prefix(es))-	Root-(Noun)-Final	-Direct/Inverse-Order-Person/Number-Number-Clitic(s)
	Stem	

Figure 7.2 *Blackfoot verbal template*

(Bliss 2005). This functional equivalence is reflected in the formal implementation. To see this, consider the examples in (60) and (61) along with their structural representations. The direct marker *-a* associates with *κ:PoV* and values its coincidence feature as [+coin] (60a). Accordingly, direct marking asserts that the PoV-participant coincides with the initial event participant (i.e., the subject) (60b). Conversely, the inverse marker values the coincidence feature as [−coin], thereby asserting that the PoV-participant does not coincide with the initial event participant (61a). Since, by hypothesis, there has to be a PoV-participant, the next available participant, i.e., the final event participant, will serve this function (61b).

(60)   Direct = [+coin]
   a.   *Nitááwayakiaa.*
        nit-(w)aawayaki-a-wa
        1-hit-DIR-3SG
        'I hit him.'

   b.

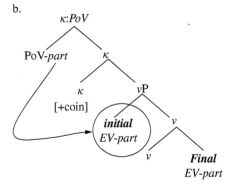

(61)   Inverse [−coin]
   a.   *Nitááwayakioka.*
        nit-(w)aawayaki-ok-wa
        1-hit-INV-3SG
        'He hit me.'

b.

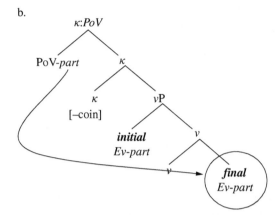

This analysis captures DeLancey's (1981: 641) insight according to which direct/inverse is a *"mechanism for marking the identity or non-identity of natural viewpoint and natural starting-point"* (see also Lochbihler [2012] for the claim that direct/inverse marking is a nominal licensing mechanism based on person).

Supporting evidence for the view that direct/inverse marking is fundamentally about which participant is the PoV holder comes from the fact that it is restricted to transitive animate verbs. That is, PoV marking is restricted to contexts where there are two potential point of view holders. For example, when the internal argument is inanimate, it cannot serve as a PoV holder and consequently, direct/inverse marking is not attested (see the discussion around (54) above).

In addition, there is also a syntactic constraint: the two PoV holders must be grammatical arguments of the verb. That is, verbs that are formally intransitive are compatible with objects, including animate objects. In such cases, there are two potential PoV holders available. Nevertheless, direct/inverse marking is not attested. This is shown based on the minimal pair in (62). If the verb is formally intransitive (62a), direct/inverse marking is absent despite the presence of an animate (pseudo-) object, but if the verb is formally transitive (62b) direct marking is obligatory.

(62)   a. *Íhkaniyaapiyaawa*   *píítaa*
           ii-ohkan-yaapi-yi-aawa   piitaa
           IC-all-see.AI-PL-3PL.PRN   eagle
           'They all saw an eagle.'

        b. *Íhkaniyaapiyaawa*   *oma*   *pííta*
           ii-ohkana-ino-a-yi-aawa   om-wa   piitaa
           IC-all-see.TA-DIR-PL-3PL.PRN   DEM-PROX   eagle
           'They all saw an eagle.'

                                          adapted from Glougie 2001: (7/6)

Thus, while there are two potential PoV holders, the pseudo-object does not function as a grammatical argument and can therefore not interact with the functional category above *v*P. This confirms the claim that direct/inverse marking is a grammatical category that picks out the PoV holder.

In sum, we have seen that direct/inverse marking found in Blackfoot is amenable to a PoV analysis. Both in terms of its formal properties and in terms of its functional properties it behaves a lot like temporal aspect marking of the familiar kind. Its morphological expression appears in the position between κ:*anchoring* and κ:*classification*, and its function is to introduce a point of view, albeit not defined based on temporal properties, but instead based on participants. Thus, like temporal aspect, the direct/inverse system serves to mediate between the event situation and the utterance situation.

Note that, given that Blackfoot is participant-based in its anchoring category, it does not come as a surprise that its PoV category as well is participant-based. In particular, since aspect mediates between event situations and the utterance situation, it follows that the particular aspect of the situations that are ordered must be compatible. That is, one cannot order participants relative to times. However, in principle it should be possible that the entire situation is ordered. This is what I argue to be the case in Squamish, to which we turn now.

7.4.4   An aspectual analysis of Squamish control marking
As introduced above (Section 7.2.4.2), Squamish has a series of transitivizers, which not only introduce the agent but also seem to mark the amount of control this agent has over the event. One of the markers appears to mark full control, whereas the other marks limited control. A minimal pair is repeated in (63) for convenience.

(63)   a. *chen*   *cháy-n-t-umi.*
         1SG.S   chase-TR-TR-2S.OBJ
         'I chased you.'

     b. *chen*   *cháy-n-umi.*
         1SG.S   chase-LC.TR-2S.OBJ
         'I caught up to you.'

                                      Jacobs 2011: 12 (20)

In previous examples, we have also seen that it is quite difficult to pin down the exact interpretation of these control markers. Thus none of the attempts that seek to define the difference between the two transitivizers in terms of their meaning are able to account for the full range of facts.

This is of course the hallmark of a grammatical category: it is not definable based on meaning. Here I propose that control marking introduces a κ-contrast which is amenable to an analysis in terms of viewpoint aspect, as in (64).

(64)   *c*:CONTROL = UoL + κ:*PoV*

To develop this analysis, I build on Jacobs (2011) whose main insight is that a control-marked predicate focuses on the initial sub-event but does not commit the speaker to anything having to do with the final sub-event.[11] In contrast, a predicate marked with a limited control transitivizer focuses on the final sub-event and does not commit the speaker to anything having to do with the initial sub-event. To formalize this insight, I again utilize the aspectual head, which introduces the PoV and which comes with an unvalued coincidence feature. Specifically, I propose that control marking realizes the [+coin] value associated with κ:*PoV* (65). It differs from temporal aspect as well as participant-based PoV marking in that it does not focus on a particular facet of the situation. Instead, it orders the entire situation. Thus, control marking asserts that the PoV situation coincides with the initial sub-event situation, as in (65).[12]

(65)   a. *c*:CONTROL = UoL + [κ:*PoV*,+coin] [13]

---

[11] The analysis developed here differs from that of Jacobs (2011). Whereas I analyze control marking as in instance of *viewpoint aspect*, Jacobs (2011) analyzes it as an instance of *situation aspect*. His main evidence against a viewpoint aspect analysis stems from the fact that it can co-occur with the imperfective marker, as shown in (i):

(i) *chen   wa   kw'ach-n-umi.*
    1SG.S   IMPF   look-LC.TR-2S.OBJ
    'I can see you.'
    Context: An adult is playing peek-a-boo with a child.

                                                        Jacobs 2011: 195 (15a)

If *wa* is indeed an imperfective marker of the familiar sort, the present analysis will have to be modified. However, as we have seen again and again, we cannot determine categorical identity based on the meaning of a given morpheme. It is thus entirely possible that *wa* instantiates a category different from viewpoint aspect. I leave this question for future research.

[12] Given that the UoLs that mark control serve double duty in that they also serve as a transitivizer (i.e., they introduce the agent), it follows that they must simultaneously associate with two heads. This may be modeled as a function of head-to-head movement (Travis 1984), or else as an indication that a given form may *span* over more than one head position (Williams 2003).

[13] For description and analysis of the UoLs that are used in control marking see Jacobs (2011).

b.

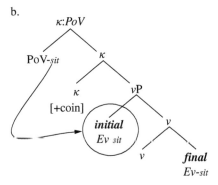

In contrast, limited control marking realizes [−coin] (66). Since, by hypothesis, there must be a PoV situation, the non-coincidence with the initial sub-event situation is interpreted as coincidence with the final sub-event situation. In other words, limited control marking is interpreted as terminal coincidence, as in (66).

(66)   a. *c*:LIMITED CONTROL = UoL + [κ:*PoV*,−coin]
       b.

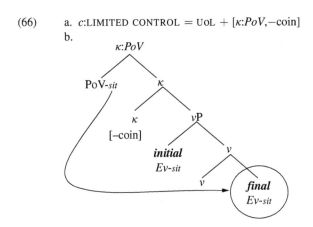

Whether the event is viewed from the PoV of the initial event or from the PoV of the final event has predictable consequences for interpretation. In particular, if the event is viewed from the initial event, then the properties of the final event are not calculated. And indeed, a control predicate is compatible with events that do not culminate (Bar-el *et al.* 2005). This is shown in (67). A sentence containing a control predicate can be followed by a sentence that denies the completion of the event.

(67)   na   p'ayak-en-t-Ø-as   ta   John   ta   snexwílh-s ...
        RL   fix-TR-TR-3OBJ-3SUB   DET   John   DET   canoe-3POSS ...
        'He (John) fixed his canoe, ...
        ... welh   haw   k'as   i   húy-nexw-Ø-as.
        ... but   NEG   SBJ-3CONJ   AUX   finish −LC.TR-3OBJ-3S
        ... but he didn't finish (fixing) it.'

Bar-el *et al.* 2005: (12)

Note that control predicates do not explicitly deny event completion as part of their meaning and thus they are compatible with contexts in which the event does in fact culminate, as shown in (68).

(68)   na   xel'-t-Ø-as   ta   sxwexwiy'ám'   lha   Mary.
        RL   write-3OBJ-3S   DET   story   DET   Mary
        'Mary wrote a story.'
        Speaker's comments: 'She wrote it ... she's finished.'

Bar-el *et al.* 2005: (6a)

The compatibility of control predicates with situations where the event culminates as well as with situations where the event does not culminate is predicted by the analysis in (65). Viewing the event from its initial sub-event does not place any requirements on the final sub-event. This is compatible with a context of use where the event culminates as in (69a) but also with a context where the event does not come to its natural endpoint, as in (69b).

(69)   a.

(69)   b.

Contrast this with limited control predicates. According to (66), they assert that the point of view does not coincide with the initial sub-event. By hypothesis, non-coincidence results in terminal coincidence, and the final event serves as the PoV situation. Consequently, culmination is necessary and cannot be denied; hence the infelicity of the continuation to the sentence in (70).

(70)   na p'ayak-**nexw**-Ø-as   ta   John   ta   snexwílh-s ...
        RL fix-LC.TR-3OBJ-3S   DET   John   DET   canoe-3POSS
        'John fixed his canoe, ...

# ... welh	haw	k'as	i	húy-nexw-Ø-as.
... but	NEG	SUBJ-3CONJ	AUX	finish –LC.TR-3OBJ-3S

'... but he didn't finish (fixing) it.'

Jacobs 2011: 23 (30b)

In contrast, limited control predicates place no requirement on the initial sub-event. Consequently, such predicates are compatible with a context in which the initial event does not come about as part of the normal course of events. This is, for example, the case if the agent initiates an event, but it does not end in the intended way, as in (71a). Similarly, the limited control predicate is compatible with a context in which the agent has no intention to initiate an event, but it happens anyway (i.e., accidentally), as in (71b). And in a similar vein, the limited control predicate is compatible with contexts in which event culmination is difficult (the agent may have initiated the event several times before it came to completion).

(71)   a.   Context: I was aiming at another target (e.g. a bottle) but I mistakenly shot the window.

chen	kwélash-nexw-Ø	ta	nkw'ekw'chústn.
1SG.S	shoot-LC.TR-3O	DET	window

'I accidentally shot the window.'

      b.   Context: he was cleaning his gun and he accidentally pushed the trigger and shot himself.

na	kwelash-númut-Ø.
RL	shoot-LC.REFL-3S

'He accidentally shot himself.'

Jacobs 2011: 227 (51)

      c.   Context: This phrase can be used as a greeting, and said jokingly when arriving somewhere; meaning that even though circumstances were difficult for me to get here, I was so determined to get here that I overcame them to be here.

chen	tl'ik-númut.
1SG.S	shoot-LC.REFL

'I managed to arrive (here).'

Jacobs 2011: 230 (52a)

But, as was the case with control predicates, where we have seen that event culmination is not explicitly denied, it is also the case that with limited control predicates, event initiation is not explicitly denied. Thus, a limited control predicate is compatible with contexts in which the event came about in its normal way, as for example in (72).

(72)   a. *ta   Peter   na   xélḵ'-nexw-Ø-as*   *ta lhách'ten.*
DET   Peter   RL   drop-LC.TR-3O-3S   DET knife
'Peter, it's his fault that the knife dropped.'

   b. *chen   ts'is-nexw-Ø   ta   míxalh.*
1SG.S   nail-LC.TR-3O   DET   bear
'I hit the bear right on.'

Jacobs 2011: 224 (46d, f)

The compatibility of limited control predicates with situations where the event
is initiated in unusual ways (non-intentionally or with difficulty), as well as
with situations where it is initiated as expected, is predicted by the analysis in
(66). Viewing the event from its final sub-event does not place any requirements on the initial sub-event. This is compatible with contexts with or without
natural starting points, as illustrated in (73).

(73)   a.

   b.

ie = natural starting point

In sum, we have seen that control marking in Squamish may be understood
without reference to a notion like control or volition. Rather, following the
insights of Jacobs (2011), I have developed an aspectual analysis according to
which control predicates are characterized as viewing the event from the point
of view of the initial sub-event, thus placing no restrictions on the final sub-
event. In contrast, limited control predicates are characterized as viewing the
event from the point of view of the final sub-event, thus placing no restrictions
on the initial sub-event.

7.4.5   *Implications for temporal viewpoint aspect*

We have now seen that it is possible to analyze the direct/inverse system of
Blackfoot and the control system of Squamish as aspectual systems. The
level of abstraction we needed was the assumption that the core function of
temporal aspect is to introduce a point of view. In a system of temporal
aspect, the point of view is defined as a time. But we have already seen with
the anchoring category that the temporal content is but one facet of
the abstract situation argument that one can access. Thus temporality can
be replaced with other facets of the situation to achieve identical function.
The same holds for the PoV category. In Blackfoot, the PoV argument is

person-based. That is, the core function of direct/inverse marking is to identify which of the event participants is the PoV holder. In Squamish, the PoV argument is the situation as a whole, and not only a particular aspect of the situation. That is, the core function of control marking is to identify which of the sub-events serves as the PoV. What was crucial in developing a unified analysis was the assumption that the PoV argument is identified with (aspects of) the initial sub-event or (aspects of) the final sub-event. Everything else being equal, we might expect to find temporally-based aspectual systems that identify either the initial or the final sub-event as the PoV time. Consider first the scenario in (74) where the PoV time is identified with the time of the initial sub-event.

(74)

Natural languages do indeed make use of an aspectual category that can be characterized in this way. Inceptive, ingressive, and inchoative aspects are all types of aspects that highlight the initial point of an event. According to traditional classification, the *inchoative* denotes the beginning of a state (75a), the *ingressive* refers to the beginning of an atelic process (75b), and the *inceptive* marks the beginning of a telic process (75c).

(75)   a. *John got tired.*   INCHOATIVE

       b. *The soup came to a boil.*   INGRESSIVE

       c. *He began to build the house.*   INCEPTIVE

While, in English, these meanings can be approximated with aspectual verbs such as *get, come,* and *begin,* there are languages with dedicated aspectual markers of this sort. In line with other aspectual systems that are sensitive to initial and final sub-events, we perhaps could analyze such markers as in (76).[14]

(76) c:INCHOATIVE = UoL + [κ:PoV,+coin]

In terms of its syntactic context, the inchoative mirrors Blackfoot direct marking and Squamish control predicates in identifying the initial sub-event as the PoV by realizing the [+coin] value of κ:PoV.

---

[14] Tough only if all other diagnostics fall into place as well. Recall that we cannot simply categorize UoLs on the basis of their substantive content alone.

(77)

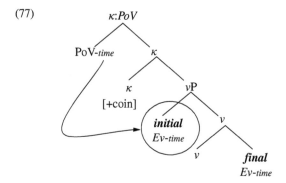

Now consider the alternative strategy, whereby the PoV time is identified with the final event, as in (78).

(78)

Perfect aspect may be analyzed in this way. Recall the original formalization of the present perfect based on Demirdache and Uribe-Etxebarria (1997), introduced in Section 7.4.1. The relevant example and representation are repeated below for convenience.

(79)   PRESENT PERFECT
a. *Kim has eaten lunch*

b. [TP Utt-time [T [+coin] [AspP POV-time [Asp [−coin] [VP Ev-time V]]]]]

c.

Given the modification to the topology of aspect that I introduced in the course of this section, we can reinterpret the analysis of perfect in the following way. Under the present conceptualization of the [−coin] feature associated with *κ:PoV*, it corresponds to terminal coincidence. In particular, the PoV time is identified with the final sub-event by virtue of asserting that the PoV does not coincide with the initial sub-event. Moreover, perfect aspect is often assumed to make available a resultant state interpretation (Parsons 1990; Kratzer 1998). In other words, the final event becomes a resultant (perfect) state (Nishiyama and Koenig 2004). The present perfect interpretation (*Kim has eaten lunch*)

arises because the final event is asserted to be the PoV event, but since the final event is also interpreted as a state, it will still hold at the utterance situation. This is illustrated in (80).

(80)   PoV time coincides with final event

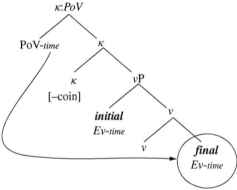

Thus, the perfect is amenable to an analysis according to which it realizes the [−coin] value, as in (81).

(81)   *c*: PERFECT = UoL + [*κ:PoV*,−coin]

In terms of its syntactic context, it mirrors Blackfoot inverse marking and Squamish limited control predicates in (indirectly) identifying the final sub-event as the PoV by realizing the [−coin] value of *κ:PoV* as shown in (82).

(82)   Perfect aspect

This subsection was not meant to provide a full-fledged analysis of temporal aspect cross-linguistically. What I hope I have shown, however, is that temporal aspect is compatible with an analysis that takes into consideration the initial and final sub-events.

7.5   Towards a typology of viewpoint aspect

Our starting point in this chapter was the standard assumption that expressions of viewpoint aspect are associated with a position in the clausal architecture which is located above *κ:classification* (*v*P) but below *κ:anchoring* (INFL). Superficially, we observe that not all languages make use of a point of view category. For example, in Upper Austrian German, the same form is used, no matter whether the event is viewed from inside or from outside.[15] Moreover, we have seen that the expression of aspect differs considerably across languages. In particular, we have seen that in Blackfoot, the markers of imperfective and perfective aspect are located in a position much lower than we would expect, given certain versions of the UBH. On the other hand, we saw that in the area of the spine where aspect would be expected, we find a different grammatical category in Blackfoot, namely direct/inverse marking. And in Squamish this area is associated with yet another grammatical category, namely control marking. According to the USH, language-specific categories are constructed, and they can be constructed in different ways. This is because a language-specific category c is constructed with the categorizers of the universal spine κ but also with language-specific UoLs, as in (83).

(83) $c = \kappa + \text{UoL}$

Thus I conclude that in the languages investigated here, there are three different types of language-specific categories, which are all constructed based on the same universal categorizer, whose core function is to introduce a point of view.

(84)   a. $c{:}\text{ASPECT} = \kappa{:}PoV + \text{UoL}$
        b. $c{:}\text{DIRECT/INVERSE} = \kappa{:}PoV + \text{UoL}$
        c. $c{:}\text{CONTROL} = \kappa{:}PoV + \text{UoL}$

Inasmuch as this analysis is on the right track, it establishes that categories that are notionally very different from each other can be analyzed as instantiating the same universal category. Conversely, categories that appear to be notionally similar, in that they seem to mark similar contrasts as perfective and imperfective, cannot always be analyzed as instantiating $\kappa{:}PoV$.

Thus, when developing a formal typology of viewpoint aspect, we should not be led solely by the substance of the category. When analyzing the aspectual categories in a given language, we must ask two questions:

(i)   What (if any) category is constructed based on $\kappa{:}PoV$?
(ii)   How do notional aspectual categories associate with the spine?

This leads to two distinct types of formal typologies: one based on the notional content of temporal aspect, and one based on the hypothesized abstract

---

[15] According to the logic of the USH, the absence of viewpoint aspect in Upper Austrian leads us to expect that there be another aspectual category in its place. Identifying this category remains a question for future research.

category κ:*PoV*, which is defined based on its hierarchical position, but also based on its function.

In addition, a formal typology of aspectual categories will also have to take into consideration the interplay with other categories: κ:*anchoring* on the one hand, and κ:*classification* on the other hand. The formalization developed here makes predictions about the ways these categories interact with each other. For example, if a given language uses temporal content in its anchoring category, then it will also do so in the viewpoint category.

While in many respects κ:*PoV* parallels κ:*anchoring* (they both order abstract arguments via their intrinsic coincidence feature), there are also certain differences. In particular, for κ:*PoV* we have assumed that the [+coin] value corresponds to Hale's notion of *central coincidence*, whereas the [−coin] value corresponds to his notion of *terminal coincidence*. That is, if the PoV argument is asserted to not coincide with the initial event argument, it is interpreted as coincident with the final event argument (see Chapter 8, Subsection 8.6.2.1 for further discussion).

Summing up, my main objective in this chapter was to show that even such typologically rare categories as direct/inverse marking and control marking can be analyzed as instantiating an abstract universal category; and moreover that substantively different categories – temporal aspect, direct/inverse marking, and control marking – all instantiate the same abstract universal category. In pursuing this goal, we saw once again that substance-based comparisons can be misleading, in that even if two categories appear to mark similar contrasts, they do not necessarily do so in the same way formally. This chapter is meant to set the stage for a novel approach towards aspect, one that is based on the assumption that language-specific categories are constructed and that universal categories cannot be defined based on their substantive content. However, many questions have been left unanswered. I mention a few of them in turn.

What is the content of the UoLs that instantiate point of view categories? Is there a common denominator? Note that I have refrained from analyzing the UoLs that define the language-specific instantiations of κ:*PoV* in terms of the valuation typology developed in previous chapters. There are several logical possibilities. [κ:*PoV,u*coin] may be valued via morphological marking or via the substantive content associated with a higher head. If aspectual morphology would serve m-valuation, we would expect it to be associated with substantive content, and we would expect it to be part of the pre-syntactic lexicon. In contrast, if [κ:*PoV,u*coin] were valued by an external head, we would expect aspectual morphology to be of the realizational, post-syntactic kind, and thus not intrinsically associated with substantive content. At this point I have not found a language that would instantiate this case, but it is certainly predicted to be possible.

Another prediction that arises in light of the analysis thus far developed is that there should be a language-specific instantiation of $\kappa{:}PoV$ that is based on location. I have no reason to believe that this is not an option.

Furthermore, we predict that there is a nominal instantiation of $\kappa{:}PoV$. It is sometimes claimed that nominal viewpoint aspect is not attested (Schmidtke 2006) but this claim is based on the assumption that aspect must be temporally based. However, if we abstract away from the temporal content, we may in fact find nominal equivalents of viewpoint aspect. For example, if indeed the core function of aspect is to make it possible to view an event from inside or outside then we may expect a similar function to hold in the nominal domain. A possible equivalent of viewpoint aspect is thus number marking and its kin. Intuitively, a distributive interpretation makes it possible to view a plural referent from inside, whereas a collective interpretation views it as a whole.

Finally, we have seen that not all temporal aspectual markers are constructed in the same fashion. It remains to be seen how the aspectual markers that are not constructed based on $\kappa{:}PoV$ are interpreted. The prediction is that they do not necessarily introduce a PoV. Again, I will have to leave a detailed semantic analysis of such categories and UoLs for future research. As with other grammatical categories, care must be taken to distinguish between those UoLs that associate with κ via the "*is-a*" relation and those that modify κ. Thus, the grammatical categories that we would classify as viewpoint aspect based on their meaning alone are not all constructed in the same way, hence they have different formal properties.

While there are many unanswered questions that the USH leaves for future research into the formal typology of aspect, it is also the case that it makes it possible to ask questions we have not previously considered. It is my hope that future research dedicated to answering these questions will make it possible to formulate a comprehensive formal typology for aspect.

8 *Towards a formal typology*

Form follows function – that has been misunderstood.
Form and function should be one, joined in a spiritual union.

Frank Lloyd Wright

8.1   Introduction

We have in this monograph explored the universal structure of categories: the way categories are structured and the structures they build. The main thesis put forth here is that all language-specific categories (c) are constructed based on a universal categorizer κ and a language-specific UoL.

(1) $c = \kappa + \text{UoL}$

Based on this thesis we can start developing a formal typology for constructing categories, one which represents the synthesis of two contradictory claims about the linguistic reality of universal categories. According to the Universal Base Hypothesis (UBH), there is a set of universal categories that serves as a repository for language-specific categories. The opposing view is held by many typologists, and I have referred to it as the No Base Hypothesis (NBH). According to this view there are no universal categories. We have shown throughout this monograph that both theses run into problems. Neither the UBH nor the NBH are empirically adequate.

The thesis that categories are constructed as in (1) sheds light on this conundrum. The key is to recognize that there are two notions of categories involved. Typologists talk about language-specific categories (c), which are indeed not universal. But they run into problems in light of universal generalizations about categorial patterns. In contrast, generative linguists talk about universal categories (κ), but the problem is that the standard conceptualization of such categories includes substantive content. Instead, what I tried to show here is that substantive content is necessarily supplied by language-specific UoLs.

In this chapter, I present the basis for a formal typology of categorization, based on the Universal Spine Hypothesis (USH). I start in Section 8.2 with a brief overview of the difference between linguistic typology and formal grammar. Linguistic typology is typically associated with functional explanations. This is however not a necessary correlation. There is no intrinsic reason as to why a typology could not be formal. And indeed, I argue in Section 8.3 that a formal typology is not only possible but is also necessary. I then show in Section 8.4 that there are indeed some existing formal criteria for classification, typically assumed to be universally applicable. However, I also show that these criteria are insufficient at best and misleading at worst. In section 8.5, I distill the formal classification criteria based on the USH. In section 8.6 I draw conclusions and raise open questions. And finally, in section 8.7, I identify the USH as a research agenda.

8.2   Linguistic typology and formal grammar

The languages of the world differ, yet they do so in systematic ways. Linguistic typology is inherently concerned with cross-linguistic comparison. It refers to a *"classification of structural types across languages"* (Croft 2003: 1). There are two principal goals:

i)   to explore linguistic **diversity** by classifying categories and structures
ii)   to explore language **universals** by seeking patterns that occur systematically across related and unrelated languages

Linguistic typology is often presented as being in opposition to *formal grammar* (see Polinsky [2010] for a recent overview). This opposition manifests itself in the primary goals associated with each approach. Linguistic typology primarily seeks to describe and explain linguistic diversity, whereas formal grammar seeks to uncover and explain universality in order to draw conclusions about the human language faculty and thus the nature of the human mind. As a consequence, the empirical basis for the two is typically quite different. Linguistic typology requires large-scale investigations of unrelated languages. In contrast, formal grammar is often characterized by in-depth investigations of a single language. In fact, it was one of the basic assumptions in the early days of generative grammar that the properties of the language faculty can be deduced on the basis of a single language.

Finally, linguistic typology and formal grammar typically differ in their modes of explanation. Here the opposition manifests itself in a number of ways. First, they differ in terms of seeking either *external* and *functional* or *internal* and *formal* explanations (Hall 1992: ch. 1; Newmeyer 1998: ch. 3). External explanations seek to explain linguistic universals and diversity by means of external factors, such as general cognitive abilities or communicative function. This often leads to functional explanations, which seek to explain linguistic universals by means of general communicative needs: the formal properties of language are to be understood as following from their communicative function. In contrast, internal explanations seek explanations within the language faculty, which is viewed as an autonomous system. This leads to the prominence of formal explanations, which seek to explain linguistic form independent of its meaning, use, or communicative function. This opposition is summarized in Table 8.1.

The distinction between linguistic typology and formal grammar is presented above in its extreme instantiations. Both formal and typological approaches come in a variety of guises, and the opposition is not always as clear-cut as it is here presented (see Newmeyer [1998] for detailed discussion). Many scholars working within the generative tradition, for example, are studying and comparing a variety of languages. These studies are sometimes on a few related languages, such as in the work pioneered by Richard Kayne in the 1970s on comparative Romance linguistics; but also on a smaller sample of unrelated languages, such as for example in Mark Baker's work on noun incorporation and polysynthesis (Baker 1988, 1996). The cartographic approach initiated by Cinque in the 1990s is probably the most large-scale approach within the generative framework (with a survey of over 500 languages; see Baker and McCloskey [2007]). It does not come as a surprise that Cinque does "*not consider ('formal') linguistic theory and linguistic typology as two separate approaches*" (Cinque 2007: 93).

Table 8.1 *Formal grammar vs. linguistic typology*

	Linguistic typology	Formal grammar
PRIMARY GOAL	understanding linguistic **diversity** by systematic **classification**	understanding the language **faculty** by uncovering language **universals**
EMPIRICAL BASIS	based on **large-scale** samples across unrelated languages	often based on a **single** language
MODES OF EXPLANATION	**external** (e.g., via general cognitive abilities) **functional** (form follows function)	**internal** (autonomy) **formal** (form is independent of function)

As for the mode of explanations, here too the emphasis has shifted. With the advent of the minimalist program (Chomsky 1995 and subsequent work) the autonomy thesis has been weakened to some extent. In particular, the computational system (narrow syntax) is conceived of as computing formal features in ways that meet constraints imposed by two interfaces: the articulatory–perceptual system (responsible for sound) and the conceptual–intentional system (responsible for meaning). In this respect formal grammar is approaching functional explanations.[1] Similarly, many formal explanations have long included some form of global economy conditions, which in turn have a functional flavor. And the field has also seen an increase in efforts to try to understand language use by incorporating the investigation of *information structure* (Rochemont [1986] is an early example), which is essentially concerned with the structuring of information flow, which is itself rooted in communicative function.

On the flip side, many functionalists use formal explanations in tandem with functional ones (Foley and Van Valin 1984; Croft 2001). Thus, the functional orientation of typology does not entail rejection of structure (Nichols 2007; Polinsky 2007: 273).

Despite this, the opposition between formal grammar and linguistic typology is still emphasized by some, and the dialogue is still not really ongoing. When it is, it remains hostile, as witnessed by the recent publication of Evans and Levinson (2009) in *Behavioral and Brain Sciences*. Here the division between the two approaches is indeed exacerbated, as already indicated by the controversial title: "The myth of language universals: Language diversity and its importance for cognitive science." In discussing the generative concept of universal grammar, Evans and Levinson (2009: 429) comment as follows:

> *The true picture is very different: languages differ so fundamentally from one another at every level of description (sound, grammar, lexicon, meaning) that it is very hard to find any single structural property they share. The claims of Universal Grammar, we argue here, are either empirically false, unfalsifiable, or misleading in that they refer to tendencies rather than strict universals. Structural differences should instead be accepted for what they are, and integrated into a new approach to language and cognition that places diversity at center stage.*

But, as discussed in Chapter 1 (Section 1.5), comparison between languages requires some standard of comparison and – perhaps more importantly – a

---

[1] See Golumbia (2010) who makes this point rather forcefully with the provocative title: 'Minimalism is functionalism.'

method of discovery. It is essential for any linguistic typology to provide a framework to classify the categories and structures of any language in a way that does not superimpose preconceived notions of the predominant languages of investigation (i.e., Indo-European). At the same time, however, there are no data without theory (Goldsmith forthcoming). Consequently, Nichols' (2007: 231) plea for "*framework neutral definitions*" as the essentials of typology is not a viable option. Any linguist will have to make assumptions about the way form, meaning, and categorial identity relate to each other. If assumptions appear to be theory-neutral, it is probably because we have gotten so used to them that we have forgotten that they are in fact assumptions. The postulate of the Saussurian sign (an arbitrary pairing of sound–meaning) is one of them. I hope to have shown, however, that the relation between a given form and its interpretation is multidimensional, and crucially in some cases mediated by syntactic context.

The goal of the present monograph is precisely to develop a formal way to talk about categories in all languages. I submit that a formal typology must serve as a pre-requisite for two essential linguistic tasks: ***discovery*** *of* and ***comparison*** *between* language-specific categories.

First, the *discovery* of the categories of a given language requires assumptions about the way forms and meanings are associated with categorical identities. This is what I mean by *the structure of a category:* the way form and meaning relate to categorial identity. Our assumptions about the way categories are structured influences the way we discover categories. Second, the *comparison* between categories across different languages (related or not) requires assumptions about what is to be compared and what is to be identified as being categorically identical. Thus, it is essential to have a heuristic which allows us to talk about languages in their own terms. I submit that a formal typology based on universalist assumptions will allow us to do just that. It is my hope that this monograph will contribute to the dialogue between formal grammar and linguistic typology.

8.3   Why do we need a formal typology of categorization?

The claim that all language-specific categories are constructed provides the basis for the development of a formal typology of categorization. In particular, I have argued that the universal categorizer mediates the relation between form (UoLs) and their interpretation, in much the same way as syntactic computation mediates between form (PF) and interpretation (LF) within the generative approach. In addition, I have introduced and developed the idea that there is a universal syntactic spine consisting of several domains, which are hierarchically organized, and which can be identified by their respective function. In this way, the present approach takes form and function to be intrinsically intertwined rather than one being subordinate to the other.

The idea that language-specific categories are constructed is in line with the basic premise of generative theorizing. That is, it was one of the hallmarks of the shift from the rule-based framework of the (Extended) Standard Theory (Chomsky 1965, 1973) to a framework based on principles and parameters (Chomsky 1981, 1986, 1993) that syntactic constructions (e.g., passive, yes/no-questions, etc.) are no longer viewed as primitives. The insight was that such constructions are in fact constructed based on universal building blocks (argument structure and case theory), language-specific features, and a general syntactic operation (Move α). Hence, constructions that we refer to as *passive* or *yes/no-questions* may be constructed in different ways, accounting for the observed linguistic diversity in grammatical constructions. In the same vein, I argue that categories are constructed based on the universal categorizer (κ), language-specific UoLs, and a general syntactic operation (Associate). Hence, categories that we refer to as *tense* or *pronouns* may be constructed in different ways, accounting for the observed linguistic diversity in categorial inventories.

In this light, consider Evans and Levinson's (2009) argument against UG. They present a list of features that, according to Pinker and Bloom (1990), all languages share in common. Those that are relevant for the present discussion, because they involve grammatical categories, are replicated in (2).

(2)   Proposed substantive universals
    a. Rules of linear order to distinguish, for example, subject from object, or case affixes which can take over these functions
    b. Verb affixes signaling aspect and tense (including pluperfects)
    c. Auxiliaries
    d. Anaphoric elements including pronouns and reflexives
             Pinker and Bloom (1990), cited from Evans and Levinson (2009)

Evans and Levinson (2009: 430) point out that "*none of these 'uncontroversial facts' are true of all languages.*" They cite a list of counter-examples for each of the purported universals in (2). But the non-universality of these categories should not come as a surprise by now. The categories listed in (2) are all of the type we have here identified as constructed, and thus are necessarily language-specific. Hence, we do not expect that all languages will have them. However, as I have attempted to show throughout this monograph, the non-universality of language-specific categories cannot be taken as evidence against UG.

Crucially, there are systematic patterns in the construction of categories that would be coincidental if we were to deny the existence of an underlying categorizing mechanism. Thus, when talking about universal categories, Evans and Levinson (2009) have in mind those categories that we have identified as *c* (constructed and thus necessarily language-specific). The notion of a universal category, as conceived of here, is fundamentally different. We have identified it as a universal categorizer *κ*, which associates with language-specific UoLs to construct language-specific categories *c*. I have further argued that the assumption of *κ* is necessary for the discovery and comparison of *c*. It serves as the *tertium comparationis* in the sense of Humboldt, which is meant to replace substance-based comparison, which has guided both formal and functional typologists. Consequently, the task of the linguist is to explore universals and variation in the construction of categories, i.e., a formal typology of categorization.

8.4   Classic criteria for formal classification and their problems

The essence of a formal approach is the postulate of the independence of form from function, at least to some degree. I here define *formal* as relating to the form, structure, and relation of the individual components, rather than to content alone. In other words, it is concerned with the way form, meaning, and categorical identity relate to each other.

If categories are not defined based on substance, but instead based on their formal properties, we need discovery procedures that are based on purely formal criteria (Wiltschko 2013). There are existing criteria for classification that are purely based on formal properties in this sense. Consider, for example, the division between *derivational* and *inflectional* morphology, and the distinction between *fusional, agglutinative,* and *isolating* languages. These classification criteria are formal in the sense that they are not based on substantive content. Nevertheless, they are not always useful heuristics in the discovery of categories.[2]

For example, on the basis of an investigation of Halkomelem plural and diminutive marking, Hukari (1978: 162f.) writes that:

---

[2] The Algonquian classification of morphemes that comprise the verb stem (initial, medial, and final: Bloomfield 1927) is based on linear position only. Hence it does not count as formal in the sense defined here, which requires that generalizations be made regarding the relation between form and function.

> *[t]he plural and diminutive fall somewhere in between ... in that there are no clear-cut reasons for considering them to be either inflectional or derivational (beyond, perhaps, a meta-linguistic assumption that categories of their semantic domains should be considered inflectional if they are productive).*

Thus, the contrast between derivation and inflection, while purely formal, does not allow for a straightforward classification of the Halkomelem plural marker. It is phenomena like this that have motivated some to conclude that the divide between derivation and inflection is not categorical but instead defines a gradient continuum with more or less prototypical instances (Bybee 1985; Dressler 1989; Payne 1997). When faced with such a non-categorical distinctions, there are two conclusions possible: (i) universal categories do not exist or (ii) non-categorical categories are constructs rather than primitives. Typologists often settle on the first conclusion. For example, in a recent post on *Diversity Linguistics Comment* (a scholarly blog on language typology and description) Martin Haspelmath writes:

> *it seems best to stop worrying whether an element is inflectional or derivational, and to concentrate on its properties. Bauer and Bauer note that "it is often difficult to determine from descriptive grammars precisely what should be considered inflection and what derivation in that particular language" (2012: 20). This must be because descriptive grammars often do the right thing: They describe the language with categories that are needed for it, not with categories inherited from Western tradition.* (http://dlc.hypotheses.org/388)

While I agree with the specific conclusion, that we should not use categories inherited from Western traditions to describe and compare languages, I do not agree with the broader conclusion that there cannot be any type of universal categories but only universal concepts (Haspelmath 2007). But then we are back to the question as to how compare languages to each other.

The other possible conclusion in light of non-categorical categories is the one I advocate, which is to consider these types of classifications as constructs rather than as primitives. As constructs, we do not expect them to be universal. In this vein, Wiltschko (2008) analyses the problematic plural marker of Halkomelem as a UoL that modifies roots, accounting for its distributional properties. Recognizing two parameters of variation, namely manner and place of association with the spine, the distinction between derivation and inflection no longer plays a role. Rather, UoLs display the prototypical inflectional characteristics if they associate as heads within one of the two core grammatical domains (*κ:anchoring* and *κ:PoV*). And they display the prototypical derivational characteristics if they associate as heads within the domain of classification. Any UoL that associates with the spine as a modifier will have properties that fall in between the inflection/derivation divide.

This brings us back to our quest for discovery procedures based on formal criteria, rather than being substance-based. While the inflection/derivation distinction meets the criterion of being formal (in the sense defined above), rather than substance-based, it nevertheless fails, because it is not a distinction that is universally attested. Hence it cannot be used as a universal discovery procedure. Interestingly, despite the widely recognized problematic nature of the inflection/derivation divide, it is still widely used both in linguistic typology as well as in formal grammar. For example, in WALS, five feature entries refer to *inflectional* forms (i) prefixing vs. suffixing in inflectional morphology; (ii) obligatory possessive inflection; (iii) fusion of selected inflectional formatives; (iv) exponent of selected inflectional formatives; and (v) inflectional synthesis on the verb. Similarly, within formal grammar, *inflectional* morphology is still often treated as if it were a natural class across languages (see, for example, Wunderlich and Fabri 1995; Bobaljik 2002, 2008, among others). That is, even if the properties of inflection are derived, the problem does not go away if they are derived in a way that will only derive the properties of prototypical inflectional categories but does not allow for the type of variation we actually observe.

The same point can be made for the other formal classification criterion often used in linguistic typology, namely the one based on morphological structure. That is, morphological typology traditionally recognizes four or five types,[3] each defined by a formal characteristic of typical word types and word formation strategies, as summarized in Table 8.2. In particular, *isolating* languages (also known as analytic languages) are characterized by the fact that their morphemes typically function as words. All other language types are *synthetic* in that they build complex words, albeit in different ways. *Agglutinative* languages are characterized by complex words consisting of more than one morpheme, where each morpheme expresses a single meaning or function. Languages of the *fusional* type (also known as inflecting) are characterized by forming at least some complex words via fusing several features into one form. That is, it is best described by a one-to-many correspondence between form and function. A single (superficially simplex) form is

---

[3] Classic morphological typology does not recognize intro-flecting as a separate type.

Table 8.2 *Morphological typology*

Type		Word types	Form of complex words	Classic example
ANALYTIC	ISOLATING	word = morpheme	n/a	Chinese
SYNTHETIC	AGGLUTINATIVE	word>morpheme	affixation	Turkish
	FUSIONAL	word>morpheme	fusion	French
	INTRO-FLECTING	word>morpheme	non-concatenative	Arabic
	POLYSYNTHETIC	word = sentence	incorporating	Algonquian

used to express more than one (grammatical) meaning or function. For example, English *-s* on verbs encodes 3rd person singular present tense. Consequently, in fusional languages a word is typically complex even if the morphological decomposition is not always detectable based on the form alone. *Intro-flecting* languages are characterized by non-concatenative morphology. And finally *polysynthetic* languages are characterized by the fact that many, if not all, arguments are incorporated into the predicate and thus what looks like a single word may serve as a sentence.

It has long been known that these types are not mutually exclusive, and thus any given language may simultaneously instantiate several types (Sapir 1921: 99). The problem is that it conflates different parameters (Haspelmath 2008), and thus classification of languages according to these morphological types is "incoherent and useless" (Spencer 1991: 38).

Just like the classification based on derivation and inflection, the classic morphological typology meets the criterion of being based on formal properties rather than substance. Nevertheless it fails because it does not return categorical distinctions. From the present perspective, the incoherence of this typology is not surprising. Its parameters and the concepts on which they are based are not defined. The notion *word* is not a primitive concept, and the notion *morpheme* does not define a unified class. Also, there is no reason as to why an entire language should be defined by a single lexicalization pattern.[4]

In sum, the classic criteria of morphological classification do not work, despite the fact that they meet the criterion of being formal (they are not based on substance). This is not surprising, since assumptions about how

---

[4] The question remains, however, whether the predominance of certain lexicalization patterns is a significant fact that deserves explanation.

form, meaning, and categorial identities relate to each other have changed dramatically over the years. In particular under classic assumptions, any given UoL is conceptualized as an arbitrary sound–meaning association, which can be categorized based on its syntactic distribution. Our assumptions about the architecture of grammar have been modified and refined over the last decades, and thus our conceptualization of UoLs has changed as well, even though classification criteria for UoLs based on these developments have not explicitly been established. As a consequence, more often than not, it is the output of structuralist analyses that serves as the starting point for generative analyses (Van Valin 2007: 255), especially when it comes to lesser-studied languages. It is tempting to use traditional morpheme analyses and classifications, only to realize that the resulting classifications are messy. I hope to have shown throughout the case studies presented in Chapters 4–7 that this is because traditional classification criteria miss several parameters of variation along which UoLs may differ. And as a consequence, the categorial patterns of the language in question are unnecessarily exoticized. The USH is meant as a contribution towards developing criteria for classification that are based on contemporary assumptions about the architecture of language.

8.5 Formal classification criteria based on the Universal Spine Hypothesis

The central thesis introduced here is that language-specific categories are constructed as in (1), repeated below.

(1) $c = \kappa + \text{UoL}$

As a consequence, categories can be constructed in different ways, accounting for language variation. We can thus distinguish between the universal structure underlying all categories and their language-specific surface manifestations, as illustrated in Figure 8.1.

The essential characteristic of this approach towards categories is that it distinguishes between language-specific categories, the UoLs that are used to construct them, and the linguistic function they manifest, which is in turn supplied by κ. The dissociation of category, form, and function captures apparent discrepancies between UoLs and their interpretations, as manifested in various patterns of multifunctionality. The interpretation of a given UoL may vary depending on κ and its association relation with κ.

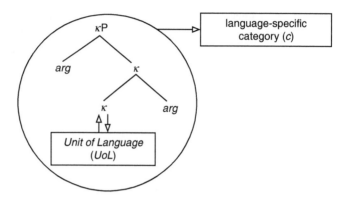

Figure 8.1 *The universal structure of categories and their language-specific instantiations*

Consequently, criteria for the classification of language-specific categories requires the identification of a given UoL, κ, and the way they associate with each other. Since only UoLs are directly observable, we have to make assumptions about κ. The USH provides the framework within which we have analyzed language-specific categories in previous chapters. In section 8.5.1 I summarize these assumptions and in Section 8.5.2 I discuss the classification criteria based upon them.

8.5.1   *Assumptions about the universal categorizer*

Our assumptions about the structure of κ are informed by contemporary theorizing about syntactic structure (as discussed in Chapter 2). At the same time, however, the USH departs from mainstream generative theorizing. On the one hand, it sides with the cartographic approach (Cinque 1999 and subsequent work) in the assumption that there is a universal spine, a series of hierarchically organized categories. In this respect, it differs from some versions of minimalism, according to which pre-established categories do not exist. At the same time, it departs from standard cartography (as well as some versions of minimalism) in denying the intrinsic association between κ and its substantive content. Rather, substantive content is associated with κ via a UoL, and hence the substantive content of a given category is always language-specific. There is however a residue of meaning intrinsically associated with κ, namely the spinal function, which may be instantiated by both nominal and verbal instantiations of κ. The spine, with its functions as assumed here, is repeated in (3).

(3)   The universal spine

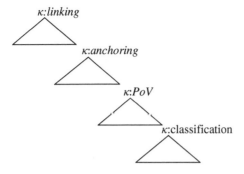

Inasmuch as the analyses of individual language-specific categories developed here are successful, we have evidence for the linguistic reality of κ. We have seen that κ is recursively applied, defining a series of domains, where each is associated with a dedicated linguistic function.

What else can we say about κ? While it is not directly observable, we can glean its characteristics by exploring those of c. There are two strategies for this: (i) to identify recurrent patterns in the formal properties of c and (ii) given the logic of the USH, essential qualities of κ may be deduced as in (4).

(4) $\kappa = c - \text{UoL}$

Since the interpretation of c depends on UoL as well as κ, it follows that whatever is not directly encoded in UoL must derive from κ.

Based on these two strategies to explore κ, we have arrived at the following conclusions about its structure and intrinsic content. (i) κ is transitive; (ii) κ establishes a relation between abstract arguments; and (iii) κ must be substantiated by virtue of a UoL.

(i)   *Transitivity.* All grammatical categories are transitive: they relate two abstract arguments to each other. For verbal categories, these are situation arguments (arg_{sit}) and for nominal categories these are individual arguments (arg_{ind}).

(ii) *Relationality.* The type of relation between the two arguments is restricted by a feature intrinsically associated with κ. For verbal categories, this feature is [coincidence] and for nominal categories it is [identity]. The feature intrinsic to κ has several effects:

It serves as the interface between κ and the UoL, in that it requires further substantiation. This requirement is modeled as an unvalued feature, [$u$coin] and [$u$ident], which is valued by the substantive content (Σ) of the UoL it associates with. Moreover, the substantive content that serves to value [*u*coin] and [*u*ident] may also have the effect of focusing on a particular aspect of the abstract arguments it relates. In particular, both situation arguments and individual arguments include spatio-temporal coordinates. In addition, situation arguments also include a variable for event participants. The universal structure of the categorizers is represented in (5a) for verbal categories and in (5b) for nominal categories.

(5)   The universal structure of categories

        a. verbal categories   b. nominal categories

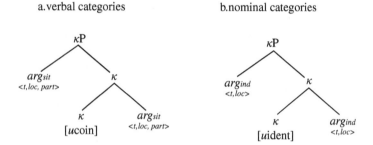

(iii) *Substantiation.* The unvalued features [*u*coin] and [*u*ident] can be substantiated by an appropriate UoL in three different ways. The UoL may directly associate with κ via the "*is-a*" relation. We have referred to this as internal or m(orphological)-valuation. Alternatively, it may be valued by a UoL that is associated with a position external to κP, i.e., higher in the structure. The valuing UoL may either be a higher l(exical)-predicate or else a higher functional head. We have referred to the former as pred(icate)-valuation and to the latter as f-valuation. This is summarized in Figure 8.2.

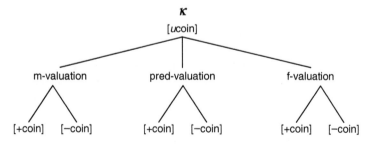

Figure 8.2 *Valuation typology for* κ

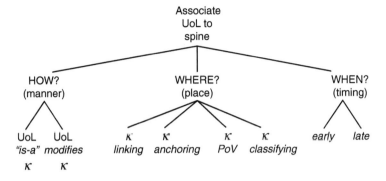

Figure 8.3 *Typology of association relations*

These are the key ingredients to derive surface categories (*c*). Consequently, criteria for classifying categories must be based on the UoLs that are used to construct them; they are the only directly observable ingredients. The classification criteria for UoLs we have used here are summarized below.

8.5.2   *Classifying the units of language*

The association relation between UoLs and the spine is characterized by three different parameters of variation. In particular, UoLs differ as to how, where, and when they associate with *κ*, as summarized in Figure 8.3. Concerning *how* a UoL associates with *κ*, there are **two** manners of association: by means of the *"is-a"* relation, or by means of the modification relation. As for *where* a UoL associates with the spine, there are four areas in the spine: *κ:linking*, *κ: anchoring*, *κ:PoV*, and *κ:classifying*. Note that manner of association cuts across place of association, in that both manners are available in all areas of the spine. Finally, regarding *when* a given UoL associates with the spine, there are two options: before or after the syntactic computation (i.e., *early* or *late*).[5]

---

[5] The classification in terms of timing may in fact be more fine-grained. That is, just like in current theorizing some assume cyclic spell out based on phases rather than a simple division between early and late insertion (Uriagereka 1999; Chomsky 2001, 2008), so too could we postulate the existence of more than two repositories of UoLs. In particular, it is conceivable that each domain in the spine is associated with its own "lexicon." This receives initial support from the fact that some UoLs associated with a certain domain are characterized by specific phonological properties. For example, English /ð-/ is restricted to functional categories in the domains of anchoring and linking. This assumption would simultaneously solve the problem of accounting for UoLs that associate as modifiers and thus are not associated with categorial information. If they are intrinsically associated with a domain-specific lexicon, then their distribution would follow.

As discussed in Chapter 3, the association relations can be diagnosed by patterns of contrast and patterns of multifunctionality. Moreover, there are certain implicational relations between different types of association and valuation relations.

Specifically, associating a UoL with κ via the "*is-a*" relation implies that the UoL serves to m-value the unvalued feature intrinsic to κ. Hence, the fact that the manner of association can be diagnosed by means of the complementary contrast relation originates with the intrinsic feature of κ, [$u$coin] and [$u$ident], respectively. Since these features must be valued, it follows that in the absence of an overt UoL that derives one value, there must be a silent one to derive the complementary value. Hence, if a given grammatical category is identified via the "*is-a*" relation, it will license zero marking. Note that silence is only one option to mark the complementary value; alternatively, an overt UoL may also mark the contrasting value. Thus, grammatical categories that seem to be identified by morphological marking are those that associate UoLs with κ by the "*is-a*" relation.

Note further that the dissociation of UoLs from their linguistic functions derives certain patterns of multifunctionality. In particular, if the UoL associates with κ via the "*is-a*" relation it will acquire the function intrinsic to κ. But since UoLs exist independently of the spine it follows that they can – in principle – associate with the spine differently, in which case they will lose the linguistic function supplied by κ. This is the case for those patterns of multifunctionality that are generally referred to as *fake* (e.g., fake past and fake indexicals).[6] Units of Language that associate as modifiers are different in this respect. Since they do not become κ, they also do not acquire the properties of κ. Thus, unlike the interpretation of m-valuing UoLs, the interpretation of modifiers is solely dependent on the content of the UoL. The syntactic spine does not mediate their interpretation; rather its interaction with the spine manifests itself in terms of scope.

Next we turn to the interaction between valuation patterns and timing of association. As summarized in Table 8.3, there are implicational relations imposed by the architecture of grammar.[7] If a given UoL manifests the unvalued feature, it must be associated early. By hypothesis, an unvalued feature has to be valued during the syntactic computation. Hence, no post-syntactic UoL may spell out an unvalued feature. The same logic applies to m-valuation, which implies early association of the valuing UoL. Late insertion

---

[6] See Déchaine and Wiltschko (2009) for an analysis of fake indexicals along these lines.
[7] See Chapter 2 (Section 2.4) and Subsection 8.6.2.4 below.

Table 8.3 *Interaction between valuation strategies and timing of association*

	Early association	Late association
[$u$coin]	✓	✗
[m-val:±coin]	✓	✗
[pred-val:±coin]	✗	✓
[f-val:±coin]	✗	✓

is not an option because it would imply the presence of an unvalued feature after spell-out. In contrast, if a given UoL realizes an externally valued instance of κ, it must do so via late association. This follows because external valuation requires syntactic computation.

Note further that late association UoLs cannot themselves be associated with substantive content. This follows because the substantive content of the UoL can no longer be interpreted. Instead, late insertion UoLs are the realization of grammatical configurations. In Chapters 5 and 6, we examined core instances of such UoLs, namely in the form of subjunctive markers (Chapter 5) and case markers (Chapter 6). These are grammatical categories that have long been difficult to analyze. The key towards developing a typology that covers such categories is to recognize the independence of UoL, κ (including the function it introduces), and c. In light of the common assumption that categories are defined based on substance, in tandem with the assumption that categorial labels do not exist, such categories give rise to non-trivial problems. In fact, there are two UoLs involved in the making of such categories: (i) those that serve to value the unvalued feature in κ (either a higher predicate or a higher functor), and (ii) those that are used to realize this value. As we have seen in Chapters 5 and 6, these late association UoLs may give rise to syncretic forms, another pattern of multifunctionality.

In sum, to classify UoLs it is essential to recognize that not all UoLs are intrinsically associated with categorial information. Rather, early association UoLs have a linguistic reality in their uncategorized form (i.e., as simple sound–meaning correspondences $\{\pi,\Sigma\}$). Since categorization via κ introduces a particular linguistic function, the interpretation of UoLs is affected as a result of categorization, giving rise to the patterns of multifunctionality that I introduced in Chapter 1. Thus, patterns of multifunctionality can serve as a key diagnostic in the identification of categories and the core of the UoLs that are used to construct them. In particular, to identify the very core of a given UoL, we can use the category and subtract the effects of the universal categorizer κ (including its function) as in (6).

(6) $\text{UoL} = c - \kappa$

In light of this approach, we eventually may want to reconsider our glossing conventions or at least make explicit whether glossing reflects grammatical categories (c) or the UoLs that serve to construct them. And, if UoLs are glossed then we may want to indicate whether the gloss reflects the UoL before or after the syntactic computation. Current glossing conventions do not make these distinctions.

8.6   Conclusions and open questions

8.6.1   *Conclusions*

We started out in Chapter 1 with three questions: What are grammatical categories? How do we identify them? And are they universal? The answers we have developed evolve around the idea that grammatical categories are constructed, as in (1), and hence they can be constructed in different ways.

(1) $c = \kappa + \text{UoL}$

Thus, in order to compare categories across languages, we have to decompose them into their respective ingredients: language-specific UoLs and universal categorizers which are intrinsically associated with linguistic function. To identify these ingredients, we have introduced several heuristics based on patterns of contrast as well as patterns of multifunctionality.

The parameters of variation we have identified range over differences in UoLs, differences in association relations, and differences in the patterns of valuation. As a consequence, there are numerous ways to construct language-specific categories, and thus surface explorations of individual languages yield the impression of massive diversity. This diversity has led some to repudiate the very concept of a universal grammar. Instead of postulating universal categories, it is argued that we are – at best – dealing with statistical tendencies (Bickel 2007; Nichols 2007; Evans and Levinson 2009). At the same time, however, we have observed significant systematicity in categorization patterns casting doubt on this conclusion. The postulation of a universal categorizer organized along the universal spine is a way to deal with the antithesis between massive diversity and universal systematicity. It plays a vital role in the construction of categories as well as the UoLs that realize them. In this way the universal spine is essential in the construction of language-specific grammars. It differs from previous instantiations of the Universal Base Hypothesis in that it is not conceived of as a repository of grammatical categories from which languages chose. Thus, the language-specific categories are not those we find on the underlying universal spine. Instead, universally the spine consists of a series of κs, and κ is the basis for the construction of categories.

It follows that, when we use traditional labels to identify categories across different languages, we are not likely to pick out a natural class. Even if two categories appear to be identical in terms of their substantive content, they may be constructed in different ways. As a result, we observe gradient rather than categorical properties. Gradience is an inevitable outcome of comparative and typological explorations that seek to compare the grammars and categories of individual languages directly to each other. We need instead a comparative approach, which recognizes an abstract universal grammar, in the sense of Humboldt, which serves as a third element for comparison, a *tertium comparationis*. The USH is meant as a step towards such a universal grammar. It requires extensive abstraction, but it does not automatically become unfalsifiable (*contra* Evans and Levinson 2009). In particular, the system that I have introduced here makes clear predictions about possible grammatical categories, possible UoLs, as well as possible association relations.

Given the scope of the research agenda I have set out to delineate here, it comes as no surprise that there are numerous open questions and implications, to which I will turn now.

8.6.2   Open questions
The USH as developed here raises a series of questions regarding all aspects of the proposal, including the proper characterization of κ, the areas in the spine, the UoLs, and the association relations. I introduce some of these questions here.

8.6.2.1   The proper characterization of [coincidence]
One of the key ingredients of our exploration of grammatical categories in this monograph is the postulation of a universal categorizer κ. I have made several assumptions based on previous generative insights, but I have also introduced some original claims. Specifically, the present approach is defined by the rejection of the often assumed intrinsic association between κ and its substantive content. Nevertheless, I have postulated some residue of content to be associated with all instances of κ namely the *coincidence* feature. The postulation of this cross-categorial feature is in the spirit of Hale (1986), who first noticed its pervasiveness within and across languages. Hale's insight can be gleaned from the following quote:

> *The coincidence theme manifests itself in the meanings of certain grammatical elements, including case endings, complementizers and tense-aspect morphology. If I am correct in my claim about the semantics of these elements, the theme which seems to me detectable in them is especially interesting, and instructive, because of the fact that it is not uniformly marked, morphologically speaking, and because of the fact that it is to be observed in parts of the grammar which are not otherwise intimately related. The theme is therefore difficult, if not impossible, to learn on the basis of the data which a language learner would have in the normal course of language acquisition, suggesting that the semantic opposition involved is universal.*   (Hale 1986: 238)

The USH exploits this notion of coincidence and models it as an unvalued feature that plays a critical role in deriving patterns of contrast. It is one of the key ingredients that provides the interface between κ and UoLs. Some of the open questions regarding the formal properties of the coincidence feature are as follows.

First, I have introduced the idea that nominal and verbal grammatical categories can be distinguished in terms of the particular characteristic of this feature. Specifically, I have proposed that *coincidence* is the essential characteristic of verbal categories, while *identity* defines nominal categories. Behind this distinction lies the insight that verbal categories deal with situations (and thus events) while nominal categories deal with individuals. Since the former unfold over time it is possible to establish relations that are not defined by strict identity, but allow for overlaps instead. In contrast, when relating single individuals to each other, it is only identity which plays a role; overlap does not play a role, even though, in principle, overlap and thus coincidence may be applicable to plural individuals. Whether this is indeed so, and how it would play out is an open question. It may lead us to abandon the distinction between coincidence and identity, or else we may expect that plural nominal constituents might behave more like verbal categories than their singular counterpart.

If indeed there is a distinction between coincidence and identity, then the question arises as to what the relation is between the two, and what determines which one is in fact associated with κ. On the one hand, identity may be viewed as a special case of coincidence, if we view identity as complete or perfect coincidence. On the other hand, identity may be the more basic relation, with coincidence introducing a complexity in the form of temporal overlaps. The question of whether one of the two relations is basic and the other one derived is an empirical question. It will require detailed cross-linguistic explorations of patterns of nominal and verbal grammatical categories, recategorization patterns (i.e., nominalization and verbalization) as well as the acquisition and grammaticalization paths associated with such categories.

In addition, if one is derived from the other, we need to determine how this is achieved. Are there dedicated UoLs that govern the distribution of these features? Or is it a matter of grammatical configurations?

A second way in which I depart from Hale's conceptualization of the coincidence feature concerns the interpretation of the negative value [−coin]. In particular, in Chapters 4–6 [−coin] was simply conceived of as non-coincidence. Two situation or individual arguments are asserted to be distinct. However, in Chapter 7, where I explored viewpoint aspect, I adjusted this conceptualization of [−coin]. Specifically, I introduced the idea that [−coin] may be conceived of as *terminal coincidence*. The latter view is more in line with Hale's (1986) original proposal, according to which the two relevant features are *central* and *terminal coincidence* (as opposed to [+coin] and [−coin]). The precise characterization of coincidence has to be explored more carefully. Is [−coin] always a form of terminal coincidence? And if not, under what conditions is it interpreted as such? Or do central and terminal coincidence both exist as bivalent features [±central coincidence] and [±terminal coincidence]. The latter view is explored in Ritter (2013).

8.6.2.2 How does substantive content value [ucoin]?

In addition to the questions about the characterization of coincidence, there is also the question as to what can serve to provide it with a value. In the course of the case studies reported in Chapters 4–7, I have assumed with Ritter and Wiltschko, (forthcoming) that coincidence is an inherently unvalued feature, which is valued and thus substantiated by the substantive content of UoLs. We have discussed three sources for this valuation operation: dedicated UoLs (m-valuation), higher predicates (pred-valuation), and higher functors (f-valuation). What they all have in common is that it is the substantive content of a given UoL that contributes to the valuation process. It is worth pointing out that valuation so conceived differs substantially from the valuation relation as conceived of in the minimalist program. There are two crucial differences. First, if valuation of [ucoin] is indeed dependent on substantive content, it follows that functional categories are associated with substantive content. This departs from Chomsky (1995: 54), who asserts that *"[i]tems of the lexicon are of two general types: with or without substantive content."* For Chomsky, lexical categories are those that have substantive content; functional categories are those that do not. Under the present conceptualization, all categories may have substantive content. The difference between functional and lexical categories lies in the fact that the substantive content of lexical categories is interpreted relative to the real world, whereas that of functional categories is interpreted relative to the grammatical context. And moreover, functional categories are characterized by non-substantive content as well.

Another way in which the present approach to valuation departs from standard minimalist assumptions is in the characterization of the UoL that values the unvalued feature. Following Ritter and Wiltschko (forthcoming), I have assumed that it is the substantive content alone that values [$u$coin]. This departs from existing approaches, according to which an unvalued feature [uF] is valued by an interpretable feature [iF] via the operation AGREE. While it would be possible to associate corresponding interpretable features with the relevant UoLs this does not seem to be a necessary assumption and I therefore have not adopted it here.

Whether or not the valuation via substantive content approach is on the right track is of course an empirical question. But if it is, it raises a series of other questions. First, does it replace the existing approach where [uF] is valued by [iF] or do the two types of valuation coexist? And if they coexist how do we diagnose them?

Moreover, if substantive content is indeed a possible source of valuation, then the question arises what determines which substantive content can serve that function. Take, for example, nominal classification systems. While there is a seemingly limitless amount of substantive content that may be realized as a noun, not every one of these contents is used to classify. Instead, there is likely a limited set of such substantive elements that may substantiate κ:*classification*. But what determines membership in this set? Is it determined by the language faculty or is it a matter of general cognition? And of course we are invited to rethink the time-honored question of linguistic relativism (the Sapir–Whorf hypothesis). While we have found support for one of the key ingredients of linguistic relativism, namely that languages differ, we have yet to address the implications of the USH for the other aspect of linguistic relativism: does the inventory of grammatical categories of a given language have an effect on the perception and conceptualization of the world and vice versa? It seems to me that this conceptualization of feature valuation as an essential ingredient in the construction of categories provides us with a new way of approaching the topic. And in the same vein, it sheds light on an old insight, according to which every language has a structural *genius*. According to Sapir (1921: 120): *"This type or plan or structural 'genius' of the language is something much more fundamental, much more pervasive, than any single feature of it that we can mention, nor can we gain an adequate idea of its nature by a mere recital of the sundry facts that make up the grammar of a language."* As we have seen, the substance associated with one category (e.g., *κ:anchoring*) influences the type of content we may find in other categories. Thus in Blackfoot, person and animacy marking pervade the entire grammar, both in the nominal and in the verbal domain.

A related question concerns the limits of valuation of UoLs. Are languages limited to one type of substantive content to value [*u*coin], or is it possible for a single language to use more than one type of substantive content for valuation? A candidate for such a category might be *κ:anchoring* in Standard German where we find both *c*:TENSE and *c*:SUBJUNCTIVE (recall that the latter has been analyzed to replace *c*:TENSE in Upper Austrian German: see Chapter 4, Section 4.4.3). It may however be significant that in Standard German, synthetic subjunctive marking is leaving the language (Fabricius-Hansen and Sæbø 2004). This contrasts with Upper Austrian German, which does not use *c*:TENSE. The drift towards complementarity might be indicative of a preference for having just one type of substantive content to m-value [*u*coin].

Another question that arises in this context is whether the other criterial component of sound–meaning correspondences may also play a role in valuation. In particular, everything else being equal, we may expect that, just like meaning (Σ) may value [*u*coin], so may sound (π). That this may in fact be the case is implicated by recent findings reported in Fujimori (2011). In particular, vowel quality in Yamato Japanese is a perfect predictor for the telicity of verbs: while monosyllabic verbs containing /e/ or /u/ are always telic, those with /i/ or /o/ are always atelic (verbs with /a/ can be either telic or atelic). Furthermore, Fujimori (2011) shows that Japanese speakers are sensitive to this distinction even in nonce verbs. This is precisely the type of behavior we may expect from a system where a particular sound serves to value [*u*coin]. Thus, the USH provides a new way of dealing with unconventional associations between sound and meaning, namely those that are often classified as ideophonic or iconic.

In this way, I believe that the USH allows for a new way of thinking about language, one that bridges the gap between formalists and functionalists by taking both form and function into consideration. Furthermore, by denying the primacy of the Saussurian sign (i.e., simple sound–meaning correspondences) it opens the way to approach multifunctionality as well as iconicity in a new way.

8.6.2.3 Other areas of the spine

We have here explored the USH on the basis of case studies involving categories that are located in the core of the spine, the domain where grammatical relations are established (*κ:anchoring* and *κ:PoV*). The question remains, however, as to whether categories in other areas of the spine behave in similar ways. Everything else being equal, we expect that to be the case. Déchaine *et al.* (forthcoming) develop an analysis of Shona noun class suffixes based on the universal spine. In Wiltschko (2012), I argue that nominal classification is not universally based on the same substantive content. Instead of a grammaticized mass/count distinction, Blackfoot grammaticizes animacy. This is not really surprising, given the pervasiveness of person marking in the language. As for the linking domain (C and K), this area is explored in Bliss (forthcoming) on the basis of Blackfoot. Furthermore, Thoma (forthcoming) explores discourse particles in Bavarian German within the framework of the USH. Initial findings suggest that there might be yet another layer above κ: *linking* which serves in the negotiation and management of the common ground. Hence, this area is labeled κ:*grounding* (Lam *et al.* 2013). Thus, the exact number of areas in the spine is still subject to investigation. Moreover, it is necessary to address the question regarding the proper characterization of a single area in the spine. Is there a one-to-one correspondence between κ and the area of the spine where it appears (as well as its function)? Again this is an empirical question. Thus far we have assumed that there is indeed only one κ per area, but this is not a necessary assumption (see, for example, Grohmann's [2003] notion of prolific domains, which recognizes the potential to expand the number of categories found within a single area in the spine). Whether the areas are indeed prolific, and, if so to what extent, remains an open question under the USH.

8.6.2.4   Beyond linguistic reality

One of the core goals of this monograph was to establish the linguistic reality of κ: it plays an integral role in the construction of grammatical categories. What I have not (yet) been concerned with is the question of whether or not κ also has psychological reality. My focus on linguistic reality stems primarily from my background as a fieldworker studying some lesser-studied languages. In doing this work, the prevailing question that arises for a syntactician is deceptively simple: how do we draw a tree for a sentence in a language that has not been analyzed to the same degree as English within the generative tradition? Even if one adopts a strict version of the UBH, such as cartography, it is not immediately clear how to map the UoLs of a given language on the hypothesized universal tree. The grammatical categories can be so different from the familiar ones that a direct mapping is simply not possible. The result is the temptation to postulate a number of silent categories on the one hand, and on the other hand to treat some of the grammatical categories (even if they are pervasive) as merely instantiating some messy morphology that plays no role in syntactic analyses. This might seem justified in light of Givón's (1971) maxim *"Today's morphology is yesterday's syntax."* However, especially in many of the languages indigenous to North America, which are (descriptively) highly agglutinative and/or polysynthetic, this would mean that core aspects of the language are treated as being syntactically irrelevant. But while many categories are indeed realized by means of morphological marking, it is far from messy and we observe the same types of patterns that are indicative for grammatical categories. This systematicity in morphological marking is indicative of a syntactic phenomenon after all, and it led, for example, Baker (1988, 1996) to treat noun incorporation and polysynthesis in the languages of North America as syntactically derived.

Thus, it was this diversity of grammatical categories and its practical implications for the theoretically inclined fieldworker that led me to formulate the thesis that grammatical categories are constructed based on a universal categorizer κ and language-specific UoLs. The next step is to explore the question regarding the psychological reality of κ. Does it have primitive status within the language faculty, or is it further derivable? To answer this question, we will have to follow standard practice within the generative enterprise and explore categorization patterns from a number of perspectives.

First, more languages will have to be explored in light of the USH. Do we find the same categorization patterns? What is the range of variation in the substantiation of grammatical categories? Second, we will have to explore the predictions of the USH for language acquisition. Just like the fieldworker can use patterns of contrast and multifunctionality as heuristics for the analysis of unfamiliar languages, so can the child acquiring a language. And indeed it appears that children are sensitive to the effects of κ. That is, while research in the 1970s was characterized by semantic bootstrapping, later on the field of language acquisition was characterized by distributionalist models. According to the latter, children are sensitive to the distribution of syntactic categories (Labelle 2005). Third, it will be useful to also look at another aspect of psycholinguistic research, namely patterns of categorization in populations characterized by language deficiencies. For example Christodoulou (2011) establishes that in the language of people with Down syndrome, the grammatical categorizer is intact but the association between κ and its substantive content may be affected. Fourth, the USH needs to be explored from a diachronic perspective including questions about grammaticalization. Thus, it will be by answering questions about language acquisition, language deficiencies, and language change that we may be able to gain some insights into the psychological reality of κ.

Finally, once we have a clearer idea about the psychological reality of κ, we can also draw some conclusions about the implications for the architecture of grammar. That is, in a sense, the USH is concerned with analyzing the construction of language-specific grammars (their grammatical categories and their UoLs) rather than with analyzing the derivation of individual sentences. Theorizing about implications of the USH for the architecture of grammar will also require a rethinking of its interfaces. For example, current formal semantic theory is characterized by Frege's principle of compositionality.

(7)   The principle of compositionality
       The meaning of a complex expression is determined by the meaning of its
       parts and the way those parts are combined.

According to standard treatments, the meaning of the (atomic) parts is a matter of the lexicon and the way these parts are combined is determined by the semantic rules of combination. On this conceptualization of compositionality, every meaning is supplied by a lexical entry. This can be characterized as a kind of *semantic lexicalism*. But it runs counter to the USH, according to which certain aspects of meaning are supplied by the positions of UoLs along the spine. Crucially, standard semantic treatments do not distinguish between different types of UoLs (i.e., our early vs. late association UoLs) and as such they miss a crucial dimension in the composition of meaning. Consequently, any form of syntactically conditioned multifunctionality has to be treated as a form of homophony. In contrast, according to the USH, catgorial identity mediates between form (the UoL), and its interpretation as in Figure 8.4.

This mirrors the standard assumption that syntax mediates the relation between form and interpretation. The mediating role of syntactic computation is reflected in the fact that there has not been a direct relation between PF (form) and LF (interpretation) in models of grammar since Government and Binding Theory (Chomsky 1981). The current minimalist model, known as the

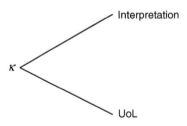

Figure 8.4 κ *mediates between UoL and its interpretation*

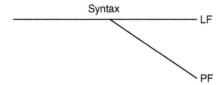

Figure 8.5 *Syntax mediates between form and interpretation*

Y-model, is given in Figure 8.5. The extent to which standard semantic theorizing has to be adapted in light of the USH remains to be explored.

There are of course many more questions the USH raises. In essence, it opens up a new way of exploring grammatical categories. As such, it defines a new research agenda.

8.7   The Universal Spine Hypothesis as a research agenda

In answering the three questions introduced at the outset of this monograph I have developed a new research agenda. These questions, the answers I have developed here, and the research questions they lead to, are summarized below.

(i)   What are grammatical categories?

Grammatical categories are constructs. They are built based on a universal categorizer κ, language-specific Units of Language (UoLs), and different association relations between the two. The research agenda that this defines is to identify and analyze the grammatical categories of the languages of the world. What are the UoLs that are used to construct them? What are the functions they acquire by means of associating with κ? And what are the attested patterns of association between the two?

(ii)   How do we identify grammatical categories?

The diagnostics for language-specific categories must be language-specific. This follows from the thesis that categories are constructed in language-specific ways. Distributional diagnostics for c are based on the interaction between c and other categories, which are also constructed. Hence, criterial diagnostics for categories must also be language-specific. This is another way of saying that each language should be described "*in its own terms*" (Boas 1911).

(iii)   And are grammatical categories universal?

To answer the universality question, it is essential to compare grammatical categories from different languages to each other. But if they must be discovered and described in their own terms, then what are the terms we can use to compare them? I have argued that these terms are formal in nature, rather than substance-based. The goal of this monograph was to start to develop a formal typology for grammatical categories in the form of universal diagnostics for categorial patterns. What remains to be done is to analyze categories of more natural languages within this framework.

References

Abney, Steven Paul. (1987). The English noun phrase in its sentential aspect. Unpublished Ph.D. dissertation. Massachusetts Institute of Technology, Cambridge, MA.

Agouraki, Yoryia. (1991). A Modern Greek complementizer and its significance for UG. *UCL Working Papers in Linguistics*, *3*, 1–24.

Aissen, Judith. (1997). On the syntax of obviation. *Language*, *73*(4), 705–750.

Albright, Adam, and Eric Fuss. (2012). Syncretism. In Jochen Trommer (ed.), *The Morphology and Phonology of Exponence*, pp. 236–287. Oxford: Oxford University Press.

Alexiadou, Artemis. (2009). Tense in the nominal domain: implications for grammar architecture. *Linguistic Variation Yearbook* 2008, *8*(1), 33–65.

Alexiadou, Artemis, and Elena Anagnostopoulou. (1999). EPP without Spec, IP. In David Adger, Susan Pintzuk, Bernadette Plunkette, and George Tsoulas (eds.), *Specifiers: Minimalist Approaches*, pp. 93–109. Oxford: Oxford University Press.

Alexiadou, Artemis, and Melita Stavrou. (1998). (A)symmetries in DPs and clauses: evidence from derived nominals. *The Linguistic Review*, *15*(2), 257–276.

Anderson, John. (1971). *The Grammar of Case: Towards a Localistic Theory*. Cambridge: Cambridge University Press.

Anderson, Stephen. (1992). *A-Morphous Morphology*. Cambridge: Cambridge University Press.

Armoskaite, Solveiga. (2008). Blackfoot stem initial predicates: shape-shifting perfectives. In Karl Hele and Regna Darnell (eds.), *Proceedings of the 39th Algonquian Conference Proceedings*, pp. 1–23.

(2011). The destiny of roots in Blackfoot and Lithuanian. Unpublished Ph.D. dissertation, University of British Columbia, Vancouver, BC.

Aronoff, Mark. (1976). *Word Formation in Generative Grammar*. Cambridge, MA: MIT Press.

(1994). *Morphology by Itself: Stems and Inflectional Classes*. Cambridge, MA: MIT Press.

Austin, Peter. (1981). *A Grammar of Diyari, South Australia*. Cambridge: Cambridge University Press.

Bach, Emmon. 1968. Nouns and noun phrases. In Emmon Bach and Robert T. Harms (eds.), *Universals in Linguistic Theory*, pp. 90–122. New York: Holt, Rinehart and Winston.

327

Baerman, Matthew. (2009). Case syncretism. In Andrei Malchukov and Andrew Spencer (eds.), *The Oxford Handbook of Case*, pp. 219–230. Oxford: Oxford University Press.

Baker, Mark. (1985). The mirror principle and morphosyntactic explanation. *Linguistic Inquiry*, *16*(3), 373–415.

(1988). *Incorporation: A Theory of Grammatical Function Changing*. Cambridge, MA: MIT Press.

(1996). *The Polysynthesis Parameter*. Oxford: Oxford University Press.

(2002). On category asymmetries in derivational morphology. In Sabrina Bendjaballah, Wolfgang U. Dressler, Oskar E. Pfeiffer, and Maria D. Voeikova (eds.), *Morphology 2000*, pp. 17–35. Amsterdam: John Benjamins.

(2003). *Lexical Categories*. Cambridge: Cambridge University Press.

Baker, Mark, and Jim McCloskey. (2007). On the relationship of typology to theoretical syntax. *Linguistic Typology*, *11*(1), 273–284.

Baker, Mark, and Nadya Vinokurova. (2010). Two modalities of case assignment: case in Sakha. *Natural Language and Linguistic Theory*, *28*(3), 593–642.

Bar-el, Leora, Henry Davis, and Lisa Matthewson. (2005). On non-culminating accomplishments. Paper presented at the Proceedings of NELS 35.

Barker, Chris. (1998). Episodic *-ee* in English: A thematic role constraint on new word formation. *Language 74*(4), 695–727.

(1999). Quantification and individuation. *Linguistic Inquiry 30*(4), 683–691.

(2010). Nominals don't provide criteria for identity. In Monika Rathert and Artemis Alexiadou (eds.), *The Semantics of Nominalizations across Languages and Frameworks*, pp. 9–24. Berlin: Mouton de Gruyter.

(2012). Quantificational binding does not require *c*-command. *Linguistic Inquiry*, *43*(4), 614–633.

Barker, Chris, and Chung-Chieh Shan. (2008). Donkey anaphora is in-scope binding. *Semantics and Pragmatics*, *1*(1), 1–46.

Barss, Andrew, and Howard Lasnik. (1986). A note on anaphora and double objects. *Linguistic Inquiry*, *17*(2), 347–354.

Bayer, Josef. (1984). COMP in Bavarian syntax. *Linguistic Review*, *3*(3), 209–274.

Beard, Robert. (1995). *Lexeme–Morpheme Base Morphology: A General Theory of Inflection and Word Formation*. Albany, NY: SUNY Press.

Beck, David. (2000). Semantic agents, syntactic subjects, and discourse topics: How to locate Lushootseed sentences in space and time. *Studies in Language*, *24*(2), 277–317.

Bejar, Susana, and Milan Rezac. (2009). Cyclic agree. *Linguistic Inquiry*, *40*(1), 35–73.

Belletti, Adriana. (1988). The case of unaccusatives. *Linguistic Inquiry*, *19*(1), 1–34.

Bendix, Edward H. (1998). Irrealis as category, meaning, or reference. *Anthropological Linguistics*, *40*(2), 245–256.

Benveniste, Émile. (1966). *Problèmes de linguistique générale*. Paris: Gallimard.

(1971). *Problems in General Linguistics*, trans. Mary E. Meek. Coral Gables, FL: University of Miami Press.

Bernstein, Judy. (2001). The DP hypothesis: Identifying clausal properties in the nominal domain. In Mark Baltin and Chris Collins (eds.), *The Handbook of Contemporary Syntactic Theory*, pp. 536–561. Oxford: Blackwell.

  (2008). Reformulating the determiner phrase analysis. *Language and Linguistics Compass*, 2(6), 1246–1270.

Besten, Hans den. (1983 [1977]). On the interaction of root transformations and lexical deletive rules. In Werner Abraham (ed.), *On the Formal Syntax of the Westgermania*, pp. 47–131. Amsterdam: John Benjamins.

Bickel, Balthasar. (2007). Typology in the 21st century: Major current developments. *Linguistic Typology*, 11(1), 239–251.

Binnick, Robert. (1991). *Time and the Verb: A Guide to Tense and Aspect*. Oxford: Oxford University Press.

Bittner, Maria, and Kenneth Hale. (1996). The structural determination of case and agreement. *Linguistic Inquiry*, 27(1), 1–68.

Blake, Barry. (1994). *Case*. Cambridge: Cambridge University Press.

Bliss, Heather. (2005). Formalizing point-of-view: The role of sentience in Blackfoot's direct/inverse system. MA thesis, University of Calgary, Alberta, Canada.

  (2008). Structuring information in Blackfoot: Against the A'-agreement analysis of cross-clausal agreement. In Susie Jones (ed.), *Proceedings of the 2008 Canadian Linguistics Association Annual Conference*. http://homes.chass.utoronto.ca/~cla-acl/actes2008

  (2011). A unified analysis of Blackfoot it-. *Proceedings of the 2011 Western Conference on Linguistics*. Fresno, CA: California State University.

  (2013). The Blackfoot configurationality conspiracy: parallels and differences in clausal and nominal structure. Unpublished Ph.D. dissertation, University of British Columbia, Vancouver.

Bliss, Heather and Bettina Gruber. (2011). Decomposing Blackfoot proclitics. Paper presented at the *34th Generative Linguistics in the Old World Colloquium*. University of Vienna.

Bliss, Heather, Rose-Marie Déchaine, and Tomio Hirose. (2013). A comparison of locative PPs in Blackfoot and Plains Cree. Paper presented at the *45th Algonquian Conference*. University of Ottawa.

Bliss, Heather, Elizabeth Ritter, and Martina Wiltschko. (2011). A comparative analysis of theme marking in Blackfoot and Nishnaabemwin. Paper presented at the *42nd Algonquian Conference*. St. John's, Newfoundland.

  (2012). Blackfoot nominalization patterns. Paper presented at the *44th Algonquian Conference*. Chicago, IL: University of Chicago.

Bloomfield, Leonard. (1927). The word-stems of Central Algonquian. In *Festschrift Meinhof*, pp. 393–402. Hamburg: L. Fiedrischsen.

Boas, Franz. (1911). Introduction. In Franz Boas, (ed.), *Handbook of American Indian Languages*, vol. 1. Washington, DC: U.S. Government Printing Office.

Bobaljik, Jonathan David. (1995). Morphosyntax: The syntax of verbal inflection. Unpublished Ph.D. dissertation, Massachusetts Institute of Technology, Cambridge, MA.

(2002). Realizing Germanic inflection: Why morphology does not drive syntax. *Journal of Comparative Germanic Linguistics*, *6*(2), 129–167.

(2008). Where's phi? Agreement as a post-syntactic operation. In D. Harbour, David Adger, and Susana Bejar (eds.), *Phi-Theory: Phi Features across Interfaces and Modules*, pp. 295–328. Oxford: Oxford University Press.

Bonet, Eulalia. (1991). Morphology after syntax: Pronominal clitics in Romance. Unpublished Ph.D. dissertation, Massachusetts Institute of Technology, Cambridge MA.

(1995). Feature structure of Romance clitics. *Natural Language and Linguistic Theory*, *13*(4), 607–647.

Bonomi, Andrea. (1997). Aspect, quantification and when-clauses in Italian. *Linguistics and Philosophy*, *20*(5), 469–514.

Borer, Hagit. (1994). The projections of arguments. In Elena E. Benedicto and Jeffrey T. Runner (eds.), *Functional Projections*, pp. 19–49. Amherst, MA: GLSA, University of Massachusetts.

(2005). *The Normal Course of Events*. Oxford: Oxford University Press.

Brandner, Ellen. (1993). The projection of categories and the nature of agreement. In Gisbert Fanselow (ed.), *The Parameterization of Universal Grammar*, pp. 73–122. Amsterdam: John Benjamins.

Branigan, Phil, and Marguerite MacKenzie. (2002). Altruism, A-movement, and object agreement in Innu-aimun. *Linguistic Inquiry*, *33*(3), 385–407.

Brittain, Julie. (1999). *A reanalysis of transitive animate theme signs as object agreement: Evidence from Western Naskapi*. In Papers of the 30th Algonquian Conference, Winnipeg.

Brown, Jason, and James Thompson. (2006). The emergence of determiner clisis in upriver Halkomelem. In L. Harper (ed.), *Proceedings of the 9th Workshop on American Indigenous Languages*. Santa Barbara Papers in Linguistics, vol. 18. www.linguistics.ucsb.edu/research/papers_vol18.htm

Bruening, Benjamin. (2001). Syntax at the edge: Cross-clausal phenomena and the syntax of Passamaquoddy. Unpublished Ph.D. dissertation, Massachusetts Institute of Technology, Cambridge, MA.

(2005). The Algonquian inverse is syntactic: Binding in Passamaquoddy. Unpublished ms., University of Delaware, Newark, DE.

(2009). Algonquian languages have A-movement and A-agreement. *Linguistic Inquiry*, *40*(3), 427–445.

(forthcoming). Precede-and-Command revisited. *Language*.

Brugmann, Karl. (1904). Die Demonstrativpronomina der indogermanischen Sprachen: Eine bedeutungsgeschichtliche Untersuchung. *Abhandlungen der königlich sächsische Gesellschaft der Wissenschaften, Philosophisch-historische Klasse 22*, 6.

Bugenhagen, Robert D. (1993). The semantics of irrealis in Austronesian languages of Papua New Guinea: A cross-linguistic study. In Ger Reesink (ed.), *Topics in Descriptive Austronesian Linguistics*, pp. 1–39. Leiden: Rijksuniversiteit Leiden.

Bühler, Karl. (1934). *Sprachtheorie: Die Darstellungsfunktion der Sprache*. Jena: Gustav Fischer.

Burton, Strang. (1997). Past tense on nouns as death destruction and loss. *Proceedings of NELS*, *27*, 65–78.

Butler, Lindsay Kay. (2012). The morphosyntax and processing of number marking in Yucatec Maya. Unpublished Ph.D. dissertation, University of Arizona, Tuczon, AZ.

Bybee, Joan L. (1985). *Morphology: A Study of the Relation between Meaning and Form*, vol. 9. Amsterdam: John Benjamins.

Bybee, Joan L., and Suzanne Fleischman. (1995). *Modality in Grammar and Discourse*. Amsterdam: John Benjamins.

Bybee, Joan L., Revere Perkins, and William Pagliuca. (1994). *The Evolution of Grammar: Tense, Aspect, and Modality in the Languages of the World*. Chicago, IL: University of Chicago Press.

Cable, Seth. (2013). Beyond the past, present, and future: towards the semantics of 'graded tense' in Gĩkũyũ. *Natural Language Semantics*, *21*(3), 219–276.

Caha, Pavel. (2009). The nanosyntax of case. Unpublished Ph.D. dissertation, University of Tromsø, Tromsø, Norway.

Cardinaletti, Anna. (1990). Subject/object asymmetries in German: Null topic construction and the status of SpecCP. In Joan Mascaro and Marina Nespor (eds.), *Grammar in Progress*, pp. 75–84. Dordrecht: Foris.

Cardinaletti, Anna, and Michal Starke. (1999). The typology of structural deficiencies: A case study of the three classes of pronouns. In Henk van Riemsdijk (ed.), *Clitics in the Languages of Europe*, pp. 145–233. New York: Mouton de Gruyter.

Carlier, Anne, and Walter de Mulder. (2010). The emergence of the definite article in Late Latin: *ille* in competition with *ipse*. In Kristin Davidse, Lieven van de Lanotte, and Hubert Cuyckens (eds.), *Subjectification, Intersubjectification and Grammaticalization*, pp. 241–275. The Hague: Mouton de Gruyter.

Carlson, Greg. (1982). Terms and generic sentences. *Journal of Philosophical Logic*, *11*(2), 145–181.

Carnie, Andrew. (2005). Flat structure, phrasal variability and VSO. *Journal of Celtic Linguistics*, *9*(1), 13–31.

Carnie, Andrew, and Eloise Jelinek. (2003). Argument hierarchies and the mapping principle. In Andrew Carnie, Heidi Harley, and MaryAnn Willie (eds.), *Formal Approaches to Function*, pp. 265–296. Philadelphia, PA: John Benjamins.

Chomsky, Noam. (1975 [1955]). *The Logical Structure of Linguistic Theory*. Manuscript, published in 1975. New York: Plenum Press.

  (1957). *Syntactic Structures*. The Hague: Mouton.

  (1965 [1964]). *Aspects of the Theory of Syntax*. Cambridge, MA: MIT Press.

  (1970). Remarks on nominalization. In Roderick Jacobs and Peter Rosenbaum (eds.), *Readings in English Transformational Grammar*, pp. 184–221. Waltham, MA: Ginn.

  (1973). Conditions on transformations. In Stephen Anderson and Paul Kiparsky (eds.), *A Festschrift for Morris Halle*, pp. 232–286, New York: Holt, Rinehart, and Winston.

  (1980). On binding. *Linguistic Inquiry*, *11*(1), 1–46.

  (1981). *Lectures on Government and Binding*. Dordrecht: Foris.

  (1986). *Barriers*. Cambridge, MA: MIT Press.

(1993). A minimalist program for linguistic theory. In Kenneth Hale and Samuel J. Keyser (eds.), *The View from Building 20: Essays in Linguistics in Honor of Sylvain Bromberger*, pp. 1–52. Cambridge, MA: MIT Press.

(1995). *The Minimalist Program*. Cambridge, MA: MIT Press.

(2000). Minimalist inquiries. In Roger Martin, David Michaels, and Juan Uriagereka (eds.), *Step by Step: Essays on Minimalist Syntax*, pp. 89–155. Cambridge, MA: MIT Press.

(2001). Derivation by phase. In Michael Kenstowicz (ed.), *Ken Hale: A Life in Language*, pp. 1–54, Cambridge, MA: MIT Press.

(2008). On phases. In Robert Friedin, Carlos Otero, and Maria-Luisa Zubizarreta (eds.), *Foundational Issues in Linguistic Theory: Essays in Honor of Jean-Roger Vergnaud*, pp. 133–166. Cambridge, MA: MIT Press.

Christodoulou, Christiana (2011). Cypriot Greek Down syndrome: their grammar and its interfaces. Unpublished Ph.D. dissertation, University of British Columbia, Vancouver.

Christodoulou, Christiana, and Martina Wiltschko. (2012). Function without content: Evidence from Greek Subjunctive na. In Anna-Maria Di Sciullo (ed.), *Towards a Biolinguistic Understanding of Grammar: Essays on Interfaces*, pp. 117–140. Amsterdam: John Benjamins.

Cinque, Guglielmo. (1999). *Adverbs and Functional Heads: A Cross-Linguitstic Perspective*. Oxford: Oxford University Press.

(2007). A note on linguistic theory and typology. *Linguistic Typology*, *11*(1), 93–106.

Cohen, Henri, and Claire Lefebvre. (2005). *Handbook of Categorization in Cognitive Science*. Amsterdam: Elsevier.

Collins, Chris. (2002). Eliminating labels. In Samuel D. Epstein and T. Daniel Seely (eds.), *Derivation and Explanation in the Minimalist Program*, pp. 42–64. Malden, MA: Blackwell.

Comrie, Bernard. (1976). *Aspect*. Cambridge: Cambridge University Press.

(1980). Inverse verb forms in Siberia: evidence from Chukchee, Koryak and Kamchadal. *Folia Linguistica Historica*, *1*(1), 61–74.

(1989). *Language Universals and Linguistic Typology: Syntax and Morphology*. Oxford: Blackwell.

Corbett, Greville G. (2000). *Number*. New York: Cambridge University Press.

Corver, Norbert, and Henk van Riemsdijk. (2001). *Semi-Lexical Categories: The Function of Content Words and the Content of Function Words*. Berlin: Mouton de Gruyter.

Cover, Rebecca. (2006). The focus on 'ko': the syntax, semantics and pragmatics of identificational focus in Pulaar. M.Sc. thesis, University of California, Berkeley.

Cowper, Elizabeth. (1998). The simple present tense in English: A unified treatment. *Studia Linguistica*, *52*(1), 1–18.

(2005). The geometry of interpretable features: Infl in English and Spanish. *Language*, *81*(1), 10–46.

Cowper, Elizabeth, and Daniel Currie Hall. (2004). The pieces of π. In Marie-Odile Junker, Martha McGinnis, and Yves Roberge (eds.), *Proceedings of the 2004 Annual Conference of the Canadian Linguistic Association*. University of Toronto Press.

Creissels, Denis. (2008). Spatial cases. In Andrei Malchukov and Andrew Spencer (eds.), *The Handbook of Case*, pp. 609–624. Oxford: Oxford University Press.

Cresswell, Maxell J. (1973). *Logics and Languages*. London: Methuen.

Croft, William. (1990). *Typology and Universals*. Cambridge: Cambridge University Press.

(2001). *Radical Construction Grammar: Syntactic Theory in Typological Perspective*. Oxford: Oxford University Press.

(2003). *Typology and Universals*, 2nd edn. Cambridge: Cambridge University Press.

Currie, Elizabeth. (1997). Topic time: The syntax and semantics of SqwXwu7mish temporal adverbs. Unpublished M.A. thesis, University of British Columbia, Vancouver.

Cysouw, Michael. (2001). The paradigmatic structure of person marking. Ph.D. dissertation, Radboud University, Nijmegen, Netherlands.

Dahl, Östen. (1985). *Tense and Aspect Systems*. Oxford: Blackwell.

Dahl, Östen, and Viveka Velupillai. (2011). The past tense. In Matthew Dryer and Martin Haspelmath (eds.), *The World Atlas of Language Structures Online* (online edn). Munich: Max Planck Digital Library. (Retrieved from http://wals.info/chapter/66.)

Dahlstrom, Amy. (1988). Morphological change in Plains Cree verb inflection. *Folia Linguistica Historica*, *9*(2), 59–71.

(1991). *Plains Cree Morpho-Syntax*. New York: Garland.

(1995). Topic, focus and other word order problems in Algonquian: The 1994 Belcourt Lecture. Winnipeg: Voices of Rupert's Land.

Danon, Gabi. (2002). Case and formal definiteness: The licensing of definite and indefinite noun phrases in Hebrew. Unpublished Ph.D. dissertation, Tel Aviv University.

(2006). Caseless nominals and the projection of DP. *Natural Language and Linguistic Theory*, *24*(4), 977–1008.

Davidson, Donald. (1968). On saying that. *Synthese*, *19*, 130–146.

Davis, Henry. (2005). On the syntax and semantics of negation in Salish. *International Journal of American Linguistics*, *71*(1), 1–55.

Davis, Henry, Lisa Matthewson, and Hotze Rullmann. (2009). 'Out of control' marking as circumstantial modality in St'át'imcets. In Lotte Hogeweg, Helen de Hoop, and Andrei Mal'chukov (eds.), *Cross-Linguistic Semantics of Tense, Aspect, and Modality*, pp. 205–244. Amsterdam: John Benjamins.

Davis, John. (1980). The passive in Sliammon. *Proceedings of the 6th Annual Meeting of the Berkeley Linguistics Society*, pp. 278–286.

de Belder, Marijke. (2011). *Roots and Affixes: Eliminating Lexical Categories from Syntax*. Utrecht: LOT Publications.

Déchaine, Rose-Marie. (1993). Predicates across categories: Towards a category-neutral syntax. Unpublished Ph.D. dissertation, University of Massachusetts, Amherst, MA.

(1999). What Algonquian morphology is really like: Hockett revisited. In Leora Bar-el, Rose-Marie Déchaine, and Charlotte Reinholtz (eds.), *Papers from the Workshop on Structure and Constituency in Native American Languages*, pp. 25–72. Cambridge, MA: MIT Press.

Déchaine, Rose-Marie, and Charlotte Reinkoltz. (2008). Case theory meets linking theory: Algonquian direct/inverse as split case. Paper presented at the *13th*

Workshop on the Structure and Constituency of the Languages of the Americas, Queens University.

Déchaine, Rose-Marie, and Martina Wiltschko. (2002). Decomposing pronouns. *Linguistic Inquiry, 33*(3), 409–422.

(2010). Interface syntax. Unpublished ms. University of British Columbia, Vancouver.

(2012). Micro-variation in agreement, clause-typing and finiteness: Comparative evidence from Plains Cree and Blackfoot, *Proceedings of the 42nd Algonquian Conference.* Memorial University, St. John's, Newfoundland.

(to appear). When and why can 1st and 2nd person pronouns be bound variables? *Northeast Linguistic Society Workshop.*

Déchaine, Rose-Marie, Raphael Girard, Calisto Mudzingwa, and Martina Wiltschko (forthcoming). The internal syntax of Shona noun class prefixes. *Language Sciences.*

Demirdache, Hamida, and Myriam Uribe-Etxebarria (1997). A uniform approach to tense and aspect. In Emily Curtis, James Lyle, and Gabriel Webster (eds.), *Proceedings of the 16th West Coast Conference on Formal Linguistics,* pp. 145–159. Stanford, CA: CSLI Publications.

(2007). The syntax of time arguments. *Lingua, 117*(2), 330–366.

DeLancey, Scott. (1981). An interpretation of split ergativity and related patterns. *Language, 57*(3), 626–657.

Den Dikken, Marcel. (2006). *Relators and Linkers: The Syntax of Predication, Predicate Inversion, and Copulas.* Cambridge, MA: MIT Press.

Deprez, Viviane. (2003). Haitian Creole *se*: a copula, a pronoun, both or neither? On the double life of a functional projection. In Dany Adone (ed.), *Recent Developments in Creole Studies,* pp. 137–173. Tübingen: Max Niemeyer.

de Schepper, Kees. (2012). You and me against the world? First, second and third person in the world's languages. Unpublished Ph.D. thesis, Radboud University, Nijmegen.

Di Sciullo, Anne-Marie, and Edwin Williams. (1987). *On the Definition of Word.* Cambridge, MA: MIT Press.

Diekhoff, Tobias J.C. (1911). Functional change of the subjunctive in German. *The School Review, 19*(9), 624–630.

Diercks, Michael. (2012). Parameterizing case: Evidence from Bantu. *Syntax, 15*(3), 253–286.

Diessel, Holger. (1999). *Form, Function and Grammaticalization.* Amsterdam: John Benjamins.

(2005). Distance contrasts in demonstratives. In Martin Haspelmath, Matthew Dryer, David Gil, and Bernard Comrie (eds.), *World Atlas of Language Structures,* pp. 170–173. Oxford: Oxford University Press.

(2006). Demonstratives, joint attention, and the emergence of grammar. *Cognitive Linguistics, 17*(4), 463–489.

Diver, William. (1995). Theory. In Ellen Contini-Morava and Barbara Sussmann Goldberg (eds.), *Meaning as Explanation: Advances in Linguistic Sign Theory,* pp. 43–114. Berlin: Mouton de Gruyter.

Dixon, Robert M.W. (1994). *Ergativity*. Cambridge: Cambridge University Press.
  (2003). Demonstratives: a cross-linguistic typology. *Studies in Language*, *27*(1), 61–112.
Dobrovie-Sorin, Carmen. (1994). *The Syntax of Romanian*. Berlin: Mouton de Gruyter.
Dressler, Wolfgang U. (1989). Prototypical differences between inflection and derivation. *Zeitschrift für Phonetik, Sprachwissenschaft und Kommunikationsforschung*, *42*(1), 3–10.
Dryer, Matthew S. (1997). Are grammatical relations universal? In Joan Bybee, John Haiman, and Sandra Thompson (eds.), *Essays on Language Function and Language Type: Dedicated to T. Givon*, pp. 115–143. Amsterdam: John Benjamins
Dunham, Joel. (2007). The "durative" in Blackfoot: Understanding imperfectivity, *Proceedings of SULA 4: Semantics of Underrepresented Languages in the Americas*, pp. 49–64.
Eckardt, Régine. (2002). Reanalyzing Selbst. *Natural Language Semantics*, *9*(4), 371–412.
Elliott, Jennifer. (2000). Realis and irrealis: forms and concepts of the grammaticalization of reality. *Linguistic Typology*, *4*(1), 55–90.
Elouazizi, Noureddine, and Martina Wiltschko. (2006). The categorial status of (anti-)(anti-) agreement. In Donald Baumer, David Montero, and Michael Scanlon (eds.) *Proceedings of the 25th West Coast Conference on Formal Linguistics*, pp. 150–158. Somerville, MA: Cascadilla Proceedings Project.
Enç, M. (1987). Anchoring conditions for tense. *Linguistic Inquiry*, *18*(4), 633–657.
Ernst, Thomas. (2002). *The Syntax of Adjuncts*. Cambridge: Cambridge University Press.
Evans, Nicholas, and Stephen C. Levinson. (2009). The myth of language universals: Language diversity and its importance for cognitive science. *Behavioral and Brain Sciences*, *32*(5), 429–448.
Fabricius-Hansen, Cathrine, and Johan Sæbø, Kjell. (2004). In a mediative mood: The semantics of the German reportive subjunctive. *Natural Language Semantics*, *12*(3), 213–257.
Falk, Yehuda. (1991). Case: Abstract and morphological. *Linguistics*, *29*(2), 197–230.
Filip, Hana. (2011). Aspectual class and *Aktionsart*. In Claudia Maienborn, Klaus von Heusinger, and Paul Portner (eds.), *Semantics: An International Handbook of Natural Language Meaning*, pp. 1186–1217. Berlin: Mouton de Gruyter.
  (2012). Lexical aspect. In Robert Binnick, (ed.) *The Oxford Handbook of Tense and Aspect*, pp. 721–751. Oxford: Oxford University Press.
Filmore, Charles. (1968). The case for case. In Emond Bach and R. Harms (eds.), *Universals in Linguistic Theory*, pp. 1–88. New York: Holt, Rinehart, and Winston.
Finegan, Edward. (2008). *Language: Its Structure and Use*, 5th edn. Fort Worth, TX: Harcourt Brace.
Foley, William A., and Robert Van Valin. (1984). *Functional Syntax and Universal Grammar*. Cambridge: Cambridge University Press.
François, Alexandre. (2005). A typological overview of Mwotlap, an oceanic language of Vanuatu. *Linguistic Typology*, *9*(1), 115–146.
Frantz, Donald. (1991). *Blackfoot Grammar*. Toronto: University of Toronto Press.
  (2009). *Blackfoot Grammar*, 2nd edn. Toronto: University of Toronto Press.

Frantz, Donald, and Norma Russell. (1995). *Blackfoot Dictionary of Stems, Roots and Affixes*, 2nd edn. Toronto: University of Toronto Press.

Fries, Charles. (1952). *The Structure of English: An Introduction to the Construction of English Sentences.* New York: Harcourt Brace.

Fujimori, Atsushi. (2011). The correspondence between vowel quality and verbal telicity in Yamato-Japanese. Unpublished Ph.D. dissertation, University of British Columbia, Vancouver.

Galloway, Brent D. (1993). *A Grammar of Upriver Halkomelem.* Berkeley, CA: University of California Press.

(2009). *Dictionary of Upriver Halkomelem.* Berkeley, CA: University of California Press.

Gast, Volker. (2006). *Grammar of Identity: Intensifiers and Reflexives in Germanic Languages.* London: Taylor & Francis.

Geach, Peter. (1962). *Reference and Generality.* Ithaca, NY: Cornell University Press.

Gelderen, Elly van. (2004). *Grammaticalization as Economy.* Amsterdam: John Benjamins.

Gerdts, Donna B. (1979). Out of control in Ilokano, *Proceedings of the 5th Annual Meeting of the Berkeley Linguistics Society*, pp. 81–93.

(1988). *Object and Absolutive in Halkomelem Salish.* New York: Garland.

Gerdts, Donna B., and Thomas E. Hukari. (2004). Determiners and transitivity in Halkomelem texts. In M. Dale Kinkade, Donna B. Gerdts, and Lisa Matthewson (eds.), *Studies in Salish Linguistics in Honor of M. Dale Kinkade*, pp. 150–170. Missoula, MT: University of Montana.

(2008). The expression of noun phrases in Halkomelem texts. *Anthropological Linguistics*, *50*(3/4), 324–364.

Gerdts, Donna B., and James H. Youn. (1999). Case stacking and focus in Korean. In S. Kuno *et al.* (eds.), *Harvard Studies in Korean Linguistics*, pp. 325–339. Seoul: Hanshin Publishing Company.

Giannakidou, Anastasia. (2009). The dependency of the subjunctive mood. *Lingua, 119* (12), 1837–1858.

Gibson, Jeanne Darrigrand. (1980). Clause union in Chamorro and in universal grammar. Unpublished Ph.D. dissertation, University of California, San Diego, CA.

Gil, David. (2001). Escaping Eurocentrism: Fieldwork as a process of unlearning. In Paul Newman and Martha Ratliff (eds.), *Linguistic Fieldwork*, pp. 102–132. Cambridge: Cambridge University Press.

Gillon, Carrie Samantha. (2006). The semantics of determiners: domain restriction in Skwx̱wú7mesh. Unpublished Ph.D. dissertation, University of British Columbia, Vancouver.

(2009). Deictic features: Evidence from Skwx̱wú7mesh. *International Journal of American Linguistics*, *75*(1), 1–27.

Giorgi, Alessandra. (2009). Toward a syntax of the subjunctive mood. *Lingua, 112*(12), 1837–1858.

Giusti, Giuliana. (1993). *La sintassi dei determinanti.* Padua, Italy: Unipress.

(1995). A unified structural representation of (abstract) case and article: Evidence from Germanic. In Hubert Haider, Susan Olsen, and Sten Vikner (eds.), *Studies in Comparative Germanic Syntax*, pp. 77–93. Dordrecht: Kluwer.

Givon, Talmy. (1971). Historical syntax and synchronic morphology: An archaeologist's field trip. In *Proceedings of the 7th Regional Meeting of the Chicago Linguistics Society*, 394–415.

(1994). Irrealis and the subjunctive. *Studies in Language*, *18*(2), 265–337.

Glougie, Jennifer. (2001). Topics in the syntax and semantics of Blackfoot quantifiers and nominals. Unpublished M.A. thesis, University of British Columbia, Vancouver.

Goldsmith, John. (forthcoming). Theory, kernals, data, methods. In *46th Annual Meeting of the Chicago Linguistic Society*, Chicago, IL.

Golumbia, David. (2010). Minimalism is functionalism. *Language Sciences*, *32*(1), 28–42.

Greenberg, Joseph H. (1963). Some universals of grammar, with particular reference to the order of meaningful elements. In Joseph H. Greenberg (ed.), *Universals of Language*, pp. 73–113. Cambridge, MA: MIT Press.

Grimes, J. (1985). Topic inflection in Mapudungun verbs. *International Journal of American Linguistics*, *51*(2), 141–163.

Grimshaw, Jane B. (2005). *Words and Structure*. Stanford, CA: Center for the Study of Language and Information, Stanford University.

Grohmann, Kleanthes K. (2003). *Prolific Domains: On the Anti-Locality Movement Dependencies*. Amsterdam: John Benjamins.

Gruber, Bettina. (2011). Indexical pronouns: generic uses as clues to their structure. *Poznan Studies in Contemporary Linguistics*, *47*(2), 331–360.

(2013). The spatiotemporal dimensions of person: A morphosyntactic account of indexical pronouns. Ph.D. dissertation, LOT dissertation series, Utrecht University.

Guldemann, Tom. (1999). The genesis of verbal negation in Bantu and its dependency on functional features of clause types. In Jean-Marie Hombert and Larry M. Hyman (eds.), *Bantu Historical Linguistics: Theoretical and Empirical Perspectives*, pp. 545–587, Stanford, CA: CSLI Publications.

Gupta, Anil. (1980). *The Logic of Common Nouns: An Investigation in Quantified Modal Logic*. New Haven, CT: Yale University Press.

Hacquard, Valentine. (2010). On the event relativity of modal auxiliaries. *Natural Language Semantics*, *18*(1), 79–114.

Haider, Hubert. (1982). Dependenzen und Konfigurationen. *Groninger Arbeiten zur Germanistischen Linguistik*, *21*, 1–16.

(1993). *Deutsche Syntax, Generativ: Vorstudien zur Theorie einer projektiven Grammatik*. Tübingen: Narr.

Haïk, Isabelle. (1990). Anaphoric, pronominal and referential INFL. *Natural Language and Linguistic Theory*, *8*(3), 347–374.

Hale, Kenneth. (1982). Preliminary remarks on configurationality. *Proceedings of the North Eastern Linguistic Society 12*, 86–96.

(1983). Warlpiri and the grammar of non-configurational languages. *Natural Language and Linguistic Theory 1*(1), 5–47.

(1986). Notes on world view and semantic categories: Some Walpiri examples. In Pieter Muysken and Henk van Riemsdijk (eds.), *Features and Projections*, pp. 233–254. Dordrecht: Foris.

(1989). On non-configurational structures. In László Marácz and Pieter Muysken (eds.), *Configurationality: The Typology of Asymmetries*, pp. 293–300. Dordrecht: Foris.

Hale, Kenneth, and Samuel Keyser. (2003). *Prolegomenon to a Theory of Argument Structure*, 2nd edn. Cambridge, MA: MIT Press.

Hall, Christopher J. (1992). *Morphology and Mind: A Unified Approach to Explanation in Linguistics*. London: Routledge.

Halle, Morris. (1997). Distributed morphology: Impoverishment and fission. In Benjamin Bruening, Yoonjung Kang, and Martha McGinnis (eds.), *Papers at the Interface*, pp. 425–449. Cambridge, MA: MIT Working Papers in Linguistics.

Halle, Morris, and Alec Marantz. (1993). Distributed morphology and the pieces of inflection. In Kenneth Hale and Samuel Keyser (eds.), *The View from Building*, pp. 111–176. Cambridge, MA: MIT Press.

Han, Chung-Hye. (2000). *The Structure and Interpretation of Imperatives: Mood and Force in Universal Grammar*. New York: Routledge.

(2001). Force, negation and imperatives. *Linguistic Review*, *18*(4), 289–325.

Harley, Heidi. (1995). Abstracting away from abstract case. In Jill Beckman (ed.), *Proceedings of NELS 25*, pp. 207–221. Amherst, MA: Graduate Linguistics Students Association, University of Massachusetts.

(2009). Roots: identity, insertion, idiosyncracies. Paper presented at the Root Bound Workshop, University of Southern California.

Harley, Heidi. (forthcoming). The syntax/morphology interface. In Artemis Alexiadou and Tibor Kiss (eds.), *Handbook of Syntax*. Berlin: Mouton de Gruyter.

Harley, Heidi, and Rolf Noyer. (2003). Distributed morphology. In Lisa Cheng and Rynt Sybesma (eds.), *The 2nd GLOT International State-of-the-Article Book*, pp. 463–496. Berlin: Mouton de Gruyter.

Harley, Heidi, and Elizabeth Ritter. (2002). Person and number in pronouns: A feature-geometric analysis. *Language*, *78*(3), 482–526.

Haspelmath, Martin. (2007). Pre-established categories don't exist: Consequences for language description and typology. *Linguistic Typology*, *11*(1), 119–132.

(2008). An empirical test of the agglutination hypothesis. In Elisabetta Magni, Sergio Scalise, and Antonietta Bisetto (eds.), *Universals of Language Today*, pp. 13–29. Dordrecht: Springer.

Heim, Irene. (1988). *The Semantics of Definite and Indefinite Noun Phrases*. New York: Garland.

Heine, Bernd. (1994). *Auxiliaries: Cognitive Forces and Grammaticalization: Cognitive Forces and Grammaticalization*. New York: Oxford University Press.

Heine, Bernd, and Tania Kuteva. (2002). *World Lexicon of Grammaticalization*. New York: Cambridge University Press.

Hewson, John. (1985). Are Algonquian languages ergative? In *Papers from the 18th Algonquian Conference, Ottawa*, pp. 147–153.

Himmelmann, Nikolaus P. (1997). *Deiktikon, Artikel, Nominalphrase: Zur Emergenz syntaktischer Struktur*. Tübingen: Narr.

Hjelmslev, Louis. (1935). *La catégorie des cas: Étude de grammaire générale*. Copenhagen: Munksgaard.

Hopper, Paul J., and Elizabeth Traugott. (2003). *Grammaticalization*, 2nd edn. Cambridge: Cambridge University Press.

Hukari, Thomas E. (1978). Halkomelem nonsegmental morphology, in *13th International Conference on Salishan Languages*, pp. 157–208.

Humboldt, Wilhelm von. (1963[1829]). Über die Verschiedenheiten des menschlichen Sprachbaues. In Andreas Flitner and Klaus Giel (eds.), *Schriften zur Sprachphilosophie*, pp. 144–367. Darmstadt: Wissenschaftlich Buchgesellschaft.

Hung, Henrietta. (1988). The structure of derived nouns and verbs in Malagasy: A syntactic account. Unpublished ms., McGill University, Montreal.

Iatridou, Sabine. (2000). The grammatical ingredients of counterfactuality. *Linguistic Inquiry*, *31*(2), 231–270.

Jackendoff, Ray. (1977). *X-Bar Syntax: A Study of Phrase Structure*. Cambridge, MA: MIT Press.

(1997). *The Architecture of the Language Faculty*. Cambridge, MA: MIT Press.

Jacobs, Peter William. (2011). Control in Skwxwu7mesh. Unpublished Ph.D. dissertation, University of British Columbia, Vancouver.

Jacobson, William H. Jr. (1983). Typological and genetic notes on switch reference systems in North American Indian languages. In John Haiman and Pamela Munro (eds.), *Switch Reference*, pp. 151–186. Amsterdam: John Benjamins.

Jakobson, Roman. (1984[1932]). *The Structure of the Russian Verb*. Berlin: Mouton de Gruyter.

(1936). *Beitrag zur allgemeinen Kasuslehre*. Prague: Travaux de Cercle linguistique.

James, Deborah. (1982). Past tense and the hypothetical: A cross-linguistic study. *Studies in Language*, *6*(3), 375–403.

Joos, Martin (1957). *Readings in Linguistics: The Development of Descriptive Linguistics in America since 1925*. Washington, DC: American Council of Learned Societies.

Katz, Aya. (1996). Cyclical grammaticalization and the cognitive link between pronoun and copula. Unpublished Ph.D. dissertation, Rice University, Houston, TX.

Kayne, Richard S. (1984). *Connectedness and Binary Branching*. Dordrecht: Foris.

(1994). *The Antisymmetry of Syntax*. Cambridge, MA: MIT Press.

(2000). *Parameters and Universals*. Oxford: Oxford University Press.

(2010). *Comparisons and Contrasts*. New York: Oxford University Press.

Keenan, Edward. (1988). On semantics and binding theory. In John Hawkins (ed.), *Explaining Language Universals*, pp. 105–144. Oxford: Blackwell.

Kiparsky, Paul. (1973). 'Elsewhere' in phonology. In Stephen Anderson and Paul Kiparsky (eds.), *A Festschrift for Morris Halle*, pp. 93–106. New York: Academic Press.

(1998). Partitive case and aspect. In Miriam Butt and William Geuder (eds.), *The Projection of Arguments: Lexical and Compositional Factors*, pp. 265–308. Stanford, CA: CSLI.

Kiparsky, Paul, and Carol Kiparsky. (1970). Fact. In Danny Steinberg and Leon Jakobovits (eds.), *Semantics*, pp. 345–369. Cambridge: Cambridge University Press.

Kiss, Katalin E. (1987). *Configurationality in Hungarian*. Dordrecht: Reidel.

(2006). *Event Structure and the Left Periphery: Studies on Hungarian*. Dordrecht: Springer.

Kiyota, Masaru. (2008). Situation aspect and viewpoint aspect: From Salish to Japanese. Unpublished Ph.D. dissertation, University of British Columbia, Vancouver.

Klein, Wolfgang. (1994). *Time in Language*. New York: Routledge.

(1995). A time-relational analysis of Russian aspect. *Language*, *71*(4), 669–695.

Koopman, Hilda. (2005). On the parallelism of DPs and clauses in Kisongo Maasai. In Andrew Carnie, Sheila Dooley, and Heidi Harley (eds.), *Verb First: On the Syntax of Verb-Intial Languages*, pp. 281–302. Philadelphia, PA: John Benjamins.

Koopman, Hilda, and Dominique Sportiche. (1991). On the position of subjects. *Lingua*, *85*(2/3), 211–258.

Kratzer, Angelika. (1996). Severing the external argument from its verb. In Johan Rooryck and Laurie Zaring (eds.), *Phrase Structure and the Lexicon*, pp. 109–137. Dordrecht: Kluwer.

(1998). More structural analogies between pronouns and tenses. *Proceedings from Semantics and Linguistic Theory*, *8*, 92–110.

(2009). Making a pronoun: Fake indexicals as windows into the properties of pronouns. *Linguistic Inquiry*, *40*(2), 187–237.

Krifka, Manfred (1998). The origins of telicity. In Susan Rothstein (ed.), *Events and Grammar*, pp. 197–235. Dordrecht: Kluwer.

Kroeber, Paul. (1995). Rhetorical structure of a Kalispel narrative. *Anthropological Linguistics*, *37*(2), 119–140.

Kuipers, Aert H. (1967). *The Squamish Language: Grammar, Texts Dictionary*. The Hague: Mouton de Gruyter.

Kyriakaki, M. (2006). The geometry of tense, mood, and aspect in Greek. Unpublished M.A. thesis, University of Toronto.

Labelle, Marie. (2005). The acquisition of grammatical categories: A state of the art. In Henri Cohen and Claire Lefebvre (eds.), *Handbook of Categorization in Cognitive Science*, pp. 433–457. Amsterdam: Elsevier.

Lakoff, George. (1970 [1966]). *Irregularity in Syntax*. New York: Holt, Rinehart and Winston. [Originally Harvard Ph.D. thesis, 1966]

Lam, Wai Man, Sonja Thoma, and Martina Wiltschko. (2013). *Thinking about You*. Paper presented at the Workshop on Interfaces at the Left Periphery, University of Michigan, July 2013.

Lamontagne, Greg, and Travis, Lisa. (1987). The syntax of adjacency. *Proceedings of The West Coast Conference on Formal Linguistics*, *6*, 173–186.

Lancelot, Claude, and Arnaud, Antoine. (1660). *Grammaire générale et raisonnée de Port-Royal Paris*. Paris.

Landau, Idan. (2004). The scale of finiteness and the calculus of control. *Natural Language and Linguistic Theory*, *22*(3), 811–877.

Langdon, Margaret. (1970). *A Grammar of Diegueño: The Mesa Grande Dialect*. Berkeley, CA: University of California Press.

Lapointe, S. (1980). A theory of grammatical agreement. Unpublished Ph.D. dissertation, University of Massachusetts, Amherst, MA.

Larson, R.K. (1988). On the double object construction. *Linguistic Inquiry*, *19*(3), 335–391.

Lecarme, Jacqueline. (2004). Tense in nominals. In Jaqueline Gueron and Jaqueline Lecarme (eds.), *The Syntax of Time*, pp. 441–475. Cambridge MA: MIT Press.

Lee, Felicia. (2003). Anaphoric R-expressions as bound variables. *Syntax*, *6*(1), 84–114.

Legate, Julie. (2008). Morphological and abstract case. *Linguistic Inquiry*, *39*(1), 55–101.

Leiss, Elisabeth. (2005). Submorphematische Motiviertheit als Grammatikalisierungsergebnis: Zur Grammatikalisierung von Reflexivpronomen. *Zeitschrift für germanistische Linguistik*, *32*(2), 233–244.

Leu, Thomas. (2008). Internal syntax of determiners. Unpublished Ph.D. dissertation, New York University.

Levinson, Stephen C. (2000). *Presumptive Meanings: The Theory of Generalized Conversational Implicature*. Cambridge, MA: MIT Press.

(2004). Deixis and pragmatics. In Larry Horn and Gregory Ward (eds.), *The Handbook of Pragmatics*, pp. 97–121. Oxford: Blackwell.

Lieber, Rochelle. (1992). *Deconstructing Morphology: Word Formation in Syntactic Theory*. Chicago, IL: University of Chicago Press.

(2004). *Morphology and Lexical Semantics*. Cambridge: Cambridge University Press.

Lin, Jo-Wang. (2006). Time in a language without tense: The case of Chinese. *Journal of Semantics*, *23*(1), 1–53.

Linder, Karin. (1991). 'Wir sind ja doch alte Bekannte': the use of German ja and doch as modal particles. In Werner Abraham (ed.), *Discourse Particles*, pp. 303–328. Amsterdam: John Benjamins.

Lochbihler, Bethany. (2012). Aspects of argument licensing. Unpublished Ph.D. dissertation, McGill University, Montreal.

Louie, Meagan. (2008). Blackfoot's non-affirmative endings: Topical NPIs with existential wide-scope. Unpublished ms. University of British Columbia, Vancouver.

(forthcoming). The temporal semantics of actions and circumstance in Blackfoot. Unpublished Ph.D. dissertation, University of British Columbia, Vancouver.

Lyons, Christopher. (1999). *Definiteness*. Cambridge: Cambridge University Press.

MacDonald, Jonathan. (2008). *The Syntactic Nature of Inner Aspect: A Minimalist Perspective*. Amsterdam: John Benjamins.

Mahajan, Anoop. (1990). The A/A-bar distinction and movement theory. Unpublished PhD dissertation, Massachusetts Institute of Technology, Cambridge, MA.

Malagardi, Ioanna. (1994). Problems of Greek aspect morphology and the identification of projection for tense and aspect. In Irene Philippaki-Warbuton, Katerina Nicolaidis, and Maria Sifianou (eds.), *Themes in Greek Linguistics: Papers from the 1st International Conference on Greek Linguistics*, pp. 161–167. Amsterdam: John Benjamins.

Malamud, Sophia. (2012). Impersonal indexicals: *one, you, man*, and *du*. *Journal of Comparative Germanic Linguistics*, *15*(1), 1–48.

Malchukov, Andreij and Andrew Spencer. (2008). *Oxford Handbook of Case*. Oxford: Oxford University Press.

Manzini, M. Rita, and Leonardo Savoia. (2010). Case as denotation: Variation in Romance. *Studi Italiani di Linguistica Teorica e Applicata (SILTA)*, *39*, 409–438.

Marantz, Alec. (1991). Case and licensing. In Germán Westphal, Benjamin Ao, and Hee-Rahk Chae (eds.), *Proceedings of the 8th Eastern States Conference on Linguistics*, pp. 234–253. Columbus, OH: Ohio State University.

   (1997). No escape from syntax: Don't try morphological analysis in the privacy of your own Lexicon. In Alexis Dimitriadis (ed.), *Proceedings of the 21st Annual Penn Linguistics Colloquium*, pp. 201–225. Philadelphia, PA: University of Pennsylvania.

Matthewson, Lisa. (1998). *Determiner Systems and Quantificational Strategies: Evidence from Salish*. The Hague: Holland Academic Graphics.

   (2005). On the absence of tense on determiners. *Lingua, 115*(12), 1697–1735.

   (2006). Temporal semantics in a supposedly tenseless language. *Linguistics and Philosophy, 29*(6), 673–713.

   (2010). Cross-linguistic variation in modality systems: The role of mood. *Semantics and Pragmatics, 3*, 1–74.

Matthewson, Lisa, Hotze Rullmann, and Henry Davis. (2007). Evidentials as epistemic modals: Evidence from St'át'imcets. In Jeroen Craenenbroeck (ed.), *Linguistic Variation Yearbook*, vol. 7, pp. 201–254. Amsterdam: John Benjamins.

May, Robert. (1985). *Logical Form: Its Structure and Derivation*. Cambridge, MA: MIT Press.

McFadden, Thomas. (2004). The position of morphological case in the derivation: A study on the syntax-morphology interface. Unpublished Ph.D. dissertation, University of Pennsylvania, Philadelphia, PA.

McGinnis, Martha. (1999). Is there a syntactic inversion in Ojibwa? In Leora Bar-el, Rose-Marie Déchaine, and Charlotte Reinholtz (eds.), *Papers from the Workshop on Structure and Constituency in Native American Languages*, vol. 17, pp. 101–118. Cambridge, MA: MIT Occasional Papers in Linguistics.

Megerdoomian, Karine. (2000). Aspect and partitive objects in Finnish. *Proceedings of the West Coast Conference on Formal Linguistics, 19*, 316–328.

   (2008). Parallel nominal and verbal projections. In Robert Freidin, Carlos Otero, and Maria-Luisa Zubizarreta (eds.), *Foundational Issues in Linguistic Theory: Essays in Honor of Jean-Roger Vergnaud*, pp. 73–103. Cambridge, MA: MIT Press.

Meillet, André. (1934). *Le slave commun*. Paris: H. Champion.

Mezhevich, Ilana. (2008). A feature-theoretic account of tense and aspect in Russian. *Natural Language and Linguistic Theory, 26*(2), 359–401.

Mithun, Marianne. (1995). On the relativity of irreality. In Joan L. Bybee and Suzanne Fleischman (eds.), *Modality in Grammar and Discourse*, pp. 367–388. Amsterdam: John Benjamins.

Mühlbauer, Jeffrey T. (2008). kâ-yôskâtahk ôma nêhiyawêwin : The representation of intentionality in Plains Cree. Unpublished Ph.D. dissertation, University of British Columbia, Vancouver.

Musan, Renate. (1997). *On the Temporal Interpretation of Noun Phrases*. New York: Garland.

Newmeyer, Frederick J. (1998). *Language Form and Language Function*. Cambridge, MA: MIT Press.

   (2002). Optimality and functionality: A critique of functionally-based optimality-theoretic syntax. *Natural Language and Linguistic Theory, 20*(1), 43–80.

(2007). Linguistic typology requires crosslinguistic formal categories. *Linguistic Typology*, *11*(1), 133–157.

Nichols, Johanna. (2007). What, if anything, is typology? *Linguistic Typology*, *11*(1), 231–238.

Nishiyama, Atsuko, and Jean-Pierre Koenig. (2004). What is a perfect state? In Benjamin Schmeiser, Vineeta Chand, Ann Kelleher, and Angelo Rodriguez (eds.), *Proceedings of the 23rd West Coast Conference on Formal Linguistics*, pp. 101–113. Somerville, MA: Cascadilla Press.

Noonan, Michael. (2007). Complementation. In Timothy Shopen (ed.), *Language Typology and Syntactic Description*, pp. 52–150. Cambridge: Cambridge University Press.

Nordlinger, Rachel, and Louisa Sadler. (2008). When is a temporal marker not a tense? Reply to Tonhauser 2007. *Language*, *84*(2), 325–331.

Nordström, Jackie. (2010). *Modality and Subordinators*. Amsterdam: John Benjamins.

Noyer, Robert Rolf. (1992). Features, positions and affixes in autonomous morphological structure. Unpublished Ph.D. dissertation, Massachusetts Institute of Technology, Cambridge, MA.

Palmer, F. R. (2001). *Mood and Modality*, 2nd edn. Cambridge: Cambridge University Press.

Parsons, Terence. (1990). *Events in the Semantics of English: A Study in Subatomic Semantics*. Cambridge, MA: MIT Press.

Partee, Barbara Hall. (1973). Some structural analogies between tenses and pronouns in English. *Journal of Philosophy*, *70*(18), 601–609.

(1989). Binding implicit variables in quantified contexts. In Caroline Wiltshire, Randolph Graczyk, and Bradley Music (eds.), *Papers from CLS 25*, pp. 342–356. Chicago, IL: Chicago Linguistic Society.

Pasha, Siraj. (2010). 'Accidental' ter-in Malay as an anti-bouletic modifier, Paper presented at 17th Austronesian Formal Linguistics Association, Stony Brook University, New York.

Payne, Doris L. (1990). The Tupi–Guarani inverse. In Barbara Fox and Paul J. Hopper (eds.), *Voice: Form and Function*, pp. 313–340. Amsterdam: John Benjamins.

Payne, Thomas Edward. (1997). *Describing Morphosyntax: A Guide for Field Linguists*. Cambridge: Cambridge University Press.

Percus, Orin. (2000). Constraints on some other variables in syntax. *Natural Language Semantics*, *8*(3), 173–229.

Pereltsvaig, Asya. (2001). On the nature of intra-clausal relations: a study of copular sentences in Russian and Italian. Unpublished Ph.D. dissertation, McGill University, Montreal.

Perez, Carolyn Harford. (1986). Aspects of complementation in three Bantu languages. Unpublished Ph.D. dissertation, University of Wisconsin–Madison, Madison, WI.

Perlmutter, David M. (1971). *Deep and Surface Structure Constraints in Syntax*. New York: Holt, Rinehart, and Winston.

Pesetsky, David, and Esther Torrego. (2001). T-to-C movement: Causes and consequences. In Michael Kenstowicz (ed.), *Ken Hale: A Life in Language*, pp. 355–426. Cambridge, MA: MIT Press.

Pesetsky, David, and Esther Torrego. (2011). Case. In Cedric Boeckx (ed.), *The Oxford Handbook of Linguistic Minimalism*, pp. 52–72. Oxford: Oxford University Press.

Philippaki-Warbuton, Irene. (1987). The theory of empty categories and the pro-drop parameter in modern Greek. *Journal of Linguistics*, *23*(2), 289–318.

Philippaki-Warbuton, Irene, and Ioannis Veloudis. (1984). The subjunctive in complement clauses. *Studies in Greek Linguistics*, *5*, 87–104.

Picallo, C. (1985). Opaque domains. Unpublished Ph.D. dissertation, City University of New York.

Pinker, Steven, and Paul Bloom. (1990). Natural language and natural selection. *Behavioral and Brain Sciences*, *13*(4), 707–727.

Plungian, Vladimir. (2005). Irrealis and modality in Russian and in typological perspective. In Bjorn Hansen and Petr Karlik (eds.), *Modality in Slavonic Languages: New Perspectives*, pp. 135–146, Munich: Sagner.

Poletto, Cecilia. (2000). *The higher Functional Field: Evidence from Northern Italian Dialects*. Oxford: Oxford University Press.

Polinsky, Maria. (2011). Linguistic typology and formal grammar. In Jae Jung Song (ed.), *The Oxford Handbook of Linguistic Typology*, pp. 1–19. New York: Oxford University Press.

Polinsky, Maria, and Robert Kluender. (2007). Linguistic typology and theory construction: Common challenges ahead. *Linguistic Typology*, *11*(1), 273–283.

Pollock, Jean Yves. (1989). Verb movement, universal grammar and the structure of IP. *Linguistic Inquiry*, *20*(3), 365–424.

Portner, Paul. (1997). The semantics of mood, complementation and conversational force. *Natural Language Semantics*, *5*(2), 167–212.

(2004). The semantics of imperatives within a theory of clause types. In Kazuha Watanabe and Robert B. Young (eds.), *Proceedings of Semantics and Linguistic Theory*, vol. 14, pp. 235–252. Ithaca, NY: Cornell University Press.

Pustejovsky, J. (1995). *The Generative Lexicon*. Cambridge, MA: MIT Press.

Quer, Josep. (2006). Subjunctives. In Martin Everaert, Henk van Riemsdijk, Rob Goedemans, and Bart Hollebrandse (eds.), *The Blackwell Companion to Syntax*, vol. 4, pp. 660–684. Oxford: Blackwell.

(2009). Twists of mood: The distribution and interpretation of indicative and subjunctive. *Lingua*, *119*(12), 1779–1787.

Quinn, Conor M. (2006). Referential-access dependency in Penobscot. Unpublished Ph.D. dissertation, Harvard University, Cambridge, MA.

Raible, Wolfgang. (2001). Foundations: Theoretical foundations of language universals and language typology. In Martin Haspelmath, Ekkehard König, and Wulf Oesterreicher (eds.), *Language Typology and Language Universals*, pp. 1–39. Berlin: Mouton de Gruyter.

Ramchand, Gillian. (2008). *Verb, Meaning and the Lexicon*. Cambridge: Cambridge University Press.

Reichenbach, Hans. (1947). *Elements of Symbolic Logic*. New York: Macmillan.

Reinhart, Tanya Miriam. (1976). The syntactic domain of anaphora. Unpublished Ph.D. dissertation, Massachusetts Institute of Technology, Cambridge, MA.

Reinhart, Tanya Miriam, and Eric Reuland. (1991). Anaphors and logophors: An argument structure perspective. In Jan Koster and Eric Reuland (eds.), *Long Distance Anaphora*, pp. 283–321. Cambridge: Cambridge University Press.

Reis Silva, Amélia, and Lisa Matthewson. (2007). An instantaneous present tense in Blackfoot. In Amy Rose Deal (ed.), *Proceedings of SULA 4: Semantics of Under-Represented Languages in the Americas*, pp. 197–213. University of Montana Occasional Publications in Linguistics 35. Missoula, MT: University of Montana Press.

Rhodes, R.A. (1976). The morphosyntax of the Central Ojibwa verb. Unpublished Ph.D. dissertation, University of Michigan.

Richards, Norvin. (2012). Lardil "case stacking" and the timing of case assignment. *Syntax 16* (1) 42–76.

Rice, Keren. (2000). *Morpheme Order and Semantic Scope: Word Formation in the Athapaskan Verb*. Cambridge: Cambridge University Press.

Riemsdijk, Henk van, and Edwin Williams. (1981). NP-structure. *Linguistic Review*, *1*(2), 171–217.

Rigsby, Bruce. (1986). Gitksan grammar. Unpublished ms, University of Queensland, Brisbane, Australia.

Rijkhoff, Jan N.M. (1991). Nominal aspect. *Journal of Semantics*, *8*(4), 291–309.

(2008). Synchronic and diachronic evidence for parallels between noun phrases and sentences. In Folke Josephson and Ingmar Söhrman (eds.), *Interdependence of Diachronic and Synchronic Analyses*, pp. 13–42. Amsterdam: John Benjamins.

Ritter, Elizabeth. (1995). On the syntactic category of pronouns and agreement. *Natural Language and Linguistic Theory*, *13*(3), 405–443.

(2013). Personalizing the clausal spine: INFL and aspect in Blackfoot. Paper presented at Tel Aviv University, Hebrew Univesity of Jerusalem, and Ben Gurion University.

(2014). Nominalizing inner aspect: Evidence from Blackfoot. In Ileana Paul (ed.), *Cross-Linguistic Investigations of Nominalization Patterns*, pp. 25–50. Amsterdam: John Benjamins.

Ritter, Elizabeth, and Sara Thomas Rosen. (2005). Agreement without A-positions: Another look at Algonquian. *Linguistic Inquiry*, *36*(4), 648–660.

(2010). Animacy in Blackfoot: Implications for event structure and clause structure. In Malka Rappaport-Hovav, Edit Doron, and Ivy Sichel (eds.), *Lexical Semantics, Syntax and Event Structure*, pp. 124–152. Oxford: Oxford University Press.

Ritter, Elizabeth, and Martina Wiltschko. (2004). The lack of tense as a syntactic category. Evidence from Blackfoot and Halkomelem. In Jason C. Brown and Tyler Peterson (eds.), *Proceedings of the 39th International Conference on Salish and Neighbouring Languages*. University of British Columbia Working Papers in Linguistics, vol. 14, pp. 341–370.

(2005). Anchoring events to utterances without tense. *Proceedings of the 24th West Coast Conference on Formal Linguistics*, pp. 343–351.

(2009). Varieties of INFL: TENSE, LOCATION, and PERSON. In Jeroen Craenenbroeck (ed.), *Alternatives to Cartography*, pp. 153–201. Berlin: Mouton de Gruyter.

(forthcoming). The composition of INFL: An exploration of tense, tenseless languages and tenseless constructions. *Natural Language and Linguistic Theory*.

Rivero, Maria Luisa. (1994). Clause structure and V-movement in the languages of the Balkans. *Natural Language and Linguistic Theory*, *12*(1), 63–120.

Rivero, Maria Luisa, Ana Arregui, and Ewelina Frackowiak. (2009). Variation in circumstantial modality: Polish versus St'át'imcets. *Linguistic Inquiry*, *41*(4), 704–714.

Rizzi, Luigi. (1997). The fine structure of the left periphery. In Liliane Haegeman (ed.), *Elements of Grammar: A Handbook in Generative Syntax*, pp. 281–337. Dordrecht: Kluwer.

Roberts, Ian G., and Anna Roussou. (2003). *Syntactic Change: A Minimalist Approach to Grammaticalization*. Cambridge: Cambridge University Press.

Roberts, John. (1990). Modality in Amele and other Papuan languages. *Journal of Linguistics*, *26*(2), 363–401.

Roberts, Taylor. (1994). Subject and Object in St'át'imcets (Lillooet Salish). Unpublished M.A. thesis, University of British Columbia, Vancouver.

Rochemont, Michael S. (1986). *Focus in Generative Grammar*. Amsterdam: John Benjamins.

Rosenbaum, Peter. (1967). *The Grammar of English Predicate Complement Constructions*. Cambridge, MA: MIT Press.

Ross, John Robert. (1970 [1968]). On declarative sentences. In Roderick Jacobs and Peter Rosenbaum (eds.), *Readings in English Transformational Grammar*, pp. 222–272. Waltham, MA: Blaisdell.

Rouveret, Alain, and Jean-Roger Vergnaud. (1980). Specifying reference to the subject: French causatives and conditions on representations. *Linguistic Inquiry*, *11*(1), 97–202.

Rullmann, Hotze, and Aili You. (2006). General number and the semantics and pragmatics of indefinite bare nouns in Mandarin Chinese. In Klaus v. Heusinger and Ken Turner (eds.), *Where Semantics Meets Pragmatics*, pp. 175–196. Amsterdam: Elsevier.

Sampson, Geoffrey. (1974). Is there a universal phonetic alphabet? *Language*, *50*(2), 236–259.

Sapir, Edward. (1921). *Language: An Introduction to the Study of Speech*. New York: Harcourt Brace.

Sauerland, Uli. (2008). On the semantic markedness of Phi-features. In Daniel Harbour, David Adger, and Susana Béjar (eds.), *Phi Theory: Phi-Features across Modules and Interfaces*, pp. 57–82. New York: Oxford University Press.

Saussure, Ferdinand de. (1967 [1916]). *Cours de linguistique générale*. New York: Philosophical Library.

Saxon, Leslie. (1984). Disjoint anaphora and the binding theory. In Mark Cobler, Susannah MacKaye, and Michael Wescoat (eds.), *Proceedings of the 3rd West Coast Conference on Formal Linguistics*, pp. 242–251. Stanford, CA: Stanford Linguistics Association.

Schlenker, Philippe. (2005). The lazy Frenchman's approach to the subjunctive: speculations on reference to worlds, presuppositions, and semantic defaults in the analysis of mood. In Twan Geerts, Ivo van Ginneken, and Haike Jacobs (eds.), *Romance Languages and Linguistic Theory*, pp. 269–309. Amsterdam: John Benjamins.

Schmidtke, Karsten. (2006). A look beyond English. Tense and aspect systems in the languages of the world, handout, University of Jena.

Schütze, Carsten T. R. (1997). INFL in child and adult language: Agreement, case, and licensing. Unpublished Ph.D. dissertation, Massachusetts Institute of Technology, Cambridge, MA.

(2001). Korean case-stacking isn't: unifying non-case uses of case particles. In Kiyomi Kusumoto, (ed.), *Proceedings of the North East Linguistic Society*, vol. 26, pp. 351–365. Amherst, MA: CLS.

Seely, T. Daniel. (2006). Merge, derivational c-command and subcategorization in a label-free syntax. In Cedric Boeckx (ed.), *Minimalist Essays*, pp. 182–217. Amsterdam: John Benjamins.

Selkirk, Elizabeth. (2011). The syntax–phonology interface. In John Goldsmith, Jason Riggle, and Alan C. L. Yu (eds.), *The Handbook of Phonological Theory*, 2nd edn. New York: John Wiley.

Seok Koon, Chin (Shujun). (2007). Aspectual classification of Blackfoot predicates. Unpublished ms, University of British Columbia, Vancouver.

Shackle, C. (1972). *Punjabi*. London: English Universities Press.

Siegel, L. (2009). Mood selection in Romance and Balkan. *Lingua*, *119*(12), 1859–1982.

Siewierska, A. (2004). *Person*. Cambridge: Cambridge University Press.

Sigurðsson, Halldór Ármann. (1991). Icelandic case-marked PRO and the licensing of lexical arguments. *Natural Language and Linguistic Theory*, *9*(2), 327–363.

(2001). *Case: Abstract vs. Morphological*. Working Papers in Scandinavian Syntax No. 67. Lund.

Smith, Carlota. (1991). *The Parameter of Apect*. Dordrecht: Kluwer.

(1997). *The Parameter of Aspect*, 2nd edn. Dordrecht: Kluwer.

Speas, Peggy. (2010). Evidentials as generalized functional heads. In Anna-Maria Di Sciullo and Virginia Hill (eds.), *Edges, Heads and Projections: Interface Properties*, pp. 127–150. Amsterdam: John Benjamins.

Speas, Peggy, and Carol Tenny. (2003). Configurational properties of point of view roles. In Anna-Maria Di Sciullo (ed.), *Asymmetry in Grammar*, pp. 315–343. Amsterdam: John Benjamins.

Spencer, Andrew. (1991). *Morphological Theory: An Introduction to Word Structure in Generative Grammar*. Oxford: Blackwell.

Sproat, Richard. (1985). On deriving the lexicon. Unpublished Ph.D. dissertation, Massachusetts Institute of Technology, Cambridge, MA.

Starke, Michal. (2009). *Nanosyntax: A Short Primer to a New Approach to Language*. Tromsø: CASTLE.

Steele, Susan. (1975). Past and irrealis: just what does it all mean? *International Journal of American Linguistics*, *41*(3), 200–217.

Steriopolo, Olga. (2006). Form and function of expressive morphology. Unpublished Ph.D. dissertation, University of British Columbia, Vancouver.

Stowell, Tim. (1981). Origins of phrase structure. Unpublished Ph.D. dissertation, Massachusetts Institute of Technology, Cambridge, MA.

(1995). The phrase structure of tense. In Johan Rooryck and Laurie Zaring (eds.), *Phrase Structure and the Lexicon*, pp. 277–291. Dordrecht: Kluwer.

Stump, Gregory T. (2001). *Inflectional Morphology: A Theory of Paradigm Structure*. New York: Cambridge University Press.

Suttles, Wayne. (2004). *Musqueam Reference Grammar*. Vancouver: University of British Columbia Press.

Svenonius, Peter. (2002). Icelandic case and the structure of events. *Journal of Comparative Germanic Linguistics*, *5*(1), 197–225.

Szabolcsi, Anna. (1983). The possessor that ran away from home. *Linguistic Review*, *3*(1), 89–102.

Taglicht, Josef. (1998). Constraints on intonational phrasing in English. *Journal of Linguistics*, *34*(1), 181–211.

Taylor, Allan R. (1969). A grammar of Blackfoot. Unpublished Ph.D. dissertation, University of California, Berkeley, CA.

Tenny, Carol. (1987). Grammaticalizing aspect and affectedness. Unpublished Ph.D. dissertation, Massachusetts Institute of Technology, Cambridge, MA.

(1994). *Aspectual Roles and the Syntax–Semantics Interface*. Dordrecht: Kluwer.

(2000). Core events and adverbial modification. In Carol Tenny and James Pustejovsky (eds.), *Events as Grammatical Objects: The Converging Perspectives of Lexical Semantics and Syntax*, pp. 285–329. Stanford, CA: CSLI Publications.

Thoma, Sonja. (forthcoming). The syntax of discourse: evidence from Bavarian discourse particles. Unpublished Ph.D. dissertation, University of British Columbia, Vancouver.

Thompson, Chad. (1990). On the treatment of topical objects in Chepang: Passive or inverse? *Studies in Language*, *14*(2), 405–427.

(1994). Passives and inverse constructions. In Barbara Fox and Paul J. Hopper (eds.), *Voice, Form and Function*, pp. 47–64. Amsterdam: John Benjamins.

Thompson, Ellen (2006). The structure of bounded events. *Linguistic Inquiry*, *37*(2), 211–228.

Thompson, James J. (2012). Syntactic Nominalization in Halkomelem Salish. Unpublished Ph.D. dissertation, University of British Columbia, Vancouver.

Thompson, Laurence C. (1979). The control system: A major category in the grammar of Salishan languages. In Barbara S. Efrat (ed.), *The Victoria Conference on Northwestern Languages*, pp. 156–176. Victoria, BC: Provincial Museum.

Thompson, Laurence C., and M. Terry Thompson. (1992). *The Thompson Language*. Missoula, MT: University of Montana.

Tomasello, Michael. (2003). *Constructing a Grammar: Towards a Usage Based Theory of Language Acquisition*. Cambridge, MA: Harvard University Press.

Tonhauser, Judith. (2011). Temporal reference in Paraguayan Guaraní, a tenseless language. *Linguistics and Philosophy*, *34*(3), 257–303.

Travis, Lisa. (1984). Parameters and effects of word order variation. Unpublished Ph.D. dissertation, Massachusetts Institute of Technology, Cambridge, MA.

(1988). The syntax of adverbs. *McGill Working Papers in Linguistics*, pp. 280–310. Toronto: McGill University.

(1992). Inner Tense with NPs: the position of number. Paper presented at the Conference of the Canadian Linguistics Association, University of Toronto.

(2000). The l-syntax/s-syntax boundary: evidence from Austronesian. In Ileana Paul, Vivianne Philips, and Lisa Travis (eds.), *Formal Issues in Austronesian Linguistics*, pp. 167–193. Dordrecht: Kluwer.

(2006). Syntactic categories: lexical, functional, cross-over, and multifunctional. In Henri Cohen and Claire Lefebvre (eds.), *Handbook of Categorization in Cognitive Science*, pp. 319–346. Amsterdam: Elsevier.

(2010). *Inner Aspect: The Articulation of VP.* Dordrecht: Springer.

Trubetzkoy, Nikolai Sergeevich. (1939). *Grundzüge der Phonologie.* Göttingen: Vandenhoek & Ruprecht.

Tsoulas, George. (1995). The nature of the subjunctive and formal grammar of obviation. In Karen Zagona (ed.), *Grammatical Theory and Romance Languages*, pp. 293–306. Amsterdam: John Benjamins.

Uchibori, Asako. (2000). The syntax of subjunctive complements: Evidence from Japanese. Unpublished Ph.D. dissertation, University of Connecticut, Storrs, CT.

Uhlenbeck, Christianus Cornelius. (1938). *A Concise Blackfoot Grammar: Based on Material from the Southern Peigans.* Amsterdam: Noord-Hollandsche Uitgeversmaatschappij.

Uriagereka, Juan. (1999). Multiple spell-out. In Samuel D. Epstein and Norbert Hornstein (eds.), *Working Minimalism*, pp. 251–282. Cambridge, MA: MIT Press.

Van Gelderen, Elly. (1993) *The Rise of Functional Categories.* Amsterdam: John Benjamins.

van Hout, Angeliek. (1996). Event Semantics of verb frame alternations. Unpublished Ph.D. dissertation, Tilburg University, Tilburg, Netherlands.

(2000). Projection based on event structure. In Peter Coopmans, Martin Everaert, and Jane B. Grimshaw (eds.), *Lexical Specification and Lexical Insertion*, pp. 403–428. Amsterdam: John Benjamins.

Van Valin, Robert D. (2007). Some speculation about the reason for the lesser status of typology in the USA as opposed to Europe. *Linguistic Typology, 11*(1), 253–257.

Vendler, Zeno. (1967). Verbs and times. *The Philosophical Review, 66*(2), 143–160.

Vergnaud, Jean-Roger. (1982). Dépendances et niveaux de représentation en syntaxe. Unpublished Ph.D. dissertation, Université de Paris VII.

Verkuyl, H. J. (1972). *On the Compositional Nature of the Aspects.* Dordrecht: Reidel.

(1993). *A Theory of Aspectuality: The Interaction between Temporal and Atemporal Structure.* Cambridge: Cambridge University Press.

Vikner, Sten. (1995). *Verb Movement and Expletive Subjects in Germanic Languages.* Oxford: Oxford University Press.

Wiese, Bernd. (1999). Unterspezifizierte Paradigmen: Form und Funktion in der pronominalen Deklination. *Linguistik online, 4*/3 99. *Syntax and Morphology.* Available at www.linguistik-online.de/3_99/

Whistler, Kenneth W. (1985). Focus, perspective and inverse person marking in Nootkan. In Johanna Nichols and Anthony C. Woodbury (eds.), *Grammar Inside and Outside the Clause: Some Approaches to Theory from the Field*, pp. 227–265. Cambridge: Cambridge University Press.

Williams, Edwin. (1981). Argument structure and morphology. *Linguistic Review*, *1*(1), 81–114.

(1994). Remarks on lexical knowledge. *Lingua*, *92*(1–4), 7–34.

(1997). Blocking and anaphora. *Linguistic Inquiry*, *28*(4), 577–628.

(2003). *Representation Theory*. Cambridge, MA: MIT Press.

Wiltschko, Martina. (1995). IDs in syntax and discourse: An analysis of extraposition in German. Unpublished Ph.D. dissertation, University of Vienna.

(1998). On the internal and external syntax of Independent pronouns in Halq'eméy-lem. *Papers for the 33rd International Conference on Salish and Neighboring Languages*. Seattle, WA, pp. 428–447.

(2002a) Sentential negation in Upriver Halkomelem. *International Journal of American Linguistics*, *68*(3), 253–286.

(2002b). The syntax of pronouns: Evidence from Halkomelem Salish. *Natural Language and Linguistic Theory*, *20*(1), 157–195.

(2003). On the interpretability of Tense on D and its consequences for Case Theory. *Lingua*, *113*(7), 659–696.

(2005). Why should diminutives count? In Hans Broekhuis, Norbert Corver, Riny Huijbregts, Ursula Kleinhenz, and Jan Koster (eds.), *Organizing Grammar: Linguistic Studies in Honor of Henk van Riemsdijk*, pp. 669–678. Berlin: Walter de Gruyter.

(2006a). Inlocatives in Halkomelem Salish. In Masaru Kiyota, James Thompson, and Noriko Yamane-Tanaka (eds.), *Papers for the 41st Conference on Salish and Neighbouring Languages*, University of British Columbia Working Papers in Linguistics, vol. 18, pp. 286–310.

(2006b). On ergative agreement and anti-agreement in Halkomelem Salish. In Shannon Bischoff, Lindsay Butler, Peter Norquest, and Daniel Siddiqi (eds.), *Studies in Salishan*, MIT Working Papers on Endangered and Less Familiar Languages, vol. 7, pp. 241–273.

(2006c). On 'ergativity' in Halkomelem Salish: And how to split and derive It. In Alana Johns, Diane Massam, and Juvenal Ndayiragije (eds.), *Ergativity: Emerging Issues*, pp. 197–227. Dordrecht: Springer.

(2008). The syntax of non-inflectional plural marking. *Natural Language and Linguistic Theory*, *26*(3), 639–694.

(2009). What's in a determiner and how did it get there? In Jila Ghomeshi, Ileana Paul, and Martina Wiltschko (eds.), *Determiners: Universals and Variation*, pp. 25–66. Amsterdam: John Benjamins.

(2011). Nominal Licensing via case or deictic anchoring. In L. Armstrong (ed.), *Proceedings of the Annual Conference of the Canadian Linguistic Association*. http://homes.chass.utoronto.ca/~cla-acl/actes2011/

(2012). Decomposing the mass–count distinction: evidence from languages that lack it. In Diane Massam (ed.), *Count and Mass Across Languages*, 146–171. Oxford University Press.

(2013). The anatomy of universal categories: Developing discovery procedures. In Stefan Keine and Shayne Sloggett (eds.), *Proceedings of the 42nd Meeting of the North East Linguistic Society*, pp. 257–276.

(2014). Patterns of nominalization in Blackfoot. In Ileana Paul (ed.), *Cross-Linguistic Investigations of Nominalization Patterns*, pp. 189–214. Amsterdam: John Benjamins.

Wiltschko, Martina, and Strang Burton. (2004). On the sources of person hierarchy effects. *Canadian Journal of Linguistics*, *49*(1), 51–71.

Wiltschko, Martina, Valerie Marshall, Andy Matheson, and Audra Vincent. (forthcoming). Independent pronouns in Blackfoot. *Proceedings of the 43rd Algonquian Conference.*

Wunderlich, Dieter, and Ray Fabri. (1995). Minimalist morphology: An approach to inflection. *Zeitschrift fur Sprachwissenschaft*, *14*(2), 236–294.

Wurmbrand, Susi. (2001). *Infinitives: Restructuring and Clause Structure*. Berlin: Mouton de Gruyter.

Yip, Moira, Joan Maling, and Ray Jackendoff. (1987). Case in tiers. *Language*, *63*, 217–250.

Zagona, Karen. (1990). *Times and Temporal Argument Structure*. Seattle, WA: University of Washington Press.

(1995). Temporal argument structure: Configurational elements of construal. In Pier-Marco Bertinetto, Valentina Bianchi, James Higginbotham, and Mario Squartini (eds.), *Temporal Reference, Aspect, Actionality*, vol. 1, pp. 397–410. Turin: Rosenberg and Sellier.

(2003). Tense and anaphora: Is there a tense-specific theory of coreference? In Andrew Barss, (ed.), *Anaphora: A Reference Guide*, vol. 3, pp. 140–171. Malden, MA: Blackwell.

Zirkov, L.I. (1955). *Lakskij jazyk*. Moscow: Izdatel'stvo Akademii Nauk SSSR.

Zlatic, Larisa. (forthcoming). Slavic noun phrases are NPs not DPs. In Loren Billings (ed.), *Comparative Slavic Morphosyntax*. Bloomington, IN: Slavica Publishers.

Zúñiga, Fernando. (2006). *Deixis and Alignment: Inverse Systems in Indigenous Languages of the Americas*. Amsterdam: John Benjamins.

Zwicky, Arnold. (1974). Hey, whatsyourname! In Michael La Galy, Robert Fox, and Anthony Bruck (eds.), *Papers from the 10th Regional Meeting of the Chicago Linguistics Society*, pp. 787–801. Chicago, IL: Chicago Linguistics Society.

Index

For EU product safety concerns, contact us at Calle de José Abascal, 56–1°,
28003 Madrid, Spain or eugpsr@cambridge.org.

www.ingramcontent.com/pod-product-compliance
Ingram Content Group UK Ltd.
Pitfield, Milton Keynes, MK11 3LW, UK
UKHW020807190625
459647UK00032B/2269